GUILFORD COURT HOUSE, N.C.

SLIPCASE: In Edward Hicks's primitive painting, the drafting committee presents the Declaration on July 2, 1776.

ENDSHEET: Thomas Hooker leads dissidents from Massachusetts to settle in the Connecticut River valley in 1636.

FRONTISPIECE: This drum beat the American troops to battle at Guilford Courthouse eight months before Yorktown.

TITLE PAGE: George Washington reviews his forces at Cumberland, Maryland, while suppressing the Whisky Rebellion of 1794.

200 YEARS

A Bicentennial Illustrated History of the United States

BOOKS by U.S.NEWS & WORLD REPORT

Books by
U.S.News & World Report
A Division of U.S.News & World Report, Inc.

Directing Editor
Joseph Newman

BOARD OF CONSULTANT HISTORIANS
John R. Alden
Professor of History, Duke University

John A. Garraty
Professor of History, Columbia University

Kenneth M. Stampp
*Professor of American History,
University of California, Berkeley*

STAFF FOR *200 YEARS*
Project Editor
Russell Bourne

Art Director
Donald McCarten

Picture Editor
Joyce Wellde

Text Editor
Linda Glisson

Researchers
Carol Breckon, Dee McRae

Writers for Volume One

Ralph Andrist (Chapters 2,8, and 12) Wayne Barrett (4,9)
Russell Bourne (1) Burke Davis (7)
Kenneth S. Davis (3) Jake T. Hubbard (6,10)
David Lavender (11) Stephen W. Sears (5)

❀ ❀ ❀

Contents

Volume One

Introduction

It is peculiarly fitting that we should look back at our history at this time, two centuries after the founding of the Republic. Americans have long been accustomed to think of themselves as a new and youthful people with a special mission to demonstrate the capacity of free men to govern themselves, to protect and extend personal liberties, and to achieve equality of opportunity for all men and women. Six generations ago the American colonists secured their independence and set up a novel system of government, which most European nations thought would never last. But both America and its institutions have survived, and today, whatever else may be said about them, it can no longer be asserted that they are immature. Yet it may now appropriately be asked whether Americans are progressing toward the fulfillment of their special mission.

Migrating across the Atlantic, the English, together with important contingents of other west European peoples and large numbers of enslaved Africans, displaced the Indians along the seaboard of North America in the 1600s. By 1763 the colonists, although their language and institutions remained English, were thinking of themselves as a distinct people, as Americans. They controlled their internal affairs through elected legislative bodies established in all of the Thirteen Colonies. Confronted by efforts on the part of British politicians to increase British authority over them, they rebelled against the Mother Country in 1775. The next year they proclaimed their independence, though only in 1783 after a long war fought with some help from Spain and much more from France did they win recognition of their freedom from Britain.

The Revolution was much more than division from Britain, important as was that separation. The Americans put forward in the Declaration of Independence two earth-shaking propositions: that all men are created equal and that government must not exist without the consent of the governed. These principles heralded the ultimate end of colonialism; and in the Northwest Ordinance of 1787, they put these ideas into practice by providing that as the nation expanded westward, new states would enter the Union as equal partners, not as dependencies.

Many learned European observers felt that a democratic republic could not long survive the flux of changing majorities and the wiles of demagogues. In large measure, the history of the United States for nearly a century after the Revolution was a test of this belief. Americans moved swiftly to strengthen their union by drafting a strong Constitution, which gave the central government a great deal of power, but at the same time protected local interests and individual freedom in the Bill of Rights and by dividing federal authority among the executive, legislative, and judicial branches. During this era also, the rights of white citizens were greatly expanded. Some of the limitations on the right to vote were removed; educational opportunities were made more widely available; true religious liberty was established. To a very large degree, Americans were able to indulge their materialistic urge to accumulate wealth without seriously conflicting with one another in the process. In part, the system worked so well because the country was rich—the natural resources and energizing opportunities provided by the vast undeveloped west lubricated the body politic and thus reduced social friction to a minimum. The nation also benefited from its relative isolation from the aggressive and powerful nations of Europe and from European internal struggles, which distracted the powers and enabled the United States to play off one against another for its own protection.

As a 15-star flag stirs in the breeze and a fiddler sets the tune, Americans prepare to celebrate the Fourth of July in J. L. Kimmel's early 19th century painting opposite. Washington's portrait and a war poster back up the patriotism of the old veteran's toast.

7

Thus the new nation developed. It grew (first steadily and then with increasing swiftness) larger, more populous, richer, more efficient. As time passed, American farms yielded ever larger harvests of wheat and cotton and corn. New factories spewed forth their riches. Roads, canals, and finally railroads linked the sections together, providing ever swifter and cheaper means for moving goods, people, and ideas from place to place. And the governmental system smoothly accommodated itself to changing needs and interests in the name of economic opportunity.

By the time Andrew Jackson was elected President in 1829, the American political experiment was clearly a success. During his two terms, the removal of property restrictions on voting in most of the states and the rise of a new and vigorous two-party system prepared the way for the democratization of American politics and the idealization of the Common Man.

Jacksonian Democracy, however, had its limitations, and none was more serious than its exclusive concern for the welfare of white men. Jackson's goal was to destroy all vestiges of special privilege and to open avenues to material success for all white Americans. Negroes had no place in this democratic society, except as servants. And as for the only "real" Americans, the Indians, they were systematically driven west and exterminated by the advancing waves of "civilization."

Black slavery was an obvious blot on a society whose ideological commitment was to liberty for the individual. It was also the basic cause of a growing sectional conflict that threatened the survival of the federal Union. Eventually nearly every major question of public policy came to be judged first in terms of sectional advantage or disadvantage.

During the 1840s, as Americans pursued their "Manifest Destiny" in a war with Mexico, in the acquisition of California and New Mexico, and in the settlement of Oregon, the country was nearly torn apart as free-soil Northerners resisted the demands of proslavery Southerners that the territories be opened to slavery. A series of tenuous compromises on slavery expansion and federal economic policy had seen the country through earlier crises, and many hoped that the great Compromise of 1850 would be a final settlement of all troublesome sectional issues.

But the truce of 1850 lasted less than four years. In 1854, when Senator Stephen A. Douglas introduced his Kansas-Nebraska Bill, he reopened the question of slavery expansion and set in motion a train of events that culminated in secession and Civil War.

In the 1850s the newly formed Republican party, morally opposed to slavery and fearful of the boundless expansion of the institution, determined to oppose it. Convinced that a "house divided against itself cannot stand," the Republicans decided to put slavery, in Abraham Lincoln's words, on "the course of ultimate extinction." Six years after its birth, the Republican party swept the Northern states and won a presidential election. The states of the Deep South, responding in panic and anger, proclaimed the dissolution of their ties with the federal Union and in February, 1861, joined to form the Confederate States of America. This time all efforts at compromise failed. Since most Northerners and many Border State people refused to accept secession as a constitutional remedy for Southern grievances, they rallied to the support of President Lincoln when the Confederates, on April 12, 1861, opened fire on Fort Sumter.

"Both parties deprecated war," Lincoln told Congress the following July, "but one of them would *make* war rather than let the nation survive, and the other would *accept* war rather than let it perish, and war came." With these words Lincoln acknowledged that the democratic process, at this crucial point in American history, had somehow failed. The Republic could only march on after an inner plague had been healed.

PART ONE

The Spirit of Seventy-Six 1763-1776

Chronology:

Pre-Revolutionary Events

1754-1763 French and Indian (Seven Years') War
1765 Stamp Act passed
1770 Boston Massacre
1773 Boston Tea Party
1774 Jefferson's *Summary View of the Rights of British America*
1774 First Continental Congress

First Blows for Independence

April 1775 Battles of Lexington and Concord
June Washington named commander in chief
June Battle at Bunker and Breed's Hill
August Expedition against Quebec
December Virginia's Gov. Dunmore defeated by patriots at North Bridge

Declaration and First Victories

June 1776 Successful defense of Charleston
July Declaration of Independence signed
September British occupy New York
November Patriots retreat to New Jersey
December Victory at Trenton
January 1777 Victory at Princeton

"The Flame Is Kindled"

1

Lieutenant William Dudingston served the Royal Navy well. And by so doing, brought on what might be called a preliminary action of the American Revolution in the year 1772.

With admirable vigilance, Dudingston spotted, pursued, and captured smugglers who operated among the many tricky channels and rocky coves of Rhode Island's Narragansett Bay. And he served himself well, too. When his swift patrol ship, the revenue cutter *Gaspée,* succeeded in catching one of the smugglers, and the victim's goods were sold after court action, Lieutenant Dudingston got a handsome share of the proceeds.

He was fierce toward American merchantmen who dared bring in such goods as molasses from the French West Indies. For he was determined to force obedience to the Acts of Trade, which sought to keep colonial business within the confines of the British mercantile system. And he was equally fierce toward skippers of whatever law-abiding ships he stopped and inspected—for who knew what they might be carrying? The colonists had begun to demonstrate a rebellious mood, and the navy must be on the alert.

This officiousness was intolerable for such aristocratic and enterprising merchants as John Brown of Providence. His firm, Nicholas Brown and Company, had been doing business in many parts of the world for the better part of the century. His ships, and those of other Rhode Islanders, would one day reach China and the East Indies and were presently plying between Europe, Africa, and the West Indies. If the cargo from Africa often consisted of slaves, and if the cargo from the Antilles was not always British-produced—wasn't that the way fortunes were made?

Father Time blames the American Revolution on France in this 1775 British cartoon. The French cock pumps the bellows to produce disaster for British forces. Grieving Europe watches the picture show, flanked by Africa and Asia; America crouches Indian style at far left.

On the afternoon of June 9, 1772, Lieutenant Dudingston pressed his luck a bit too far when chasing a smuggler close to shore: he ran aground on a sandspit below Providence. Hearing of the *Gaspée's* accident, John Brown recalled how Rhode Islanders had wrecked another customs vessel some four years earlier. And, collecting a band of armed men ready for any act of mischief against the crown, he rowed out to the helpless ship, wounded the lieutenant, forced the crew into longboats, then set the *Gaspée* ablaze.

Somehow the culprits could not be found, even though the outraged British cabinet demanded that the offenders be brought to justice and the privy council offered a reward of £500 for information leading to conviction. Parliament, for its part, had declared four months before that setting fire to a naval vessel was a treasonous crime, punishable by death. But the investigation could accomplish nothing—besides persuading many Americans by the severity of its language that England was determined to put a noose around the neck of all who believed in freedom.

The *Gaspée* assault was but a prelude to many other battles, including the one on April 19, 1775, at Concord and Lexington which is generally treated as the opening engagement of the American Revolution.

Before that critical turning point of the eighteenth century, in the time when relations between the colonies and the mother country were still harmonious, English ministers made plans to impose certain new taxes on the prosperous Americans to help pay for the recently concluded Seven Years' War and for the maintenance of a large imperial force. In 1763, Lord Egremont, a secretary of state, inquired how the Americans might be led to support a larger share of Britain's empire. "In what Mode least Burthensome and most palatable to the Colonies can they contribute . . .?"

But gentle measures in regard for colonial sentiment

George Grenville

First monarch since the Stuarts to speak English natively, George III won Englishmen's hearts. Less comely than as painted by court artist Allan Ramsay at his coronation (left), he suffered from instability and an unstable cabinet. His search for ministers to do his imperial will included George Grenville (who put through the Stamp Act) and Charles Townshend. Their acts made the colonists cry out against taxation without representation. Finally the king's quest for a strong prime minister ended with Lord North, who helped him mismanage the Revolution.

William Pitt won renown as "The Great Commoner" by his leadership of the House of Commons during the reign of George II. Alone among English leaders he possessed a clear vision of empire; yet George III dismissed him as war minister for his desire to pursue the expensive war with France and Spain. He opposed many of George III's impositions on the American colonies—as a statesman, not as a lover of liberty. In the dramatic painting by John Copley at right, Pitt (then the Earl of Chatham) has risen to protest a motion in the House of Lords and has been stricken with a heart attack that would prove fatal.

Charles Townshend

Lord North

interested England's new king, George III, not at all. Ignorance of and unconcern for the colonies characterized his reign at its outset. Indeed, the king could scarcely comprehend the vast empire, the world's largest, that he had inherited from his grandfather in 1760 at the age of twenty-two.

At first, aided by the coming of peace abroad, George III won greater popularity than any monarch since Charles II a century before. Religious, temperate, and devoted to his queen and family, he preferred to spend his days at outdoor sports and on his farm. He plunged into the business of being king, dismissing the very statesmen who had previously sustained the ties between the colonies and England. First he appointed his "dearest friend" and former tutor Lord Bute as prime minister, heeding his advice that monarchy was a sacred trust. Then, when Bute resigned for reasons of health and political ineptitude, he named George Grenville to the post.

Though Grenville was a brother-in-law of William Pitt, the "Great Commoner"—who had a truly global view of the empire and a statesman's respect for the parliamentary process—the new prime minister was an insular financial specialist who knew next to nothing about colonial affairs.

Grenville struggled to consolidate the crown's old and new territories in North America. Toward that end a standing army seemed called for—an army that the Americans must support. Indians still threatened the security of the lands beyond the Allegheny Mountains. The French citizens of newly won Canada could hardly be expected to be quiescent. And the Spanish in western Louisiana would seize any opportunity to extend their control. So an army was mustered, an army that would cost some £300,000 annually and that would ultimately prove to be a major cause of the American Revolution.

The king retained General Jeffery Amherst, who had been commander in chief of all British forces in North America since 1758, as head of the new army and gave him seventeen regiments of infantry. Many of these 8,000 men Amherst stationed at relatively isolated forts along the frontiers of the Thirteen Colonies. To the colonists, that seemed a strange procedure. Had that hero of the French and Indian War and the captor of Montreal forgotten how easily Indians could penetrate such a thin screen? And would the army not have the adverse effect of stirring up the Indians? Soon such fears were realized as Pontiac's painted warriors swept through the backwoods settlements of Pennsylvania, Maryland, and Virginia.

Yet another question haunted many colonial minds: was perhaps the real purpose of the army to keep a rein on their own independent spirit? Writing home from London in April, 1764, Eliphalet Dyer of Connecticut conjectured, "It seems determined to fix upon us a large Number of regular troops under pretence for our Defense; but rather designed as a rod and check over us!"

American agents raised warning signals from England; Amherst might move his troops into coastal cities in order to support Grenville's customs officers. Such talk of increased British control played upon the worst fears of Americans of all classes. If British laws long on the books taxing certain imports (notably molasses) were actually enforced, a traditional aspect of American life would be threatened. And of course smuggling, a well-established business of the day, would perish as an industry!

Also alarming was the Royal Proclamation of 1763, which closed the rich lands beyond the Alleghenies to settlement by Americans. Frontiersmen beyond the proclamation line in northwestern Pennsylvania were ordered to retreat, to abandon their cabins and forsake the freedom of settlement which they had always thought was theirs. Refusing to move out, they saw

Wolfe's Triumph at Quebec

"The Year of Miracles," 1759, gave England victory after victory in the Seven Years' War for empire against France. Greatest miracle of all: 32-year-old General James Wolfe's capture of "impregnable" Quebec from the Marquis de Montcalm. After victory came peace—the 1763 Treaty of Paris which virtually banished France from North America. Americans rejoiced and began to think continentally. "We doubt not," resolved Massachusetts Bay, "but as we are delivered from foreign wars, we shall be equally free from intestine Divisions."

Finding a cleft in Quebec's 200-foot-high cliffs, Wolfe led his 4,000 men up to the Plains of Abraham (below). Outwitted but still superior French forces made the mistake of leaving their citadel and counterattacking. Decimated by fire from the well-drilled British ranks, they collapsed beneath the thrust of Wolfe's victory charge.

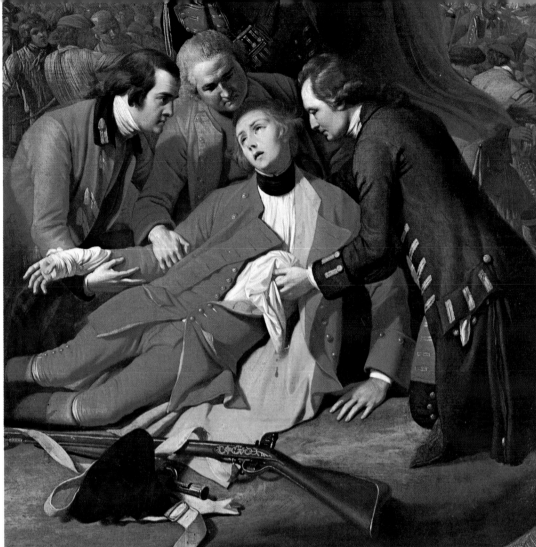

Against the threat of an amphibious assault from Britain's globe-girdling navy and audacious army, Montcalm pledged he would "save this unhappy colony or die in the attempt." Wolfe, no less morbid, recited Gray's "Elegy in a Country Churchyard" on his way to the landing site. Their fears were both realized—Montcalm's chest was ripped open by an exploding British shell; Wolfe took two wounds and fell beneath a third after ordering the climactic charge. It had been an age of heroes, and Wolfe's death was recorded heroically by Benjamin West (above). But in the next few months the British almost lost their hold on battered Quebec (below). A new age was dawning in which lesser mortals' ability to fight and fight again would win all.

Gen. Jeffery Amherst (caricatured at left) lost his reputation as England's best New World fighter when he failed to protect American frontiersmen from Pontiac's warriors. During the Revolution, Britain's Indian allies (right) harassed American settlements.

their cabins burned to the ground by the king's men.

Yet as George III and his ministers tightened the screws of the imperial system, few Americans presumed to challenge the king's rule.

From the Atlantic to the mountains, from Georgia to Maine, they numbered about a million and a half loyal souls. A major fraction of the colonists (a fifth or more) were black. A large minority of the population (one out of twenty) lived in cities, towns, or villages. Of the cities, the largest were Boston, Philadelphia, and New York, which had roughly the same populations as England's Bristol, Sheffield, and Leeds. Nonetheless, America presented a rural and even a wild appearance. Farmer families still dwelled in log cabins. Children raised in these outpost communities knew no lifestyle other than fathers with gun and plow, mothers with gun and treadle; they had never seen a city, never heard the rumble of iron-sheathed wagon wheels over cobblestoned streets.

Children both in the boundless wilderness and in the industrialized cities were multiplying with astonishing rapidity. Benjamin Franklin estimated that the population of the Thirteen Colonies was doubling every generation.

Secure in their New World haven, the colonists bustled to profit from its bounty. Raids from rival colonial powers had now ceased. Prosperous and peaceful, Americans enjoyed more personal freedom and more social equality than any other group of people in the eighteenth century world.

Though separated from each other by vast distances and by unfordable rivers—as well as by profound cultural differences—they enjoyed a certain sense of community. With some exceptions, they spoke or understood English. They were sustained by a financial network whose agents and merchants corresponded with each other from the port cities. Despite religious antagonisms, they shared an appreciation of their Christian heritage. And they were fascinated by what the lively and enterprising newspapers had to say about events in England and in the other American colonies.

A violent wrench of mind and spirit was required to turn the colonists from that early and happy mood of dependence toward revolution. And in the opinion of John Adams—the sober lawyer from Braintree, Massachusetts, who became the revolutionary nation's second President—the change occurred in 1761 when Boston was inflamed over the Writs of Assistance.

The British government displayed unusual zeal that year in an effort to enforce the Acts of Trade and Navigation Act. All shipped articles would be liable for inspection on the sole authority of the royal "Writs." No special search warrants would be necessary; customs inspectors could forcibly open all cargoes that entered or left their ports.

For the merchants of Massachusetts, many of whom had built their fortunes on a volume of illicitly handled goods (particularly wine from the Azores and molasses from the non-British West Indies), such inspection and taxation was not only ruinous . . . it was unconstitutional! They believed they had certain privileges as Englishmen, privileges which protected them from arbitrary assessment. And certain lawyers nodded their heads in agreement, quoting Bacon and Locke, basing abstract arguments on "natural rights."

When the test came to court, the burden of pleading for the defense was put on the shoulders of young James Otis. For all his youth, he represented the best training and legal knowledge that Boston as a cultural center had to offer (though some pointed out that his anticrown sentiments might have resulted from his father's having been turned down for the post of chief justice of Massachusetts). Both he and his partner in pleading the case, Oxenbridge Thacher, had been

trained by the eminent barrister Jeremiah Gridley—who was that day arguing for the crown. Gridley, filled with pride at his pupils' performance, later said, "I raised up two young eagles. They pecked out both my eyes."

James Otis had but one central argument: the classical case for freedom. For five hours he hammered away at that basic theme. "This writ is against the fundamental principles of English law!" "An act against natural equity is void."

Although the governor and judges eventually found a way of deciding the case in favor of the crown, Otis had been heard. He had seized the bugle of freedom and blown it with such clarity that the heads of Americans would never stop ringing until true political freedom had been won. John Adams (who kept the notes from which our knowledge of the trial comes) could not forget Otis's performance. Fifty years later,

North Carolina's Royal Governor William Tryon, backed by militia, faces down an overtaxed and angry mob of frontiersmen called "Regulators." This 1769 uprising preceded the Regulators' defeat in the 1771 Battle of the Alamance—a battle indicative of pre-1775 tensions throughout the colonies.

he wrote, "Here this day, in the old Council Chamber, the child Independence was born."

Others would disagree with Adams, dating the upsurge of American sentiment against the crown to the passage of Grenville's American Act of 1764. This bill, plus another that aggravated the critical shortage of currency in the colonies, was passed in a severe depression. "Trade is become dull, Money very scarce, Contracts decrease, Law Suits increase . . ." wrote a merchant of Philadelphia. Resentment rose against British customs men and mercantile agents who personified the new restrictions. One of them, operating in Virginia's tidal waterways, fearfully began toting a pistol. He reported, "Particularly at this time when the Planters are pressed for old Ballances, we find it necessary to carry with us some defensive weapons." Richard Henry Lee wrote from Virginia's House of Burgesses to a friend in London: "Poverty and oppression . . . may produce a fatal resentment of parental care being converted into tyrannical usurpation."

Americans had easily borne a variety of poorly enforced restrictions (see box, page 22). But they began to bridle at the imposition of duties that sought in the king's name to squeeze every last possible sixpence out of the colonists' trade. Traditionally, the favorite route for an American ship was one leg or another of the "triangular trade" between Africa, the West Indies, and the colonies. New England rum and barrel staves were shipped out to Europe and Africa's Gold Coast; slaves there were forced on board and transported to the vast sugar plantations of the West Indies; molasses and sugar came thence to American ports where they were brewed into rum and more rum.

Totally at odds with this free-flowing and long-accepted system, the new duties of Grenville seemed unjust, disruptive, and recklessly provocative. Then in the summer of 1764 the news of Grenville's plans to have Parliament impose stamp duties on the colonies

Gravestone rubbing: Massachusetts preacher

reached America. The colonists were driven beyond expressions of individual outrage to constructing official petitions for redress. The New York General Assembly addressed that colony's governor in September, 1764, with the words: "We hope your Honour will join with us in an Endeavor to secure that great badge of English liberty, of being taxed only with our own Consent . . ."

George III's ministers would not listen to such messages of discontent as were relayed to them. Instead, they went ahead and invoked the notorious Stamp Act "towards further defraying the Expenses of defending, protecting and securing the colonies."

The Stamp Act demanded that colonists buy stamps from royal distributors for a whole range of documents and activities. The troublesome and expensive stamps would have to be affixed to playing cards and insurance policies, legal documents, wills and bills of lading, liquor licenses, and newspaper advertisements. Grenville estimated that all those purchases might add up to nearly £100,000 a year. That would give him almost a third of what he needed to balance the outlay for the North American Army whose commander now,

after Amherst's failure in Pontiac's war, was General Thomas Gage.

A few courageous members of Parliament spoke against the Stamp Act. The most daring was Colonel Isaac Barré, a follower of William Pitt, who predicted that the Americans would rise in revolt. But the crown easily swept opposition aside, and a vote for the bill in the Commons was 245 to 49.

Reaction on these shores was instant and vituperative. The *Maryland Gazette* called the colonists "THUNDERSTRUCK."

In Williamsburg, a new member of the House named Patrick Henry rose to address his fellow burgesses. He had already acquired a public reputation for strong language. In 1763, when he was little more than a failed storekeeper and novice lawyer, he had spoken against the royally established Church of England in a case that became famous as the "Parson's

New England's tradition of Protestant learning—sustained by such venerable institutions as Harvard College (below)—gave rise to a highly literate upper class, characterized by piety and legalism. Yet those attributes did not interfere with the merchants' strenuous pursuit of "that coy mistress, trade."

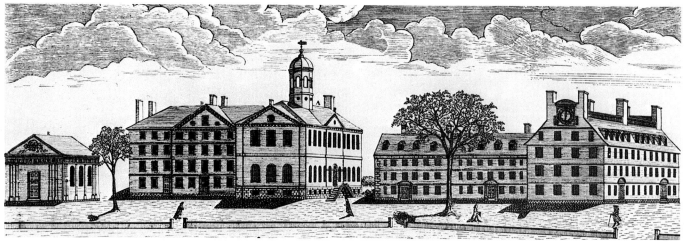

Eloquent lawyer James Otis, called a "flame of fire," raises his hand (below) to plead for the rights of Massachusetts merchants against the crown's Writs of Assistance that would have subjected their shipments to inspection and taxation. Otis's near classmate at Harvard, Sam Adams (left) was even more radical and more successful in translating principles into popular rallying cries. In this portrait by J.S. Copley, he points to the charter of 1629 which made Massachusetts a self-governing colony. His scholarly cousin John Adams (right) based his defense of liberty on Englishmen's ancient privileges.

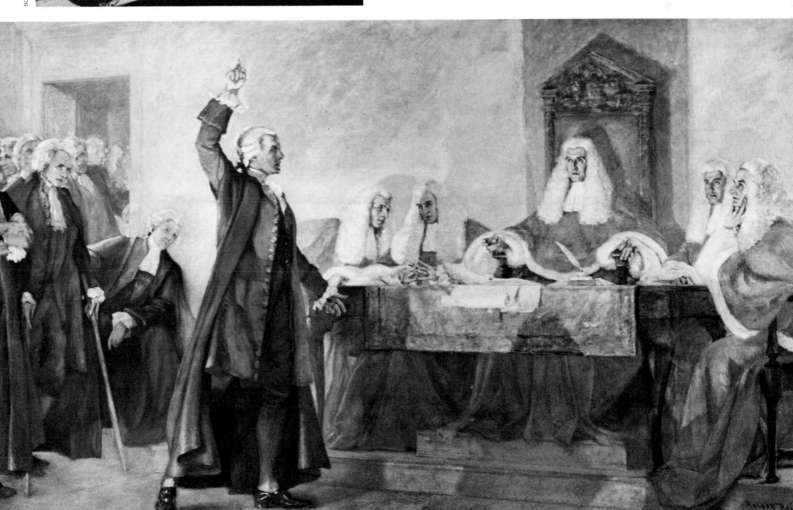

Documentary stamps—such as this one that cost a mere two shillings sixpence—provoked the American colonists to their first united defiance of the king.

Cause." Some while before, the Virginia legislature had ruled that clergy of the church in Virginia would have to accept payment in the much-depreciated form of local currency. This would give the clergy far less than the 16,000 pounds of tobacco each year to which earlier laws entitled them. The king had then annulled the Virginia statute, but the local parishes had protested, pleading that they not be forced to pay the larger salaries. By his eloquence, Patrick Henry had translated the "Parson's Cause" into a plea for human freedom. He had dared assert, it was said, that "a king, by annulling or disallowing salutary acts . . . degenerates into a tyrant, and forfeits all right to his subjects' obedience."

Now, with passions heightened by the debate on the Stamp Act, he presumed to use even stronger language. Now, as the story of his defiance came to be told, he called down doom upon the head of the king. "Caesar had his Brutus; Charles the First his Cromwell; and George the Third . . ." Interrupted by the mounting furor, he managed to press on: ". . . and George the Third may profit by their example. If this be treason, make the most of it!"

Throughout all the colonies, men of all classes were inspired by Patrick Henry's words and encouraged by post-riders' reports that the House of Burgesses had passed his Virginia Resolves. (Actually, only a watered-down version had survived the cautious scrutiny of the conservatives.) Following the Virginians' lead, men of South and North strove to express their hatred of the stamps.

By mob action and personal assaults, radicalized colonists frightened officials appointed as stamp distributors. And generally their actions had the desired results: the appointees declined to serve. In Charleston, South Carolina, a terrified stamp officer wrote in dismay that he had noted friends, relatives, business associates in the mob that had attacked him. So this was more than a mere upsurge of the common herd.

In New York City, a crowd of men shouting "Liberty!" marched to Fort George on the evening before the Stamp Act was to take effect. They seized and burned the governor's coach, broke into the commandant's house, guzzled his wine, and smashed his furniture. In Boston, outraged "Sons of Liberty" destroyed the stamp collector's office; in Newport, they built gallows and hanged the king's appointees in effigy.

Site of Patrick Henry's
outburst against the
Stamp Act, Williamsburg's
H-shaped House of Burgesses
served as capitol
for Britain's
most populous colony.

The Massachusetts legislature sent out a call for common action. And in October, 1765, delegates from nine colonies met in New York's Wall Street. In that unprecedented convention, they vowed mutual support and declared the Stamp Act unconstitutional.

"Liberty, Property, and No Stamps," were key words emblazoned on American banners. Unified in opposition to Grenville's act, the colonists determined to enter into no business activity that required the stamps.

Trade came to a standstill; in some colonies even the courts closed. The *Boston Gazette* threatened Grenville in verse:

> *To make us all Slaves, now you've*
> *lost Sir! the Hope,*
> *You've but to go hange yourself—*
> *we'll find the Rope.*

Hurt by the American boycott, British merchants clamored for parliamentary action. In the colonies, several loyal governors appealed to General Gage for protective troops. Gage managed to avoid an open clash with the Americans, but the crisis intensified.

By the time the news of American resistance reached Britain, the reins of parliamentary power had changed hands. George III had fired Grenville (not because of the Stamp Act but because of the prime minister's failure to put the queen mother on a council empowered to act for the king in the event of illness) and replaced him with the Marquis of Rockingham. The new ministry wanted to avoid another uprising and therefore sought to bring about the termination of the Stamp Act.

Repeal was also urged by William Pitt, the colonists' aged friend. In the course of one debate, he declared, "I rejoice that America has resisted." He also claimed that the Americans were right, that taxation without representation was unconstitutional. Parliament and the ministry disagreed. The Declaratory Act, which was passed by large majorities in both houses, declared that the crown had the right to tax the colonies. Therein lay the essential and rankling disagreement between Britain and most loyal colonists.

Soon after the repeal, new taxes were imposed by

Before admiring Virginians and a weeping justice (left), country lawyer Patrick Henry berates the crown in the "Parson's Cause" of 1763. He spoke out even more vigorously in the Stamp Act debate of 1765; among his seven resolutions before the House of Burgesses, one said Parliament could not constitutionally tax Virginia for revenue.

Parliament under the leadership of Charles Townshend, George III's chancellor of the exchequer. Townshend gained the appealing nickname "Champagne Charlie," but there was in fact nothing very gay about him. Walpole wrote of him: "He [would have] had almost every talent . . . if he had but had common truth, common sincerity, common honesty, common modesty, common steadiness, common courage and common sense." His tax program of 1767 included a long list of imports to America on which it laid duties. Taxed were such essentials as glass, lead, and paint.

The colonists, who had but recently rung bells and commissioned statues of the king to celebrate the repeal of the Stamp Act, quickly struck back against the Townshend Acts. Boston imposed a boycott of British goods. Samuel Adams of Boston, the down-at-the-heel lawyer and radical genius who had become the rallying point for the Sons of Liberty, was asked by the Massachusetts legislature to draft a protest to the king that would be even stronger than the one he had drawn up against the Stamp Act. In Virginia, the members of the House of Burgesses were dismissed by the governor after they voted to support the protest of Massachusetts. In New York, "Liberty Boys" provoked clashes in the street with the king's soldiers.

The presence of swaggering redcoats, many of whom had arrived in the city when New York was made the headquarters of the British Army of North America, was particularly hard for prideful Americans to accept. The obligation of quartering the troops had been placed on the citizens in the so-called Mutiny Act of 1765. Popular but overbearing General Gage wrote home that "the colonists are taking large strides toward independency; . . . it concerns Great Britain by a speedy and spirited conduct to shew them that these provinces are British colonies dependent on her, and that they are not independent states."

Amid legislative protests and mob outbursts, one notably firm and serious voice could be heard. It emanated from John Dickinson, a public-spirited and conservative attorney, whose *Letters from a Farmer in Pennsylvania* had won a wide readership in both the colonies and England. Deploring violence but criticizing England's recklessness, he again asserted the classic argument that such legislation as the Townshend Acts violated the colonists' constitutional rights. And he appealed to his fellow gentlemen and to English Whigs who were friendly to Americans, asking that they recognize the principle of federalism. This ideal, which would allow the Thirteen Colonies to

Timetable of Repression

Parliament regulated colonial imports and exports for more than a century before the Revolution. During much of that time the Thirteen Colonies prospered, as their trade was valuable to Britain, but after 1763 restrictions upon America became increasingly onerous. Even more serious in creating American discontent were efforts on the part of Britain to tax the colonies for revenue to support the British army and officials in North America.

1660-1672	**Acts of Trade and Navigation** made England the control center for nearly all the colonies' foreign trade.
1762	**Writs of Assistance** permitted British customs officers in Boston to search premises for smuggled goods.
1764	**Currency Act** restricted supply of legal paper money in the Thirteen Colonies.
1765	**Stamp Act** levied duties by means of stamps on wide range of colonial documents.
1765	**Quartering Act** (also known as Mutiny Act) required colonists to provide barracks for Gen. Gage's army.
1767	**Townshend Acts** imposed duties on glass, lead, tea, paper, paint; set up special courts for offenders.
1773	**Tea Act** gave British East India Company monopolistic privilege to sell tea in the colonies.
1774	**Coercive Acts** (also known as Intolerable Acts) punished Boston by closing port and controlling government.

Violence flared in the colonies during the Stamp Act controversy: in New Hampshire a stamp agent was hanged in effigy (opposite); in the Pennsylvania *Journal* a skull and crossbones warned of death (right).

exist under British rule, had come to be regarded by many moderates—Franklin included—as the most sensible solution. Dickinson stressed that Americans were "as much dependent on Great Britain as a perfectly free people can be on one another."

Perfectly free! He had said it, and he meant it. And others heard him in the depths of their being—though reasons for agreeing varied among all men.

In restless Boston, where muscular laborers were idled by the boycott and the decline of shipping activity, attention focused on the sloop *Liberty*. Owned by the rich young merchant John Hancock (who was known to be an openhanded supporter of the Sons of Liberty), the sloop had been seized by customs commissioners on June 10, 1768. The charge was that wine from the West Indies was secreted in the ship's holds. Now, towed out to the warship *Romney* for complete

inspection, she swung captive on her tether. To the waterfront crowd, she seemed a symbol of British highhandedness.

Each day the men became more aggressive, hurling first insults then stones at the customs officials when they dared appear in public. Soon they made an even bolder move and attacked the home of Benjamin Hallowell, comptroller of customs, smashing his windows and driving him to the island sanctuary of Castle William. Roaring through the streets to the wharves, they next hauled the customs collector's own barge ashore, hefted it up to the common in front of Hancock's Beacon Hill mansion, and burned it there as a flaming demonstration of their sympathy.

Royal customs commissioners raised a cry for help, claiming that the Bostonians were "in open revolt." The British government barely restrained the Massachusetts legislature from summoning a congress of the colonies and labeled that attempt "seditious." To the customs men's great relief, two warships bearing regiments from the British garrison in Halifax sailed into Boston Harbor in September. Delegates sent by Boston's town meetings to issue a call to arms pondered the consequences, and hesitated. Their ardor dimming in the face of British might, they passed but a few moderate resolutions and dissolved.

The troops did present a formidable appearance: the Fourteenth West Yorkshires, the Twenty-ninth Worcestershires, plus cannoneers of the Royal Artillery, all in their distinctive colors and gleaming equipment. General Gage, who had traveled up from New York to find quarters for them, succeeded in quieting the city by the tramp of boots. Yet a spirit was at work here that would not be quelled. As John Adams expressed it, "certain busy characters [operating] between the inhabitants of the lower classes and the soldiers . . . [tried] to enkindle an immortal hatred." And they succeeded.

Crispus Attucks, one of the five men slain by British guns in the Boston Massacre of 1770 (above), was a robust runaway slave. The victims received a common, well-publicized burial. A newspaper of the day reported, "the peculiar solemnity with which the whole Funeral was conducted surpassed description."

23

Sword and spyglass mark Providence merchant Abraham Whipple (opposite), who joined disguised citizens in burning the pesky British revenue cutter *Gaspée* (below) in 1772. Privateering profitably during the Revolution, he once bagged ten British ships in as many nights.

The next year Boston celebrated Guy Fawkes Day (November 5, 1769) with a special passion. A crowd rounded up a customs informer and tarred and feathered him. Another mob of celebrants broke into the office of a publisher whose newspaper had dared suggest that certain colonists were actually importing British-taxed goods in secret—and paying the taxes! The publisher saved his life only by brandishing a brace of pistols.

Just three months later occurred the Revolution's first fatality. A threatened customs officer, goaded beyond tolerance, fired his musket into a crowd of tormentors and killed a lad named Christopher Snyder.

The customs officer, spared a lynching, was later convicted of murder, though he was not executed as the deed had been perpetrated "in self-defence."

The winter air tingled with excitement; the stars seemed to dance in tension. Thomas Hutchinson, Massachusetts's lieutenant governor, predicted, "there is going to be a Rumpus—a Riot." He warned the population of the penalties for treason, rioting, unlawful assemblage. But others (particularly Sam Adams) kept Boston in a high political fever.

John Adams, considerably more cautious than his cousin Sam, worried that the political activists might make unscrupulous use of the small boys—each one a

potential Christopher Snyder. To such youngsters, snowballs were objects of play, not war; to them British soldiers were natural targets, not defenders of a fragile empire. The boys had no idea what a conflict might be set off by a hunk of ice.

Hutchinson, having become acting governor, took intelligent steps to cool the fever. The soldiers were instructed not to deprive any man of his liberty. The legislature, which Hutchinson had disbanded until March 15, would meet across the river in Cambridge rather than in Boston. It was too late, however, for sense to rule.

On Monday morning, March 5, 1770, snow fell upon a layer of ice. By nighttime, every boy who wanted something to throw had all the ammunition he could use. And the perfect target came along when a British sentinel who could not take teasing whacked one of the boys. Friends let fly at the sentinel, overwhelming him in a barrage of snowballs. Finally, the captain of the guard, knowing the nature (and the danger) of the game, recalled the soldiers for the night.

Then another boy managed—with the help of what political leader?—to enter the North End's Brick Church, where he rang the bell so clamorously that alarmed citizens thought it must be the fire call. Out into the moonlit street they rushed, looking for other excitement when the fire alarm proved false. More citizens converged from other parts of the city, having been told that the sentinel now on guard near the Customs House was the same one who had "attacked" the boy earlier in the evening.

Under a storm of ice and wood missiles, the sentinel called for help. Seven soldiers and an officer dashed across Boston's main square to his aid, pushing back the growing crowd with their bayonets. An officer of the Twenty-ninth Regiment, Captain Thomas Preston, also came forth and took command of the beleaguered men at the sentry box. He ordered that none of the men fire, but that they load and ready their muskets.

The skillfully led crowd taunted the soldiers. "Lobsters! Lobsters!" they chanted, "Let's see your fire! You dare not fire!"

Then one of the soldiers slipped, or was knocked down. And the others, alarmed, leveled their muskets, one firing, then the next, into the crowd. Five Americans fell before order could be restored . . . three dead, the others dying.

In a few moments, Hutchinson himself appeared on the scene. He was able to prevent further bloodshed by making his way to the balcony of the State House, and from there pleading for the crowd to disperse. He promised that the soldiers would be put on trial immediately. And tried they were—with John Adams speaking for the squad's defense, in the American tradition of judicial equity. Captain Preston and six of the "lobsterbacks" were acquitted, but the harm had been done. Colonists up and down the length of the land, hearing the news of the "Boston Massacre," knew now that they were all under the British guns. Martyrs had been found whose deaths (when narrated with dramatic imagination and embellished with patriotic passion) made each fear for his own life.

By a great stroke of irony, it happened that on the very day of the massacre, March 5, 1770, Lord North urged repeal of the Townshend duties which had impelled the whole crisis. Lord North, the new prime minister—the man who finally fulfilled the king's hopes for a minister with the strength to stay in power—discerned that the Townshend duties were economically unsound. Yet in canceling the duties, the royal government kept one fatal restriction in effect: a high duty on tea.

A time of truce came to the colonies. As the colonists abandoned their trade boycott, and as the British commanders withdrew their troops from Boston's streets, it almost looked like a time of peace. But peace would not be allowed by that firebrand, Sam Adams. As described by Samuel Eliot Morison, Adams was "austere and implacable." He was, further, "a genuine revolutionary, resembling in several respects the communist agitators of our time. . . . A master of propaganda, he realized that the general run of people prefer drama and ritual to a well-argued exposition."

Incessantly he worked to perfect his propaganda system. He created an interlocked network of town committees; other Americans joined in forming Committees of Correspondence that extended throughout the colonies. Through these he regularly communicated with such kindred spirits as Isaac Sears in New York and Christopher Gadsden in South Carolina. And, always looking for the spectacular example of patriotic behavior or of British perfidy, he seized on such events as Rhode Island's burning of the royal revenue schooner *Gaspée*. By 1774, all colonies but Pennsylvania were tightly linked through Adams's sensitive alarm system. One of the riders who pounded the trails carrying the news was Paul Revere, who seemed those days to live on his horse.

"Tea!" was the cry that Revere and the other patriots kept raising: the king's ministers were keeping the tax on tea, the very wellspring of the colonists' life. Tea stood for tyranny and should not be bought. Smugglers profited as propagandists preached.

Radical propaganda was in this case not far from the truth. Lord North was persuaded to help save the crown-financed East India Company from bankruptcy. His ingenious proposal (a concept which Ben Franklin sarcastically called "a noble piece of chicanery") gave the East India Company the opportunity to sell taxed tea to the colonies at a price considerably below that offered by American smugglers.

Immediately a new cry went up from patriotic throats: the British were forcing an "illegal monopoly" upon America. Ships bearing the monopolistic tea should not be allowed to land at the four ports scheduled to receive the shipments.

Sensing the serious mood of this rebellion over a pot of tea, John Adams's wife Abigail wrote, "The flame is kindled, and like lightning it catches from Soul to Soul."

At Charleston, Christopher Gadsden forced the captain of the East India Company ship to lock the 257 chests of tea in a sturdy warehouse, from which it would not be sold. Below Philadelphia and at New York, the ship captains were informed by patriots that they had better take the tea back whence it came. And so they did.

But it was Boston, where the tea arrived first, that set the pace. Three East India Company ships had arrived by December, 1773; their spars seemed to hover menacingly over the city, for the ships had been secured in the Inner Harbor. Through its town meetings, the city declared that the governor must arrange to have the tea sent back to England. When Hutchinson refused to issue clearance papers for the ships, citizens became Indians in disguise. In the course of a drizzly evening, 342 chests were taken out of the holds and dumped into Boston harbor by unrecognizable "Mohawks."

Ben Franklin, anxious that the colonies maintain a good, law-abiding image, was shocked at the "Boston Tea Party." Throughout England there was dismay, followed by anger.

To George III, the Bostonians' action was treasonous. The king's ministers pushed into law a series of bills known to history as the Intolerable Acts—which were designed to punish Boston and to prevent future trouble by changing Massachusetts's system of government. By their severity they also convinced many Americans that none who loved freedom could any longer take the king's part. The struggle was now begun.

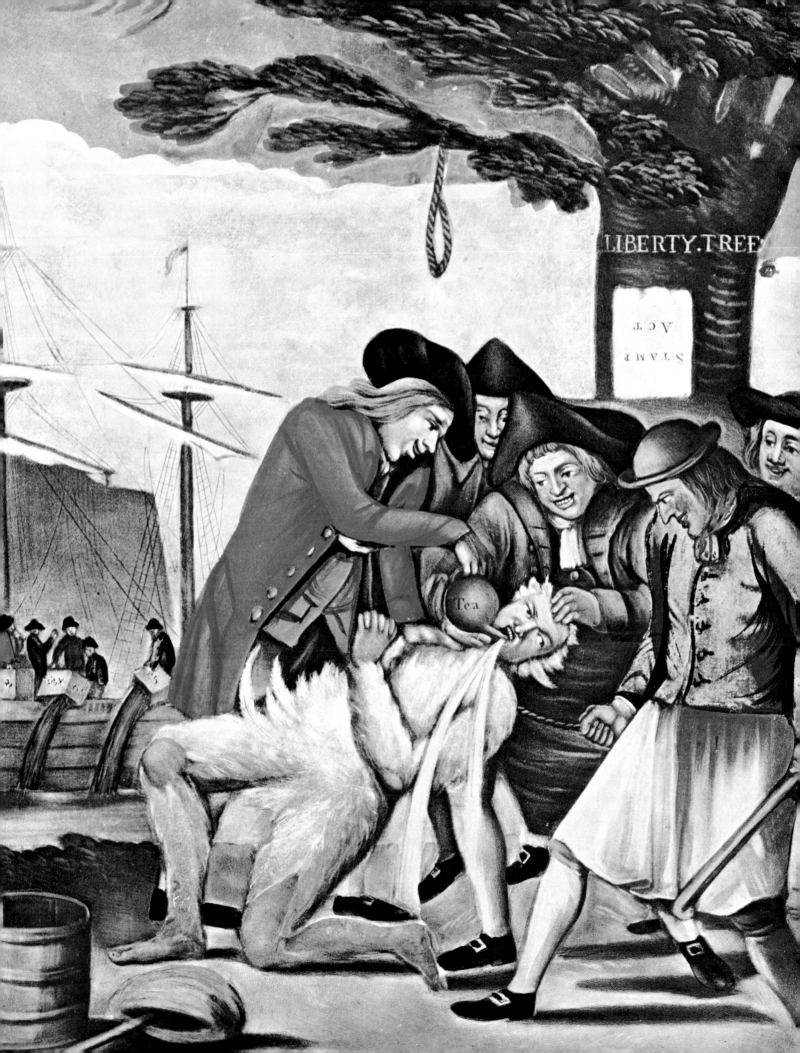

A Shot Heard 'Round the World

2

Boston was a dead port. Under the watchful eye of the Royal Navy, nothing disturbed the waters of Boston Harbor except an occasional vessel bringing supplies for the garrison of British troops. The city was being punished for the Boston Tea Party. An act of Parliament, which had gone into effect on June 1, 1774, had closed the port to all shipping until the rebellious people paid £15,000 for the destroyed tea in order to satisfy the king that they would in future show due respect to the crown.

Yet Parliament was not satisfied with merely closing off Boston; all of Massachusetts should be made to suffer for the deeds of the Boston hotheads. Thus, between March and June, 1774, Parliament passed a number of bills which Americans called collectively the Intolerable or Coercive Acts. Two of the acts clearly violated the Massachusetts charter of 1691.

In May, 1774, a new governor, Lieutenant General Thomas Gage, arrived to preside over the chastisement of Boston. He interpreted his mandate literally: by his reading the Port Bill made it unlawful for any vessel to load or unload goods at any "island, creek, landing-place, bank, or other place" within Massachusetts Bay. No scow with hay or lumber could move across the bay, no ferry, not even a farmer in a rowboat with a few melons to sell.

The blockade set up by Gage would shortly have starved Boston if it had not been for an outpouring of help from other colonies. From Connecticut came hundreds of sheep; other New England states sent cattle, fish, flour, money. The Carolinas sent rice and money, and from Virginia came corn and wheat and flour. The colonies were united in their generosity—and with the

gifts came an exhortation to the Bostonians to stand fast, to refuse to pay for the destroyed tea.

Gage had little success in applying either the Port Bill or the Intolerable Acts. In September, 1774, a session of the supreme court was called in Boston, but not one man on the jury panel would agree to be sworn. Sheriffs, judges, and other officers refused to serve since it meant they would be king's men instead of servants of Massachusetts. The assembly refused to consider making payment for the Boston Tea Party; instead it echoed the Virginia House of Burgesses's call for a congress of the colonies and nominated five delegates to attend.

On September 5, 1774, the first Continental Congress convened in Philadelphia to discuss the Massachusetts situation and the threat it constituted to Americans' rights. Of the Thirteen Colonies, only distant Georgia was not represented.

The delegates were debating a plan for American-British relations when the clatter of hoofbeats interrupted the meeting. Paul Revere, silversmith, engraver, craftsman—and official courier for the Boston Committee of Correspondence—had arrived with copies of a group of resolutions passed by a convention of the towns of Suffolk County of which Boston was a part.

As the "Suffolk Resolves" were read to the Congress, silence stole over the hall. The liberal delegates were elated; the conservatives were shocked. The aroused townsmen of Suffolk County had declared that the Coercive Acts were unconstitutional and so to be ignored. They called on the people of Massachusetts to arm themselves in case of attack and to suspend all trade with Britain until the Coercive Acts were repealed. The Congress talked down the fainthearted among its members and enthusiastically endorsed the Suffolk Resolves. No one yet was using the word independence—but Sam Adams was probably thinking it.

Meanwhile, in Massachusetts the tension mounted.

An advance guard of redcoats fires at blue-coated militiamen on Lexington Green in this 1775 drawing by Amos Doolittle, a militiaman himself. Tradition says that Lexington's Capt. John Parker told his men, "Stand your guard! Don't fire unless fired upon! But if they want to have a war, let it begin here!"

Commander of British forces in America, Gen. Thomas Gage (right) was also named governor of Massachusetts after the troublesome "Tea Party." With an American wife and reputation for bravery if not brilliance in the French and Indian War, Gage had colonial friends as well as foes. The foes recalled his role in landing and quartering troops in Boston after the Townshend riots of 1768 (below). He perceived that New Englanders would fight if further oppressed, and therefore made Boston a British citadel in a hostile land.

A VIEW OF PART OF THE TOWN OF BOSTON IN NEW ENGLAND AND BRITTISH SHIPS OF WAR LANDING THEIR TROOPS! 176

On friday Sept.r 30.th 1768, the Ships of War, armed Schooners, Transports, &c. Came up the Harbour and Anchored round the Town; their Cannon loaded, a Spring on their Cables, as for a regular Siege. At noon on Saturday October the 1.st the fourteenth & twentynineth Regiment, a detachment from the 59.th Reg.t and Train of Artillery, with two pieces of Cannon, landed on the Long Wharf; there Formed and Marched with insolent Parade, Drums beating, Fifes playing, and Colours flying, up KING STREET. Each Soldier having received 16 rounds of Powder and Ball.

ENGRAVED, PRINTED, & SOLD by PAUL REVERE, Bos

In October, the assembly organized itself as a Provincial Congress, free of control by king and governor, and thereafter governed Massachusetts (with the exception of Boston) virtually as an independent state. General Gage, who with his meager army could not hope to control the interior of the colony, entrenched himself in Boston, steadily built up his troop strength, and began to fortify the city. With the help of his loyalist informers, moreover, he managed to keep an eye on the patriots' movements. At Charlestown, across the river from Boston, there was a magazine in which nearby towns communally stored powder for their militia. During August those towns had been quietly removing their powder and storing it nearer home, a move that seemed ominous to Gage. On September 1 he sent a force of 260 soldiers to seize the remaining powder; at the same time another detachment was sent to Cambridge to confiscate two cannon recently acquired by the militia of that town. Both operations went off smoothly and without violence, but as news of the actions spread, fact was obscured by rumor. Soon it was being said that six men had been killed at Cambridge resisting the British. By the next day 4,000 patriots were in Cambridge and more were on the way. By September 4 the story had reached New York; within a week it had spread to Philadelphia where Congress was in session. "The effect of the news we have both upon the Congress and upon the inhabitants of this city, was very great," John Adams wrote to his wife. "Great indeed! Every Gentleman seems to regard the bombardment of Boston as the bombardment of the capital of his own province." Twenty to thirty thousand men were said to have been on the march toward Cambridge before the rumors proved false.

Massachusetts lapsed into uneasy quiet. Throughout the province, throughout all New England, militia began drilling with new earnestness. In Massachusetts the old militia companies were disbanded and reorganized in order to purge them of officers and men with Tory sympathies. One-fourth of the men were to be organized into minuteman companies—a goal not always met. The patriots were also gradually accumulating military stores.

General Gage was not oblivious to these actions for there were plenty of loyal Tories to keep him well informed, but he refused to commence hostilities without direct orders. His seizure of the cannon at Cambridge had given him a sobering view of how quickly and thoroughly the countryside could be aroused.

Ultimately, however, the decision was taken out of his hands. On April 14, 1775, new orders arrived from London. Massachusetts had been declared in a state of rebellion—as indeed it was—and Gage was ordered to take immediate action.

The provincials had assembled their military stores in Worcester and Concord. Worcester was too distant to reach through a hostile countryside, but Concord was near enough for a surprise foray. Gage went quietly to work, but his plans were soon discovered. On April 15, a British officer noted in his diary that certain troops had been relieved of duty to learn new maneuvers: "This I suppose is . . . a blind. I daresay they have something for them to do." There were also other signs that something momentous was afoot.

With hundreds of unemployed men loitering on street corners and along the waterfront, little went unnoticed. Paul Revere had his organization of spies, and there were similar groups throughout the city. They patrolled the streets and met secretly to exchange information. Among other things, they noticed that the boats belonging to the troop transports, which had been pulled up on shore for repairs, were no longer there. This news they immediately reported to Dr. Joseph Warren, who concluded that Gage was planning to raid Concord. Moreover, as the preparation of

Paul Revere: Silversmith and Propagandist

Craftsmanlike revolutionary, Paul Revere (1735-1818) lavished on liberty the same skill he gave to silver trays, bowls, and tableware. Though humbly born of a Yankee mother and French Huguenot father (Apollos Rivoire), he soon emerged as Boston's best silversmith and stood proudly among the city's fraternity of artisans and masons. Over clay pipes and punch bowls these independent-spirited tradesmen hammered out a program to depose the aristocratic oligarchy of Massachusetts. Bold, swarthy, full of love for his two successive wives and energy for his booming business, Revere was short only in stature, in philosophy, and in artistic originality. Through his propagandistic designs and his tireless riding to spread news through New England and distant colonies, he served the Revolution vigorously and well.

John Singleton Copley's portrait of his friend Paul Revere shows him holding a newly made, pear-shaped teapot, pondering what to engrave on its face.

Marring the chastity of Revere's silver punchbowl, slogans and symbols clutter its classical sides to honor 92 legislators who refused to "recind" the Massachusetts letter against the Townshend Acts. Revere's design ideas came mostly from London, then enraptured by the rococo style; he simplified and reworked them with his keen eye and strong hand.

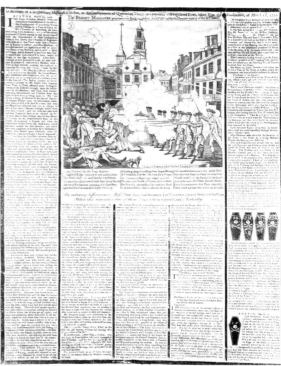

BLOODY MASSACRE perpetated in King——Street BOSTON on March 5th 1770 by a party of the 29th REGT

BUTCHER'S HALL

Engrav'd Printed & Sold by PAUL REVERE BOSTON

The bright red of British coats and American blood in Paul Revere's engraving of the Boston Massacre (above) inflamed patriots. They could buy the poster for eightpence soon afterwards. The crudely effective drawing, copied from a more artistic original, shows neither the British captain's restraint nor the mob's weapons; it concentrates instead on the citizens' death throes. The engraving also appeared in the *Boston Gazette* (opposite), accompanied by "coffings."

33

the ships' boats showed, Gage was not going to march his troops out across Boston Neck; he was going to ferry them across the Charles River, a shorter route and one that avoided most villages, thereby making it possible to take Concord by surprise—or so Gage thought. Having reached this conclusion, Warren sent Paul Revere off the next day, April 16, to warn John Hancock and Samuel Adams who were staying in Lexington and to tell the people of Concord to hide the weapons and supplies.

On his way home that evening, Revere stopped in Charlestown to talk to Colonel William Conant "& some other Gentlemen." He arranged "that if the British went out by water, we would show two lanthorns in the North Church Steeple, and if by land one, as a signal." Longfellow's poem notwithstanding, the lamps were not a signal to Revere; they were a signal from Revere to alert other couriers, especially in case he did not himself get across with the message.

Long after dark on the night of April 18, sergeants moved among the sleeping redcoats, waking their men, cautioning them to be quiet as they sleepily dressed, forming them up outside their barracks, marching them toward the waterfront. There were six to eight hundred men—ten companies of light infantry, ten of grenadiers, one of marines—and no matter how silently their sergeants tried to move them, they were observed by many eyes. Word was brought to Dr. Warren that

In Boston's Old North Church (properly called Christ Church), young Paul Revere had served as youthful bellringer. Patriotic parishioners discharged the loyalist rector just before lanterns were put in the steeple to signal Gage's plans.

the regulars were abroad and heading for the waterfront. Warren sent one of his dispatch riders, William Dawes, off to Lexington and Concord by way of the road that led across Boston Neck. Paul Revere waited only long enough to see that the two signal lanterns in North Church were lit; then two friends rowed him across to Charlestown. On the opposite shore Colonel Conant and others waited. Revere mounted a horse and galloped off. His fellow patriots disappeared down other dark roads to alert minutemen and militia in many quarters.

Revere raced toward Lexington, rousing farmers along the road, awakening the villages of Medford and Menotomy (now Arlington), and galloping on again. Once he ran into two officers of Gage's patrol but wheeled about in time to dash down another road and escape in the dark. He reached Lexington about midnight, roused Hancock and Adams, and while they prepared to flee, waited about half an hour until Dawes arrived by his longer route. Then the two, along with Dr. Samuel Prescott, who had lingered long courting a young lady in Lexington, continued on toward Concord. About halfway there two of Gage's redcoats suddenly appeared and stopped them at pistol point. The three broke and ran. Dawes turned and headed back toward Lexington. Prescott jumped his horse over a stone wall, escaped, and went on to give the alarm in Concord. Revere headed for a wood,

Lacking but a flame, one of the lanterns used to alert the couriers is still serviceable. It gleamed above a peninsula city of 20,000 connected to the mainland by a causeway and by mutual fear of a British attack.

but was hopelessly surrounded when half a dozen more British guards appeared. When questioned, Revere boldly informed his captors that 500 American militia were even then assembling on Lexington Green. At the sound of shots—a rallying signal used by the Americans—the British became alarmed and set Revere free after putting him afoot. He walked back to Lexington, arriving there in time to help Hancock and Adams load a last chest of papers in their carriage. He then climbed in and rode away with them. Thus ended Paul Revere's ride.

In the meantime, the British force, commanded by Lieutenant Colonel Francis Smith and Major John Pitcairn, had set out for Lexington. As the redcoats trudged silently through the dark countryside, they soon realized that they were not the only men stirring in the night. They heard the eerie tolling of church bells in the darkness, now near, now far; they heard musket shots and knew that no hunters were in the field at that hour. Now and then they caught glimpses of shadowy figures stealing by on mysterious errands, and a general unease grew in the ranks. By the time they reached Menotomy, even their slow-witted leader, Colonel Smith, was aware that a great many Americans were abroad in the night, and he sent an express rider back to Boston to ask Gage for reinforcements.

The sun rises about five o'clock on April 19, and it

Roused from sleep on April 18, 1775, Paul Revere was then hustled past guardposts, put aboard a skiff, and rowed quietly across moonlit Boston Harbor past anchored British ships (below).

was above the horizon when the British column came over a gentle hill and saw the Lexington village green. The green was—and still is—triangular in shape, with one side of the triangle formed by the road to Concord. Drawn up on the green were some seventy-five men, about two-thirds of the Lexington Minute Company, under the command of Captain John Parker.

Upon seeing the minutemen, Major Pitcairn, who was at the head of the British column, led his men off the road and onto the green, at the same time changing them from column into line; then, as the redcoats swept toward the forlorn band of minutemen, he called on the Americans to disperse. At first Parker ordered his men to stand their ground; then, realizing the hopelessness of their situation, he commanded them to disband.

Pitcairn had orders to disarm any rebels he came upon; now, as the minutemen were leaving the field in response to his command, he bawled out to his men the somewhat contradictory order to surround the Americans. Don't fire, he shouted, but disarm them.

At this uneasy moment, as the redcoat line bore down on the minutemen and extended its flanks to surround them, there was a shot, followed by two or three more. No one knows who fired that first shot. It may have been discharged by a minuteman, probably panicked by the line of regulars bearing down on him. One redcoat was very slightly wounded, and Pitcairn's horse was grazed. The British troops, ignoring Pitcairn's orders not to fire, began a general and enthusiastic blasting at the retreating minutemen. Some shouted that the village should be set afire; a number headed for a tavern whence, it was claimed, shots had come. Eventually their officers got them under control again, and as they formed up in ranks on the green where eight minutemen lay dead—another nine were wounded—they gave three cheers. They resumed the march to Concord with fifes and drums playing since there was no longer any need to keep up the pretense of secrecy.

Concord was awake and ready. Dr. Prescott, after escaping from the redcoat patrol, had alerted the village some time before two in the morning. The militia had been called out and assembled on the green; the villagers had resumed the work of hiding the military supplies in attics, cellars, and haymows.

Near dawn, however, the militia grew restless. Was this just another false alarm? Reuben Brown, the local saddler and one of the Concord militia, volunteered to find out for his uneasy fellows where the redcoats were. He rode toward Lexington and arrived in time to see the flash and gleam of British uniforms, to hear the rattle of musketry, and to see gunsmoke rising in the early morning air. Shaken, he hurried back to report that not only were redcoats on the way but that there had been a clash of some kind at Lexington.

The Concord militia, now reinforced by men from nearby Lincoln, deliberated and decided to reconnoiter in force. Some 150 strong, they marched toward Lexington until they saw the British column approaching and heard its fifes and drums. It took no second look at the long redcoat ranks to tell the Americans that they were outnumbered. Whereupon they very sensibly countermarched; their fifes and drums picked up the British cadence, and the provincial militia preceded the regulars almost like an escort of honor. Corporal Amos Barrett afterwards remembered the odd scene: "We thought we wood go and meet the Britsch . . . . We marched Down to wards L[exington] about a mild or a mild[and a] half and we see them acomming. we halted and stayd till they got within about 100 Rods then we was orded to the about face and marchd before them with our Droms and fifes agoing and also the B[ritish]. we had grand musick."

The Americans retreated through Concord village, across North Bridge over the Concord River, and up

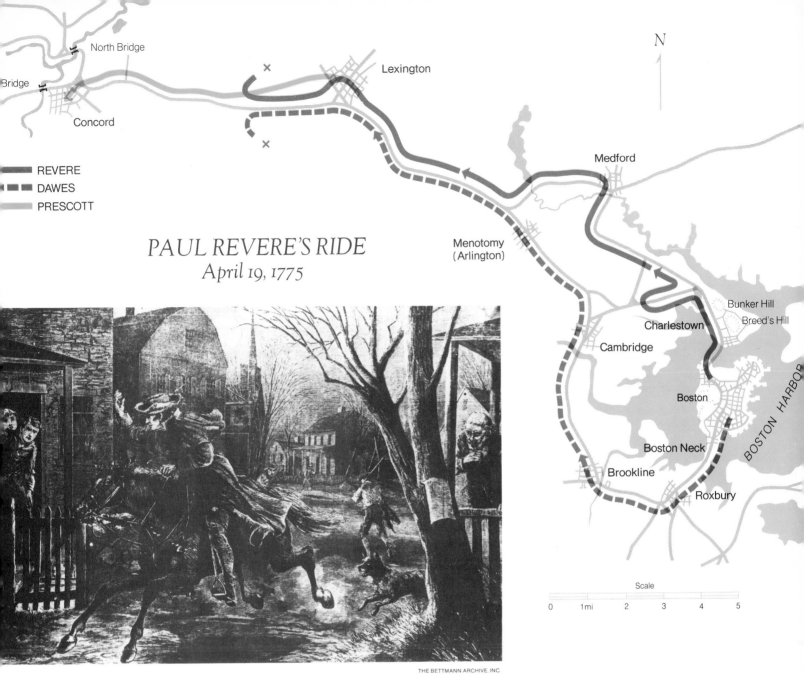

REVERE
DAWES
PRESCOTT

PAUL REVERE'S RIDE
April 19, 1775

THE BETTMANN ARCHIVE, INC.

"The regulars are coming out!" Paul Revere cried to patriots protecting Sam Adams and John Hancock in Lexington. Then, having warned those leaders that they might be captured, he pounded further along his route (above) accompanied by William Dawes, a second messenger. Slippery enough to have fooled sentries on Boston's causeway, Dawes (left) slipped away again when the couriers were halted by a British patrol. Revere finally won his release—but lost his borrowed horse—when the soldiers discerned that the countryside was aroused.

a hill on the other side. The British stationed three light infantry companies to guard North Bridge and sent four more to search for arms and supplies at the farm of Colonel James Barrett, the commander of the Concord militia. The remaining three were dispatched to guard South Bridge. The grenadier companies began searching the village for military stores, and Colonel Smith established a command post on a vantage point in the village burying ground. It was then about eight o'clock in the morning.

The search of the village was far from thorough or ruthless. Three cannon were found and smashed, but were later repaired. A few tents and a number of tools were destroyed, and some barrels of flour and bags of musket balls were found and thrown into the millpond. But the barrels were not broken nor the bags cut, and everything was fished out after the British left, with only minor damage to the flour. In many cases soldiers accepted the word of villagers that their houses concealed no forbidden items; one lady turned searchers away from a closed room by saying that an invalid lay inside, when in fact it was filled with military goods. A number of wooden gun carriages were found in the meetinghouse, dragged outside, and set afire, but when the meetinghouse eaves began smouldering, grenadiers yielded to the entreaties of an old woman and doused the flames with water.

Across the river the Americans had moved down the

"Disperse ye rebels! Lay down your arms!" called Maj. John Pitcairn (at far right in engraving below) before his skittish troops started firing. One victim, Jonathan Harrington, managed to reach home, dying in his wife's arms (foreground).

Personable Maj. Pitcairn (opposite) lost his silver-mounted pistols (right) at Concord. His British marines, long held on shipboard, had to wade ashore after a sloppy landing maneuver, then hike 13 miles through a night of spooky alarms.

LEXINGTON HISTORICAL SOCIETY

hill to a position nearer North Bridge and the British. They had been joined by men from Acton, Bedford, and other nearby towns; their numbers had grown to several hundred, far outnumbering the British at the bridge. While they were discussing their course of action, they saw the pillar of smoke from the burning gun carriages and drew the obvious but wrong conclusion: the British were putting the torch to Concord. They decided they could no longer stand indecisive, but must "march into the middle of the town for its defence or die in the attempt." Colonel Barrett gave the order, and they filed off toward the bridge, an Acton company in the van, its two fifers and two drummers setting the pace.

Captain Laurie, commanding the British at the bridge, withdrew his men to the Concord side of the river when he saw the Americans coming, leaving only a small detail to take up the bridge planking. This gross mistreatment of town property outraged the Americans, and an officer shouted to the British to leave the bridge alone, whereupon the men meekly stopped what they were doing and joined the rest of the redcoats across the bridge. Captain Laurie, greatly outnumbered, sent to Colonel Smith for reinforcements, and that officer, when he received the message, personally took command of a company of grenadiers and headed for the bridge. But, as British Lieutenant John Barker, who was present at the bridge, somewhat caustically wrote, Smith "put himself at their head by which means he stopt 'em from being [in] time enough, for being a very fat heavy man he wou'd not have reached the Bridge in half an hour tho' it was not half a mile to it."

Smith and his rescue force were still on the way when the American column reached the bridge. The British opened fire, first a few harmless shots, then a volley that killed Captain Isaac Davis and drummer boy Abner Hosmer of the leading Acton company and injured several provincials. The American muskets fired in return, and three redcoat soldiers fell dead or dying; four officers and five men were wounded. Then, incredibly, these disciplined British troops broke and fled in utter panic, leaving their dead and wounded. On their way they met Colonel Smith at the head of his grenadiers; Smith restored some order and all returned to the village.

The Americans did not know what to do with their victory. After pursuing the enemy a short distance, some went back across the bridge and up the hill again. Others continued on a short distance toward Concord and took up positions behind a stone wall on a ridge. While the Americans were thus divided, the four redcoat companies returning from a fruitless search at Barrett's farm were able to cross the bridge unopposed and reach Concord unscathed.

Smith, back at his vantage point in the cemetery, could see that the number of provincials across North Bridge was growing steadily larger; he also saw that American units were drifting down and spreading out on all sides of the village. His force was not only outnumbered, it was being surrounded. He called in the three companies that had been uneventfully watching South Bridge, got his troops in marching order, and at noon led his force out of Concord, carrying his wounded in commandeered carriages.

About a mile out of Concord the Bedford road from the north joins the Lexington road at a point called Meriam's Corners. Now striding down the Bedford road came minutemen from more distant towns: Billerica, Reading, Chelmsford, Wilmington, Woburn. These men, some of whom had come as far as fifteen miles on foot, were informed of the situation by messengers from Concord. They took up positions along the Lexington road, where they were joined by many Concord men who had circled ahead of the British. There is disagreement over what happened when the redcoats came down the road. The British claim that the Americans fired first. The American story is that the rear ranks of the redcoat force, exasperated by the way the provincials dogged their steps, turned and fired a harmless volley. The American reply killed two redcoats and wounded others, and the shooting that began there did not stop for hours—not until, as one American was later to recall, "A grait many Lay dead and the Road was bloddy."

From Meriam's Corners on, the provincials kept up a constant fire. They fought not as military units but as individuals, and their strategy was simple: to shoot, then run to keep abreast of the British column, and shoot again. Many dropped out as their ammunition gave out or they became weary or perhaps when courage flagged at the whistling of English bullets. But there were always plenty of fresh men to fill the gaps, for the alarm that had been sounded the preceding night had spread far and fast.

The Americans did not come off untouched. British fire from the road got some; others were so absorbed in getting close for a good shot that they did not see British flankers behind them, and more than one was thus shot in the back. But by and large the regulars could only plod their nightmare way along, leaving their dead and badly wounded where they fell, not even daring to think of all the miles that still lay between them and safety. Though the fight was continuous, there were places where it raged especially hot. Scarcely a mile beyond Meriam's Corners, the American fire rose again to a crescendo at Hardy's Hill where several companies of minutemen lay in ambush in the thick woods that bordered the road. Beyond Hardy's Hill the road turned sharply to the left and, some 500 yards farther on, swung back to the right again. In this double angle, where heavy undergrowth kept the British flankers in, American muskets took a heavy toll. Beyond the angle a pasture full of large boulders gave

excellent protection to snipers until the British drove them out; beyond that John Parker's minutemen, reorganized and inspirited after their savage treatment on Lexington Green that morning, got satisfying revenge when they set up their own private ambush and shot down a number of redcoats. Colonel Smith himself was struck in the thigh during this concentrated fire and knocked off his horse.

A short way beyond Parker's ambush, Major Pitcairn rallied his force in the protection of a small hill and got the column organized into reasonable marching order again. The respite was brief and costly. Several ma-

Climax of the Lexington-Concord action: confrontation at Concord's North Bridge. As depicted in Amos Doolittle's sketch below, the redcoats retreated when minutemen attacked to save Concord. British commander Lt. Col. Francis Smith (shown at left viewing the action from cemetery command post) then found himself nearly cut off from the retreat route to Boston.

rines were killed holding back the provincials from the hill, and the stop gave the rebels a chance to catch up with the head of the column again. When the redcoats resumed their march, the leading companies were raked by a withering fire; Pitcairn was thrown from his horse, but was unhurt. From this point on British morale began to collapse. The light infantry companies were so exhausted from crashing through woods and swamps that they were no longer able to operate as flankers, and the main body of troops on the road became completely demoralized as men continued to fall dead and wounded from the muskets of a swarming but largely unseen enemy. As one man remarked, "It seemed as if men came down from the clouds." By the time the column neared Lexington most of the men were no longer making an attempt to return the rebels' fire. The American farmers and townspeople were on the verge of victory.

On the edge of Lexington village the British officers still on their feet resorted to a desperate measure to bring the column back to some semblance of order and discipline: they put themselves at the head of it and threatened to shoot their own men if they did not stop and straighten up their ranks. Even as they made this hopeless gesture, the officers were astounded to hear their men break into cheers; turning around they saw the leading company of a powerful force of redcoats about to enter Lexington from the other direction. At the same time they heard the report of a cannon.

The rescue force was the one Smith had sent for

A Boston broadside lists 62 men killed and wounded at Concord.

early that morning. As a matter of fact, Gage himself had had second thoughts after Smith had left and had made plans to send relief under the command of Earl Percy even before he received Smith's message.

As the brigade, one thousand strong, entered Lexington, the men of Smith's battered command staggered onto Lexington Green and fell down in utter collapse, while Percy's two cannon boomed and the firing of the bewildered Americans died down.

Percy allowed the exhausted men to rest for an hour; then at 3:30 he started for Boston. Once more the rebel muskets began firing. Hundreds of fresh men were arriving from eastern towns now, all eager for their chance at the redcoats. By this time the British troops were not only searching every roadside home; they were looting as well. The fighting was especially bitter in Menotomy where the British had to march between rows of houses and other buildings held by rebel snipers. There was house-to-house and often hand-to-hand fighting. The British lost forty men killed and about eighty wounded at Menotomy, just about half their casualties for that entire bloody day.

Ahead of Menotomy lay Cambridge village, and beyond that Brookline and Roxbury—and evening was approaching. Percy did not fancy any more house-to-house fighting, especially in the dark. In a surprise move he took the fork leading to Charlestown, a much shorter route than the road to Boston. A force of rebels held a hill beside the Charlestown road, but Percy's cannon and men forced them off. Now the way was clear. Soon the grimy, dazed redcoats had crossed the

42

A propagandist cartoon portrays British troops as ''Wild Irish Asses'' looting and burning during the retreat from Concord.

narrow neck of land that connected the Charlestown peninsula with the mainland. In the river between Boston and Charlestown lay British warships, their guns ready. The redcoats were safe at last.

That day 73 regulars had been killed, 174 wounded, and 26 missing, not a rousing tribute to the shooting of the Americans. Still, it must be remembered that the musket was not a sharpshooter's weapon and that the

Americans were farmers, not marksmen. The Americans lost 49 killed, 41 wounded, and 5 missing.

That night the British force camped upon Bunker Hill, and many of the rebels, instead of going home, began to ring Boston with the campfires that would soon become siege lines. In less than two months many of those same men would die facing each other in another bloody encounter. The battle would take its name from the hill where the redcoats slept that night, but the actual site was not much more than a musket shot away, and the late-rising moon revealed its outlines. It was called Breed's Hill.

''There was not a stone-wall or house . . . from whence the Rebels did not fire upon us,'' reported Lord Percy, whose British relief forces assisted in the retreat. In Alonzo Chappell's painting (below), some redcoats reload while others hold off snipers.

Battle for Boston

Quietly by moonlight Col. William Prescott's men erect hasty defenses atop Breed's Hill.

"Possession of Bunker's Hill appears of Importance to the Safety of this Colony," concluded a meeting of the Committee of Safety two months after Concord and Lexington. The committee and its leader, handsome Dr. Joseph Warren, saw that Boston was vulnerable; it rode on the water like a sitting duck between two headlands. To the north and west across the Charles River rose Bunker Hill, which was joined to a lesser prominence known as Breed's Hill above the village of Charlestown. There the British occupation troops, in trying to dislodge a hastily entrenched, ill-organized provincial army task force, suffered more than 1,000 casualties (nearly half those engaged). To the south and east across Boston Harbor rose Dorchester Heights. There George Washington, the Americans' new commander, would emplace cannon brought from Ticonderoga in March, 1776, forcing the British to flee into the sea, and winning a major victory for the patriots.

Weighted with full field packs, Gen. Howe's redcoats march resolutely forward (opposite) in the frontal attack that failed to take Breed's Hill from the Americans (who, according to tradition, withheld fire till they saw British eye whites). Royal marines led by Maj. Pitcairn launched the final successful charge, killing Dr. Warren and wounding Col. Prescott (left and right respectively in detail from John Trumbull's painting above).

OVERLEAF:
Before the battle, shells from
Boston set Charlestown ablaze.

45

BOSTON

CH

Assault on the North

3

News of the battle of Bunker Hill reached Philadelphia on June 22, 1775, stunning the delegates to the Second Continental Congress, which had formally convened in that city on May 10. The news was of special interest to a tall, powerfully built, forty-three-year-old Virginia planter named George Washington. For on the morning of June 16, as the Americans in Cambridge had been preparing their advance to Breed's Hill, Washington had accepted an appointment as "General . . . to command all the continental forces, raised, or to be raised, for the defense of American liberty."

The nomination of a Virginian as commander in chief of the Continental Army had come as a surprise to many delegates; they had expected a New Englander to be named. But the man behind the nomination, John Adams, had realized the importance of making the struggle against Britain a truly united effort, not one centered in New England alone.

The new commander in chief immediately prepared to depart for Cambridge where he would establish his headquarters and assume command of the troops surrounding Boston. There, in 1776, after many long months of siege operations, he would force the British to flee by threatening to bombard the city with cannon captured almost a year earlier in a raid on Fort Ticonderoga—a raid led by two flamboyant fighters, Ethan Allen and Benedict Arnold. The effects of the raid were twofold: not only did it help lift the siege of Boston, it also served as a prelude to another campaign— the patriots' assault on the north. As a bold beginning to a disastrous campaign, the saga of Ticonderoga perhaps deserves retelling.

Echoes of the shots at Lexington and Concord had

Carrying sprung boats and spare provisions, Col. Benedict Arnold's men trudge through the Maine wilderness on a mission to seize Quebec and unite all American colonies against the crown.

brought thousands of patriots to the environs of Boston to help drive out the British. Among these men was one Benedict Arnold, a short, stocky man in his mid-thirties whose long black hair and swarthy complexion contrasted sharply with his pale eyes. A natural leader, Arnold possessed far more than the normal share of driving ambition, fighting courage, and general ability.

As soon as he heard about the first battle with the British, Arnold, who was then a captain of the Connecticut militia, summoned his men and set out for Cambridge. On the way he met Colonel Samuel H. Parsons who was on the road to Hartford to recruit troops for Boston. Parsons deplored the lack of cannon in patriot hands, and Arnold pointed to ill-defended Ticonderoga as a place where cannon could be easily obtained. Both then went their separate ways.

At Cambridge, Arnold sought out the Massachusetts Committee of Safety and informed them too that there were many cannon at Ticonderoga, that the fort was in a "ruinous condition," and that it was manned by "not more than fifty men at most." The committee was interested in Arnold's information, and for a variety of reasons. Ticonderoga not only contained artillery; it also occupied a position of extreme strategic importance. Situated on a headland between Lake Champlain and Lake George, Ticonderoga seemed to control the one easy route to and from Canada—a water passageway consisting of the St. Lawrence River, the Richelieu, Lake Champlain, and the Hudson. Since Canada was in British hands, the northern waters were potentially dangerous as an attack route.

Consequently, on May 3, 1775, the committee offered Arnold a colonel's commission and authorized him to lead an expedition up through the New Hampshire Grants (now Vermont) to Fort Ticonderoga. Arnold ordered supplies and sent out officers to recruit militiamen; then he hurried north alone. He arrived at Castleton in the Grants, twenty-odd miles southeast of Ti-

Ethan Allen and the Green Mountain Boys

"Ever since I arrived to a state of manhood, I have felt a sincere passion for liberty."

So Ethan Allen explained how he became the Revolution's champion in the New Hampshire Grants (as Vermont was then called) on a May day in 1775. His brother had galloped up to the Catamount Inn in Bennington soon after daybreak with news that the revolutionary Committee of Correspondence wanted Fort Ticonderoga taken from the British *at once*. While other Granters debated loyalty to the crown —a crown that had finally supported their property claims against those of settlers from New York—Ethan Allen scorned their caution. He persuaded his Green Mountain Boys and other followers to fight for freedom against tyranny.

A natural leader who stood six foot six and had a reputation for strangling wildcats with his bare hands, he had been born in Litchfield, Conn. on January 21, 1738. His frontier farmer family gave him what education they could, and he grew up a mighty brawler and original philosopher.

He organized five companies of Green Mountain Boys (above) to cast the hated Yorkers out of the Grants. Back over the western borders he flung surveyors and magistrates, earning from them the title "Outlaw." With motives both magnanimous and mercenary (for he himself had invested in Grants land speculation), he protected the original settlers' property.

Then, having accepted the order to take Ticonderoga as his personal calling, he prepared to put brain and brawn on the line for the freedom of all Americans.

---

conderoga, on the evening of May 8 and was directed to the house of one Richard Bentley. There he encountered obstacles to his immediate glory—obstacles which, ironically, he had helped create.

After meeting Arnold on the road, Colonel Parsons had continued on to Hartford and had immediately told that town's Committee of Correspondence about the condition of Fort Ticonderoga. Simultaneously, the committee had had laid before it another proposal for seizing the fort, accompanied by a request for help in the enterprise. The author of the proposal, a colorful Grants fighting man named Ethan Allen who commanded a group of men known as the Green Mountain Boys, was awaiting a reply in Bennington. The coincidence of the two reports prompted swift action. The Hartford Committee withdrew £300 from the Connecticut Colony treasury for the purchase of supplies and recruitment of men.

Some fifty of these recruits had arrived in Castleton by the morning of May 8. Their officers, along with several of Allen's chief subordinates, were gathered at Bentley's house when Arnold arrived there, displayed his commission, and announced in confident tones that he had come to assume command of the expedition.

"The hell you will!" was, in effect, the immediate reply of Ethan Allen's men. Astonishment gave way to taunting laughter; ridicule yielded to flaming anger. But Arnold, though he stood solitary (his own recruits were yet several days south of him), stood with rock-like firmness. The one vestige of legality that this whole operation possessed had been bestowed upon it by the commission in Arnold's hand, and the commission named him commander. He must, he did insist!

Ethan Allen was not present in person during this acrimonious discussion. Having dispatched couriers to round up every Green Mountain Boy in the area, he had set out for Hand's Cove, the final rendezvous point, before Arnold arrived in Castleton. It was to Hand's Cove, therefore, that the quarrel over command was now transferred. A coldly aloof Arnold, escorted by a hotly angry group of Allen's subordinates, arrived there sometime after midnight on May 10.

Allen was already plagued with anxiety. The boats he needed to ferry his men across Lake Champlain had not yet arrived, and he feared the approach of dawn, which would render surprise impossible. Then came this stranger's bold challenge to his authority.

Finally, after much argument it was decided that

Arnold would march at Allen's side when the attack
was made. Arnold, accepting this arrangement because he had to, chose to interpret it as an equal share
of the command. All that is known for certain, however, is that he was among those present when two
boats arrived at last, two only, barely in time to permit
a single secret crossing of the lake before dawn.

Allen jammed the boats to capacity—but could
squeeze in no more than eighty-five men. Theirs were
the only rifles mustered when he moved upon the fort.

The assault was full of sound and fury that signified,
as it turned out, a great deal for the American cause.
Complete surprise was achieved. A single British
sentry, posted outside the fortress, aimed his flint-
lock point-blank at Allen as the latter charged at the
head of his men toward a break in the southern wall.
The musket misfired. The sentry fled into the fort, pursued by a yelling, sword-waving Allen who, in turn,
was followed by Arnold and the others, all of them
save Arnold emitting Indian war whoops in terrifying
volume. Inside the walls a single British regular,
emerging from barracks, rushed Allen with fixed bayonet and was promptly knocked down by the flat of
Allen's sword. It was he, lying prone with Allen's
sword at his throat, who pointed out his commandant's
headquarters. Toward these Allen at once made his
roaring way. He charged up the stairway allegedly
shouting, "Come out of there, you damned old rat!"

A British lieutenant, trousers in hand, appeared at
the top of the stairs. To him Allen addressed a loud
demand for the fort's surrender.

"In whose name?" asked the bewildered lieutenant.

"In the name of the Great Jehovah and the Continental Congress!" cried Ethan Allen, according to his
own later account, thereby asserting a piety he wholly
lacked and an authority he did not possess; he had had
no communication whatever with the gentlemen in
Philadelphia.

Patroon and patriot, Philip Schuyler (left), received one of Congress's four major generalships in 1775. He suffered from gout and ambitious juniors, particularly dashing Richard Montgomery (opposite).

Shortly thereafter the fort's commandant, Captain William de la Place, appeared and, helpless to do otherwise, surrendered his fort to the invaders.

Two days later Allen's second in command, Seth Warner, occupied Crown Point, several miles up the lake from Ticonderoga, without firing a shot. A few days after that, Arnold, the only patriot present who knew how to sail a ship, took command of a schooner which had been seized by the Green Mountain Boys from a wealthy Tory at Skenesboro and sailed for Fort St. John's at the northern end of the lake. There he surprised a fourteen-man garrison (no shots were fired) and briefly occupied the place. But he could not remain. The arrival of a contingent of British regulars much too large for him to handle was hourly expected. However, he did capture some supplies and a seventy-ton sloop, which he sailed triumphantly southward.

In Philadelphia the Second Continental Congress hastened to disown the rash attack on Ticonderoga. It recommended immediate retirement from the captured forts and the removal of all war material to a place of storage at the southern end of Lake George.

It was a recommendation that aroused vehement protests not only from the fiery leaders of the expedition, but also from the colonies themselves. Popular spirits had been lifted high by news of Ticonderoga's fall, and many colonists wanted to push northward and wrest all of Canada away from Britain.

Such sentiments, conveyed to Philadelphia from men of authority in New England and New York, had their effect upon the Congress. It was an effect soon augmented by intelligence from American agents in Canada. Reportedly, the mass of Canadian French, the *habitants* as they were called, remained restive under British rule. If the colonies were to send a strong force northward, the majority of the French might embrace the patriot cause. Reportedly, also, British troop strength in Canada was woefully small. The bulk of

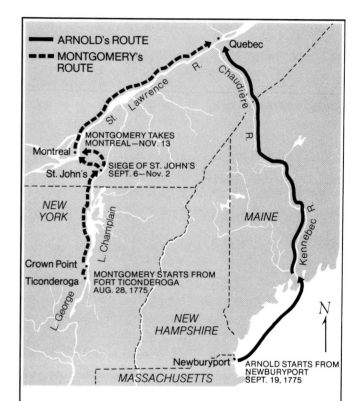

Two Routes North

Like a gangplank into Canada, Lake Champlain thrusts north from New York, inviting would-be conquerors to come across. From his Fort Ticonderoga base (junction of Lakes Champlain and George) Gen. Philip Schuyler prepared to move north on Congress's orders on August 28, 1775, three weeks before Washington approved Benedict Arnold's plan to attack Canada by way of Maine.

Even before Schuyler's replacement, Richard Montgomery, took St. John's by siege, rash Americans urged immediate seizure of Montreal. In one such assault, Ethan Allen was captured.

Allen barely survived two years' imprisonment. But a worse consequence of Montreal (which fell on November 13) was Gen. Guy Carleton's escape. That skilled British commander would be waiting for Montgomery and Arnold on the heights of Quebec.

the British forces in America were now cooped up in Boston; in Canada, General Guy Carleton had but four regiments under his command, of whom only 550 men were fit for duty. These, moreover, were widely scattered among various posts. On the other hand, it was certain that by the spring of 1776 Carleton would be greatly reinforced from across the sea and, meanwhile, he was attempting to recruit troops to defend Canada.

Finally, after weeks of deliberation, the Congress reversed its policy on Canada. By this time, Washington had reached Cambridge and was considering his situation. Plagued by a munitions shortage, he needed the artillery captured at Ticonderoga, and that winter he would send a young man named Henry Knox north to bring back the guns. Long before Knox's trip, however, the assault on the north would be under way.

On June 27, 1775, Congress authorized General Philip Schuyler, the patriot commander in New York, to move into Canada and seize any positions vital to colonial security. General Schuyler, however, was a better officer of supply than combat commander. For many weeks he remained at Ticonderoga gathering men and supplies, boats for transport, and intelligence of dubious accuracy from the north. In fact when his force was finally set in motion, on August 28, it was not by his order at all (he was absent from Ticonderoga, attending a conference in Albany) but by that of his second in command, General Richard Montgomery.

Montgomery's period as temporary commander was brief but intense. He led 1,200 men toward St. John's, held then by 700 seasoned British troops. In preliminary skirmishing along the approaches to the fort, the redcoats handled the Americans roughly. Schuyler rejoined his command just as these first fights were taking place and at once halted offensive operations to erect defensive works. Soon, however, reinforcements arrived, swelling his ranks to nearly two thousand. Schuyler, a decision determined by his great preponderance of force, was about to resume the offensive when he suddenly fell ill, so ill that he was forced to relinquish his command to Montgomery and go back to Ticonderoga.

Montgomery was thereby enabled to press the offensive, although he did so with deliberate speed. He was acutely aware that his great numerical superiority over the enemy was offset by their possession of strong defensive works and by his lack of cannon powerful enough to reduce them. His men, moreover, were a various, undisciplined crew of short-term enlistment, having small respect for military authority: they could be led but not commanded. Montgomery therefore wisely decided against any attempt to carry St. John's by storm; he besieged it instead.

The St. John's garrison held out for fifty-five days. Its commandant, Major Charles Preston, on November 2, when it had long been obvious that his position was untenable and that he and his men faced starvation, accepted Montgomery's generous terms of surrender. Weeks earlier, patriot artillery, impotent against thick stone walls, had pounded into submission the only

other obstacle to an advance on Montreal, this point being the wooden fort named Chambly. The way to Montreal was now open, and Montgomery did not hesitate. Enriched by the booty he had captured at St. John's, which included cannon, stocks of muskets, bountiful supplies of ammunition, and some, though not enough, warm clothing for his men, he moved as swiftly as possible to the St. Lawrence. He crossed the river without difficulty and, on November 13, occupied Montreal without a fight. General Carleton, who had barely 150 troops with him in the town, fled by boat downstream to Quebec.

And there, safely in the citadel, Carleton heard more bad news. Montgomery's was not the only American force that threatened him. On November 8, to the astonishment of the Canadians who saw them, there had abruptly appeared on the southern shore of the St. Lawrence, directly opposite Quebec, a ragged scarecrow band of 650 armed and incredibly determined American fighting men, under the command of Colonel Benedict Arnold!

Back in August, George Washington had written to General Schuyler, then in command at Ticonderoga, asking for his advice about a "Plan of an Expedition which has engaged my thoughts for several days. It is to penetrate into Canada by Way of Kennebeck River and so to Quebeck. . . ." The route had been suggested some months earlier by a Colonel Jonathan Brewer. He had described to the authorities how a force could travel by boat up the Kennebec River to a point separated by a "Great Carrying Place" from a sharp upstream bend, north to northwest, in the Dead River; then overland westward across a few miles of carrying; then by boat up the Dead to a point near its source where a height of land formed the natural boundary between Maine and Canada; then over the height to the headwaters of the Chaudière River; and finally,

down the Chaudière to its mouth on the St. Lawrence, a few miles above Quebec. Washington had received a favorable reply from Schuyler and soon thereafter had decided to send the expedition. The man he chose to lead it was Benedict Arnold.

Arnold, having been frustrated in his attempt to lead an invasion northward from Ticonderoga, accept-

Painted in 1776 when he looked like the colonies' fiercest general, this portrait of 35-year-old Benedict Arnold shows him above Quebec dressed as the traditional hero: silver gorget at throat, red sash at ample waist, sword and hand idly at hip.

"Very troublesome indeed," remarked Arnold of progress up Maine's Kennebec River, across half-frozen bogs, and over the 2,000-ft. height of land (right). Of 1,092 who started, 675—including two wives—made it.

DRAWINGS BY PAUL HOFFMASTER

ed with alacrity and immediately went to work. An order went at once to Reuben Colburn, a boat-builder in the tiny settlement of Gardinerstown, on the shore of the Kennebec, for the construction of 200 bateaux; each was to be large enough to carry six or seven men with baggage and provisions, yet light enough for easy portage. Other orders called for the accumulation of needed supplies at Gardinerstown. Some 1,100 men, most of them volunteers, made up the expeditionary force: ten companies of New England musketmen, two companies of Pennsylvania riflemen, and one company of Virginia riflemen under the command of a giant woodsman, Captain Dan Morgan. As his personal aide Arnold chose a personable young man by the name of Aaron Burr.

On September 11, Arnold began the march to Newburyport. From this point some days later the entire force sailed in eleven vessels to the mouth of the Kennebec. There, at Gardinerstown, the commander encountered his first bad omen. The bateaux he had ordered were shoddily made, and many were smaller than specified. Much green pine had been used, so that the boats were heavier than if made of seasoned timber (each bateau weighed at least 400 pounds) and were bound to spring leaks as the green wood warped and opened at the seams. Arnold did not hesitate to proceed, however. A scouting party was sent forward in two birchbark canoes to reconnoiter and mark portage trails. The main force was separated into four divisions, the leading one composed of the three companies of riflemen. They loaded their supplies into the bateaux and began to pole their way upstream.

At first all went well. Not until the expedition passed the site of present-day Augusta did its troubles begin. The portages proved longer, more numerous, and much more difficult than indicated by the map Arnold followed. The labor of carrying supplies and the overly heavy bateaux across them reduced the strongest men to exhaustion. Across parts of the Great Carrying Place, heavily burdened men were forced to wade through knee-deep mud. Then as the expedition entered the rugged northwest Maine wilderness, the weather turned bad. Incessant, cold rain soaked the men to the skin and brought the Dead River to flood height. By that time nearly all the bateaux had sprung leaks. Several were swamped. Arms were lost; so were provisions. And the provision loss, added to the fact that the expedition now lagged behind the original schedule, meant extreme hardship and danger.

The forward units were the first to suffer from food shortage. Of all Arnold's men they performed the heaviest labor and ran the greatest risks. They were the trailblazers who cleared clogged river channels and cut back the dense undergrowth in forests. The pioneers among them were usually Morgan's riflemen, although there was some rotation of leadership. Arnold himself remained at the head of this straggling column, with the ever resourceful Burr at his side, his example of high courage and good cheer being an inspiration to his men.

As October advanced, the early northern winter closed down: one morning the expedition awoke to find six inches of snow on the ground. By then clothing repeatedly soaked and brush-torn was so tattered that it gave inadequate protection against the increasing chill. Nor was there any protection against lengthening cold nights. Inevitably, there was much sickness. The rear division became heavily cumbered with men left behind by the forward divisions—men whose weight was often added to that of the supplies which the rear division carried from one water-passage to another.

Of the expedition's total food supply, this division, under the command of Lieutenant Colonel Roger Enos of Connecticut, had a disproportionately large share. The expedition's surgeon, Dr. Isaac Senter, recorded

55

Newville.

Cul de Sac

River St. Laurence

The Siege of Quebec

"I think our fate extremely doubtful," Governor Guy Carleton wrote London as the siege began. Only Quebec stood against the invading Americans' drive to claim all Canada for the Revolution.

But with a veteran's wisdom Carleton knew Quebec's defensive secret: never sally forth to meet the superior enemy as had Montcalm. Besides artillery, he commanded loyalty—even from French inhabitants. As revolutionaries shivered and deserted, the defenders' resolve grew stronger.

For three December weeks the city endured constant shelling. Then on the night of December 30, 1775, the Americans came on amid a blizzard.

Savior of Quebec, Gov. Sir Guy Carleton (above) was a wounded veteran of Wolfe's memorable victory over Montcalm in 1759. When Benedict Arnold arrived before Quebec 16 years later, he stood at Point Nevis (numbered 20 in the 18th century print at left) and pondered how to breach the citadel's defenses. A lofty city, Quebec was divided between the Lower Town (17) and the Upper Town with its churches and official buildings (4-8).

"Liberty or death" slogans pinned to their uniforms gave American attackers courage. And the giant-sized Virginian Dan Morgan gave them new heart when Arnold fell. But none of this availed as they hurled themselves on the final barrier in Quebec's well-defended Lower Town (opposite).

in his diary entry for Wednesday, October 25, 1775, that when the four divisions were established by Arnold "the provisions were distributed according to the supposed difficulty or facility attending the different dispositions." Since Enos's men, with the way prepared for them, would have the easiest travel, they could bear the heaviest burden. However, the men up front naturally assumed that this supply was for the expeditionary force as a whole, to be equally shared among all.

It was on the day of this diary entry (October 25), amid a "direful howling wilderness, not describable," as Senter wrote, that a fateful "council of war" was held by the officers of the second division and those of Enos's fourth division. Immediately ahead of the men lay the curving headwaters of the Dead River, beyond which was the most difficult of all land travel thus far,

the passage over trackless mountains to Canada's Lake Megantic and the rising of the Chaudière. Despite the hazardous difficulties ahead, the second division's officers were determined to go forward and sought to dissuade those of the fourth from turning back. They argued in vain. The officers of the fourth had already made up their minds not only to quit the expedition but also to take with them the provisions they carried. Thus, when they marched southwestward next day, they weakened the assault force by 350 men and, taking with them desperately needed provisions, placed the whole of the enterprise in seemingly fatal jeopardy.

Contemporary artists tended to portray Montgomery's fate romantically. But the painting below realistically shows the steep trail he took around Cape Diamond. When he perished beneath fire from a strategically located blockhouse (at right), his junior officers abandoned the plan to join Arnold's thrust.

But the rest went on. Not only did they manage to cross over the "height of land," they also took with them a few of the bateaux so that military stores otherwise impossible to carry might be floated down the Chaudière. The iron-willed, iron-thewed Morgan and his men carried seven, an "intolerable labor" whose witnessing "would have made your heart ache." Some of the men "had the flesh worn from their shoulders even to the bone." Yet this anguish counted for nothing in the end, for soon thereafter all the bateaux were wrecked in the swift rapids of the Chaudière.

By then famished men had eaten the few dogs that accompanied them. "Our bill of fare last night and this morning consisted of the jawbone of a swine destitute of any covering," wrote Senter in his entry for Friday, October 27. "This we boiled in a quantity of water . . . with a little thickening [of flour] . . . ."

Nor did their sufferings diminish after they reached Canadian soil. Arnold, by this time, had pushed on ahead of the foremost of the rifle units in order to obtain food from sympathetic *habitants* in nearby settlements. While he was gone, his expeditionary force was daily reduced as men crazed by pain and hunger wandered off the trail, never to be seen again; others collapsed beside the trail and were left to their fate. At almost the last moment possible for survival, the starving men obtained relief; the first food came back from Arnold, who found the French of the Chaudière region not hostile to the patriot cause and certainly very kind and helpful to sick, famished men.

A few days later, after what is assuredly one of the epic marches of history, Arnold stood upon the St. Lawrence shore. A share of his force's fighting strength was already restored, for these were men of great toughness and resiliency. They were ready, even eager, to move against Quebec, visible to them atop its fabled rock across the broad river.

Had they arrived a day or two earlier, they might have taken Quebec with little trouble and significantly altered the course of American history.

The Canadian lieutenant governor, Hector Cramahé, who was responsible for Quebec's defense in Carleton's absence, despaired of holding the city when he first learned of Arnold's arrival on the river's south bank—news that coincided with that of Montgomery's advance to Montreal. He had in all nearly a thousand men, but several hundred of them were French Canadians of doubtful loyalty; moreover, the walls of Quebec were so long that the men had to be very thinly spread. However, before Arnold could cross the river (he did so on the day of Montreal's occupation, November 13), there arrived back in the citadel, after a futile attempt to relieve the British garrison at Fort St. John's, a remarkably able British officer, Lieutenant Colonel Allen Maclean. He brought with him eighty men. Maclean and his men immediately took charge of the city's defense and provided the margin by which Canada, at that crucial point, was saved for the crown. Soon his mettle was backed up by newly arrived Carleton's authority.

On November 14 the Americans stood upon the Plains of Abraham. Twice Arnold demanded Quebec's surrender. Twice his demand was answered by gunfire. He could not attack "without too great a risk," as he later wrote (probably to General Schuyler):

> we therefore invested the town and cut off their communication with the country. We continued in this situation until the 20th, having often attempted to draw out the garrison in vain. On a strict scrutiny of our ammunition, found many of our cartridges (which to appearance were good) inserviceable and not ten rounds each for the men . . . and as the garrison was daily increasing . . . we thought it prudent to retire.

He withdrew to Pointe Aux Trembles, some twenty

Benjamin Franklin

Samuel Chase

Charles Carroll

miles up the river, where General Montgomery joined him "with about 300 men" and "with artillery, clothing, etc.," on the morning of November 27.

On December 5, Montgomery moved onto the Plains of Abraham to begin siege operations. He did so under highly disadvantageous conditions. Carleton contemptuously rejected Montgomery's formal calls for surrender. The capable governor of Canada, later knighted for his role in her salvation, saw that he possessed ample stocks of food and fuel; he could hold out if necessary until the spring of 1776 when he was virtually certain of being reinforced. He and his men were sheltered against the rigorous Canadian winter, as the Americans emphatically were not. Moreover, Montgomery had no assurance that the militiamen whose terms expired at the end of the year would remain with him. Consequently, he felt forced to launch an attack on the city, although he realized the hazards of such an attempt.

The assault was planned to achieve a maximum of deception and surprise, since without these it must surely fail. Montgomery awaited a dark stormy night on which to launch a perhaps unduly complicated tactical maneuver, one requiring a dangerous dispersal of his limited forces. Two noisy rocket-firing feints were to be made against the Upper Town, where the British garrison was strongest. These were to be followed by a two-pronged main assault upon the Lower Town. When that was secured, the Upper Town would be attacked. Montgomery and 300 men were to attack the town from its south or river-facing side while Arnold, with 600, attacked from the north; the two forces were to meet and become one at a designated point in the eastern part of the Lower Town.

The awaited northwester arrived with a vengeance on the evening of December 30. The snowfall was tremendous, and there was a high wind. Around two o'clock in the morning on the last day of 1775, the main attacks got underway. Montgomery and his men, laden with scaling ladders, struggled toward the town through huge drifts and over great jagged cakes of ice piled up from the river. The general, at the head of his men, was forced repeatedly to pause and wait while the column closed up behind him. Finally he arrived at a narrow snow-heaped approach to a fortified house. Pausing again, he called back along the howling wind, "Come on, my good soldiers. Your general calls upon you to come on." Then, while the column yet straggled too far behind, he charged the house, believing its occupants to be unaware of him. He was fatally mistaken. There were four pieces of artillery in the house. These and a score of muskets opened fire at close range. Montgomery and several others were killed instantly. Abruptly the column's command devolved upon a Colonel Donald Campbell. As gunfire continued ahead, he ordered the column to retreat, leaving the dead and wounded behind on bloodstained snow.

Meanwhile, Arnold and his 600 men had forced their way into the Lower Town. They were, alas, expected—the two feints at the Upper Town had wholly failed to distract Carleton. Heavy fire from palisades and house windows took its toll as the assaulting troops advanced. Arnold, who was leading the way, was wounded in the leg at the first barricaded street and had to be taken to the rear. Big, brave Dan Morgan took over the forward command. He reached the rendezvous point and advanced beyond it when Montgomery failed to appear. But as he approached the gateway to the Upper Town, and before the main part of the American column could catch up with him, he and his men were cut off and surrounded. They fought desperately, suffering heavy casualties, until their ammunition gave out. They then perforce surrendered, while the remainder of the patriots withdrew from the town, out onto the Plains of Abraham.

Nearly half of the assault force had been killed, wounded, or captured, whereas the British garrison had suffered but five fatal casualties.

Arnold, despite his wound and his depleted forces, refused to retreat; instead he began to erect defensive works about a mile from Quebec. There he and his men remained until April of 1776—a ragged, tiny band hopelessly besieging a heavily fortified city.

To the patriot leaders in Philadelphia and Boston, the news of the defeat at Quebec came as a shock. Nevertheless, they refused to abandon Canada—which they had come so close to winning—as a lost cause. Instead Congress sent a diplomatic delegation north to try and convince the *habitants* to join the patriot cause; it also began to raise troops for a second assault on Quebec. Had this effort been made a year earlier,

Breaking through ice at the St. Lawrence's mouth, a British relief squadron reached Quebec on May 6, 1776 (below). Reinforced, Carleton drove the smallpox-racked patriots from Canada.

MARINERS MUSEUM, NEWPORT NEWS, VIRGINIA

Battle of Valcour Island

With vengeance in mind and a north wind behind him, Canada's Governor Guy Carleton sailed south on Lake Champlain in the fall of 1776 accompanied by "the greatest expeditionary force Great Britain had ever sent out from its shores."

To stop the amphibious British juggernaut, Benedict Arnold and a crew of Yankee shipbuilders had hammered together that summer a tiny little fleet of 5 warships, 20 gunboats, and 28 longboats. They alone, with Fort Ticonderoga at their back, would face the enemy.

Now the British foamed down the lake—little suspecting that sea-wise Arnold had a trick up his sleeve. He had hidden his boats behind Valcour Island on the western shore of the lake. When the British discovered him, they had already sailed past; each ship then had to beat back up to meet his massed power.

By the time Carleton finally got his ships in order and began to inflict severe damage, darkness had fallen and Arnold was able to slip away.

The Continental Gunboat *Philadelphia*

Salvaged from the bottom of
Lake Champlain, one of Arnold's
homemade fleet survives in
the Smithsonian's Museum of
History and Technology. The
oak-built *Philadelphia* measures
some 57 feet long, with a
beam of 17 feet and draft of
no more than 2. The 12-pounder
in the bow was backed up by
9-pounders amidships
plus swivelguns.

In this contemporary watercolor (which still hangs in Windsor Castle),
a British artist shows Arnold's fleet in its snug hideaway behind Valcour Island.
Carleton's more powerful ships are struggling into position against the wind.

Quebec and Canada would surely have fallen. As it was, the move came too late.

For as thousands of American troops were pushing northward in May, a fleet bearing an army of British regulars and Hessian mercenaries under the command of General John ("Gentleman Johnny") Burgoyne appeared on the St. Lawrence River. The very sight of the British ships spread panic among the Americans who were besieging Quebec; they fled up the St. Lawrence to the Richelieu River.

The next few months were disastrous for the American campaign. Burgoyne's arrival quieted the *habitants*, convincing them that the patriot cause was hopeless. The Americans, hoping to renew their assault on Quebec, attacked Trois Rivières, the principal settlement between Montreal and Quebec. But to their surprise, they encountered there the bulk of Burgoyne's army—experienced, disciplined professionals who sent the patriot forces reeling backward with heavy losses. Pursued by Carleton and Burgoyne, the Americans retreated. They gave up Montreal, fled down the Richelieu to Lake Champlain, surrendered St. John's, and finally came to a halt at Crown Point, where they came under the command of General Schuyler. However, even Crown Point, whose defenses were weak, was soon abandoned as Schuyler concentrated his forces at Ticonderoga.

The patriot position was desperate. Carleton and Burgoyne came down the Richelieu into northern Lake Champlain in decisive force. Schuyler could not hope to hold out against them if they converged on Ticonderoga. Moreover, there was the possibility that the British, after capturing Ticonderoga, would split the colonies in two by advancing from Canada all the way to the mouth of the Hudson.

This almost certainly would have been the case but for the ingenuity, audacity, and cold nerve of Benedict Arnold (he was now General Arnold). Schuyler had given him command of the few armed craft that made up the patriots' fleet on Lake Champlain. Arnold promptly began to augment this meager naval force by building a dozen or so additional craft and mounting cannon on them, an enterprise that forced Carleton to tarry at the northern end of the lake until he, too, could enlarge his fleet. This naval armaments race ended in the early autumn of 1776. The British were far superior. Carleton's fleet not only had well over twice the firepower of Arnold's; it was also manned by veteran seamen and skilled artillerymen, whereas Arnold's crews were made up primarily of landlubbers who barely knew how to load and fire cannon. Hence it was seemingly the height of folly for Arnold to meet the British when, on October 11, they sailed overwhelmingly toward him.

But meet them he did.

All day long Arnold fought from behind Valcour Island, losing many of his vessels and using up nearly all his ammunition while inflicting only minor injuries upon his enemy. By nightfall even the possibility of retreat seemed denied by British gunboats positioned south of him. Almost any other man would have surrendered. Instead, as fog closed down upon the darkened lake, Arnold managed to slip between the British vessels and escape. Next day, action was resumed by the pursuing Carleton. More patriot vessels were sunk; others were captured. With only five of his original vessels left, Arnold ordered his fleet to head for the eastern shore of the lake. There he beached his boats, set them afire, and retreated inland.

Despite Arnold's losses, the battle proved to be a defensive victory for the patriots. Arnold had bought time—desperately needed time. Carleton felt that Ticonderoga was too strong to attack and that the season was too far advanced to allow siege operations. Thus the British withdrew to Fort St. John's. They would drive down from that point in the spring of 1777.

"We Hold These Truths"   4

On June 12, 1775, Governor Thomas Gage of Massachusetts issued a proclamation in His Majesty's name, promising pardon to all rebels in the colony if they would lay down their arms—with two exceptions: Samuel Adams and John Hancock. Their offenses were of "too flagitious a nature to admit of any other consideration than that of condign punishment."

Palsied, fifty-three-year-old Sam Adams, "that Machiavel of Chaos," as a Tory dubbed him, had been inciting riot for a decade. He "eats little, drinks little, sleeps little, thinks much," muttered Joseph Galloway (a less than ardent defender of American rights who eventually became a loyalist). In Philadelphia, where he went as a delegate to the Continental Congress, Adams sought to "instruct the unenlightened, convince the doubting and fortify the timid." While Congress, hoping for reconciliation, dawdled throughout the fall and winter of 1775, Adams argued for independence. Adams made enemies, but he also made sense, especially to the rowdies in the taverns and dockside gangs. Adams called them Sons of Liberty. "Would you believe it," a British officer wrote, "that this immense continent from New England to Georgia is moved and directed by one man?" To Jefferson, Adams was the "Man of the Revolution."

The other traitor, Hancock, cut quite a different figure. Elegant, vain, well-to-do, he was in appearance the direct opposite of frugal, plainly dressed Sam Adams. King Hancock, as he was called, pranced about Philadelphia in a handsome coach attended by liveried servants and escorted by saber-rattling horsemen. Sam and John Adams had engineered Hancock's appointment as president of the Continental Congress

Thomas Jefferson fought the Revolution with pen rather than sword. Young and sandy-haired when he composed the Declaration of Independence, he was 53, white-haired, and President when Charles B.J.F. de St. Memin drew this "physiognatrace."

when Peyton Randolph, called back to Virginia, stepped down. Hancock, having drilled the governor's cadets on the Boston Common, hoped for at least a complimentary nomination as commander of the Continental Army. When John Adams rose in Congress to nominate Washington and Sam Adams seconded the choice, Hancock was mortified. He turned decidedly cool toward the Adamses. In turn they denounced him for cozying up to Philadelphia's John Dickinson and other moderates and suggested he resign. Hancock, not about to step out of the limelight, ignored them.

If old friends sworn to the cause of liberty could fall out over trivialities, it followed that strong-willed men from different colonies would find scant room for agreement. "Jealousies, ill natured observations and recriminations take the place of reason and argument," lamented Joseph Hewes of North Carolina. "Our tempers are soured." John Adams characterized the fifty or so congressional delegates—the number constantly changed—as strangers "not acquainted with each other's language, ideas, views, designs. They are, therefore, jealous of each other—fearful, timid, skittish." His cold blue eyes took the measure of every man there, and his busy pen scathingly recorded what he saw: Benjamin Harrison of Virginia—"an indolent, luxurious, heavy gentleman, of no use in Congress or committee, but a great embarrassment to both." Edward Rutledge of South Carolina—"uncouth and ungraceful speaker; he shrugs his shoulders, distorts his body, nods and wiggles with his head . . . looks about with his eyes from side to side, and speaks through his nose, as the Yankees sing." James Duane of New York—"a very effeminate, weak voice, a sly surveying eye." Francis Hopkinson of New Jersey had a head "not bigger than a large apple." John Dickinson of Pennsylvania was "but a shadow. Tall, slender as a reed, pale as ashes."

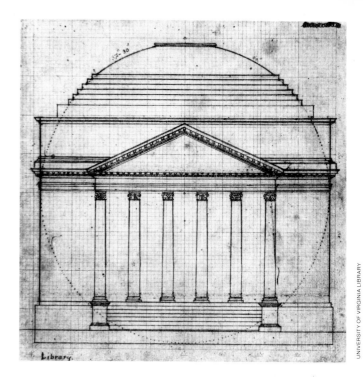

Beyond Jefferson's political and literary genius stretched interests ranging from natural science to economics (in 1783 he proposed the decimal system to Congress). His architectural talents shine forth in the University of Virginia's rotunda (above) and Monticello (below).

Gentleman farmer, rich lawyer, shrewd parliamentarian, leading advocate for reconciliation with Great Britain, Dickinson in July, 1775, drafted and Congress approved the so-called Olive Branch Petition beseeching George III "to procure us relief from our afflicting fears and jealousies . . . and to settle peace through every part of our Dominions." John Adams thought the supplication puerile, and said so. "A certain great Fortune and piddling Genius, whose Fame has been trumpeted so loudly, has given a silly Cast to our whole Doings," he wrote James Warren in Boston. This letter and another in the same vein to wife Abigail were intercepted and published in Tory newspapers. Soon Adams's mail was being read by all of London, including presumably George III. The stubborn monarch did not, however, condescend to read Dickinson's humble petition. Instead he proclaimed the American colonies to be in a state of rebellion. Addressing Parliament in October, 1775, the king declared, "The rebellious war now levied . . . is manifestly carried on for the purpose of establishing an independent empire." Thus George III was among the first to perceive what the conflict would be about—independence.

Pamphleteer Thomas Paine espoused a doctrine of independence in *Common Sense*. A protégé of Ben Franklin and recent emigré from England, Paine exhorted, " 'Tis time to part." Scrambling metaphors in passionate outbursts, he raged:

> Ye that tell us of harmony and reconciliation, can ye restore to us the time that is past? Can ye give to prostitution its former innocence? Neither can ye reconcile Britain and America. The last cord now is broken, the people of England are presenting addresses against us. There are injuries which nature cannot forgive. . . . As well can the lover forgive the ravisher of his mistress, as the continent forgive the murderers of Britain. . . . Ye that dare oppose not only the tyranny but the tyrant, stand forth!

Published anonymously in January, 1776, *Common*

Sense roused public sentiment for independence as no other document could have—a notable exception being the Prohibitory Act, which also became known in the colonies as the Piratical Act or Act of Independency. Enacted December 22, 1775, it was virtually a British declaration of war on the American colonies. The act first came to the attention of Congress two months later, when a ship returned from England after being "strictly searched" and cleared by officials.

A copy of the act along with some letters stowed in the bottom of a barrel of bread had escaped detection.

The act withdrew the crown's protection from the American colonists, forbade all trade with them, and authorized a naval blockade. This "more than diabolical act," seethed Maryland's delegate Robert Alexander, meant either "absolute slavery or Independency, the latter I have often reprobated both in public & private, but am now almost convinced the measure is right. . . ." "It throws thirteen Colonies out of the Royal protection, levels all distinctions, and makes us independent in spite of our supplications and entreaties," wrote John Adams to General Horatio Gates. "It may be fortunate that the Act of Independency should come from the British Parliament rather than the American Congress; but it is very odd that Americans should hesitate at accepting such a gift from them."

But even as Adams wrote these ironic words, hesitation was giving way to decisive action. Congress issued letters of marque and reprisal, dispatched Silas Deane to France for money and gunpowder, declared American ports open to all countries except Britain, and called for the disarming of loyalists.

Sensing that sentiment for independence might be growing, the brace of Adamses collared delegates in the City Tavern or Bunch of Grapes, plotted strategy in their quarters at Mrs. Yard's, shook the high-ceilinged assembly room of the State House with forceful if not flowing oratory. Ceaselessly they labored for unanimity, trying, as John put it, to "make thirteen Clocks strike precisely alike, at the same Second."

The task was formidable. "My mind is overborne with Burdens," Adams grumbled. Borrowing a little time from his sleep, he helped draft a resolution recommending that each of the united colonies institute governments as shall "best conduce to the happiness and safety of their constituents in particular, and

Popular author Thomas Paine (left) saw his 47-page pamphlet *Common Sense* (title page opposite) sell 120,000 copies in three months of 1776. Its logical, powerful prose advanced the cause of independence.

America in general." This passed on May 10, 1776, and Adams, Edward Rutledge, and Richard Henry Lee were instructed to prepare a preamble. The product, largely if not entirely the work of Adams, indicted George III as well as Parliament for the "hostile invasions and cruel depredations" that necessitated this call for self-determination. To Carter Braxton, Virginia's token conservative delegate, preamble and resolution fell "little short of Independence."

Yet despite his and other conservatives' objections, the preamble, according to Pennsylvania delegate James Allen's count, "was carried by a majority of 7 Colonies to 4." Georgia's delegates were not present, and one colony—probably Delaware—split its vote.

On May 20, Adams exulted that support for independence was rolling in like a torrent: "The delegates from Georgia made their appearance this day in Congress with unlimited powers. . . . South Carolina has erected her government and given her delegates ample powers. . . . North Carolina have given theirs full powers. . . . This days post has brought . . . letters from Virginia, all of which breath the same spirit." Adams believed the four southern colonies "perfectly agreed now" with the four in the north, a sentiment which in the case of South Carolina was to prove premature. Edward Rutledge and the other South Carolina delegates, unlike the radicals in control of that colony's legislature, were conservative planter gentlemen, hesitant to take the final step of severing all ties with Britain. Furthermore, the five colonies in the middle—New York, New Jersey, Pennsylvania, Delaware, and Maryland—were definitely not yet ripe for independence.

While the middle colonies procrastinated, Virginia, warring with deposed Governor Dunmore then running loose in the Chesapeake, openly called for independence. The Virginia Convention sitting at Williamsburg in May had instructed its delegates to propose that Congress "declare the United Colonies free and independent states, absolved from all allegiance to, or dependence upon, the crown or parliament of Great Britain." A committee headed by George Mason was appointed to draw up a Declaration of Rights. Virginians had found George III's hiring of German mercenaries to fight for Britain particularly odious. "The infamous treaties with Hesse, Brunswick etc.," wrote Richard Henry Lee, ". . . leave not a doubt but that our enemies are determined upon the absolute conquest and subduction of N. America. *It is not choice then but necessity that calls for Independence . . .*"

On Friday, June 7, Lee as spokesman for the Virginia delegation sounded the call. A tall, spare man in his forties, the "Cicero of America" stepped forward to deliver a three-pronged resolution:

> Resolved, that these United Colonies are, and of right ought to be, free and independent States, that they are absolved from all allegiance to the British Crown, and that all political connection between them and the State of Great Britain is, and ought to be totally dissolved.
>
> That it is expedient forthwith to take the most effectual measures for forming foreign Alliances.
>
> That a plan of confederation be prepared and transmitted to the respective Colonies for their consideration and approbation.

Seconded by John Adams, the resolution touched off a debate that spilled into Saturday and Monday, the Sabbath being a time for worship and a time, no doubt, for Sam Adams to practice his "intriguing arts."

A detailed account of the debate was kept by Thomas Jefferson. The tall Virginian, although he rarely spoke on the floor of Congress, was one of its busiest and most respected members. He had first entered Congress in June of 1775, bringing with him, as John Adams put it, "a reputation for literature, science and a happy talent of composition. Writings of his

COMMON SENSE;

ADDRESSED TO THE

INHABITANTS

OF

AMERICA,

On the following interesting

SUBJECTS.

I. Of the Origin and Design of Government in general,
with concise Remarks on the English Constitution.

II. Of Monarchy and Hereditary Succession.

III. Thoughts on the present State of American Affairs.

IV. Of the present Ability of America, with some miscellaneous Reflections.

Man knows no Master save creating HEAVEN,
Or those whom choice and common good ordain.
THOMSON.

PHILADELPHIA;
Printed, and Sold, by R. BELL, in Third-Street.
MDCCLXXVI.

were handed about, remarkable for the peculiar felicity of expression." He had also impressed Adams by being "prompt, frank, explicit, and decisive upon committees and in conversation." Soon Jefferson was serving on more committees than any other delegate except Adams.

In his notes on the debate, Jefferson listed first the arguments against the resolution as voiced by James Wilson of Pennsylvania, Robert R. Livingston of New York, South Carolina's Rutledge, Dickinson, "and others." They—Jefferson didn't quote specific spokesmen—argued that the middle colonies "were not yet ripe for bidding adieu to British connection;" that some colonies "had expressly forbidden their delegates to consent to such a declaration, and others had given no instructions;" that "if the delegates of any particular colony had no power to declare such colony independent, certain they were the others could not;" that if a declaration was agreed to now, certain colonies "might

secede from the Union;" that there was "little reason to expect an alliance with France and Spain;" that by waiting, "we should have reason to expect an alliance on better terms."

In distilling the arguments of John Adams, George Wythe of Virginia, "and others," Jefferson wrote that "the question was not whether, by a declaration of independence, we should make ourselves what we are not; but whether we should declare a fact which already exists;" that allegiance to the king "was now dissolved by his assent to the late act of parliament, by which he declares us out of his protection; and by his levying war on us, a fact which had long ago proved us out of his protection;" that no delegates can be denied "a power of declaring an existent truth;" that the voices of the delegates are "not always consonant with the voice of the people, and that this is remarkably the case in these middle colonies;" that "it would be in vain to wait either weeks or months for perfect unanimity;" that "a declaration of Independence alone could render it consistent with European delicacy for European powers to treat with us."

The great debate determined, as Jefferson observed, that since "the colonies of New York, New Jersey, Pennsylvania, Delaware, Maryland & South Carolina were not yet matured for falling from the parent stem, but that they were fast advancing to that state, it was thought most prudent to wait a while for them, and to postpone the final decision to July 1."

On June 11 a committee consisting of Jefferson, John Adams, Benjamin Franklin, Robert Livingston, and Roger Sherman of Connecticut was appointed to prepare a declaration in the event Congress approved Lee's resolution. That evening Oliver Wolcott of Connecticut wrote his wife: "We seem at present to be in the Midst of a great Revolution, which I hope God will carry us safe thro with." The next day, John Adams, "drudging on, as usual," penned an expectant

71

note to Francis Dana of the Massachusetts Council: "We have greater Things, in Contemplation, than ever —the greatest of all, which We ever shall have.—Be silent and patient and time will bring forth, after the usual Groans, throes and Pains upon such Occasions, a fine Child." But it was Jefferson, not Adams, who labored to bring it forth. Years later, Adams recounted how Jefferson was selected:

> The committee met, discussed the subject, and then appointed Mr. Jefferson and me to make the draught. . . . Jefferson proposed to me to make the draught.
>
> *I said, "I will not."*
>
> "You should do it."
>
> "Oh! no."
>
> "Why will you not? You ought to do it."
>
> *"I will not."*
>
> "Why?"
>
> *"Reason enough."*
>
> "What can be your reasons?"
>
> *"Reason first—You are a Virginian, and a Virginian ought to appear at the head of this business. Reason second—I am obnoxious, suspected and unpopular. You are very much otherwise. Reason third—You can write ten times better than I can."*
>
> "Well," said Jefferson, "if you are decided, I will do as well as I can."

Turning "to neither book nor pamphlet," Jefferson set to work in his second-floor lodgings at Seventh and Market streets and spent the next two weeks molding the ideas and feelings of the moment into ringing prose.

Jefferson's manifesto for freedom was not wholly his own. His scholarship tempered with the mettle of Locke and Sidney, his mind sharpened by the teachings of Wythe, the example of Mason, and, as John Adams tactlessly put it, the ideas "hackneyed in

King George and Broadswords

Driven into the sea by North Carolina patriots, the colony's governor commanded "all his Majesty's faithful Subjects to repair to the Royal Standard."

To his call rallied upcountry Regulators who, after the Battle of Alamance (page 17), had sworn loyalty; also Highland Scots who obeyed the call of their heroine Flora MacDonald (below). She, after being pardoned for her role in helping the last Stuart Pretender escape England, had vowed faithfulness to the king and moved to this country. Now loyalists, some 1,600 men and boys in all, gathered to march down the Cape Fear River and join Royal Navy forces.

Blocking their way at Moore's Creek—about 20 miles north of Wilmington—stood a large force of patriots. They ripped up planks from the bridge across the creek, greased the girders, and prepared for the Scotsmen to attack with broadswords. Attack they did, in the face of fierce fire from the emplaced defenders (above).

The result: complete dispersal of the loyalists and relief for the Carolinians, who would thereafter vote solidly for independence.

Congress for two years," Jefferson produced something both familiar and innovative. His object in writing the Declaration of Independence was clear:

> Not to find out new principles, nor new arguments, never before thought of, not merely to say things which had never been said before; but to place before mankind the common sense of the subject, in terms so plain and firm as to command their assent. . . . Neither aiming at originality of principle or sentiment, nor yet copied from any particular and previous writing, it was intended to be an expression of the American mind, and to give to that expression the proper tone and spirit.

After submitting a preliminary draft to Adams and Franklin, who suggested several changes in wording, Jefferson made a fair copy and presented it to Congress on June 28.

The next day Edward Rutledge wrote John Jay in New York that "A Declaration of Independence . . . will be laid before the House on Monday"—July 1. Effective opposition, he asserted, "will depend in a great measure upon the exertions of the honest and sensible part of the Members."

Foremost among these was ascetic John Dickinson. He entered the white-paneled assembly room Monday morning primed for the fight of his life. Ready to oblige him was John Adams, his spirits bolstered by a letter from Maryland's Samuel Chase announcing "an Unan[imous]: Vote of our Convention for Independ-

South Carolina's governor fled from patriot-dominated Charleston in September, 1775. Then the Council of Safety could prepare defenses against Sir Henry Clinton's expected force, which would first hit islands at the channel's mouth (below).

The Defense of Charleston

While Jefferson pondered the Revolution's political concepts in Philadelphia (June, 1776), Col. William Moultrie struggled against a British fleet of ten warships in the South. The British command, learning that the patriots were fortifying Sullivan's Island in Charleston harbor, determined to seize the fort and gain control of

LIBRARY OF CONGRESS

Nine British warships vainly pound Sullivan's Island in the painting above. But for the obstinacy of the South Carolinians, Gen. Charles Lee (Moultrie's superior) would have abandoned the fort as indefensible. "As soon as they came within reach of our guns," Moultrie wrote later, "we began to fire. They were soon abreast of the fort . . . and began their attack most furiously." Another observer, his head still ringing from the booming British guns, wrote of the "Smart Cannonade, which was return'd with Coolness and deliberation from the Fort . . . an incessant fire was kept up till Eleven O'Clock at Night." He went on to describe how the British, having lost some 64 men (against 36 American casualties), "cut their Men of War's cables in the dead of Night & Stole away."

the South's major port. In the romantic depiction of the action below, South Carolina's colors fly from a jury-rigged staff above the fort's palmetto logs; the soft logs did not splinter when hit by shells and thus protected the defenders. Their cannon hulled Sir Peter Parker's flagship 70 times—and gained two years of peace for the South.

A Declaration by the Representatives of the UNITED STATES OF AMERICA, in General Congress assembled.

When in the course of human events it becomes necessary for one people to dissolve the political bands which have connected them with another, and to assume among the powers of the earth the separate and equal station to which the laws of nature & of nature's god entitle them, a decent respect to the opinions of mankind requires that they should declare the causes which impel them to the separation.

We hold these truths to be self-evident; that all men are created equal, that they are endowed by their creator with equal rights, some of which are inherent & inalienable, among which are the preservation of life, & liberty, & the pursuit of happiness; that to secure these rights, governments are instituted among men, deriving their just powers from the consent of the governed; that whenever any form of government becomes destructive of these ends, it is the right of the people to alter or to abolish it, & to institute new government, laying it's foundation on such principles & organising it's powers in such form, as to them shall seem most likely to effect their safety & happiness. prudence indeed will dictate that governments long established should not be changed for light & transient causes: and accordingly all experience hath shewn that mankind are more disposed to suffer while evils are sufferable, than to right themselves by abolishing the forms to which they are accustomed. but when a long train of abuses & usurpations [begun at a distinguished period, &] pursuing invariably the same object, evinces a design to reduce them under absolute Despotism, it is their right, it is their duty, to throw off such government & to provide new guards for their future security. such has been the patient sufferance of these colonies; & such is now the necessity which constrains them to [expunge] their former systems of government. the history of the present king of Great Britain is a history of [unremitting] injuries and usurpations, [among which appears no solitary fact to contradict the uniform tenor of the rest, but all have] in direct object the establishment of an absolute tyranny over these states. to prove this, let facts be submitted to a candid world, [for the truth of which we pledge a faith yet unsullied by falsehood.]

Thomas Jefferson hears committee members' comments on his "Rough Draft" in the engraving at right from a painting by Alonzo Chappell. Jefferson kept this scratched version all his life, recalling such emendations as "self-evident" for "sacred and undeniable" truths (7th line opposite).

ence." After spending the morning on regular business, Congress resolved itself into a committee of the whole, chaired by the Falstaffian Harrison, to consider Richard Henry Lee's resolution. Dickinson took the floor. Glancing from time to time at notes, he denounced independence. Declaring for it now, he said, "would be like destroying our house in winter . . . before we have got another shelter."

Adams, who gave a stinging rebuttal, thought the debate "an idle mispence of time, for nothing was said but what had been repeated and hackneyed in that room before, a hundred times, for six months past." Perhaps so, but Adams, Jefferson recalled, "came out occasionally with a power of thought and expression that moved us from our seats." In the course of the speech, a smile must have flickered across Ben Franklin's face when Adams, lifting his voice above the tumult of a sudden thunderstorm, proclaimed that "sink or swim," he was voting for independence.

Chairman Harrison polled the colonies, each having one vote regardless of its number of delegates. Lee's resolution passed with nine votes in favor, two—Pennsylvania and South Carolina—opposed. New York, stricken with political paralysis, abstained. Delaware, with two of its three members present, divided—George Read voting against, Thomas McKean for. South Carolina's Rutledge doubtless shocked Dickinson when he requested that the final tally be taken the next day. McKean also favored postponement, having sent for colleague Caesar Rodney in Dover. Strong for separation, Rodney would swing Delaware to the side of independence. South Carolina was leaning, its delegates willing to join the majority for the sake of unanimity, and New York was likely to remain uncommitted. Thus the key to a unanimous vote was Pennsylvania. Her seven members, McKean believed, were split four to three. One switch apparently was all that was needed. But who could be persuaded to change his

vote? The delegates, numb from nine straight hours of debate and deliberation in an ovenlike chamber, adjourned at six and filed outside.

That evening Adams answered Chase's letter, venturing a prediction. Tomorrow, he wrote, the resolution "will pass by a great majority; perhaps with almost unanimity." But, "If you imagine that I flatter myself with happiness and halcyon days after a separation from Great Britain, you are mistaken. . . . freedom is a counterbalance for poverty, discord and war and more. It is your hard lot and mine to be called into life at such a time. Yet even these times have their pleasures."

July 2 began as another uncomfortable day—warm, sticky, threatening. Flies from the stable across the street buzzed through open windows in the State House. Hands slapped at necks and stockinged legs as Hancock, speaking up so Jefferson and others at the far end of the room could hear, worked through the stack of papers before him—most of which concerned military matters. A few minutes before ten, rain began to fall. It was still coming down at noon, with no sign of letting up. Nor was there any sign of Rodney. That wasn't really surprising. In bad weather he would be fortunate to reach Philadelphia at all. But there was nothing to detain Dickinson and his fellow Pennsylvanian Robert Morris, usually punctual. On this day of decision they had every reason to be present. Otherwise, Pennsylvania's vote would shift to the majority—if McKean's assessment had been right.

As the morning wore on, it became obvious that Dickinson and Morris did not intend to make an appearance. Thus, though unwilling to betray their consciences and vote for independence, they could, by being absent, contribute in a negative way to harmony. Hancock, who had been in the chair, stepped aside for Harrison as the delegates resolved themselves into a committee of the whole. The chairman directed Secretary Charles Thomson to read Lee's

"Votaries of Independence"

First presented to Congress on July 2, 1776, the Declaration of Independence was thereafter signed by 56 patriots. John Trumbull's painting of the document's presentation (above) shows 48 men present—including the drafting committee at center—who may be identified as follows:

Group at far left: George Wythe *(Virginia)*, William Whipple *(New Hampshire)*, Josiah Bartlett *(New Hampshire)*, Thomas Lynch, Jr. *(South Carolina)*, Benjamin Harrison *(Virginia)*; **Standing in back:** William Paca *(Maryland)*, Samuel Chase *(Maryland)*, Richard Stockton *(New Jersey)*, Lewis Morris *(New York)*, William Floyd *(New York)*, Arthur Middleton *(South Carolina)*, Stephen Hopkins *(Rhode Island)*, William Ellery *(Rhode Island)*, George Clymer *(Pennsylvania)*; **Seated in first row:** Richard Henry Lee *(Virginia)*, Samuel Adams

(Massachusetts), George Clinton (New York), Thomas Heyward, Jr. (South Carolina), Charles Carroll (Maryland), Robert Morris (Pennsylvania), Thomas Willing (Pennsylvania), Benjamin Rush (Pennsylvania), Elbridge Gerry (Massachusetts), Robert Treat Paine (Massachusetts), William Hooper (North Carolina), George Walton (Georgia), James Wilson (Pennsylvania), Abraham Clark (New Jersey), Francis Hopkinson (New Jersey); **At desk:** John Adams (Massachusetts), Roger Sherman (Connecticut), Robert Livingston (New York), Thomas Jefferson (Virginia), Benjamin Franklin (Pennsylvania), Charles Thomson (Pennsylvania), John Hancock (Massachusetts); **Seated and standing beyond desk:** Thomas Nelson, Jr. (Virginia), Francis Lewis (New York), John Witherspoon (New Jersey), Samuel Huntington (Connecticut), William Williams (Connecticut), Oliver Wolcott (Connecticut), George Read (Delaware), John Dickinson (Pennsylvania), Edward Rutledge (South Carolina), Thomas McKean (Delaware), Philip Livingston (New York).

resolution of June 7 and poll the respective colonies.

Hoofbeats on cobblestones announced the arrival of Rodney. Booted and spurred, spattered with mud, he had ridden through "thunder and rain . . . to give my voice in the matter of Independence." Delaware voted aye. So did South Carolina and Pennsylvania. New York delegates, "for it themselves," Jefferson explained, but constrained to abide by year-old instructions from home, "asked leave to withdraw from the question, which was given them." Thus the vote was twelve colonies for independence, none against.

After the tally was taken, Secretary Thomson recorded the resolution in the journal of the Congress. Next to be considered was Jefferson's 1,800-word draft. Acting again as a committee of the whole, the delegates, after some deliberation, "desired leave to sit again" tomorrow "to take into their farther consideration the declaration on independence."

The next morning the Congress resolved into a committee of the whole, and the delegates painstakingly went over Jefferson's manuscript. They cut here, substituted words of their own there, and tidied up Jefferson's spelling and punctuation as they proceeded. The tall, freckled, red-haired author, turned thirty-three in April, could only watch in pained silence as one man after another tore into the document.

Eventually Jefferson saw his work reduced by about one-fourth. Several of the deletions, as he noted, rankled him: "The clause . . . reprobating the enslaving the inhabitants of Africa was struck out, in complaisance [to] South Carolina and Georgia, who never attempted to restrain the importation of slaves, and who on the contrary still wished to continue it. Our northern brethren also I believe felt a little tender under those censures; for though their people have very few slaves them selves yet they had been pretty considerable carriers of them to others."

Also cut were such stirring passages as "he has

On July 9, 1776, after George Washington had the brave new Declaration read to the citizens of New York, they rejoiced and pulled down the leaden equestrian statue of King George III.

waged cruel war against human nature itself, violating it's most sacred rights of life & liberty in the persons of a distant people, who never offended him, captivating and carrying them into slavery in another hemisphere. . . ."

All the delegates—with the obvious exception of Jefferson—could take satisfaction in a day's work well done. Tomorrow they would complete the task.

Thursday, July 4, 1776, dawned clear, with a pleasant breeze out of the southeast. Among the delegates entering the State House chamber was Robert Morris, no longer content to absent himself from events. Friend Dickinson, however, had not returned.

Taking up where they left off, the delegates resumed their hammering out of differences. When the last apostrophe had been removed from the last "its"—

80

Jefferson habitually wrote the possessive as "it's" —Harrison reported "that the committee of the whole Congress have agreed to a Declaration," which he then read:

A Declaration by the Representatives of the United States of America in General Congress assembled.

When in the course of human events, it becomes necessary for one people to dissolve the political bands, which have connected them with another, and to assume among the powers of the earth, the separate and equal station to which the Laws of Nature and of Nature's God entitle them, a decent respect to the opinions of mankind requires that they should declare the causes which impel them to the separation.—We hold these truths to be self-evident, that all men are created equal, that they are endowed by their Creator with certain unalienable Rights, that among these are Life, Liberty and the pursuit of Happiness . . . .

As Harrison continued reading, his stentorian voice spellbinding the hushed assembly, none—not even Jefferson—could deny that, with all its changes, the thing was well-knit.

. . . And for the support of this Declaration, with a firm reliance on the protection of divine Providence, we mutually pledge to each other our Lives, our Fortunes and our sacred Honor.

Congress ordered that the Declaration be engrossed, printed, and distributed and "that it be proclaimed in each of the United States, and at the head of the army."

On July 8 the Declaration was publicly read from a round, wooden platform, used for stargazing, in the courtyard. John Adams set the scene in a letter to Sam Chase:

The Declaration was yesterday published and proclaimed from that awful stage in the State-house yard; by whom, do you think? By the Committee of Safety, the Committee of Inspection, and a great crowd of people. Three cheers rended the welkin. The battalions paraded on the Common, and gave us the *feu de joie*, notwithstanding the scarcity of powder. The bells rang all day and almost all night. Even the chimers chimed away. . . .

As soon as an American seal is prepared, I conjecture the Declaration will be subscribed by all the members, which will give you the opportunity you wish for, of transmitting your name among the votaries of independence.

A few days later Congress provided that when the Declaration was "fairly engrossed on parchment," each member would sign it. On August 2, John Hancock put his flamboyant signature to the paper, writing it large so John Bull could read it without putting on his spectacles. Hancock, who like Sam Adams had a price on his head, supposedly remarked while waiting for others to sign, "we must all hang together." Franklin replied, "we must, indeed, all hang together, or most assuredly we shall all hang separately."

81

The Capture of New York

*George Washington called New York "the place that we must
keep from the British." But the fortifications hastily built
by the patriots in 1776 proved too feeble and his command too
untrained: the British easily outflanked him on Long Island (above);
then Gen. William Howe landed at Kips Bay and proudly entered
Manhattan (opposite). Washington won only a small holding victory
at Harlem Heights. Yet the slow movements of the British
allowed him to consolidate forces in Westchester and to
discourage pursuit. Now the British found themselves not
victors of the territory but defenders of a crucial city.*

Proud relatives of George III, the Howe brothers—Admiral Richard (above right) and General William (left)—handled the delicate assignment of converting or defeating the rebellious Americans in 1776. Ineptly, they insulted American generalship (their letter was addressed to ''George Washington, Etc. etc., etc.'') Tactlessly, they declined to take American independence seriously in a September meeting with Franklin. Then they tried to conquer the Americans without actually crushing them —a tactic that helped the Revolution succeed.

OVERLEAF: British ships force passage up the Hudson River between American Forts Washington (at right, on Manhattan) and Lee. The fall of these forts cost more than 3,000 American soldiers.

Across the Delaware

5

It was the crowning disaster of a disastrous campaign. New York, second largest city in the infant United States, was already in enemy hands, along with its magnificent harbor and its dependencies of Long Island and Westchester. Now the British and their German mercenary allies were preparing to take Fort Washington, the last American outpost on Manhattan Island, with its garrison of 2,900 troops and its enormous stock of supplies and munitions. On November 16, 1776, from a vantage point across the Hudson River, George Washington watched his helpless Fort Washington troops ground their muskets. "The General seemed in an agony when he saw the fort surrendered," an eyewitness recalled.

That the proud, sensitive Washington should be agonized was hardly surprising. After three months of campaigning he had nothing but negatives—successive retreats from Long Island, Manhattan, and Westchester—to show for his efforts. An army of sorts still remained under his command, but he had lost everything he had tried to defend. Moreover, what had been a force of some 28,000 men was shriveled through casualties, disease, capture, and desertion to 14,000. The American loss at Fort Washington would be exceeded only once during the Revolution, when besieged Charleston, South Carolina, fell in 1780.

Four days later came still another blow—the British seizure of Fort Lee, Fort Washington's companion stronghold across the Hudson. Washington had decided to evacuate the fort in any case, but it was hardly flattering to the American cause when Nathanael Greene and his 3,000-man garrison were forced to

flee in disorder, leaving behind valuable supplies and even their half-eaten breakfasts. "On the appearance of our troops," a Britisher gloated, "the rebels fled like scared rabbits, and in a few moments . . . not a rascal of them could be seen. They have left some poor pork, a few greasy proclamations, and some of that scoundrel Common Sense man's letters, which we can read at our leisure. . . ." Tom Paine of *Common Sense* fame was serving as Greene's aide; this experience, and others to come, would soon inspire him to take up his pen again.

When the two forts fell, the American army was divided into three parts: General Charles Lee was at North Castle in Westchester with his own division plus those of John Sullivan and Joseph Spencer, about 5,500 men all told. His task was to guard the approaches to New England. General William Heath and 3,200 troops were at Peekskill on the Hudson, with the assignment of blocking a British attempt to take the Hudson Highlands. Washington and the remaining 5,400 men were encamped at Hackensack, from which position Washington hoped to prevent Howe from moving into New Jersey. The commander in chief had expected Forts Washington and Lee to detain Howe for several months. Their surrender completely upset his plans. By so quickly disposing of the Hudson River forts, Howe had retained the military initiative. He was free to move in any direction he chose, and a dismayed Washington was well aware of that fact. His problem now, as it had been throughout the campaign, was how to guess Howe's next move.

But that was not the only problem he faced. Men were deserting the Continental Army at a frightening rate. They were not cowards, for the most part, but dispirited men, sick and cold and hungry, who had fought to their limit and simply could fight no more. Even worse, on December 1 the enlistments of 2,000 troops, most of whom were veterans, were due to ex-

Fleeing before cocksure Lord Cornwallis, George Washington ferried his defeated army from New Jersey into Pennsylvania. But then, changing the nature of the war in the North—and demonstrating for all time his courage and capability—Washington recrossed the Delaware on Christmas night, 1776, in a "storm of wind, hail, rain and snow." Edward Hicks recaptured that moment in the painting opposite.

The *American* CRISIS.

NUMBER I.

By the Author of COMMON SENSE.

THESE are the times that try men's fouls: The fummer foldier and the funfhine patriot will, in this crifis, fhrink from the fervice of his country; but he that ftands it NOW, deferves the love and thanks of man and woman. Tyranny, like hell, is not eafily conquered; yet we have this confolation with us, that the harder the conflict, the more glorious the triumph. What we obtain too cheap, we efteem too lightly :---'Tis dearnefs only that gives every thing its value. Heaven knows how to fet a proper price upon its goods; and it would be ftrange indeed, if fo celeftial an article as FREEDOM fhould not be highly rated. Britain, with an army to enforce her tyranny, has declared, that fhe has a right *(not only to* TAX, but) "*to* "BIND *us in* ALL CASES WHATSOEVER," and if being *bound in that manner* is not flavery, then is there not fuch a thing as flavery upon earth. Even the expreffion is impious, for fo unlimited a power can belong only to GOD.

WHETHER the Independence of the Continent was declared too foon, or delayed too long, I will not now enter into as an argument; my own fimple opinion is, that had it been eight months earlier, it would have been much better. We did not make a proper ufe of laft winter, neither could we, while we were in a dependent ftate. However, the fault, if it were one, was all our own; we have none to blame but ourfelves*. But no great deal is loft yet; all that Howe has been doing for this month paft is rather a ravage than a conqueft, which the fpirit of the Jerfies a year ago would have quickly repulfed, and which time and a little refolution will foon recover.

I have as little fuperftition in me as any man living, but my

* "The prefent winter" (meaning the laft) " is worth an " age, if rightly employed, but if loft, or neglected, the whole " Continent will partake of the evil; and there is no punifh- " ment that man does not deferve, be he who, or what, or " where he will, that may be the means of facrificing a feafon " fo precious and ufeful." COMMON SENSE.

pire, and on January 1, 1777, nearly all of the other enlistments would be up. At that point, Washington and his generals calculated they would have only 1,400 men left unless new forces could be recruited.

The difficulty of keeping the army together, especially with its short-term militia contingents, was candidly described by Captain Ebenezer Huntington in a letter written to his grandfather on November 25. "The Militia who have been sent for our assistance," Huntington wrote, "leave us the minute their times are out and would not stay tho' their eternal salvation was to be forfeited if they went home. The persuasion of a Cisero would not any more effect their tarry than the Niagara Falls would the kindling of a fire. . . ."

Washington called on the Congress in Philadelphia, the governor of New Jersey, and the patriot army at Fort Ticonderoga for reinforcements. He also seems to have considered the idea, if all else failed, of melting into the mountains to the west with as many men as would follow him for a campaign of guerrilla warfare. Then, under sudden pressure from the enemy, he was forced to put his ragged army on the roads.

To avoid being trapped between the Hackensack and Passaic rivers, Washington shifted southward to Newark, arriving on November 22. His respite there was brief. On the twenty-eighth, as the American rear guard pulled out, the enemy swept into Newark from the north.

These pursuing forces were commanded by Charles, second Earl Cornwallis. Not yet thirty-eight, Cornwallis was already a twenty-year man in the British army. He had arrived in America in 1776, having been appointed a major general the year before. Unlike many of the British officers who served in the Revolu-

Mud-spattered patriots on the New Jersey retreat (opposite) saw the American cause as a "melancholy situation." Again Tom Paine took pen in hand and wrote the appeal called *The American Crisis* (left); it fanned the flickering flames of the revolutionary spirit.

Captured Gen. Charles Lee gives up his sword to a British dragoon. Scholarly, eccentric, ambitious Lee had espoused independence soon after arriving in the colonies. Neither a military genius nor an American at heart, his loss was no disaster.

tion, Cornwallis was aggressive and enterprising, an ideal officer to lead the pursuit of a retreating foe.

After leaving Newark, the Continental Army traveled southward through New Jersey as fast as the miserable roads and shortage of supply wagons would allow. It was very much a ragtag army, ill-fed, ill-clothed, ill-shod. A sergeant recalled that they had no tents and "no food of any kind but a little raw flour." Despite the hardships, the troops pushed on, followed closely by Cornwallis. Writing a dispatch at New Brunswick on December 1, Washington added in a hasty footnote, "The Enemy are fast advancing, some of 'em in sight now." His best hope was to cross into Pennsylvania, putting the Delaware River between himself and the British. He pressed his dwindling army on through New Jersey, toward Princeton, Trenton, and the river.

Throughout the retreat Washington had been sending messages to General Charles Lee, urging him to bring his divisions into New Jersey. These were not

definite orders but rather "suggestions," for the American leaders treated Charles Lee with great deference. Appointed Washington's second in command by the Congress, Lee had served his military apprenticeship in the British army, had fought with distinction in Portugal during the Seven Years' War, and had later become a soldier of fortune in Russia and Poland. He was a gaunt and spindly man, with a personality as unpleasant as his looks and a broad streak of vanity. Yet the Congress, making generals out of the likes of a blacksmith (Nathanael Greene), a bookseller (Henry Knox), and an apothecary (Hugh Mercer), was flattered that Lee wanted a commission and delighted to give it to him.

Early in December, Lee moved leisurely from Westchester into northern New Jersey, replying to some of Washington's messages and ignoring others. At the same time he informed anyone who would listen that his commander ought to be replaced. "A certain great man is most damnably deficient," he remarked with little subtlety and dropped broad hints about who was best fitted to replace the commander in chief.

Meanwhile, the chase through the Jerseys grew hotter. At one point in his pursuit, Cornwallis drove his men twenty miles through a day-long rainstorm, but as he reached New Brunswick close on Washington's heels, he was ordered by Howe to halt and wait for reinforcements. Once again, Howe was allowing his enemy to slip away.

For a time Washington considered making a stand at Princeton or Trenton, but his common sense prevailed. Some reinforcements were trickling in, but hardly enough to offset the losses to sickness, expired enlistments, and desertion. He decided to retreat to Pennsylvania, and on the afternoon of December 8, he boarded one of the last boats to leave Trenton, just as Cornwallis's vanguard came into view.

Washington had perhaps 3,000 men left in his force, the veterans exhausted and hungry, the replacements ill-trained and bewildered. He had ordered his men to scour the Delaware for every boat they could lay hands on and move them to the Pennsylvania shore, so for the time being the army was safe. But Howe was in an excellent position to continue the pursuit. Trenton was well stocked with lumber yards and with blacksmiths who were equipped to make the necessary hardware should the British decide to build a flotilla. And with all of New Jersey secure in his hands, Howe had a base from which to operate.

As an American officer admitted, New Jersey was "totally deranged." Tory sentiment was strong in the state (a term the Tories did not recognize, of course; to them it was still a colony), and with the retreat of the rebel forces, many loyalists rushed forward to apply for General Howe's pardons and to swear to "remain in a peaceable Obedience to His Majesty." Washington was bitter. "Instead of turning out to defend the Country and affording aid to our Army," he wrote, "they are making their submissions as fast as they can."

It was not long, however, before many New Jersey citizens—Tories, patriots, and neutrals alike—realized that they were in not-so-gentle hands. Pillage, arson, rape, and murder marked the passage of His Majesty's forces across the state. Shopkeepers' shelves were emptied, mills were looted and burned, and silver and family heirlooms were spirited away. Anguished Tory victims vainly waved loyalty oaths signed by General Howe before uncomprehending German eyes. Each day the grim list of outrages grew longer, and Tory sentiment began to waver. New Jersey, for all its loyalist professions, was no longer a pacified area.

When all things are considered, the American cause reached rock bottom in those early weeks of December, 1776. No hours were ever darker; no prospects ever dimmer. Since August Washington had endured defeat and retreat. Yet somewhere in those days of

The power behind Washington's fire came from Col. Henry Knox's artillery—18 fieldpieces salvaged from New York's collapse. Knox located his "artillery park" (opposite) on the Pennsylvania side of the ice-clogged Delaware.

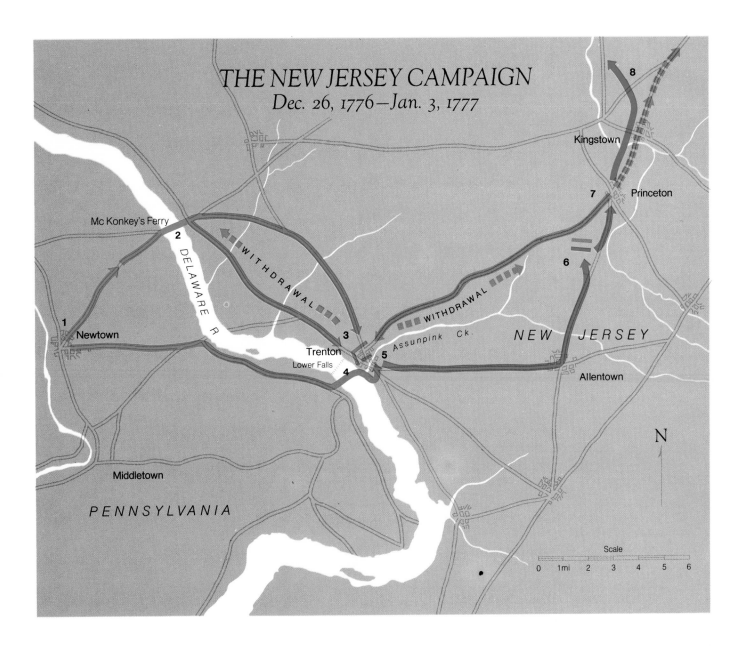

THE NEW JERSEY CAMPAIGN
Dec. 26, 1776 – Jan. 3, 1777

Based at Newtown (**1**), Washington (blue) first crossed the swift-flowing river on Christmas night at McKonkey's Ferry (**2**) for his two-pronged attack on Trenton (**3**). Next, having returned to his base, he crossed again below the Lower Falls (**4**) on December 30, 1776, to counter Cornwallis (red) at Assunpink Creek (**5**), then slipped away by night from the superior British force. Undeterred, he successfully attacked Cornwallis's rear guard (**7**) and Princeton before moving into winter quarters at Morristown (**8**) on January 4.

disaster he had glimpsed the steel in the men he commanded. Tom Paine had seen the same thing. Washington, the man of action, would soon act on his intuition. Paine, the man of letters, had already acted. Between the two of them they helped save a revolution.

After being routed out of Fort Lee, Paine had tramped along with the troops as they retreated through New Jersey and had begun to write about the cause he had adopted. The result, the first part in the series that Paine called *The Crisis,* was published in a Philadelphia newspaper on December 19 and as a pamphlet on December 23. The message that "flew like wildfire through all the towns and villages" has become almost a national cliché, yet the words still carry that solid clang of reality, that ring of deeply held beliefs. The fact is that in all the long history of man's struggle for liberty, no one has ever said it better than Tom Paine did on those icy December nights two centuries ago. He is worth listening to . . .

> These are the times that try men's souls. The summer soldier and the sunshine patriot will, in this crisis, shrink from the service of their country; but he that stands it *now* deserves the love and thanks of man and woman. Tyranny, like hell, is not easily conquered; yet we have this consolation with us, that the harder the conflict, the more glorious the triumph. . . .

Even as a Philadelphia printer was setting Paine's ringing phrases into type, Washington received a dispatch bearing more bad news. On December 12, General Charles Lee had put his little army into camp near Morristown, New Jersey, and then had decided that he would spend the night in greater comfort at a tavern a few miles away. Early the next morning a British cavalry patrol, probably tipped off by a Tory, surrounded the tavern and hauled him off to captivity. The humiliation was all the greater when Lee discovered that the dragoons who had captured him were part of the same regiment he had led so dashingly in Portugal back in 1762.

The cause, Washington wrote to his brother, had "received a severe blow in the captivity of Gen. Lee." Leaders in Congress and elsewhere bewailed the loss in more melodramatic terms. With the benefit of hindsight we know that Lee's capture was actually a blessing for the patriot cause, for he was unstable, capricious, and disposed to follow his own inclinations. Yet at the time, Lee's capture was just another measure of the growing crisis. "Our only dependence now is upon the speedy enlistment of a new army," Washington continued in the same letter. "If this fails, I think the game will be pretty well up. . . ."

Thirty miles away, a good many Philadelphians shared Washington's pessimism and fled into the countryside or behind the British lines. Being the largest city in North America and the capital, such as it was, of the emerging republic, Philadelphia was certainly a logical next target for Howe. The Congress hastily conferred upon Washington sweeping powers for the conduct of the war and adjourned to the comparative safety of Baltimore.

Howe was in no great hurry, however, for winter was advancing. In that century no proper army campaigned in winter, and General Howe—now Sir William, having been knighted for his victory at New York—was very much a man of his century. In any event, he had done quite well by the contemporary standards of European warfare. He had not completely wiped out the enemy army, to be sure, but he had captured important real estate and a secure base for future operations. Spring would be time enough to resume the fighting. On December 14 the orders went out: the army would go into winter quarters, and 14,000 troops would man a chain of defensive outposts stretching across New Jersey to the Delaware. Cornwallis returned to New York, having been granted leave to sail

Emanuel Leutze's famous portrayal of Washington crossing the Delaware is marred by romantic conceptions: the general stands erect; few of Glover's men are rowing. But Washington's determined face makes the painting true and memorable.

for home and his ailing wife, while Sir William settled in Manhattan for the winter and contemplated his spring campaign.

Manning the southern anchor of the chain of New Jersey posts at Trenton and nearby Bordentown was the corps of Colonel Carl von Donop, 3,000 Highlanders and German mercenaries. The Trenton half of this force was made up of three of the better Hessian regiments, Knyphausen's, the Lossbergs, and that of the garrison commander, Colonel Johann Gottlieb Rall. They had taken part in the capture of Fort Washington, and their opinion of the rebels was not high. Rall called his enemy "country clowns" and disdained

A primitive view of the crossing by J.O.J. Frost shows Henry Knox's cannon, plus ferries for horses and supplies. The first boatload carries the independence flag favored in New England.

the idea of building fortifications. "Let them come," he is reported to have said. "We want no trenches. We will go at them with the bayonet."

It was on one of those cold days in early December that George Washington decided to gamble on a counterstroke. Precisely when he made up his mind is not known, but it is clear that he had been aware for weeks that without some sort of revitalization the patriot cause would soon be dead. The forthcoming expiration of enlistments certainly influenced his decision, as did his somewhat improved troop situation. John Sullivan had brought in the remains of Charles Lee's force, which consisted of some 2,000 men, many of whom were in poor condition. In addition, some militia had arrived. The returns now showed 6,000 men "fit for duty," but that was a phrase more hopeful than accurate.

Carefully Washington worked out his plan. Trenton was the primary target, with Princeton and the British supply base at New Brunswick listed as secondary objectives. Since surprise was essential, Washington chose the day after Christmas for his assault; the Hessians, reports went, were planning a splendid and alcoholic celebration of the holiday. He quietly ordered three days' rations cooked for the troops and in strict security informed his principal officers. "Necessity, dire necessity, will, nay must, justify an attempt," he wrote on December 23, and that same day he had Tom Paine's newly published *Crisis* pamphlet read to the troops.

The attack plan called for three separate forces. One, under John Cadwalader, was to cross the Dela-

ware downstream from Trenton and divert the attention of Donop's force in the Bordentown area. Cadwalader had a mixed force of militia and Rhode Island veterans, about 2,000 in all. James Ewing, commanding 700 men, was to cross at Trenton's Ferry and take up a blocking position at Trenton's "back door," the bridge over Assunpink Creek on the Bordentown road. Meanwhile, at McKonkey's Ferry nine miles upstream from Trenton, Washington would cross with the main force, 2,400 men selected from his best veteran regiments. With him would go Henry Knox's eighteen cannon. The crossing was to begin at dark on Christmas Day, with the assault on Trenton scheduled for an hour before dawn on the twenty-sixth.

On Christmas afternoon Washington assembled the main force behind a concealing ridge. Rations, new flints for the muskets, and forty rounds of ammunition were issued. It was raw and cold, and many of the men had broken shoes or none at all. "It will be a terrible night for the soldiers who have no shoes," an officer wrote in his diary. "Some of them have tied old rags around their feet, but I have not heard a man complain." The march to McKonkey's Ferry could be traced by the bloody tracks in the snow.

The width of the Delaware at McKonkey's Ferry—about 350 yards—was less of a problem that night than its condition. A fierce, biting wind was blowing, and huge chunks of ice were slamming along in the swift current.

Washington's counter to these conditions was the regiment of Marbleheaders commanded by Colonel John Glover. These Massachusetts deep-water fishermen had lost their livelihood when Parliament banned them from the Grand Banks fishing grounds, and they had a score to settle. Distinctive in their heavy blue seamen's jackets, white caps, and tarred trousers, they could handle arms or oars with equal skill, and the discipline of the sea made them ideal for special as-

Roused after Christmas revelry, the Hessians (below at left) vainly resist the patriots' cannon, swords, and spontoons. Muskets failed to fire as the storm had drenched the powder.

signments. It was Glover's men who in August had spirited Washington's whole army across the East River from Long Island to Manhattan under the noses of the British. In October at Pell's Point in Westchester they had held off Howe long enough for Washington to escape with the main body of his troops to White Plains. Now they faced their greatest test.

In sweeping the Delaware clean of shipping, the Americans had been particularly careful to confiscate the local craft known as Durham boats. These flat-bottomed, shallow-draft vessels measured from forty to sixty feet in length and were used for carrying grain, whiskey, and iron ore on the Delaware and its tributaries. Propelled by oars and poles, they could carry up to fifteen tons and were thus ideal for ferrying an army and its artillery. As darkness fell, the Durham boats were hauled out of hiding and manned by Glover's Marbleheaders.

The seamen faced impossible conditions. The high water, fast current, and strong winds were bad enough, but the ice floes were worse. Tumbling and sliding over each other, pitching up out of the water at crazy angles, they tested the Marbleheaders' every skill. The ice crashed against the boats and had to be fended off with oars and poles before any headway could be made. Ice froze on thwarts, poles, and oars, and snow reduced visibility to near zero. Washington

had intended the crossing to be completed by midnight, but it was past three o'clock by the time the last troops reached shore. The Marbleheaders, however, had not lost a man or a horse or a gun.

By the time the nine-mile march on Trenton began, it was nearly four o'clock. Beyond the ferry the road divided. John Sullivan with one wing of the army and four of Knox's guns took the right fork, or River Road, which entered the town at its south or lower end. The left wing led by Nathanael Greene took the Pennington Road, which described a gentle arc and entered Trenton at its upper end. It was to be a classic pincers attack. Washington and the rest of Knox's guns traveled with Greene, as did Generals Hugh Mercer and Lord Stirling. The attack was now several hours behind schedule, but Washington's resolve never wavered. When Sullivan sent word that the rain and snow had wet the priming powder in the men's muskets, he replied, "Tell General Sullivan to use the bayonet. I am resolved to take Trenton."

In 1776, Trenton was a prosperous little village of some hundred houses. Since it was situated at the head of navigation on the Delaware and at the center of a network of roads, it had strategic significance as a communications center. The two main streets, King and Queen, ran a block apart along the town's axis, coming together at their upper, or northern, ends to

join the Pennington Road. Colonel Rall had been ordered to fortify this key junction, but he had failed to do so. Two Hessian outposts were positioned on the Pennington Road, and one was on River Road.

The German soldiers in Trenton had made the best of a lonely Christmas in a foreign land by feasting and sampling generously of their sizable rum supply. There had been a brief alarm early in the evening when a small American force staged a hit-and-run raid on one of the Pennington Road outposts. This bit of unauthorized freelancing could easily have spoiled Washington's surprise, but Colonel Rall did not take it seriously and soon had his men back in quarters. He then dined leisurely at the home of a local merchant and settled in for an evening of cards and conviviality. Around midnight a Tory farmer appeared at the door with an urgent message. Rall refused to have his game disturbed, so the Tory scribbled a note informing him that the American army was on the march. Rall thrust the note into his pocket unread. In the small hours of the morning when he finally staggered off to his quarters and bed, he was quite drunk.

At dawn the two American columns were still some two miles short of their objective, and their officers hurried them along at what one marcher described as a "long trot." It was almost 8:00 A.M. when Greene's advance guard slammed into the first of the Pennington Road outposts. The Hessian sentries retreated to the back-up post and then ran pell-mell for the town. At the same time, Sullivan's van attacked the outpost on River Road. A few minutes after eight, sentries pelted into Trenton crying *Der Feind! Der Feind! Heraus! Heraus!* (The enemy! The enemy! Turn out! Turn out!) Scattered musketry confirmed that the Battle of Trenton had begun.

Drummers summoned the Hessians to arms, and an aide rushed off to wake Colonel Rall. The latter took some doing, but at last Rall appeared at an upstairs window in his nightclothes. No doubt cursing a throbbing head, he hurried to dress. The Rall regiment formed up on King Street, while the Lossbergs were divided, part on Queen Street, part facing the sound of firing from the lower town. The Knyphausen regiment was put in reserve nearby while Rall tried to sort things out. But he was losing precious time, and Washington, Greene, Sullivan, and Knox were not wasting a moment.

Henry Knox ordered two batteries set up at the junction of King and Queen streets (the spot Rall had failed to fortify); Captain Thomas Forrest set up four guns to fire down the length of Queen Street, and nineteen-year-old Captain Alexander Hamilton placed his two guns to sweep King Street. Since rain and snow had soaked much of the infantry's powder, the artillery was crucial. Their shot and shell ripped down the two main streets, and the Hessians dived for cover.

Greene's troops deployed with almost clockwork precision—the mark of veterans. Hugh Mercer's brigade swung off to the right to link up with Sullivan's force in the lower town. The men under Lord Stirling

(he claimed a lapsed Scottish title, but he was actually plain William Alexander) were in the center, backing up Knox's guns at the head of King and Queen streets. Off to the left went the brigades of Adam Stephen and the Frenchman Alexis la Roche de Fermoy, swinging east of town toward Assunpink Creek. Meanwhile, Sullivan's corps was shouldering its way into the lower town from the River Road. The Americans had sprung the trap and were fast surrounding Trenton.

The Rall regiment tried to move up King Street, but the American artillery and Mercer's infantry, which was infiltrating through side streets, caught it in a withering cross fire. The Hessians loosed two inaccurate volleys and withdrew. Next, Stirling's troops took the offensive, charging down the two main streets with fixed bayonets. Captain William Washington was ordered to take the Rall battery, which was trying to repel the assault. As Sergeant Joseph White remembered: "I hallowed as loud as I could scream to the men to run for their lives right up to the pieces. I was the first that reach them. They had all left except one man tending vent—run you dog, cried I, holding my sword over his head, he looked up and saw it, then run. . . ." Captain Washington and young Lieutenant James Monroe (who forty-four years later would be elected President in an era of good feelings) were wounded in the charge. On Queen Street the Lossberg gunners managed to fire only two or three rounds before Knox's deadly cannoneers silenced them.

By this time, the town was in chaos. American troops were everywhere, darting between buildings, shooting and bayoneting the confused Germans. Battle smoke eddied through the streets, and sleet and snow poured down, obscuring vision. The boom of cannon, the crackle of musketry, and the yells of the fighting men combined to create an unholy din. American sharpshooters ducked into houses, dried and reprimed their guns, and from the windows began to pick off enemy soldiers. To compound the confusion, camp followers, Tory hangers-on, and some German soldiers tried to drive away wagons loaded with plunder.

Rall ordered a counterattack, but his men were smashed back by snipers and cannon fire. He then tried to rally his own regiment and the Lossbergs on the Knyphausen regiment, which was sheltering in an orchard east of town, but he was knocked off his horse and carried from the field with two bullets in his side. Major Friedrich von Dechow, his top subordinate, was down with a mortal wound. Now the fresh American brigades of Stephen and de Fermoy closed in. Quickly the Rall and Lossberg regiments grounded their muskets and dipped their colors, while their officers raised their hats on sword points to signify surrender.

The Knyphausen regiment had fallen back toward the marshy ground along Assunpink Creek, with Sullivan's corps in hot pursuit. Ewing's blocking force of militia had not been able to cross the Delaware, and some 400 Hessians fled across the bridge before Sullivan could reach it. However, the Americans soon gained control of the bridge and cut it off as an escape route. Other Germans tried to swim the brimming creek, but few made it. In the tradition of the time, the rebels fired a warning volley over the heads of the enemy before the final charge. That was enough; the Knyphausens surrendered. It was now 9:30 A.M. The Battle of Trenton had lasted about an hour and forty-five minutes.

Except for those few hundred escapees, it was a total victory for the Americans. The Hessians had suffered casualties of 114 dead and wounded and 948 captured. Six good fieldpieces and over a thousand muskets were gathered up, plus a mixed booty that included enough musical instruments to equip two complete bands. The American casualty list totaled four men wounded.

The booty was collected and the prisoners rounded up. Washington and Greene looked in on the stricken Rall and ordered what medical aid they could, but he was beyond help; he died the next day. A quick council of war debated the next move. A continued offensive beckoned, toward Princeton and beyond. But there had been no word from Cadwalader, who was supposed to be engaging Donop around Bordentown. (Cadwalader, like Ewing, had not been able to cross the Delaware—but of course neither man was blessed with Glover's Marbleheaders.) The storm still raged, and there were a thousand prisoners and walking wounded to consider. Perhaps most important, the American troops were exhausted; they had had no sleep in at least twenty-four hours. At noon Washington reluctantly gave the order to pull back across the Delaware into Pennsylvania. When they finally got back to camp, some of the troops had gone fifty hours without sleep and had marched over forty miles. But they had won a dazzling victory, and every one of them knew it.

The true measure of any military victory is not its size but its effects, and the effects of Trenton were crucial to the American cause. The Continental Army had shown the world (and itself) that it could not only fight but win. As the news spread, recruiting suddenly became easier and civilian morale shot up. "This affair has given such amazing spirit to our people," a Philadelphian reported. That spirit went up a few more notches when those 900-odd captured Hessians, looking sturdy and fit in their splendid uniforms, were paraded through the streets of Philadelphia on their way to a prison camp in Virginia.

Moreover, at Trenton George Washington had demonstrated that he was a general of considerable skill. His pincers movement achieving tactical surprise was a classic right out of the military textbooks, and the near-perfect way it had been carried out under the most atrocious conditions captured the imagination of the young nation.

Although John Cadwalader did not get his force across the Delaware on Christmas night as planned, he tried again on December 27, thinking that Washington must still be in Trenton. This time he made it. Cadwalader's action could have been disastrous, but he was lucky—there was not an enemy soldier in sight. Upon learning about the battle at Trenton, Hessian Colonel von Donop had hastily withdrawn from the Bordentown post and retreated to Princeton. Soon thereafter all the posts in the Delaware River area were abandoned.

This news aroused Washington's combative instincts. He sent word to Cadwalader to stay where he was; the rest of the army would be along shortly to resume the offensive and "beat up the rest of their Quarters." By December 30, Washington was back in Trenton.

However, before he could make another move, Washington had a problem to solve: the next day the enlistments of most of his veteran troops would expire.

If they went home, he would have only militia and a few raw recruits left. He ordered the veteran regiments paraded and appealed to them to stay on for six more weeks, until a new army could be raised. In addition, he offered a ten-dollar bounty to all who would stay. "My brave fellows, you have done all I asked you to do and more than could be reasonably expected," one of the men recalled him saying. "But your country is at stake, your wives, your houses, and all that you hold dear. You have worn yourselves out with fatigues and hardships, but we know not how to spare you." The drums rolled, calling for volunteers. With a shrug or an "I-will-if-you-will" glance at their comrades, nearly all the veterans stepped forward.

Later that day Washington wrote to Robert Morris, the Philadelphian who was chief financier for the patriot cause, urging him to do everything possible to raise the bounty money. "I thought it no time to stand upon trifles when a body of firm troops, inured to danger, was absolutely necessary to lead on the more raw and undisciplined," he explained. Pledging his own credit, Morris managed to raise $50,000.

So as the new year began, Washington still had an army. When he pulled all the scattered detachments together in Trenton, it numbered some 5,100 men. However, it was an army heavily leavened with militia and new volunteers, and Washington knew that his veterans, his "firm troops," were very near the end of their tethers; to one observer they looked like a "flock of animated scarecrows."

When Howe learned that Washington had knocked loose the southern anchor of his chain of New Jersey posts and that the situation in that "pacified" state was in danger of coming unstitched, he hastened to restore order. Princeton was designated as the assembly point for a fresh offensive, and his best general, Cornwallis, was told to forget his home leave and take charge. By New Year's Day Cornwallis had marshalled over 8,000 troops in Princeton, and before dawn on January 2 he set out for Trenton with 5,500 of them.

Upon learning that the British were on the move and that Cornwallis was in command, Washington may well have had second thoughts about his plan. He had apparently hoped to clip off another section of the British chain of posts—probably at New Brunswick, the loss of which would have made Princeton untenable—and thereby liberate the southern half of New Jersey. But by reacting much faster than expected, thanks to the aggressive Cornwallis, the British had again seized the initiative.

Trenton was a bad place in which to stand and fight. The Americans had their backs to the Delaware, and getting safely across the river if the battle turned against them would be all but impossible. Retreating downstream to another crossing, with the enemy at their heels, held no more promise. Washington realized his predicament, but he betrayed no concern as he sent forward a detachment to delay the British and then ordered his main force to dig in. He was not retreating.

Washington needed the daylight hours to prepare his position, and the delaying force gave them to him. The weather also lent a helping hand. A warm spell followed by heavy rains had thawed the ground, with the result that Cornwallis's men and guns were deep in mud. And as they slogged along, they were caught in one long ambush. From every barn, from every thicket, from behind every wall, the Americans kept up a steady fire. Thomas Forrest's two-gun battery contested the advance at natural obstacles such as creeks and ravines. Perhaps most annoying to the British were Colonel Edward Hand's Pennsylvania riflemen, whose frontier "long rifles" outranged the British and German muskets and were far more accurate as well. Repeatedly the British had to stop, shake out a battle line, and unlimber their guns, at which point the rebels faded away to their next blocking position. It took Cornwallis ten hard hours to travel ten miles. By the time he reached Trenton, it was late afternoon. The delaying force fired its last shots and then hurried across the Assunpink Creek bridge into the American lines. At the bridge Washington greeted them on his big white charger, looking, said a New Englander, "firm, composed, and majestic."

The Assunpink flows into the Delaware just below Trenton. Washington and his troops had occupied a ridge along its southern bank. It was a strong position, solidly anchored on the left by the Delaware and protected by the steep-banked creek in front; its weakness was the right, which was "in the air." If the British were to send a force upstream to where the creek narrowed, they could easily cross and outflank the whole position.

But as Washington had anticipated, by the time Cornwallis secured Trenton it was too late for any flank marching. The Britisher was not content to end the day's activities, however, and the result was the Second Battle of Trenton.

It was a very sharp battle. Hessians tried to cross the creek upstream at a ford and were repulsed by a Rhode Island regiment. The main effort, however, was at the Assunpink bridge where Knox had positioned eighteen guns. An artillery sergeant remembered how

> the enemy came on in solid columns; we let them come on some ways, then by a signal given, we all fired together. The enemy retreated off the bridge and formed again, and we were ready for them. Our whole artillery was again discharged at them. They retreated again and formed; they came on the third time. We loaded with cannister shot, and let them come nearer. We fired altogether again, and such destruction it made, you cannot conceive. The bridge looked red as blood, with their killed and wounded, and their red coats. . . .

After this repulse Cornwallis decided to end the action. More than 2,000 reinforcements were to join him the next day, at which time he planned to use a flanking march to dislodge the rebels from their entrenchments. One of his officers questioned the decision: "My Lord, if you trust those people tonight, you will see nothing of them in the morning." Cornwallis reportedly replied that they had "the old fox in the trap" and would "bag him in the morning."

It was an unfortunate statement in view of events to come, and it tends to obscure the fact that Cornwallis had made the only decision possible. A renewed frontal assault would have resulted in more casualties —and the British had already lost several hundred men that day. A flank march carried out by exhausted troops at night in unfamiliar country over roads deep in mud would have been foolish, perhaps disastrous. So the British posted sentries and settled down to rest and wait for daylight.

At eleven that night Washington convened a council of war in a house well behind the lines. It was clear to everyone that the next day would be decidedly unpleasant if they stayed where they were. Then a suggestion was made, a very bold suggestion: why not quietly pull out, take an obscure road leading off to the northeast around the British lines, and fall on the garrison at Princeton? Just who made the proposal is not clear, but there is some evidence that it was Washington himself. In any event, it was quickly seconded. One very real problem was already being solved by a weather change. A sharp temperature drop was freezing the muddy roads.

Quietly the word was passed. Campfires were built up by piling on fence rails, and a detachment of 400 men was detailed to strengthen the entrenchments at points along the line where the noise would carry to the British camp. Gun carriage wheels were wrapped with rags to muffle their passage, and at 1:00 A.M. the march began. The "play-acting" detail would keep working and then follow along just before daylight.

The escape route used by the Continental Army that pitch-black night was unguarded for the simple reason that the British probably knew nothing about it. This is not surprising, since it was hardly more than a rough track recently hacked through heavily wooded country. The column jammed up frequently, and during the halts men leaned on their muskets and fell asleep standing up. It may have been a slow march, but it was a quiet one, and the army got away clean.

By dawn the American column had reached a road junction by a Quaker meeting house, two miles short of Princeton. The column split; Hugh Mercer took 350 men off to the left toward the main Princeton-Trenton road where he was to take up a blocking position against the pursuit expected from Cornwallis. Washington and the rest of the troops took the right fork, planning to swing around Princeton and attack it from an unexpected direction.

At about this time a patriot scout and a redcoat scout from Princeton simultaneously caught sight of sunlight flashing off rifle barrels. Each galloped back to his respective commander to report that the enemy was in sight.

The day before, when he set out for Trenton, Cornwallis had left three of his regiments—the Seventeenth Leicestershires, the Fortieth South Lancashires, and the Fifty-fifth Border Regiment—behind at Princeton. When he failed to defeat Washington that day, he sent orders back for the Seventeenth and Fifty-fifth to come along at first light on January 3, leaving the Fortieth to guard Princeton. Thus Lieutenant Colonel Charles Mawhood and his two regiments were on the road to Trenton when his scout galloped up to tell him that there was a rebel force off to the east, heading right past him toward Princeton.

What the scout had seen was Washington's main column; now Mercer's force came into view from behind a hill, much closer. Patriots and redcoats rushed toward the only high ground in the area, the orchard and farm owned by William Clark. Mercer's men narrowly won the race, driving back a unit of dismounted cavalry. Then Mawhood came up with his Seventeenth Regiment of regulars and a full-scale fire fight broke out, supported by a battery or two on each side. "The battle was plainly seen from our door," a local farmer recalled. "Before any gun was heard a man was seen to fall and immediately the report and smoke of a gun was seen and heard, and the guns went off so quick and many together that they could not be numbered. We presently went down into the cellar to keep out of the way of the shot. . . ."

These British troops were sturdy veterans, fresh, well rested, and well led. After a single volley they charged with the bayonet. It was an unnerving sight, and Mercer's tired brigade began to fall apart. Mercer tried to rally his men but was caught in a melee, knocked down with a gun butt, and repeatedly bayoneted. He feigned death and the redcoats moved on. John Haslet, a Delaware colonel who had consistently done well and was marked for higher command, fell

The roar of cannon reverberates through this painting of the Battle of Princeton by William Mercer, deaf-mute son of the brigadier general who died under British bayonets. Young Mercer accurately recalled the landscape, but painted Washington's white horse brown.

dead nearby, a bullet in his brain.

Meanwhile, there was consternation back in Trenton. Cornwallis and his staff had awakened to discover no rebels at all in the entrenchments across the creek. As they were trying to puzzle this out, the thunder of artillery came faintly to them from the north. It was all too apparent that "the old fox" had slipped out of their trap and was stirring up trouble somewhere else. The drums rattled to call the men to formation.

On the battlefield near Princeton, the fight was moving across the fields and woods toward the Quaker meeting house and the farm of Thomas Clark. John Cadwalader's militia unit, the natty Pennsylvania Associators, came up from the main force to try and brace the line, but these militiamen were new to the sight of battle smoke and bodies writhing in the grass. After two or three volleys they broke and fled along with the remnants of Mercer's brigade.

Then came a scene with such larger-than-life heroics that it seems too improbable to have really happened. Yet there is ample eyewitness testimony to the facts. General George Washington, commander in chief of the Continental Army, came galloping up on his big white horse, clearly furious and with the light of battle in his eye. Behind him were some of those "firm troops" he so admired—the Rhode Islanders who had repulsed the Hessians at Assunpink Creek the evening before, Edward Hand's sharpshooting Pennsylvanians, and the crack Seventh Virginia. Washington rode past the bewildered militia toward the front shouting "Parade with us, my brave fellows! Parade with us!" Then suddenly and incredibly he was squarely between the two battle lines, not thirty paces from the enemy. Both sides fired at the same time, and he was completely enveloped in battle smoke. His aide, Colonel John Fitzgerald, later admitted pulling his hat down over his eyes to spare himself the sight of the commander in chief going down; another officer remembered "a thousand deaths flying around him." Then the smoke cleared, and there was Washington still in the saddle, untouched, still rallying his men. "Bring up the troops, Colonel Fitzgerald," he called out. "The day is our own."

Now the veterans were there, coolly firing, reloading, advancing, firing again. Knox's cannon were blazing away as fast as they could be served, pouring grapeshot into the British ranks. The militia held and began to fight back. The redcoats courageously stood their ground, but they were outnumbered and outgunned. When Mawhood finally gave the command to retreat, they began to lose their good order, and then they simply turned and ran. Washington led the charge after them, swinging his hat and bellowing, "It's a fine fox chase, my boys!"

The fragments of the once-proud Seventeenth Leicestershire Regiment fled down the road toward Trenton, while the Americans scoured the woods and creek beds for stragglers. The farmer who had taken shelter in his basement emerged and found his barnyard full of triumphant Americans: "Though they were both

103

hungry and thirsty some of them were laughing outright, others smiling, and not a man among them but showed joy in his countenance. It really animated my old blood. . . ."

With the rout of the Seventeenth, the other two British regiments withdrew into Princeton. Out of touch with their commander, they fell into confusion about their orders. Most of the redcoats simply marched straight through town and took the road to New Brunswick, but a party of some 200 sought shelter within the stone walls of Princeton College's Nassau Hall. John Sullivan's division quickly surrounded them while Alexander Hamilton brought up his battery and put a solid shot through the walls into the prayer hall, neatly decapitating a portrait of George II. After another round or two, a white flag appeared at one of the windows, and the redcoats filed out in surrender. "They were a haughty, crabbed set of men," an American sergeant noted.

So ended the Battle of Princeton, the second stunning American victory in nine days. The British suffered probably 100 dead and about 300 captured. Washington's casualties totaled 44, including General Mercer; his wounds were mortal, although he lived in agony for nine days.

Washington had the army assembled, the prisoners and booty were collected, and at about noon they marched out of Princeton on the road toward New Brunswick. Cornwallis's advance guard from Trenton was in sight, "in a most infernal sweat—running, puffing and blowing and swearing at being so outwitted," as Henry Knox imagined them (probably accurately) in a letter to his wife.

The thought of going after New Brunswick, with its stocks of supplies and its reputed war chest of £70,000, was tempting, but Washington had to face facts. The men had been up all night, they had had little or nothing to eat, and they had just been through some of the

sharpest fighting many of them had ever seen. New Brunswick was eighteen miles away and close behind was Cornwallis with a superior force, no doubt coldly furious at the humiliation he had suffered. A council of war on horseback confirmed Washington's analysis. When the army reached the crossroads at Kingston, it turned left and set out for Morristown and winter quarters. The Trenton-Princeton campaign was history.

Now at last the two armies settled down for the winter, the rebels in a naturally strong bastion at Morristown, the British in New York and in the New Jersey posts of Amboy and New Brunswick. Fighting would certainly resume in the spring, but for the moment the American rebellion was very much alive. "These feats have turned the scale," wrote Robert Morris who as fund raiser for an often unpopular cause was especially sensitive to the public mood.

In the British camp there was grudging admiration edged with some unease. While still scornful of the rebels' lack of military polish, a cavalry officer admitted that "though it was once the fashion of this army to treat them in the most contemptible light, they are now become a formidable enemy." Howe was concerned, reporting to London that "the unfortunate and untimely" actions had "thrown us further back than was at first apprehended." London was equally concerned. Colonial Secretary Lord George Germain wrote Howe, "I trust . . . that the unexpected success of the rebels will not so far elate them as to prevent them from seeing the real horrors of their situation, and tempt them to disdain to sue for pardon."

George Washington was not just then about to sue for pardon. The Revolution was a long way from being won, but miraculously it had not been lost. The crisis had been passed; the times had indeed tried men's souls, but those men had not been found wanting.

Picture Portfolio

Americans of the Revolution

By 1776 a population numbering 2 million had built Atlantic cities and begun to cross the Appalachians. This restless collection of Europe's children were already calling themselves what they would soon be—Americans. Here, a special selection of pictures shows the varied composition of the fledgling nation. These men, of numerous ancestries (though mostly British), tradesmen and aristocrats, farmers and scholars, became a people united in revolution, defiantly replacing royal images with liberty poles (below).

Prudence Punderson's embroidered biography reflects placid acceptance of birth and death, minimizes the busy life of a merchant's wife managing household and servants.

Patriot Merchants of New England

England's taxes and restraints were costly for prosperous businessmen—a large portion of New England's 700,000 souls. At Boston's Red Lyon, presided over by his friend Edward Proctor, Paul Revere met with artisans, merchants, lawyers to discuss events. In time talk turned to rebellion, then independence.

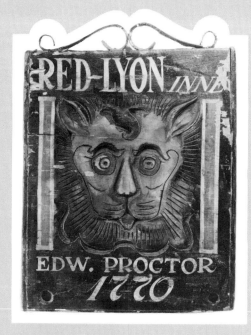

Gazing from over the mantel in his Massachusetts home, Moses Marcy considers evidences of a merchant's life: ledger and trading ship, hospitable home and punch bowl. His ties with England were strong, but stronger was resistance to acts threatening economic independence.

If any man symbolized the restless American spirit, it was Daniel Boone. As this romantic scene suggests, he led pioneers through the Cumberland Gap: by 1790, Kentuckians numbered 52,573. Many scratched a living on farms like the one at right, typical of the long, raw frontier.

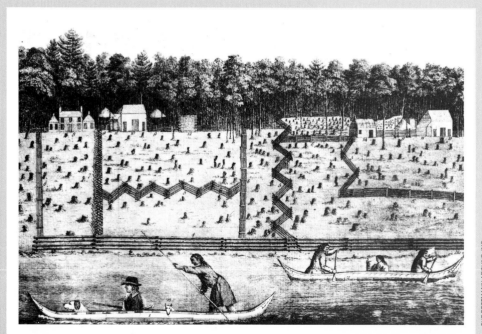

Seekers beyond the Mountains

The royal Proclamation of 1763 recognized Indian lands, forbade settlement west of the Appalachian divide. Though partly devised for colonists' protection, the law infuriated them. To ambitious men, western lands had always offered a better life. Great tracts bought from Indians by speculators for little could be sold to settlers for dollars or debts.

Painted to ornament the New York farm it depicts, this overmantel has an aura of prosperity and permanence. New York produced large crops of wheat for export as grain or bread. For these farms, trade restraints would be disastrous. On eastern farms as on the frontier a spirit of independence flourished, fostered by distance from royal authority.

Redmen in a Whiteman's War

As rebellion flared into revolution, powerful Indian tribes watched and waited. Whether they took sides, and with whom, could be vital. Sir William Johnson's heir, at whose home the council at right met, convinced many Iroquois to side with England. Sadly, their reward would be devastation and loss of ancestral lands.

COURTESY KNOX GELATINE COMPANY

SCHOOLCRAFT, HISTORY OF THE INDIAN TRIBES OF THE UNITED STATES

Known among member-tribes
as the Great Peace, the Iroquois
League was a "United Nations"
of six New York tribes.
They dated their union from
1575, when it was accepted by
Medusa-like Onondaga chief
Atotarho (opposite). The highly
sophisticated confederacy
kept peace among its members,
served as governing council
and defense league. When
most Iroquois joined England,
Seneca orator Sagoyewatha
(right) followed. For his
English coat he was known
as Red Jacket. In 1812 he
fought for the Americans.
Washington, only white man
he admired, gave him the
medal worn in this portrait.

Citizens of Philadelphia

Philadelphia, called America's London, and Benjamin Franklin, America's sage, complemented each other. The stolid Quaker city had become a leading port with 25,000 residents, setting precedents of religious liberty, enlightened medical, penal codes.

Literate and sophisticated, Philadelphians loved diversions. Their city had everything from cockfights to concerts; and later, the most elaborate theater in the country. No practical use to them, electricity was a tingling new game.

Humanist, scientist, businessman, and diplomat, Franklin symbolized American genius for the rest of the world. Printer, son of a tallow maker, he spoke easily with all society. He dreamed of an expanded empire, but finally urged independence.

Squire of a Tideland Plantation

George Washington, warrior and statesman, considered himself first of all a planter. His beloved Virginia plantation occupied his thoughts even at war; letters contain many references to crops and buildings. Neither so wealthy nor scholarly as some fellow leaders, he was respected for his prudence, integrity, and sense of justice.

MOUNT VERNON

Tobacco was the main crop but unprofitable. Washington preferred wheat (harvested at left). Herring was also a cash crop at Mount Vernon.

Like many Virginia fortunes, Washington's was founded on tobacco. But the Tidewater was changing. No longer did the farmer seal his tobacco sale with a leisurely glass at the wharf. An early experimenter, Washington tried new fertilizers and crops to rebuild exhausted soil. Eventually he could show friends, like Lafayette (above), the happy results.

115

Blue uniforms with varied coat facings had been ordered for all services, but the usual field dress was a cloth or deerskin hunting shirt and fitted leggings, "justly supposed to carry terror to the enemy, who think every such person a complete marksman." Muskets were the main weapon, but accuracy made the Pennsylvania rifle valuable in skirmishes and forest fighting.

Men at Arms

George Washington was greeted at Boston by 13,000 undisciplined, ill-equipped men, the New England militia. He saw their strength; established command, instilled discipline.

The Continental Army, about half Yankee, grew around that core. Loyalists disparaged the "rabble at arms," but Howe wrote that America's best men had joined Washington.

Some men enlisted for a hundred-acre bounty, but John Glover's Marblehead fishermen, marching to join Washington (above), fought British restriction of their livelihood. Ignorant of military discipline, they faced war in disarray. Prussian-born Gen. von Steuben drilled them and others with his *Regulations,* complete with step-by-step diagrams like the one on the recruiting poster at right.

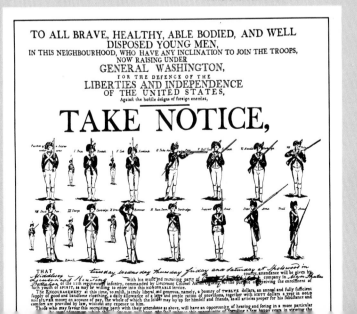

An Army Takes Shape

As tension mounted, other colonies
followed the New Englanders. The eager
volunteers leaving Annapolis on July 10, 1776,
were soon toughened into a crack regiment, one
of Washington's most valorous and loyal.

175TH INFANTRY, MARYLAND NATIONAL GUARD, BALTIMORE

PART TWO

The Young Republic 1777-1815

Chronology:

Final Battles for Freedom

First Steps as a Nation

Second War of Independence

The Way to Victory

6

On the morning of June 20, 1777, one of France's most fearsome Indian captains, Louis St. Luc de la Corne, stood in a clearing at the mouth of the Bouquet River and stared out across the waters of Lake Champlain. St. Luc was close to seventy years old, and he had come, over time, to resemble his warriors in both appearance and savagery. Around his leathery neck hung the ribbon and medallion of the coveted Order of St. Louis, presented to him by the French king for leading raids against the English-speaking colonists, first in King George's War and again in the French and Indian War. Throughout his career, the watchword of this veteran campaigner had remained sadistically simple. *"Il faut brutaliser les affaires,"* he declared to all who would listen. "It is necessary to brutalize matters."

Now, St. Luc mused as he waited by the lake, the irony was complete. Fifteen years earlier the British had accused him of murdering and scalping English women and children after the peaceable surrender of Fort William Henry. But now on a sunlit morning in June, 1777, the Frenchman had buried the hatchet with the British authorities. Indeed, he and his 400 braves had been commissioned by them to move in the van of one of the most noble and formidable armadas ever seen upon the inland waters of North America.

Gazing out across the lake, St. Luc watched the stately procession of bateaux, barges, pinnaces, and gunboats. Soon his sharp eye perceived a scurry of activity upon the decks of a small schooner lying to anchor several hundred feet from the shore. In a flutter of crimson coats, gold epaulets and white-cockaded hats the commander of the British forces, Lieutenant General John Burgoyne, clambered down the *Maria's* topsides into a waiting pinnace. When the articulate, somewhat paunchy Burgoyne stepped ashore, St. Luc greeted him ceremoniously and led the general and his staff inland to a glade where the Indian mercenaries were gathered. After a number of introductory remarks, Burgoyne, who was an amateur dramatist renowned for his pretentious style of writing, rose to his feet. "Warriors," he declared in what was to become one of the most fateful speeches of his career, "you are free—go forth in might and valor of your cause—strike at the common enemies of Great Britain and America —disturbers of public order, peace, and happiness, destroyers of commerce, parricides of state."

Burgoyne spoke at length in this fashion and then somewhat belatedly began to temper his directive. "I positively forbid bloodshed, when you are not opposed in arms," he commanded. "Aged men, women, children, and prisoners must be held sacred from knife or hatchet, even in actual conflict." Despite these restrictions, the news of Burgoyne's speech was received with grim foreboding by the colonists. In the vulnerable borderlands, patriot and Tory alike knew that swinging tomahawks were incapable of making even the bluntest political distinction.

In England, Burgoyne's ill-advised bombast exposed him to ridicule at the hands of the king's opponents. Edmund Burke denounced the hypocrisy of the speech in the House of Commons. And Prime Minister Lord North, who had originally approved the use of Indians as a tactic to frighten the colonists, is reputed to have laughed so hard at Burgoyne's disingenuous restraints on the Indians that tears ran down his cheeks.

But Lord North's laughter was misplaced. No decision could have been better calculated to create unified popular opposition to Burgoyne's advance. Nor could any decision have better ensured his defeat at Saratoga that autumn. For the time being, however,

In John Trumbull's painting begun a dozen years after the 1777 triumph at Saratoga, Gen. Gates gallantly declines Burgoyne's sword. Trumbull included in the scene buckskin-clad Dan Morgan and Philip Schuyler (in civilian clothes, at far right), but not Benedict Arnold—by then anathema to all patriots.

Burgoyne fondly believed that his Indian terror campaign would play an important part in the destruction of the colonists' "unnatural Rebellion." After the speeches at the Bouquet River, the Indians received a liberal ration of rum and staged a war dance that pierced the night with the "most hideous yells." In the morning, St. Luc and his men were gone.

The British fleet was soon under way again, heading down Lake Champlain toward Ticonderoga, its first target. Burgoyne's plans for this expedition were based on his experience as General Carleton's second in command on Lake Champlain during 1776. After that campaign he had returned to England and had written a paper entitled "Thoughts for Conducting the War from the Side of Canada," which he had presented to the king and Lord George Germain, the colonial secretary. Correctly assuming that the British ministry desired another invasion from the north, Burgoyne proposed that an army of 8,000 regulars be sent south from Canada down Lake Champlain. Ticonderoga would be attacked, if all went according to plan, in the summer of 1777. Then the army would proceed to Albany, its main objective, by way of Lake George and the Hudson River. Along the way Burgoyne planned to set up a chain of posts to establish a line of communications between Canada and New York. At the same time an auxiliary force would advance down Lake Ontario and the Oswego and Mohawk rivers. The two armies were to meet on the Hudson above Albany, capture the city, and then establish contact with General Howe in New York.

Predictably, the king liked the plan, and Burgoyne was promoted to command the Champlain thrust with the new rank of lieutenant general. Late in March, 1777, Germain wrote to the capable Sir Guy Carleton in Canada, informing him that he had been superseded by his former deputy. Burgoyne was to have the bulk of the troops for the Champlain expedition, while a

further 675 would be sent under Colonel Barry St. Leger to Oswego, on Lake Ontario, with instructions to proceed down the Mohawk.

Howe, in the midst of preparing his own campaign for 1777, displayed little interest in the invasion from Canada. He planned to attack Philadelphia, and early in April, 1777, he wrote to Germain saying he intended to take the bulk of his force out of New York and approach the American capital by sea. Burgoyne would thus be on his own. This was not entirely unexpected. Burgoyne did not believe he needed assistance to reach Albany, nor did the British ministry. Besides, both Germain and Howe believed that the attack on Philadelphia would be over by September (Burgoyne's projected time of arrival at Albany) and that Howe would then have men to spare. By early May, however, Germain had begun to have second thoughts about the wisdom of letting Burgoyne advance unprotected. He wrote to Howe and mentioned the idea of coordinating the two armies, but by the time the letter reached America it was too late.

Burgoyne landed at Quebec on May 6. By June 13 he had marshalled his army of 7,213 men in St. John's on the northern tip of Lake Champlain. This force was split into two parts: the British infantry division, numbering 3,700 rank and file, under Major General William Phillips; and the Germans, numbering 3,000, under the resourceful Baron von Riedesel. General Simon Fraser, a distinguished Scots officer who had served for some time in America, commanded the light reconnaissance troops. The army, expecting to encounter a force of 12,000 Americans at Fort Ticonderoga, carried a field train of forty-two heavy guns, including mortars and two massive twenty-four pound siege guns.

Instead of the 12,000 troops the British expected, Ticonderoga was held by a thoroughly demoralized force of only 2,500 men. Much of the blame for their

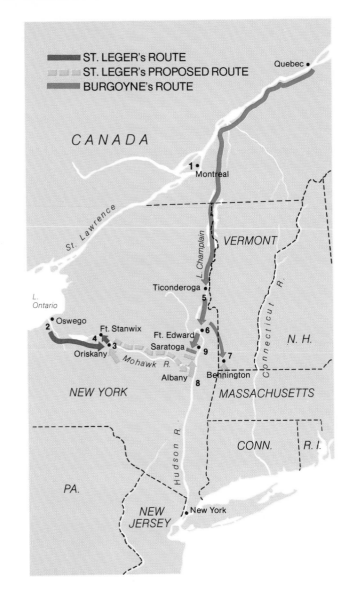

Blunting the Combined Assault

By a pincer movement from Montreal (**1**) the British sought to bisect the colonies in June, 1777.

Relying on New York Tories and Iroquois Indians, Barry St. Leger drove down the Mohawk Valley from a base at Oswego (**2**). After his defeat of old settler Nicholas Herkimer's force at Oriskany (**3**), his siege of Ft. Stanwix (near present-day Rome—**4**) was relieved by Benedict Arnold.

Gen. John Burgoyne (portrait by Joshua Reynolds below), who headed the major attack force, captured Ft. Ticonderoga (**5**) on July 6, then swept southward. His Indian hatchetmen turned passive farmers into zealous patriots by their atrocities, such as the scalping of Jane McCrea (shown below at left) near Ft. Edward (**6**); then his Hessian allies were smashed by John Stark's Hampshire Grantsmen near Bennington (**7**).

With St. Leger in retreat, the two armies failed to meet for the planned move on Albany (**8**). Instead, weakened Burgoyne faced an entrenched Gen. Horatio Gates near Saratoga (**9**).

Heroism at Freeman's Farm

Gen. Gates stands crowned by victor's laurels for Saratoga. He displayed good sense by fortifying Bemis Heights and forcing Burgoyne to attack the entrenched Americans or retreat. History, however, credits the win to Benedict Arnold who here fought his last battle for the revolutionaries.

The fight began at Freeman's Farm, a clearing where unharvested wheat still waved on September 19 when Burgoyne's men emerged from the forest. Immediately Dan Morgan's longriflemen (who had unnerved the British by turkey-gobbling signals) opened fire, knocking out every red-coated officer in the advance (above). Arnold fiercely pressed the British center. They were saved from disaster only by the arrival of German troops.

When Arnold's success was hailed and when he wrote Congress directly, Gates raged and took away his command. But as the Second Battle of Freeman's Farm burst forth on October 4, Arnold could not be restrained. After sharpshooters had dispatched Burgoyne's Gen. Simon Fraser (carried from the field in the painting below), Arnold led the crucial attack on the British redoubt. His heroism won him little save another wound and the enmity of the high command.

condition can be laid to the squabbles of two generals who, though both better suited to desk jobs, were vying for the command of the Northern Army. Major General Philip Schuyler had nominally filled the post since the summer of 1775. But when difficult decisions had been required of him, he had frequently retired to his tent with "a bilious fever and violent rheumatic pains," thus abdicating responsibility, but not command, to his subordinates. When the Americans had encountered serious reverses in Canada in the summer of 1776, Congress had ordered Major General Horatio Gates to take command "in that province." The jovial but somewhat devious Gates was, like Schuyler, better equipped for the maneuvers of the council chamber than of the field. The chief problem with Gates's first big command, however, was that by the time he reached the shores of Lake Champlain all American troops had long since retreated out of Canada. Instead of superseding Schuyler, as he expected, he had to serve as his second in command.

Burgoyne's fleet landed above Ticonderoga, at the southern narrows of Champlain, on July 1. Four days later British engineers hauled two twelve-pound guns to the top of a nearby hill that the Americans had mysteriously failed to fortify. Before the British had fired a shot, the patriots began a precipitous withdrawal down the road to Hubbardton, a few miles through the forest to the southeast. A week later, after fighting a number of bitter rearguard actions, the bulk of the American force scrambled into Fort Edward on the upper Hudson. There they found a worried Schuyler encamped with about 3,000 men. Washington, hoping to push Schuyler into action, dispatched further reinforcements and two New England major generals, one of whom was the popular and demoniacally aggressive Benedict Arnold. Schuyler, however, still felt that it was necessary to retreat and therefore withdrew another twenty-five miles down the west bank of the Hudson to the village of Stillwater, New York.

As he withdrew, Schuyler put 1,000 axmen to work. They destroyed dozens of bridges between Skenesboro, where Burgoyne was camped, and Fort Edward. They also flooded the woodland trails and covered the main road from Skenesboro with a shambles of felled pine and hemlock. These tactics delayed Burgoyne, but they did not stop him. He sent out hundreds of men to clear the obstructions, and finally after three weeks of hard work, the British forces reached Fort Edward, only twenty-three miles away. There Burgoyne was forced to stop and wait for the guns and supplies coming via Lake George.

The delay was an anxious one for Burgoyne. On August 3 he received definite word that there would be no help from Howe. In a letter dated July 17, Howe wrote that he was carrying out his plan to attack Philadelphia and would only come up the Hudson if Washington "goes northward contrary to my expectations." In that case, Howe wrote, "I shall soon be after him to relieve you." That was only the first of Burgoyne's problems. Two days before the British regulars had entered Fort Edward, St. Luc's Indians had slaughtered the family and three black servants of a farmer named John Allen. On the same day a young woman named Jane McCrea, the sweetheart of one of Burgoyne's Tory officers, was killed and scalped by an Indian named Wyandot Panther. When the brave returned to the camp proudly bearing the scalp of Miss McCrea, Burgoyne ordered his arrest and trial for murder. St. Luc warned the general that such an act would make his mercenaries desert the expedition. Burgoyne, heeding St. Luc's advice, pardoned the murderer.

The story of this barbarous deed, and its expedient exculpation, quickly reached the New England newspapers and inflamed patriot anger to fighting pitch. Militia gathered on village greens, eager to defend their homes against the British and their brutal allies.

On August 11, Burgoyne sent out a mixed force of 650 Germans, British snipers, Indians, and Tories under Colonel Frederick Baum to seize military stores supposedly kept in the village of Bennington, thirty miles to the southeast of Fort Edward.

The march had hardly begun when the Indians once again undercut the purpose of their employers by looting, destroying property, and killing milk cows for the sake of their sonorous bells. But Baum quickly ran into worse difficulties. To forestall any such "fishing expeditions" into its territory, New Hampshire had marshalled a force of 1,500 volunteers under the command of Brigadier General John Stark; these troops now lay encamped at Bennington.

Upon learning that a strong enemy force was advancing into New Hampshire, Stark sent word to Colonel Seth Warner, whose regiment of Green Mountain Boys was gathered at Manchester. Before Warner and his men could join him, however, Stark set out to meet Baum. The opposing forces met on August 14, at a ford across the Wallomsac River. Baum did not attack; so the Americans withdrew to Bennington for the night. Two days later the patriots encircled Baum and at 3:00 P.M. attacked the entrenched Germans from all sides.

At the first American volley St. Luc and his Indians fled, shrieking in fear and clanging their stolen cowbells. After two hours of close fighting, Baum's ammunition wagon exploded whereupon most of his force either surrendered or ran. Baum tried to cut his way out at the head of a few dragoons but was mortally wounded, and the rest of his men soon gave up.

Burgoyne had sent a relief force under Lieutenant Colonel Heinrich von Breymann to extricate Baum, but it had been seriously delayed by shirt-sleeved farmers who, using blunderbusses and fowling pieces, had fired repeatedly into the Hessian columns. It was late afternoon when Breymann finally collided with some of Stark's men. The Americans retired to a wooded hill on the north side of the road and began to fire into the German line—with little effect. Breymann's advance was finally slowed by the arrival of Warner's men. The action then developed into a toe-to-toe fight. At sunset, his ammunition spent, Breymann ordered a retreat. Back on the road, the Americans maintained such a murderous fire that the German drums beat a "parley" to seek terms of surrender. The sound, however, meant nothing to the New Englanders, and the slaughter continued until Breymann escaped into the night, having lost four field guns, hundreds of muskets, and nearly 1,000 men. Of these, 207 were dead, and more than 700 were either captured or missing. For their part the Americans suffered a loss of 30 dead and 40 wounded.

The debacle at Bennington, besides diminishing their strength by one-tenth, forced an agonizing reappraisal upon the British. Burgoyne was shocked to learn that his troops were viewed not as liberators but as the enforcers of a detested tyranny. Since there was no prospect of local support, Burgoyne decided to delay his advance to Albany, less than fifty miles away, until provisions and the rest of his artillery came from the north. Though the guns slowed all his movements, Burgoyne insisted that they were necessary to destroy the earthworks favored by the Americans and to prevent them from imposing another Bunker Hill upon the British infantry.

At the beginning of September, Burgoyne received news of yet another setback. After initial success, St. Leger's stroke down the Mohawk Valley had bogged down in a siege action around Fort Stanwix, the principal defensive post of that region. St. Leger defeated one relief expedition under General Nicholas Herkimer at Oriskany, but a second under Benedict Arnold, who cunningly exaggerated his strength, forced St. Leger back to Oswego. General Burgoyne would

Retreat from Philadelphia

South of Philadelphia, at sleepy Brandywine Creek, the Americans tried to stop the onrushing British at nearly the same moment as the first battle of Freeman's Farm in the North. Peculiarly, Gen. William Howe had sailed toward the rebels' capital from New York by Chesapeake not Delaware Bay. But neither American geography nor arms could keep him from his objective.

After Brandywine, the defenders met another defeat at Paoli where British bayonets "massacred" a

detachment under Anthony Wayne by night (top). Then Philadelphia fell without further struggle.

Howe made a single mistake: he rashly concentrated part of his forces at Germantown. Washington seized the offensive. But his complex plan fell apart in fog and confusion, partly because of a premature assault upon British troops in the Chew mansion (above).

Withdrawing to Valley Forge, Washington and Lafayette (right) feared for their ill-clothed soldiers. Fortunately, the winter proved mild.

Cockpits of War

Just as Gentleman Johnny Burgoyne failed to crack the rebellion by his 1777 invasion from Canada, so indulgent Gen. William Howe failed to coerce the colonies by his occupation of their capital. Nor could he perceive that the Revolution would only be won by the will of the people and the maneuvering of continental forces. Puzzled by the unconventional war, he resigned.

Gen. Henry Clinton, marching the main British force back to New York, was rattled by George Washington at Monmouth Courthouse, New Jersey—the last great battle in the North. In the romantic painting of that June-weather battle above, Washington accepts a captured British standard while riding a gigantic white horse (which, in fact, later fell dead from exhaustion). Through the smoke in the background appears the legendary Molly Pitcher (so called for the water she lugged to parched troops), standing beside her husband's smoking cannon.

Thereafter the flames of Revolution spread west and south. And, when the treaty with France had been confirmed, the allies even sought to defeat England on the sea and by amphibious operations. A number of the important engagements from the war's inconclusive middle years are pinpointed on the map at left: (**1**) Battle of Monmouth (June 28, 1778); (**2**) route of hostile navies, as France's Comte d'Estaing seeks to intercept Adm. Richard "Black Dick" Howe's evacuation from Philadelphia at the Delaware's mouth; (**3**) fleets' positions as d'Estaing declines to enter New York harbor and attack Howe; (**4**) d'Estaing seeks to assist in siege of Newport (captured by the British in 1776) but both naval forces are scattered by a great storm off the New England coast; (**5**) George Rogers Clark sets forth down Ohio River to defend western settlers against Indians and Detroit-based British (June, 1778); (**6**) Tory and Indian raids destroy settlements in Wyoming Valley (July 3, 1778); (**7**) Gen. John Sullivan defeats Iroquois Indians (August 29, 1779); (**8**) Anthony Wayne's task force, demonstrating professional dispatch, temporarily takes the Hudson River bastion Stony Point from British (July 15, 1779); (**9**) and (**10**) British capture Savannah (December 29, 1778) and Charleston (May 12, 1780).

have to take Albany—if he took it at all—on his own.

It was clear that the British could not stand on their present positions. Burgoyne must either retreat to Canada or else advance and capture Albany before winter. On September 13 he crossed the Hudson at Saratoga and began to march south toward Bemis Heights—and one of the most decisive battles in world history.

Back in August the Congress had grown tired of General Schuyler's continual retreats from Ticonderoga and had ordered Horatio Gates to take over as commander of the forces opposing Burgoyne. Gates immediately moved the American army to a position on Bemis Heights three miles north of Stillwater. The heights were rapidly fortified under the direction of Colonel Kosciusko, but work was still incomplete when scouts reported the approach of Burgoyne on the morning of September 19.

Riedesel, with most of the German troops and the baggage, commanded the British left along the riverbank. Burgoyne, with the bulk of the British infantry and guns, commanded the center, which lay on the clearing of Freeman's Farm about a mile due north of the American lines. The right under General Simon Fraser fanned out in a crescent to the west. The British plan was for their center and left wing to engage the Americans on Bemis Heights; meanwhile Fraser was to take some high ground on the American left flank, enfilade the enemy trenches, and then push the rebels into the river.

Gates at first planned to sit on his hilltop and inflict another Bunker Hill upon the British. But General Arnold, in command of the troops who had to contend with Fraser, objected: Burgoyne, he felt, should be tackled in the woods around Freeman's Farm and kept out of cannon range of the earthworks on Bemis Heights. Arnold "urged, begged and entreated" the sedentary Gates for permission to lead his division into the attack. Gates finally sent Colonel Daniel Morgan with 300 backwoods riflemen and some light infantry under Major Henry Dearborn to cover any flanking move by Fraser. Arnold's division was to stand in reserve. After considerable skirmishing, Fraser scattered Morgan's men into the woods, but they soon regrouped on the western slopes of Freeman's Farm.

The British lines were now more than two miles long, and Arnold seized the opportunity to throw his division into the gap between Burgoyne and Fraser. His men stormed across the clearing and took the British guns; but before they could haul them away, the British counterattacked with bayonets, driving the Americans back to the trees. High above the battle Morgan's men sat among the golden leaves of oak, elm, and maple and—whenever the smoke cleared—systematically picked off the gunners and gaudily uniformed officers. Only one of the artillery officers and a quarter of the gunners survived the maelstrom of fire unhurt; veterans of the Seven Years' War declared that they had "never experienced so long and hot a fire" as that around Freeman's Farm. But the thin red line held, due in large part to the personal gallantry of Burgoyne who "shunned no danger" while inspiring his men and who at all times "delivered his orders with precision and coolness."

Meanwhile, Gates rejected Arnold's repeated requests for reinforcements. Finally at dusk Riedesel placed the expedition's baggage under nominal guard by the river bank and staged a counterattack, which forced the Americans to retreat. Despite their withdrawal, the victory clearly went to the Americans, who suffered only 220 casualties to the enemy's 600.

Expensive though the battle was, Burgoyne determined to press the attack on Bemis Heights. But before he could do so, he received word from Sir Henry Clinton, Howe's lieutenant in New York, who promised to send a diversionary force up the Hudson to attack patriot fortifications in the Highlands. Burgoyne decided to dig in and wait for Clinton's sally to draw off Gates's reserves. During the delay, however, the patriots' strength increased—sometimes at the rate of 1,000 men a day—as the harvest came in and the militiamen marched up to help administer the *coup de grace* to the murderers of Jane McCrea.

By early October, Burgoyne, having heard nothing more from Clinton (his message had been intercepted), prepared to send a reconnaissance force to probe the American defenses and perhaps open a way to Albany. On the morning of October 7, Brigadier General Simon Fraser led a force of 1,500 regulars south and deployed them across a rolling wheatfield. While foragers cut straw for the horses, staff officers peered through their spyglasses, attempting to locate the American strongpoints. Gates immediately ordered flank attacks against Fraser by Morgan and Dearborn on the left and by Arnold's division on the center and right. Arnold was conspicuously absent; he had quarreled with Gates over his conduct at Freeman's Farm and, after a bitterly outspoken exchange, had been relieved of his command. For a while Arnold sat out the battle, fuming in his tent as his old division fought to contain the British in the valley below. Then, unable to stand it any longer, he leaped into the saddle and rode pell-mell into the action, hotly pursued by Major Armstrong, one of Gates's aides, who had orders to restrain him.

Arnold rode through the middle of General Learned's brigade and led its first three regiments in an impromptu assault on the British center. After fierce fighting the Americans were driven back. But Morgan, charging out of the trees further to the west, pushed in the British right wing under Lord Balcarres. On a second attack by the Americans, the British center deserted its guns and withdrew into its breastworks.

Not content with winning a skirmish, Arnold, with Major Armstrong still doggedly in pursuit, now rode to the left and led men from Patterson's and Glover's brigades against Lord Balcarres's breastworks. But the British held. Instead of retiring, Arnold spurred his huge chestnut horse yet further to the left and, riding within feet of the blazing muskets, stormed on down the British line to take command of Learned's brigade. He led it, together with Morgan's riflemen, in an assault on the redoubt that marked the western end of Burgoyne's line. As he vaulted his horse through the fort's sally port, Arnold's left thigh was smashed by a musket ball. After a brief but bitter struggle, the redoubt surrendered. When poor Major Armstrong finally galloped up, there was nothing he could do, in all propriety, but offer the wounded Arnold his heartiest congratulations. After their conquest of this fort, the rebels were in a position to roll up the entire British line and push the enemy into the Hudson. As the Americans rested upon their arms in the dusk, Arnold was carried past on a litter of blankets and poles. "Where are you hit?" asked Henry Dearborn, who had been with Arnold at Quebec. "In the same leg," his former commander replied. Then in an eerily prophetic afterthought, the hero of Saratoga supposedly added, "I wish it had been my heart."

Aware of the threat to his flanks and rear, Burgoyne withdrew his army to the bank of the Hudson. The next evening the retreat, and heavy rains, began. Leaving their wounded and much of their baggage, the British ploughed through a growing sea of mud to arrive the following evening at the Heights of Saratoga, less than a dozen miles to the north. By the morning of October 13, Burgoyne's exhausted remnant of 3,500 effectives was surrounded by a swarm of 14,000 Americans, who maintained a constant sniper fire and bombardment.

Burgoyne, the glib brutalizer, had become the victim of the fate he had so arrogantly outlined for the

The War at Sea

"I have not yet begun to fight!" bellowed John Paul Jones (right) on a moonlit September 23, 1779, when the seemingly victorious *Serapis* inquired whether the Scotch-American commodore had struck his colors. As shown in the U.S. Naval Academy painting below, the 44-gun British frigate—convoy for the type of merchant vessels Jones liked to hit—was thereupon drawn into a deathly embrace by grapples from the American ship.

Jones had named his converted merchantman *Bonhomme Richard* ("Poor Richard") to honor Ben Franklin's almanac, for diplomatic Franklin had helped get French funds for him and other privateers like Gustavus Conyngham (far right). Losses from American raiders made British businessmen think twice about continuing the war.

Treaty of Alliance.

The most Christian King, & the United States of North America, to wit, New hampshire, Massachusetts Bay, Rhode island, Connecticut, New York, New Jersey, Pennsylvania, Delaware, Maryland, Virginia, North Carolina, South Carolina and Georgia, having this Day concluded a Treaty of Amity and Commerce, for the reciprocal Advantage of their Subjects and Citizens have thought it necessary to take into Consideration the means of strengthening those Engagements ......

Alliance in Paris

"Huzza! Long live the King of France!" exulted George Washington on hearing that Louis XVI had recognized American independence on February 6, 1778. In the print at right, Washington stands before a French artist's idea of a Valley Forge tent. He holds in his hand the Treaty of Alliance (whose first page has been reproduced above right). The treaty committed France to fight as a full partner until the Revolution was won.

Franklin had arrived at Versailles late in 1776 to speed up the diplomatic efforts of Silas Deane and Arthur Lee. The three patriots met a willing foreign minister but a king reluctant to act. Franklin, dressed in fur hat and homely garb, found ways to cut through courtly indecision; his mission was made successful by the good news from Saratoga.

In the painting above Franklin is shown exercising another of his skills—charming the ladies—at a reception after the treaty's signing.

Americans at Cumberland Head four months previously. He was surrounded, with no prospect of retreat.

Realizing the hopelessness of his situation, Burgoyne opened negotiations with Gates—who was so anxious to settle that the British began to suspect that Sir Henry Clinton, unbeknownst to them, had marched up the Hudson to menace Gates's rear. Burgoyne dragged out the negotiations, arguing that his men must be permitted to return to England on agreement never to serve again in America and that his surrender must be termed a convention instead of a capitulation. General Gates readily agreed to all this (to the subsequent fury of Congress) because the British had in fact taken two important forts at the entrance to the Highlands on October 6. But neither army at Saratoga knew that Clinton had returned to New York. After further dalliance Burgoyne finally signed his "convention." On October 17 his men grounded arms and marched through the American camp between lines of troops who, despite their motley attire, stood "like soldiers, erect, with a military bearing." Even the colonels were in everyday clothes, reported one Brunswicker, and many of the rebel troops, though greybeards in their fifties, were as lean and as formidable as the much younger Europeans. In front of both armies, Burgoyne presented his sword to Gates, who bowed politely and then returned it.

News of the convention spread across the continent faster, even, than St. Luc's furiously retreating Indians. On October 18, Washington's army to the south, depressed by the loss of Philadelphia, welcomed the victory with jubilation. The commander in chief greeted this "important and glorious triumph" with a thirteen gun salute and a *feu-de-joie* by the army.

Even by European standards, the victory was impressive. Besides capturing 7 generals, 300 officers and 5,000 men, the Americans also acquired thousands of muskets, 27 guns, and tons of ammunition. Yet, more important, the victory proved that American independence was a cause to be reckoned with. For many months, Benjamin Franklin and his fellow commissioners in Paris, France, had been seeking some kind of recognition from Louis XVI. But the French king had steadfastly resisted for fear of antagonizing his old foe, England, in the name of what might be a losing cause. Believing that Saratoga would break the deadlock, Congress commissioned a young merchant named Jonathan Austin to rush the news to Paris. After a wild winter voyage across the Atlantic in the *Penet,* a small snow noted for her speed in all weathers, Austin arrived in France on November 30.

Franklin had expected bad news about a British occupation of his beloved Philadelphia. As the muddy, exhausted Austin galloped into the courtyard of Franklin's Paris residence, the old gentleman called out:

"Sir, is Philadelphia taken?"

"Yes, sir," replied Austin. Franklin clasped his hands, turned, and began to grope his way back indoors.

"But, sir," Austin shouted, "I have greater news than that." The elderly statesman stopped and turned. "General Burgoyne and his whole army are prisoners of war!" The effect, in Austin's own words, "was electrical."

On hearing the news from a beaming Franklin, King Louis's ambivalence vanished. On December 6, 1777, he promised recognition of American independence and opened negotiations that culminated two months later in a formal treaty of alliance. The nations would fight together against England, and neither would make peace without the consent of the other. Much of Europe subsequently joined the League of Armed Neutrality in opposition to Great Britain. Thus the capitulation at Saratoga transformed the American Revolution into an international war. At the same time, by enlisting the purse, the fleet, and the prestige of one of the world's great powers, it also laid the most significant and perhaps the most substantial paving block in the United States's hard road to victory.

American patriots set other paving blocks on the road to victory in the four arduous years ahead. But the road from Saratoga to Yorktown was also marked by so many defeats and wearying setbacks that we can only wonder at the soldiers' will to press on.

Perhaps the most serious challenge to the patriots' determination came in the winter following Saratoga. While General Howe—having successfully brushed aside the rebels' badly coordinated attack on the suburb of Germantown—luxuriated in the snug warmth of Philadelphia, Washington marched his 11,000-man army up the Schuylkill River to Valley Forge. He later reported that his shoeless men's "marches might be traced by the blood from their feet."

On that bleak but defensible plateau of Valley Forge some twenty miles northwest of Philadelphia, the American army endured freezing rain and frost—and on Christmas Day, 1777, four inches of snow—in canvas tents and lean-to shelters thatched with dead leaves. There was no wood for fires, and scant water. Due to muddle among the quartermasters, many soldiers were without boots, coats or blankets or proper food. "Here comes a bowl of beef soup," a surgeon wrote bitterly of the army's cuisine in December: "full of burnt leaves and dirt, sickish enough to make a Hector spue." Typhus, smallpox, typhoid, and pneumonia attacked the camp. At one time a quarter of the men were unfit for duty, and so many officers resigned their commissions that Washington, only half joking, surmised he might soon be alone with the men.

Besides wrestling with the army's supply problems, and the problem of garrisons throughout the states, Washington had also to tangle with a not consistently friendly Congress. Certain members (particularly from New England) regretted Washington's performance at Philadelphia and hinted at General Horatio Gates's su-periority. An allied officer (General Thomas Conway, an Irishman in the French army) was challenged to a duel by a supporter of Washington because Conway and the "Conway Cabal" purportedly desired to replace the commander in chief with Gates, the sedentary hero of Saratoga.

One day, late in February, 1778, when matters at Valley Forge seemed at their lowest ebb, a rotund Prussian officer named Friedrich Wilhelm von Steuben rode into camp with a letter of introduction from Benjamin Franklin. Though the cheery, red-faced Steuben spoke no English, Washington accepted his offer to train the Continental Army in drill and mass infantry maneuvers.

While the army drilled and struggled to keep warm at Valley Forge, American diplomats in Paris were negotiating a treaty (signed on February 6, 1778) in which France renounced all ambitions to the American mainland east of the Mississippi. In return, the United States agreed to assist France's struggle against British forces on the islands of the West Indies. Since 1776 France and Spain had covertly supplied the American patriots with arms and given aid to American privateers. Now, within six months of the treaty's signing, 4,000 French soldiers, borne by a fleet of four frigates and twelve ships-of-the-line, under Count d'Estaing, arrived off the Delaware Capes.

The appearance of a hostile fleet in the very waters of the Channel and news of the departure of d'Estaing's fleet for America confirmed the deepest fears of the British government in Whitehall. London had learned of Burgoyne's failure on December 2, and most sensible Englishmen, including William Pitt (Lord Chatham), decided the war in America could not be won. British spies had quickly procured copies of the new Franco-American treaty, and it was clear the home shores of England itself were in peril. (The more so since the once-vaunted British fleet had been allowed

Campaign in the West

Lanky frontiersman George Rogers Clark (below) celebrated July 4, 1778, by seizing Kaskaskia on the Mississippi, some 50 miles south of St. Louis. He and his 200 "Long Knives" had flatboated west from Virginia to liberate the Illinois country from the British. Now, as French inhabitants joined the revolutionary cause, Clark's mission seemed accomplished.

But then came word that British Lt. Col. Henry Hamilton—known as "Hair Buyer" for his supposed purchase of American settlers' scalps from the Indians—had retaken Vincennes on the Wabash. Undeterred by winter floods, Clark counterattacked. Barely surviving a 180-mile wilderness march (above), the frontiersmen captured Vincennes's Fort Sackville by ruse. The "Hair Buyer" gave his sword—and the temporary possession of western territories—into American hands (left).

British Adventures in the South

Pursuing the hope of American loyalty to the crown in the South, the British took Savannah, Georgia, as an operations base in 1778. The American and French command ordered an amphibious allied force to drive the British out.

As shown in the panorama at right, d'Estaing's fleet and Gen. Ben Lincoln's army made a mighty

show as they surrounded the city in 1779. But when Spring Hill redoubt failed to fall to the allies (a spy having revealed their attack plan), their resolve faded. Once again, d'Estaing sailed away.

The British later chased Lincoln to Charleston, bringing cannon within half a mile of the city (above) in April, 1780. Finally Lincoln and patriot leaders capitulated, surrendering some 5,500 men—the worst loss of the war.

But in South Carolina's western mountains, the patriots scored a moral and strategic victory at King's Mountain when their long hunting rifles toppled Maj. Patrick Ferguson from his horse (right). His force of Tory troops was routed by "back water men, a set of mongrels." The South was rising.

to decline, while money was lavished on Howe's red-coated battalions.) Also, the Royal Navy was burdened with the task of blockading the American coastline. Thus it could not shield British supply convoys from American privateers, who captured more than 400 vessels in the year 1777 alone. And now that the French fleets were at sea, it would be even harder to protect the sea routes to North America.

For a while it seemed possible that Lord Germain, one of the prime architects of the fiasco at Saratoga, would be sacked. Sir Henry Clinton, the dour but clear-thinking commandant at New York, replaced Howe as commander in chief. But after much speechifying and politicking, Lord North and Germain (firmly supported by George III) remained in office. In Parliamentary debates, the king's men made much use of the argument that British troops could not evacuate America for fear of exposing the faithful loyalists to the wrath of the patriots. The ministry was perpetually inclined to exaggerate the strength of Tory sentiment, which in turn prompted it to undertake a policy of active military assistance to the South, thought to be impregnated with loyalism.

Soon after a peace commission—dispatched from London with powers to grant everything short of independence—was scornfully rejected by Congress, Clinton was ordered to evacuate Philadelphia (June, 1778). Washington sallied out from Valley Forge to block his road to New York, but the maneuver dissolved into an inconclusive skirmish around Monmouth Courthouse near the village of Freehold, New Jersey. The British disengaged in good order, and Washington marched slowly northward, crossed the Hudson, and encamped at White Plains, New York.

Both commanders had learned enough from past fighting to know that, without strong French naval help, Washington had no chance of storming New York. On the other hand, Clinton could accomplish little by advancing from the city. A stalemate ensued. For this reason much of the fighting in the next four years would take place, so to speak, in the wings (see map, page 128).

As the American privateers took yet heavier tolls on British cargo ships (their total haul for the war came to £18 million worth of property and 12,000 captured sailors), the British in turn organized a number of punitive raids on the more notorious New England ports such as New Bedford. On the other side of the settled continent, the king's men sought to mobilize the Iroquois, Shawnee, Delaware, Cherokee, and Miami tribes against the American settlers on the borders of the western states.

Many of the hostile savages were supplied and directed from the British posts at Niagara, Detroit, and Fort Sackville at Vincennes, on the Wabash River. In an effort to halt the terror on the border, Colonel George Rogers Clark, aged twenty-seven, led a force of 127 backwoodsmen in February, 1779, on an epic march to the Illinois country along the Mississippi. Then, when a powerful British force recaptured Vincennes behind him, he doubled back for a surprise attack across 180 miles of frigid swampland.

The floods that winter had driven all the game from the forest; Clark's men soon ran out of food. Wading for days at a time through freezing, shoulder-deep water, the expedition took a week to cover the last nine miles before Vincennes. But Clark's approach was so unexpected that the British commander capitulated on February 25.

Clark's midwinter campaign through the icy floodlands of Illinois temporarily took pressure off the border settlements to the east. But the Tories and Iroquois continued to use Fort Niagara (at the junction of Lakes Erie and Ontario) as a base for depredations against the farmers of New York. In the summer of 1779, Major General John Sullivan—who four years before had

Southern Irregulars

Soon after Gen. Gates's Continental Army suffered a crippling defeat at Camden, South Carolina, some of his men were sprung from capture by raiders. Leader of the raid: Francis "Swamp Fox" Marion.

The famous Marion (pictured above crossing the Pee Dee on a ferry) and other southern militia commanders at first dedicated themselves to stinging the British wherever possible; ultimately they combined with the South's new American commander Nathanael Greene to sweep the British out of the Carolinas.

Less well-known southern irregulars were six-foot Nancy Hart (shown below repelling Tory attackers from her cabin) and Bunyan-sized Peter Francisco (left) who routed cavalrymen of Britain's feared leader, "Butcher" Banastre Tarleton.

tried to revitalize Arnold's dispirited army at Quebec— prosecuted a scorched earth campaign against the Indian towns of western New York. Though he demolished many native communities, raids by the notorious Butler's Rangers and by the Iroquois under Joseph Brant continued up and down the Mohawk Valley to the end of the war.

The remorseless professionalism of Sullivan's scourge had its echo in other theaters of the war. Despite their defeat at Saratoga, the British were still flirting with the idea of splitting the American colonies with a thrust up the Hudson Valley. In June, 1779, they captured a small fort at Stony Point, New York, a few miles down river from the key American fortifications at West Point. The British doggedly built up the defenses of their new fort. But to their consternation, a force of 1,350 men under Anthony Wayne, using the bayonet alone, stealthily assaulted and retook the fort on the night of July 15. Shortly thereafter the Americans withdrew, taking the British guns with them. But the cold, silent savagery of Wayne's attack against well-entrenched regulars made it clear to the British that their enemy had achieved a professionalism equal to, if not surpassing their own.

These isolated struggles, though dramatic, were peripheral to the issue of winning American independence. That, as Washington knew, could only be accomplished by a major application of force.

In the summer of 1778 he had sought to overpower Clinton by an attack on land and sea. He had requested the French fleet to attack the British in New York harbor. But the attack was abandoned when d'Estaing, loath to tangle with Admiral Howe, decided he could not move his largest vessels across the sandbar at the harbor's mouth. The French then sailed to New England to link up with the American militia in an assault on 6,000 British troops at Newport, Rhode Island. But, once again the plan miscarried; a storm damaged the French squadron, which then retired to Boston to refit.

It was now Clinton's turn to try a coordinated blow. Late in the fall of 1778 he dispatched a force of more than 3,000 regulars and loyalists to test the sentiment in Georgia. The fall of Savannah to the British on December 29, 1778, was to initiate one of the most convoluted episodes in the struggle for American independence. For nearly three years, armies marched and countermarched, collided and dispersed, through the length and breadth of the four southernmost states. At first the tide of war flowed in favor of the British, who quickly captured Augusta, Georgia, and began to recruit numerous companies of loyalist militia. A former governor of Georgia successfully reestablished a more or less orderly royalist civil government.

General Benjamin Lincoln, who had worked so effectively to destroy Burgoyne's supply lines at Saratoga, now marched 6,000 men south to expel the invader from Savannah. Though he had the help of d'Estaing's fleet and troops, Lincoln failed to dislodge the British. Then the British turned the tables. When the French admiral sailed for Europe, Clinton took advantage of his absence to transport more than 8,000 troops down from New York and trap the isolated Lincoln in Charleston, South Carolina.

On May 12, 1780, the city surrendered and the American loss in prisoners and equipment equalled that of the British at Saratoga. Clinton now controlled —with much local support—two southern states, and rumors circulated that the northern states might abandon Georgia and South Carolina to the crown. Congress, however, stoutly voted to sustain the fight for the original union. Large numbers of southern patriots under the command of such noted partisans as Andrew Pickens and Francis Marion waged an increasingly effective guerilla war against the British from southern swamps and forest hideaways. Recognizing that the

South was becoming the critical theater of war, patriot reinforcements marched southward.

On August 16, 1780, the brisk new British commander in the South, Charles, Lord Cornwallis, routed an army of 4,000 men under Horatio Gates at Camden, South Carolina. (Gates, mounted on a noted racehorse, did not stop until he reached Hillsborough, North Carolina—160 miles from the battle.)

Sir Henry Clinton believed in consolidating royal power in Georgia and South Carolina before attempting to bring the more northern states under the king's sway. But Camden convinced Clinton's ambitious subordinate Cornwallis that he should now move into both North Carolina and Virginia. If he had followed Clinton's plan, the southern colonies might just possibly form today some kind of warm-weather Canada on America's southern border.

Burgoyne, in his march south, had failed to learn the lesson of Bennington. And Cornwallis, in his march north, was not sufficiently impressed when, on October 7, 1780, a detached force of 1,000 Tories was trapped and destroyed by a lesser number of patriot "back mountainmen" at King's Mountain, thirty miles west of Charlotte, North Carolina. As he tramped north, Cornwallis found himself opposed by a new American commander—the Southern Army's fourth in two years —the intelligent and resourceful Nathanael Greene, from Rhode Island. Greene's strategy was, simply, to use the continental spaces of the South to swallow the invading British, much as the wilderness of upstate New York had swallowed Burgoyne's forces. To this end Greene—disregarding military convention—divided his small army so that it could simultaneously harass the east and west flanks of the British advance.

Brigadier General Daniel Morgan, the "Old Wagoner," commanded the flanking force that was to strike out of the west. But while Morgan's 1,000 men were moving into position, they were met by a force of similar size under the command of a ruthless, Oxford-educated cavalry colonel named Banastre Tarleton. On January 17, 1781, Morgan deployed on a wooded hill at Cowpens (ten miles northeast of Spartanburg, South Carolina). After two volleys, Morgan's militia withdrew in simulated flight. Colonel Tarleton, imagining the day to be his, then hurled his men on the seasoned American Continentals and the quickly reformed militia who inflicted great loss. The Americans counterattacked with the bayonet, and the British suffered more than 100 killed and 700 captured. Cornwallis conceded the defeat was a "very unexpected and severe blow."

After much marching, and countermarching, the British main force finally confronted Greene's recombined army, together with some 2,800 militia, at Guilford Court House (near Greensboro, North Carolina) on March 15, 1781. Like Morgan at Cowpens, Greene placed his Continentals behind his militia. But this time some militia never stopped running. They never returned to provide extra strength for the American battle line. But even then Cornwallis was only able to drive the Continentals back after a stiff struggle. One American attack was pressed with such vigor that Cornwallis only contained it by ordering his artillery to fire canister into the backs of his own hard-pressed guards. Although they won the battle, the British lost more than 500 men. In London, Horace Walpole observed, "Lord Cornwallis has conquered his troops out of shoes and provisions and himself out of troops."

Left with a depleted army (1,600 men), the earl was forced to fall back. Rather than devote himself to the defense of British posts in South Carolina and Georgia, he resumed his march to Wilmington, North Carolina, thence on to the security of Virginia. After a few days' rest, the British battalions began their trek north past the mouth of Chesapeake Bay to the destiny that awaited them at Yorktown.

Washington at Yorktown

7

An air of crisis hung over patriot headquarters in New England. The war was in its seventh year, and the Continental Army was rapidly shrinking as bone-thin, weary men reached the end of their endurance and refused to reenlist. The Comte de Rochambeau, commander of the French army that had been sent to America in 1780, described the growing crisis in a letter to a fellow officer:

> These people here are at the end of their resources. Washington has not half the troops he counted on; I believe, though he is hiding it, that he has not 6,000 men. M. de La Fayette has not 1,000 regulars with the militia to defend Virginia. . . . This is the state of affairs and the great crisis at which America finds itself.

Aware not only that it was growing increasingly difficult to keep an American army together but also that the flow of men and money from France was nearing an end, Washington and Rochambeau met in Wethersfield, Connecticut, on May 22, 1781, to plan a final campaign.

Although Rochambeau was a highly decorated veteran of forty years campaigning, he was deferential toward Washington. He had written months before, when his troops landed in Rhode Island: "The commands of the King, my master, place me under the orders of Your Excellency. I came, wholly obedient and with the zeal and the veneration which I have for you and for the remarkable talents displayed in sustaining a war which will always be memorable."

Washington's achievements were indeed remarkable. For nearly seven years, he had held the American army together through his indefatigable energy and tenacity, through his ability to bear adversity without

L.C.A. Couder's panoramic painting *The Siege of Yorktown* hangs in Versailles. It shows Washington and French commander Comte de Rochambeau in the field, planning the final allied campaign.

becoming discouraged, and through a strength of character that inspired respect and trust in all kinds of men. Time and time again, Washington and his ragged army had outmaneuvered the British, at times scoring brilliant coups, but almost always remaining on the defensive, parrying the enemy's moves. Now, with the help of the French, Washington would soon be able to take the offensive.

Although at Wethersfield, Rochambeau and Washington agreed to combine their armies for an attack, they disagreed over the target. Washington favored an assault on Sir Henry Clinton's garrison in New York. Rochambeau wanted to attack Earl Cornwallis's army in Virginia on the Chesapeake Bay. Washington objected, arguing that a major move southward would have to be made by water and thus in conjunction with a French fleet. Although Washington knew that a fleet under the command of Admiral de Grasse was due to arrive in the West Indies that summer, he did not know that the admiral had orders to cooperate in an offensive against the British. Rochambeau (who did know but had been ordered to keep it secret) asked Washington what he would do if a French fleet were to come to North America and establish naval supremacy. The American commander replied that he would still prefer an attack on New York.

Officially Washington prevailed. At the end of the conference, Rochambeau signed a document agreeing to an attack on New York should the fleet appear. Secretly he sent de Grasse a dispatch in which he noted the results of the meeting but urged the admiral to sail for the Chesapeake, "for it is there that . . . you can render the greatest services."

Four days after the conference, Washington received word from his representative in Paris, John Laurens, that the French West Indian fleet had been ordered to send a large detachment to America. According to Laurens, the ships would probably arrive in

July. More than two weeks later, Rochambeau officially notified Washington that the French fleet would definitely come to America that summer. He also informed Washington that he had not only told de Grasse about the results of the Wethersfield meeting but that he had also mentioned the alternate plan for attacking the Chesapeake region. This was a slight understatement as Rochambeau had strongly urged de Grasse to go to the Chesapeake and would continue to do so in private dispatches until the admiral selected that point as his destination.

It was not until July, after he and Rochambeau had reconnoitered Manhattan's bristling defenses, that Washington finally gave up hope of storming the city. Although he still believed that a successful attack on New York was the key to winning the war, Washington noted that he "could scarce see a ground upon which to continue my preparations against New York . . . and therefore I turned my views more seriously than I had done before to an operation to the southward." Cautiously, so as not to alert the enemy, he began to investigate the possibility of moving his combined force of some 2,000 Americans and 4,000 French southward without the help of the French navy.

On August 25 the allied army crossed to the west bank of the Hudson and moved southward through New Jersey without a challenge from the enemy. Clinton's spies reported daily on allied progress, but the British did not stir; so long as Washington and Rochambeau were in the neighborhood, Sir Henry was afraid of an attack. Washington's adroit moves increased British fears. He made a show of building ovens at Chatham, as if he planned winter quarters nearby; forage parties combed the region as if preparing for a long encampment; carpenters built boats, as if for the crossing to Manhattan; and artillerymen raised batteries on Sandy Hook, as if to aid in an assault on New York.

On August 27, Sir Henry sent Cornwallis a dispatch —by whaleboat, rowed and sailed down the coast and into the Chesapeake. Clinton was unsure of Washington's moves, but felt that the rebels would probably winter at Morristown, New Jersey. Two days later Sir Henry still believed the allies had settled about Chatham. On that day Washington, riding ahead of his troops, reached Philadelphia.

On September 1, after long delays, Admiral Thomas Graves sailed out of New York harbor with nineteen ships, urged by Clinton to locate the French fleet of de Grasse, rumored to be in American waters. Two days later, when it was too late, Clinton realized that Washington had deceived him and that the Americans were heading for Virginia. Sir Henry sent Cornwallis a warning and promised to come to his aid. He then wrote to Lord George Germain in London: "Things appear to be coming fast to a crisis . . . with what I have, inadequate as it is, I will exert myself to the utmost to save Lord Cornwallis."

Back in April, Washington had sent his twenty-three-year-old major general, the Marquis de Lafayette, to Virginia in hopes of turning back a British invasion. The wealthy young Frenchman was a plump, rather ungainly figure, tall, red-haired, articulate, and devoted to the rebel cause. "The moment I heard of America, I loved her," he later said. ". . . I burned with a desire of bleeding for her."

Leading a small force of Continentals, he had reached Richmond in time to prevent its being burned by a British force led by General William Phillips and the traitor Benedict Arnold, and then had begun a series of marches through the state.

When he learned that Cornwallis, who had left the Carolinas to join the action in Virginia, was advancing to meet him, Lafayette reported to Washington in his newly acquired English: "It now appears that I have business with two armies, and this is rather too much.

Each is more than double, superior to me. . . . Was I to fight a battle, I'll be cut to pieces. . . . Was I to decline fighting, the country would think herself given up. I am therefore determined to skarmish, but not to engage too far. . . ."

Washington approved and immediately dispatched reinforcements from Pennsylvania. These were led by General Anthony Wayne, an aggressive fighter who had won acclaim for his dashing bravery at Stony Point. Meanwhile, Baron Frederick von Steuben had arrived in Virginia to train Continentals for service in the Carolinas. The stern Prussian was soon quarreling with the easygoing Virginians, who seemed to take little interest in the war (once, when Steuben rode to a remote courthouse to meet five hundred volunteers, he found only five, three of whom deserted).

Cornwallis drove Lafayette from Richmond and moved rapidly westward up the valley of the James River. Governor Jefferson and the legislators fled, but Colonel Banastre Tarleton's cavalry captured seven assemblymen in Charlottesville and narrowly missed taking Jefferson at Monticello. Jefferson's term expired during this crisis, and he was succeeded as governor by Thomas Nelson, Jr., a militia commander.

Lafayette retreated northward to Fredericksburg—but when Cornwallis inexplicably turned back to the east, the Frenchman followed at a respectful distance. In mid-June, Wayne arrived with his Pennsylvanians, grim soldiers who had lately been mutinous and were driven south with empty muskets and ammunition wagons under guard. Lafayette now had 2,000 regulars, and Steuben was nearby with 3,000 militia. The Frenchman followed Cornwallis more rapidly, but for weeks the British seemed unaware of his presence.

Cornwallis burned Richmond and fell back to Williamsburg, moving at his own pace. When he learned that he was being followed, the earl wrote Sir Henry Clinton that he would turn on the young Frenchman, "if I can get a favorable opportunity of striking a blow at him without loss of time." The opportunity came near Williamsburg as Cornwallis prepared to cross the James, moving southward.

The impetuous Anthony Wayne encountered the British rear guard at Greenspring Plantation on July 6 and charged recklessly into a trap, suffering heavy casualties from the fire of masked cannon and concealed redcoat infantry. General Lafayette rode forward un-

der fire and extricated his troops after a brief skirmish.

Cornwallis, who had been ordered by Clinton to fortify a base on the coast of Virginia where he could be evacuated by the British navy if it became necessary, then headed east and inspected a post at Old Point Comfort. He concluded that it was unfit for a naval station and proceeded out onto the Yorktown peninsula. There the earl occupied the tobacco port of Yorktown, a straggling little town with a high proportion of black laborers, on the south bank of the York River, and the village of Gloucester Point just opposite. Cornwallis was uneasy: "The position is bad, and of course we want more troops."

Lafayette was camped a few miles away, anxiously watchful: "To speak plain English I am devilish affraid of him. . . . His Lordship plays so well that no blunder can be hoped from him. . . ."

As the two armies lay near the York, Lafayette received a hint of exciting news from Washington outside New York: "I shall shortly have occasion to communicate matters of very great importance to you." Lafayette divined his meaning—the Chesapeake was to be the scene of action. The Frenchman replied, "Should a French fleet now come to Hampton Road, the British army would, I think, be ours."

On September 1, Lafayette learned that de Grasse had arrived and blocked the Chesapeake. He wrote Washington: "I hope you will find we have taken the best precautions to lessen His Lordship's chances to escape. . . . I congratulate you upon the arrival of the French fleet. . . ."

The marquis barred the peninsula with his picket lines near Yorktown, determined at all costs to hold Cornwallis in place until Washington arrived.

Meanwhile, the allied armies had reached Philadelphia; citizens of the nation's largest city were shocked by the contrast between the Americans and the French. Washington's troops were lean, lank-haired, dirty, and ragged; the French were smartly clad in uniforms of clean linen with silk facings. But the rebels, as one French officer said, "lost no credit in the steadiness of their march and their fitness for battle."

Troops of both armies were mutinous: the Americans because they had not been paid—some of them had not seen hard cash since the opening of the war— and the French because they yearned to join civilian relatives in this new country. Washington spent several days in the city, pleading with Congress and state officials for boats, arms, and money. He asked Robert Morris to raise cash for the disgruntled troops, and the resourceful banker at last wheedled $20,000 from the French, half the money in Rochambeau's chests.

Although Washington appeared confident, he was worried about the arrival of the French fleet. He had not yet received Lafayette's dispatch of September 1 when he wrote this anxious appeal to his young friend:

> My dear Marquis, I am distressed beyond expression to know what has become of the Count de Grasse, and for fear that the English fleet, by occupying the Chesapeake . . . may frustrate all our flattering prospects. . . . Should the retreat of Lord Cornwallis by water be cut off, I am persuaded you will do all in your power to prevent his escape by land. . . . You see how critically important the present moment is.

Washington was on the road south, near the village of Chester on the Delaware, when a dispatch rider from Baltimore reached him with the thrilling news: the Admiral de Grasse's fleet of twenty-eight ships had successfully blocked the Chesapeake. Cornwallis was trapped. Washington threw off the dignity of a lifetime and to the astonishment of his staff shouted, whipped his hat in the air, laughed like a boy, and grasped Rochambeau in a bear hug. "I have never seen a man moved by a greater or sincerer joy," said Count Dumas.

A few days later the allied troops reached the head of Elk River on the northern tip of the Chesapeake, and the American army was paid at last; money kegs were broken open and silver coins rolled on the ground. A New York major wrote, "This day will be famous in the annals of History for being the first in which the Troops of the United States received one month's Pay in specie." The money, a French officer said, "raised spirits to the required level," and though there was not enough silver to go around, the men now moved southward willingly.

At the head of the Chesapeake, Washington loaded a few boats with artillery, engineers' tools, some French cavalry, and elite infantry and saw them off down the bay, a motley fleet of old craft wallowing almost to the gunwales with heavy burdens. Other troops marched overland in the direction of Baltimore. Washington and Rochambeau left General Benjamin Lincoln to lead the troops to Virginia and rode on ahead of the armies. After a few miles the impatient commander left the Frenchman far behind. On September 8, after a rapid ride with his Negro servant, Billy Lee, he entered Baltimore, where he was welcomed with a torchlight parade and an exchange of speeches. Behind him the armies made slow progress, as rain-swollen river crossings delayed the infantry and its wagons, and a storm drove the overloaded

Benedict Arnold: Hero Turned Traitor

"Treason! Treason! Treason! black as hell," exclaimed a former colleague of Benedict Arnold when learning of the general's 1780 plot to betray vital West Point. Arnold had instructed his conspirator, British major John André, to hide plans for the fort's capture in his boot (right).

LIBRARY OF CONGRESS

Patriot militiamen soon captured André (below) and hanged him as a spy. Arnold escaped. The scheme he had hatched for 16 months paid off: he won £6,315 and a British command. His career as a royal general failed to damage the revolutionary cause, but his perfidy shocked the patriots.

DAUGHTERS OF THE AMERICAN REVOLUTION MUSEUM

Comte de Grasse   Adm. Lord Graves

boats ashore; news that the British fleet had appeared and challenged the French kept the little flotilla in Annapolis for several days.

Early on September 9, Washington left Baltimore on a punishing sixty-mile ride to Mount Vernon, probably the general's longest one-day ride of the war. Washington had not seen his plantation for six years, and there was an excited homecoming. An early historian reported that servants who greeted Washington noted "a face . . . changed by the storms of campaigns and the mighty cares which had burdened his mind during more than six years of absence."

While at Mount Vernon, Washington sent dispatches to Virginia officials, urging work on the fords, ferry landings, and roads in the path of the armies and pleading for food to supply his men. He wrote Lafayette that he would meet him in Williamsburg on September 14, and added, "I hope you will keep Lord Cornwallis safe, without Provisions or Forage until we arrive."

Just after dawn on September 5, Admiral Graves brought the British fleet of nineteen ships to the capes of the Chesapeake, and his lookouts were soon bellowing warnings of French ships inside the bay. Graves

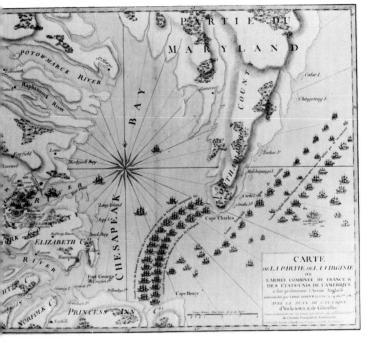

The contemporary map above shows the crucial battle seaward of Cape Charles, in which French Adm. de Grasse (opposite) defeated the British fleet. In the French painting of that contest below, British ships sail off to right. When they withdrew, Cornwallis was trapped.

had a decidedly inferior force, but when his captains reported the presence of French ships, the admiral drove boldly shoreward under a stiff breeze.

The French were disconcerted by the appearance of the enemy and ill-prepared to fight. Only twenty-four of de Grasse's ships were ready for battle; the rest were blocking the York and James rivers or sailing northward up Chesapeake Bay to meet Washington's column. The French were short-handed, as well, for nearly two thousand men had gone ashore to search for firewood and fresh water. Admiral de Grasse was forced to lie at anchor, watching the British approach, until the tide turned outward at noon. He then moved out to fight.

As the French streamed eastward, tacking to hold a straight line, Graves continued sailing toward the mainland, parallel to his enemy. The British now saw that they were outnumbered; the realization may have shaken Graves, for he failed to attack despite the impatience of his captains. Gunners of both fleets stood with slow matches ready, awaiting word to fire, but it was not until 4:00 P.M., after awkward maneuvering and confused signals from the flagship *London*, that the British opened fire. Even then some officers, including the second in command, Admiral Sir Samuel Hood, noted that Graves flew conflicting signal flags. The crowded British line fired raggedly as the battle began, and many gunners were prevented from firing by neighboring ships which blocked their way.

The vans of the fleets were soon hidden in smoke as guns rolled and shot plowed through the brittle wooden hulls where seamen were locked below decks. The French ship *Pluton* took a heavy toll with its first volley, which raked the *Shrewsbury*, ripping off her captain's leg and killing the first lieutenant and thirteen crewmen. Sixty more men were lost in the heavy exchange of fire with the *Pluton*, and then the *Shrewsbury* dropped out of line, flying a distress signal. The

149

next British ship in line, the *Intrepid*, was also raked by French shot; these two ships bore about half the British casualties of the day.

The French van also suffered. Captain Boades of the *Reflechi* was killed, and the *Pluton, Caton,* and *Diademe* were driven from the line.

Within an hour the center divisions of the two fleets came together and fought, but the most furious phase of the battle was over. Within two hours the guns fell silent. Only fifteen French ships had been heavily engaged, and Graves had maneuvered only twelve of his nineteen into close action.

The battered fleets sailed southeastward in the dusk, while carpenters labored over torn hulls and masts and gunners stood ready, awaiting orders to fire. The orders never came. Graves, who had the favorable wind position, dared not attack; and de Grasse was content to wait. For several days the fleets drifted slowly off the North Carolina coast toward Cape Hatteras.

Graves had lost four or five ships and though casualties had been light—90 dead and 246 wounded—the admiral felt that he could no longer fight. Admiral Sir Samuel Hood insisted that Graves attack the next day, but was overruled after an angry conference.

By September 10, de Grasse, having lost sight of the British, sailed back into the Chesapeake, where he was stunned to discover ships inside the harbor—and relieved to learn that they belonged to French Admiral de Barras, who had sailed down from Rhode Island with siege guns and supplies for Rochambeau and Washington. On September 13, Graves returned, found the French in the bay, and turned northward, leaving the Chesapeake to the French and Cornwallis to his fate. The admiral dismissed the decisive battle as "a lively skirmish." But when the battered fleet reached New York, a British officer wrote in his diary, "I fear the fate of the Army in Virginia will be determined before our fleet can get out of the harbour again. . . ."

In the first week of September, as Lafayette lay ill with fever, his army was reinforced by 3,500 French troops brought from the Indies by de Grasse. The young Frenchman's force of 8,500 was then able to close the trap even more tightly around Cornwallis, pushing pickets almost to Yorktown. Officers urged him to strike Cornwallis, but Lafayette was determined to wait for Washington: "Having so sure a game to play, it would be madness by the risk of an attack to give anything to chance."

Despite favorable prospects, the marquis was by no means certain of an early victory; though more militia were joining him, his small army had run out of supplies. He wrote Virginia's Governor Nelson on September 11:

> I could wish to sleep tonight but I fear it will be impossible with the prospect which is before us tomorrow. There is not one grain of flour in camp either for the American or French army. What we are to do I know not.

Only a few days later Washington arrived, to be greeted fervently by the marquis. The commander established his headquarters in the Williamsburg home of George Wythe, Thomas Jefferson's law professor and a Signer of the Declaration of Independence; and there, after midnight on September 14, he received a cheering message from de Grasse—the British fleet had been driven off, and de Barras would soon be unloading his cargoes of food, ammunition, and siege guns. Washington wrote Benjamin Lincoln to urge the main army southward: "Every day we now lose is comparatively an age. . . . Hurry on then, my dear Sir, with your troops on wings of speed."

The British earthworks around Yorktown were growing daily more formidable, Washington reported. He was also anxious about de Grasse, to whom he wrote, urging that the fleet remain in the bay until

Replacing the Union Jack with the
Stars and Stripes, Lafayette's American
task force seizes a British redoubt
before Yorktown. Covered ways
(at far left) assist the advance. Meanwhile,
allied troops shut the British escape
hatch across the York River.

Cornwallis had been defeated. The admiral was non-committal, and on September 17, Washington, Rochambeau, and Henry Knox sailed down the James to visit the fleet. De Grasse agreed to remain until the end of October, but he refused to send ships into the York River to aid in bombarding Cornwallis.

Blustery weather kept Washington at sea for almost five days. When he returned, he found Williamsburg filling with men and supplies from the North. Then, as Washington and Rochambeau prepared to march on Yorktown, just twelve miles away, they were stunned by a message from de Grasse—the admiral, alarmed by reports that the British fleet in New York had received reinforcements, had decided to leave the Chesapeake. The ring around Cornwallis was about to be broken.

De Grasse was persuaded to remain in the bay only by an urgent plea from Washington, carried to the fleet by Lafayette, who also urged the admiral to cooperate. As if fearful that the French admiral might change his mind again, Washington marched for Yorktown the next morning, September 28. The allied armies were now about 17,500 strong. Cornwallis awaited them with some 7,500 men—and with foreboding.

"This place is in no State of defense," he wrote hurriedly to Clinton. "If you cannot relieve me very soon, you must be prepared to hear the Worst."

The French and American columns invested Yorktown in an arc, pinning the British inside the small town. From the French position on the shore west of Yorktown, the line curved across the peninsula to the river marshes below the town. Washington began the conduct of his first siege by reconnoitering the enemy position. He saw ten small forts connected by trenches; Cornwallis had sixty-five cannon in line, but these were light and would be outgunned by the French weapons when they were brought up.

Behind their fortifications, British and Hessians were shaken by the sight of enemy troops settling so casually about them. One soldier in Yorktown wrote, "... the whole camp was in alarm. ... Tents were hastily removed and all the baggage taken into the town." A British artillery officer estimated Washington's strength at 21,000.

There was scattered fire from Yorktown cannon the next day, but no allied guns were in position to reply. French and American troops lay in the lines under fire, waiting. Washington forbade his men to leave camp and warned that the British were trying to spread smallpox by sending infected men into his lines.

Dawn, Sunday, September 30 brought a pleasant surprise to allied headquarters; Cornwallis had abandoned his outer line of defenses, including some strong redoubts, or small forts, which might have withstood heavy attacks. Washington and Rochambeau inspected the works and ordered them occupied; when the big guns were emplaced, they would have a better field of fire into Yorktown.

Cornwallis had made this move after receiving a dispatch from Sir Henry Clinton, who promised that a fleet would soon bring the earl a reinforcement of 5,000 troops. The fleet would sail to the entrance of the Chesapeake and fire its guns. If Yorktown still held out, Cornwallis was to signal with a column of smoke. The earl replied to Clinton almost gaily. His army's only wish, he wrote, "was that the enemy would advance." He added, "I shall retire this night within the works, and have no doubt, if relief arrives at any reasonable time, York and Gloucester will be both in possession of His Majesty's troops."

Despite the promise of relief, many of the earl's officers disapproved of Cornwallis's decision to withdraw from the outer lines. Colonel Banastre Tarleton complained, "Time would have been gained by holding and disputing the ground inch by inch." Corporal Stephan Popp, a Hessian, noted in his diary that the

Washington supervises shelling of besieged British army (opposite). Benjamin Latrobe—who would later help design the U.S. Capitol—painted the watercolor at right of a Yorktown mansion pulverized by American cannon and mortar fire.

troops pulled back about 1 A.M., "all in silence, because the enemy always came nearer." Private Johann Doehla saw eight men slip from the trenches and disappear—deserters to the enemy.

The British, now confined to the town itself, opened heavy cannon fire on the allies, but inflicted few casualties. Ignoring the British fire, the French and Americans worked steadily on their trenches and prepared for the arrival of artillery from the rear.

Lt. Col. Alexander Hamilton, once a Washington aide, broods amid the Yorktown trenches (below). When Lafayette finally let him lead the attack on the redoubt, Hamilton exulted "We have it! We have it!"

On October 1, Washington's orders of the day urged every man to help "conduct the attacks against York with the utmost rapidity . . . with the most unabating ardor. The present moment . . . will decide American Independence." Thousands of men were put to work behind the lines, making siege equipment; they cut branches and saplings in the woods to make huge rolls and tall wicker baskets which were to be filled with earth and added to the fortifications.

On the night of October 6, between dusk and dawn, the allies built a 2,000-yard, four-foot-deep trench shielded by stout earthworks. Fifteen hundred men dug in the sandy soil while almost 3,000 stood guard, in case of British attack. At sunrise Cornwallis saw the extent of the new line, which was in places only 600 to 800 yards from his works.

The huge siege mortars and cannon, which had been dragged through deep sandy roads by hundreds of men tugging at ropes, were now placed in line. Washington withheld his fire until most of the cannon were in place and on October 9 touched off the first American gun himself. One officer said of this shot, "I could hear the ball strike from house to house, and I was afterwards informed that it went through the one where many of the officers were at dinner, and over the table . . . and either killed or wounded the one at the head of the table."

The siege guns battered Yorktown day and night, giving Cornwallis's artillerymen no rest. British guns disappeared as embrasures were blown up. More batteries joined the allied chorus each day. Cornwallis's reports to Clinton became increasingly somber: "The fire continued incessant from heavy cannon . . . until all our guns on the left were silenced, our works much damaged and our loss of men considerable."

As the heavy fire continued, Cornwallis and his officers were driven into a cave beneath the river bluff. The town was in ruins; many Negroes died "in the

153

most miserable manner," and thousands of horses were slaughtered—hundreds of their corpses floated in the York River.

On October 11 the American forces dug a second parallel, even closer to Yorktown; and three nights later Washington ordered an attack on two critical British outposts which overlooked his new entrenchments. After dark on October 14 two 400-man parties crept out between the lines to assault the redoubts: a French party led by Count William Deux-Ponts and an American group led by Lieutenant Colonel Alexander Hamilton. Both works were taken after brief fights, with the loss of nine Americans killed and twenty-five wounded; fifteen French dead and seventy-seven wounded.

Washington watched the action from an exposed position with Lincoln and Knox. When Colonel David Cobb of his staff tried to persuade him to take cover, the general said sharply, "Colonel Cobb, if you are afraid, you have liberty to step back."

The opposing lines were now only 250 yards apart. Cornwallis wrote Clinton: "My situation now becomes very critical. We dare not show a gun to their old batteries, and I expect their new ones will open To-Morrow Morning. . . . We shall Soon be exposed to an assault in ruined Works, in a bad position and with weakened Numbers. I cannot recommend that the Fleet and Army should run great Risque in endeavouring to save us."

But the earl had not yet given up. The night following the loss of his redoubts he launched a counterattack against the weary allied troops. The assault was quickly driven back. The British inflicted seventeen casualties at the cost of a dozen men of their own and managed to spike only six allied guns, which were repaired and rejoined the firing the next day. Each day the pounding intensified. Soldiers in Yorktown who felt that the cannonade could grow no worse were stunned by the increased volume of pointblank fire.

One German soldier wrote: ". . . with the dawn the enemy began to fire heavily, as he had not done before . . . so fiercely as though the heavens would split. . . . Now we saw what was to happen to us."

On October 16, Cornwallis belatedly heeded the advice of his officers and attempted an escape by night across the broad, swift York River to Gloucester, but a sudden squall scattered his small boats and forced him to abandon the attempt.

Cornwallis visited one of his outermost works in the early morning of October 17, and Corporal Popp read the news in the earl's bleak face: "It looked as though there would be an early surrender, and we were heartily glad." British troops began smashing valuables and slashing their tents to ribbons.

A British council of war agreed that the end had come—the works were open to assault and all but one large cannon was out of action. "Under all these cir-

The Surrender of Lord Cornwallis by Trumbull portrays the decisive moment when "The World Turned Upside Down." Benjamin Lincoln (on white horse) offers to receive the surrender of Cornwallis's aide—after the British had tried to capitulate to Rochambeau. Their action is observed by the French at left and Americans at right.

cumstances," Cornwallis wrote, "I thought it would have been . . . inhuman to . . . sacrifice the lives of this small body of gallant soldiers."

About 9 A.M. a redcoat drummer climbed to the top of a British parapet and began a long roll. He went unheard for several moments, until, one by one, allied gunners caught sight of him. The fire dwindled and quiet fell at last. Ebenezer Denny, a Pennsylvania soldier, spoke for the besiegers: "I thought I had never heard a drum equal to it—the most delightful music to us all."

A British officer emerged with a message for Washington, a plea for surrender terms, and was led, blindfolded, through the allied lines to the rear.

Washington opened the message to find that the earl was sparring for time—he asked a truce of twenty-four hours so that officers could meet to discuss terms of surrender. Washington was not misled. He sent the British redcoat back into his lines with an ultimatum:

An Ardent Desire to spare the further Effusion of Blood, will readily incline me to listen to such Terms for the Surrender of your Posts. . . .

I wish . . . that your Lordship's proposals in writing, may be sent to the American lines; for which Purpose a Suspension of hostilities during two Hours from the Delivery of this Letter will be granted.

No sooner had the redcoat officer disappeared in his trenches than allied guns opened fire again.

Cornwallis, trying to secure favorable terms, proposed that his army be set free, both German and British troops to return home in exchange for a pledge that

155

Brought to the peace table by York-town, American negotiators pose for Benjamin West's painting (the British delegates declined to sit). Left to right: John Jay, John Adams, Benjamin Franklin, Henry Laurens; also William Temple Franklin, who served as his grandfather's secretary. George III's proclamation at right recognizes the existence of the United States.

they would fight no more. Washington declined, and messengers passed frequently for several hours, bearing dispatches between the commanders.

The next day Washington offered his terms for surrender:

All troops in Yorktown and Gloucester would become prisoners of war and be sent to inland prison camps.

British arms and supplies would be seized.

British troops could keep their personal property.

Cornwallis and a few officers could depart in one small ship, without a search.

And finally the harshest article of all:

The British army would be accorded the same honors that had been granted General Benjamin Lincoln's troops when they surrendered Charleston in 1780.

Cornwallis was given two hours in which to reply and name officers to discuss terms in detail. He appointed Lieutenant Colonel Thomas Dundas and Major Alexander Ross to negotiate with the allies. They met with Viscount de Noailles and Lieutenant Colonel John Laurens in the small white frame house of Augustine Moore, not far from the battlefield.

Both armies had expected a settlement after a brief parley, and indeed, most of the terms were soon worked out. All but one: the afternoon and most of the night passed while the officers argued heatedly over the matter of honors. According to the military etiquette of the time, an army that had acquitted itself well in the defense of a fortified place but had nevertheless been defeated would be granted the "honors of war"—in other words, it would be allowed to march out with flags flying and drums beating, while its band played a march or song of the victorious enemy.

At Charleston, General Lincoln's army had been denied these honors by Sir Henry Clinton. The defeated Americans had been forced to come out with flags furled, playing a Turkish march instead of a British air. Cornwallis's representatives at the Yorktown conference argued that the earl had not been responsible for the insult to Lincoln's garrison. But to the Americans the honor of a nation not an individual was at stake. They insisted that the term stand, and finally, the next morning, October 19, the British gave in.

At 2 P.M. that afternoon, the allied army was led into a broad field by Washington, Rochambeau, and Admiral de Barras, the latter representing de Grasse who was ill. There the American and French troops waited at attention, surrounded by hundreds of civilians from the neighboring countryside.

The British came at last, their colors cased, behind bands playing the melancholy air, "The World Turned Upside Down." Cornwallis did not appear, sending word that he was ill. His second in command, General Charles O'Hara, led the troops instead, and in an effort to embarrass the Americans, attempted to hand his sword to Rochambeau. The Frenchman passed him to Washington, who passed him in turn to General Benjamin Lincoln, whose humiliation at Charleston was finally avenged.

A "universal silence" hung over the field as 3,500 of the defeated troops lay down their arms. (Almost as many more waited in Yorktown, many of them sick and wounded.) Dr. Thacher thought the British "disorderly and unsoldierly." Some British officers wept, and a few men flung down their muskets angrily, breaking them. The breakage halted only after General Lincoln passed a stern order.

After the ceremony was over, allied soldiers inspected Yorktown, and many wondered that the enemy had been able to resist so long. Von Closen wrote, "One could not take three steps without running into some great holes made by bombs . . . with scattered white or Negro arms or legs, some bits of uniforms."

Houses were wrecked, and the remaining inhabitants were terrified. Negroes, sick and dying, lay about the streets, amid heaps of American shells which had failed to explode. The victors found mountains of supplies and ammunition. The count of British and German prisoners was 7,247; about 300 had been killed during the siege and 44 had deserted.

The next day Cornwallis wrote Henry Clinton:

> Yorktown, October 20, 1781
> I have the mortification to inform your Excellency that I have been forced to give up the posts of York and Gloucester, and to surrender the troops under my command.

It was late evening before Washington turned to the task of writing a victory dispatch. The brief message was drafted by his secretary, Jonathan Trumbull, Jr.:

> Sir: I have the Honor to inform Congress, that a Reduction of the British Army under the Command of Lord Cornwallis, is most happily effected. The unremitting Ardour which actuated every Officer and Soldier in the combined Army in this Occasion, has principally led to this Important Event, at an earlier period that my most sanguine Hope had induced me to expect.

The dispatch was entrusted to thirty-six-year-old Lieutenant Colonel Tench Tilghman, Jr., a Maryland volunteer who had served on Washington's staff for five years without pay. Although ill with malaria, Tilghman hurried northward, reaching Philadelphia in the early morning hours of October 24.

He banged on the door of Thomas McKean, and spent some moments convincing the skeptical president of Congress that his news was true. Night watchmen soon spread the report through the sleeping city, and the State House bell tolled until daybreak.

The feverish Tilghman was put to bed, but since he had arrived without a penny in his pocket, he requested a loan from Congress. The Treasury was empty, but congressmen voluntarily raised a purse by contributing $1 each to pay Tilghman's expenses. He was voted a sword, a horse, and a saddle for his services, and Congress declared a day of national thanksgiving.

On the same day the British fleet, returning belatedly from New York, approached the Chesapeake, only to discover that French ships were still there and that Cornwallis had surrendered. Two days later, Admiral Graves turned back and sent word to England, "the most melancholy news Great Britain ever received," said Admiral Hood.

A disconsolate Henry Clinton received the news in New York as "a distressed man, looking for friends and suspicious of all mankind." For many years he was to deny the blame for the loss of Cornwallis and the American colonies, protesting, "I may say with Macbeth, 'thou Canst not say I did it.'"

Lord North, the prime minister, was one of the first in London to hear about Yorktown. It is said that he accepted the news as if mortally wounded. "He reeled, threw out his arms, exclaiming wildly, as he paced up and down . . . 'Oh, God! It's all over.'" George III was so shaken that he considered abdication, rather than admit that the war with America had been lost. However, he finally accepted a new ministry which pledged to seek peace even at the cost of recognizing American independence.

Washington sent the British and German troops captured at Yorktown to prison camps in Virginia and western Maryland, then moved his troops back to the north, ready for further action. Fearful of national overconfidence, he hoped that the public would not fall into "A state of Languor and Relaxation." Tense years of waiting remained, as British troops continued to occupy American cities; but the major battles were over. Washington, with the aid of the French, had won his war; and the United States of America had joined the mainstream of world history as an independent nation, the first great modern republic.

Birth of a Nation

8

In the year 1787 the United States was united in name only. Although in theory the states were joined together into one nation by the Articles of Confederation, in practice they resisted any attempt to make the tie binding. "We do not want any goviner but the Goviner of the univarse," the citizens of Ashfield, Massachusetts, had resolved in 1776, and that feeling had grown stronger after the war. Each of the thirteen states envisioned an America in which the state would function as a separate and sovereign unit, free to conduct its own local affairs and bound to the others only for foreign affairs and defense.

This spirit of separatism had guided the authors of the Articles of Confederation with the result that the power of Congress rested on little more than the good will of the various states. Congress could not levy taxes nor pay the public debt nor defend the country. It could ask the states for money, but it could not force them to comply—and usually they did not. There was no national judiciary, nor was there an executive power to enforce the acts of Congress. Each state had one vote in Congress; the small states had refused to accept even the weak bonds of the Confederation on any other terms. The concurring votes of seven states were needed to pass any legislation, and on important matters nine were needed. As for amending the Articles, that would have taken the unanimous agreement of all thirteen states, a remote possibility.

Jealousy and rivalry increasingly dominated the states' dealings with one another. They argued over boundaries in the western territories; Massachusetts, Connecticut, Pennsylvania, New York, Virginia, the Carolinas, and Georgia all had conflicting claims to

George Washington, president of the 1787 Convention in Philadelphia, oversees the signing of the Constitution in this painting by Thomas Rossiter. Behind him rises the sun that Franklin recognized as an omen (actually it was carved into the president's chair). Jefferson called the document's framers "an assembly of demi-gods."

the land beyond the Appalachians. Although eventually settled by the Northwest Ordinance of 1787 (one of the few achievements of the Confederation Congress), these claims gave rise to several small-scale wars immediately after the Revolution.

Commerce between the states also gave rise to disputes. Since Congress lacked the power to regulate trade, each state was free to control the entry of goods into its territory. Many imposed tariff laws that applied to other states as well as to foreign nations. New Jersey, for example, exported its goods directly, but imported foreign products through the ports of Philadelphia and New York. To protect its merchants, New Jersey put a tax on foreign goods entering by way of other states. New York retaliated by imposing heavy duties on New Jersey ships that entered her harbor. In the South, Virginia passed a law providing for the seizure and prosecution of any ship that failed to pay duties; it was aimed not at Europe, but at Maryland, Pennsylvania, and Massachusetts.

It was clear to many leading Americans that unless something was done to strengthen the central government, the United States would remain, as Alexander Hamilton had described them, "a number of petty states, with the appearance only of union, jarring, jealous, and perverse, without any determined direction, fluctuating and unhappy at home, weak and insignificant by their dissensions in the eyes of other nations."

The first small seeds of change were sown in 1785. In the spring of that year, commissioners appointed by the state legislatures of Maryland and Virginia met at Mount Vernon to work out an agreement for the joint peaceful use of the Potomac River. When the resulting pact was given to the two states to be ratified, the Virginia legislature proposed that other nearby states send commissioners to Annapolis the following summer to discuss trade problems.

Twelve men from five states met in Annapolis in

September, 1786. Although the meeting was small, it included two strong nationalists: James Madison and Alexander Hamilton. Together they persuaded the other commissioners to issue a call for a convention of all thirteen states, which would meet in Philadelphia on the second Monday of the following May "to devise such further provisions as shall appear to them necessary to render the Constitution of the Foederal government adequate to the exigencies of the Union." Some states named delegates immediately; others pondered the invitation—and while they waited, an incident occurred in Massachusetts that shook the entire country.

Driven to desperation by a government that demanded taxes in cash and seized their lands and livestock when they could not pay, back-country farmers rebelled. Meeting in impromptu conventions, they demanded relief, and when their petitions went unanswered, they prevented courts from sitting so that tax judgments could not be brought against them. Massachusetts appealed to Congress, but that body had no money to raise troops. Shays's Rebellion, so named because Daniel Shays, a captain in the American army during the Revolution, had been one of the leaders, was eventually put down by militia paid with private funds. At the next election a new governor and a more friendly legislature took office. The rebel leaders were pardoned, and most of the reforms they demanded were put into effect. But the rebellion had had a chilling effect on the rest of the country. Every state had its disgruntled debtor class, and if such men could take the law into their owns hands in Massachusetts, were men of property safe anywhere? Americans saw in the uprising the need for a central government strong enough to quell such rebellions or, better yet, to prevent them by improving the economic conditions that caused them.

"What stronger evidence can be given of the want of energy in our government than these disorders?" George Washington asked in a letter to James Madison. "If there exists not a power to check them, what security has a man for life, liberty or property?"

Shays's Rebellion convinced several undecided states to name delegates to the proposed convention, but Congress continued to delay its approval. Finally, in February, 1787, it issued a cautious resolution limiting the convention to "the sole purpose of revising the Articles of Confederation, and reporting to Congress . . . such alterations . . . as shall, when agreed to in Congress, and confirmed by the States, render the Foederal Constitution adequate to the exigencies of Government, and the preservation of the Union." Thus, though referred to by many popular writers as the "Constitutional Convention," the meeting was originally planned only to revise the Articles.

May 14, 1787, was the date set for the convening of the "Foederal Convention" in Philadelphia, but when the day arrived, only eight delegates were on hand: four from Virginia and four from Pennsylvania. Each morning those present met at the State House, in the room where the Declaration of Independence had been drawn up eleven years earlier, and after solemnly noting that they did not yet have a quorum, they adjourned until the next day.

George Washington was the best known of the Virginia delegates. He had arrived in Philadelphia a day early, and his first act had been to call on eighty-one-year-old Benjamin Franklin, president of Pennsylvania. James Madison, another Virginian, had arrived a full eleven days early. Intellectually Madison would be the best prepared delegate at the Convention; he had read everything available on political theory and the law of nations. In addition to Washington and Madison, Virginia had sent its governor, Edmund Randolph, and George Mason, a respected Virginia statesman. Besides Franklin, Pennsylvania's delega-

Power Crisis

Crying ''Hurrah for Daniel Shays!'' a band of discontented Massachusetts farmers had challenged the viability of the young American nation in 1786 when they seized courthouses in the western part of the state (below) and prepared—unsuccessfully—to take over the federal arsenal at Springfield.

Fearful citizens then looked to a stronger government than that of the old Articles of Confederation. Noah Webster concluded a limited monarchy was necessary. Alexander Hamilton (right) agreed. But delegates disapproved when he proposed an elected king to the Philadelphia Convention.

At last the delegates accepted the balanced plan of an elected, short-term executive and Congress, and an appointed judiciary. During the crucial battle for the Constitution's adoption by the states, Hamilton repented of royalty and led the campaign. Below at right, a ship with his name honors New York's adoption in 1788. Yet the question remained: would the government be powerful enough?

Washington: The Royal President

First in war, first in peace, first in the hearts of his countrymen, George Washington received the expected news of his election with regret (left). He had been named President unanimously by the electoral college on February 4, 1789.

"My movements to the chair of government," he said upon leaving his beloved Mount Vernon, "will be accompanied by feelings not unlike those of a culprit, who is going to the place of his execution." Yet all along his northward route he was hailed—and held up—by formal receptions. When rowed across from New Jersey to the temporary federal capital at New York "by thirteen pilots of this harbor, dressed in white uniforms," he was saluted by flag-bedecked ships (below) and booming cannon from the Battery.

To the office of the presidency he gave a decisive character and regal manner. Pomp and ceremony attended him and "Lady" Washington in their daily rounds. When senators declined to cooperate in the framing of a treaty, Washington took negotiations into his own hands and merely sent the document on to the Senate for ratification. Yet when his advisors made a recommendation, he generally followed it, stressing his opinion only when the cabinet was divided. He was well aware that "everything *in our situation* will serve to establish a Precedent."

FROM STEFAN LORANT'S *THE GLORIOUS BURDEN* (HARPER & ROW)

tion included Robert Morris, the financial genius of the Revolution; Gouverneur Morris, one of the most brilliant men to attend the Convention; and James Wilson, who has been called the unsung hero of the Convention. There would be able and notable men from other states as well: awkward, honest Roger Sherman of Connecticut; Rufus King and Elbridge Gerry from Massachusetts; John Dickinson of Delaware; John Rutledge and Charles Pinckney of South Carolina; Alexander Hamilton of New York. Seventy-four delegates had been appointed, but only fifty-five would attend.

Delegates slowly drifted in, until on May 25, eleven days late, the New Jersey delegation arrived, creating a quorum of seven states present. That morning the delegates from Virginia, Pennsylvania, South Carolina, New York, Delaware, North Carolina, and New Jersey met in the State House and called the Federal Convention to order. Its first job was to select a presiding officer. There was only one possible choice; Franklin had intended to nominate Washington, but his ailments had kept him home; so Robert Morris made the nomination instead. Although there were no other candidates, the delegates soberly cast paper ballots, and, to no one's surprise, unanimously elected George Washington, after which the Convention adjourned for the weekend.

By Monday more delegates had arrived. Massachusetts now had a quorum, and additional men from Delaware and Pennsylvania were there. Procedural matters were discussed, ending in a decision to keep all proceedings secret. On Tuesday, James Madison, from whose voluminous notes most of our knowledge of the Convention comes, wrote, "Mr. Randolph then opened the main business."

During their wait for a majority to assemble, the Virginia delegates had prepared a plan to present to the Convention, and now thirty-three-year-old Governor Edmund Randolph presented what would become known as the Virginia Plan or Virginia Resolves. Randolph spoke first of the faults of the Articles of Confederation, of the crisis in the United States, and of the need for a stronger government. Then he unfolded the Virginia Plan, the essential point of which was that there should be a government of three parts: a legislature of two branches with the first branch elected by the people and the second chosen by the members of the first; an executive of unspecified number; and a national judiciary consisting of one or more supreme tribunals as well as inferior courts. Randolph described his resolves as corrections and enlargements of the Articles of Confederation, but it was apparent to every man present that the plan went far beyond a mere revision of the Articles. However, his audience was willing to accept it as a starting point for discussions, despite the fact that it called for a highly centralized form of government.

The next morning the Convention went into a committee of the whole to study the Virginia Plan. This parliamentary device permitted more freedom in debate, since votes were used only to learn the sentiment of the members and thus were not binding. Washington stepped down from the dais, and Nathaniel Gorham of Massachusetts took the chair. Randolph then opened the discussion by proposing that his first three resolutions be amended. A union of states that was "merely federal," Randolph argued, could not accomplish what they were there to do; he proposed instead "that a national government . . . be established consisting of a supreme legislative, judiciary and executive." Elbridge Gerry of Massachusetts disagreed. The Confederation would be destroyed if they passed Randolph's resolution, he claimed, and anyway they had no authority to pass it. Instead, he suggested, let the proposal read "for the establishment of a *federal* legislative, judiciary, and executive."

Gouverneur Morris then attempted to explain the difference between the words "federal" and "national." A federal government, he said, was merely a compact that depended on the good faith of the states making it, while a national government had "a complete and compulsive operation." With the confusion then prevailing throughout the United States, concluded Morris, "We had better take a supreme government now than a despot twenty years hence—for come he must."

The arguments of the nationalists prevailed. Massachusetts, Pennsylvania, Delaware, and the two Carolinas voted in favor of a national government. Connecticut voted no, New Jersey lacked a quorum, and New York was divided. By a good margin the delegates decided to break with the past and try to create a new order for the United States.

The thorniest problem of the whole Convention arose immediately thereafter. The next Virginia Resolve proposed "that the rights of suffrage in the national legislature ought to be proportioned to the . . . number of free inhabitants. . . ." Before it could be put to a vote, however, George Read of Delaware rose and reminded those present that Delaware had instructions not to agree to any change in the present voting rules of Congress—an equal vote for each state— and that if any change were made, he and the rest of his delegation might walk out of the Convention.

The point was a fundamental one. Madison argued that the reasons for equality of suffrage under the Confederation would not exist under a national government; just as large counties in a state had more representation in the state house than small counties, so should large states have more votes than small states in a national government. But Delaware refused to budge. During the weeks that followed, the Convention would almost be destroyed by this dispute, as small states continued to insist that the equal vote rule be retained. Rather than risk a defection so early, the question of representation was set aside until later.

The next day, June 1, the committee of the whole turned its attention to the executive branch. The Virginia Plan did not specify whether the executive should be one man or more; so James Wilson of Pennsylvania moved that he be a single person. There followed what Madison described as "a considerable pause." The members were gazing into the past at the last single executive they had known, a king who had tried to rule the colonies as a tyrant. Wilson explained his position. The executive branch, he said, needed energy, decisiveness, and responsibility—characteristics that could best be found in one person. Roger Sherman disagreed: the executive was "nothing more than an institution for carrying the will of the legislature into effect." As such, it ought to be chosen by the legislature which could name one or more men as it saw fit. Randolph, remarking that a single executive was "the fetus of monarchy," recommended three men. The final vote was seven to three in favor of a single executive, but like every decision made in the committee of the whole it could be reconsidered.

On June 6 the Convention returned to discussing the method of electing legislators. The delegates had previously agreed that the first branch of the legislature should be elected by popular vote, but by now many had had second thoughts. Charles Pinckney moved that the first branch be elected by the state legislatures because "the people were less fit judges." But James Wilson, speaking in his Scot's burr, felt that the vigor of a strong government should "flow immediately from the legitimate source of all authority—the people." George Mason agreed. Congress, he said, represented the states under the Confederation, not the people: "The case will be changed in the new plan of government. The people will be represented; they ought therefore to choose the representatives."

They returned again to the second branch of the

Rebellions and Incursions

During Washington's second administration, domestic and foreign threats to national security forced him to draw his sword once more from its scabbard.

To farmers of western Pennsylvania, the government's initial excise tax seemed cruelly aimed at their main product—whiskey made from surplus corn. In the sketch below at right, a lad warns distillers that federal excisemen are coming. Taking the offensive, the moonshiners began to terrorize tax agents and legal whiskey-makers alike; then they went on to threaten secession. The President, recognizing his constitutional power and duty, called out a force of 15,000 militiamen—one of whom sadly says "Adieu" to his sweetheart below. After organizing his troops at Fort Cumberland, Maryland (above), in the fall of 1794, Washing-

ton sent them over the Alleghenies and brought the "Whisky Rebellion" to a quick end.

On the northwestern frontier another danger threatened: the British, still savoring the Indians' defeat of a fledgling American army in 1791, sought to hold some of the Indiana Territory; they set about building a fort on the Maumee River (above present-day Toledo). Washington named "Mad Anthony" Wayne head of a task force to move up to the Maumee in the spring of 1794. The resultant Battle of Fallen Timbers, in which Wayne routed the Indian tribes under British leadership, has been called by Samuel Eliot Morison "the last phase of the War of Independence."

With Washington in the saddle, the nation seemed strong enough to survive.

Factionalism Among The Founders

President Washington hoped that "no separate views nor party animosities" would sunder his government. But that dream was soon shattered by the pull of his own faction (the Federalists, led by Hamilton) and the push of the opposition (the Republicans, led by Jefferson).

First focus of factional disagreement: John Jay's Treaty of 1794 (which in Republican eyes seemed servile because it did not force England to recognize U.S. neutrality). At left, anti-Federalists burn Jay in effigy; in the Senate, the treaty passed by only one vote.

Under President John Adams (right), whose single administration began in 1797, factionalism intensified. By passing the Alien & Sedition Acts of 1798, Federalists hoped to curb Republican "conspiracies" at home that reflected the French Revolution abroad. Congressman Matthew Lyon of Vermont soon felt the act's manacles; he was sentenced to four months' imprisonment for publishing a rather mild attack upon Adams. The cartoon below shows Lyon (with tongs) attacking a Federalist congressman who had insulted him.

To Americans of a later day, the founders bequeathed a hammer-and-tongs political legacy.

legislature, on which they had been unable to agree before. James Wilson, putting his trust in the people, argued that it too should be elected by popular vote, but at this even his republican colleagues balked. The committee agreed unanimously that the second branch should be a check on the first and as such should be appointed by the state legislatures. Thus, despite all the debate and argument, the outlines of the Constitution were slowly taking shape. Yet overshadowing everything was the seemingly irreconcilable difference between large and small states: should representation be by states or population?

On June 9, William Paterson of New Jersey rose to protect the small states' rights. All of those present, said Paterson, were under instructions only to revise the Articles of Confederation. Under those Articles, each state had an equal vote. Proportional representation would threaten the existence of small states. "I therefore declare," he stated, "that I will never consent to the present system, and I shall make all the interest against it in the state that I can. Myself or my state will never submit to tyranny or despotism!"

The large states were just as adamant. James Wilson responded to Paterson, "Shall New Jersey have the same right or council in the nation with Pennsylvania? I say no! It is unjust—I will never confederate on this plan. . . . If no state will part with any of its sovereignty it is in vain to talk of a national government." Wilson, for all his republican principles and his belief in the people, was as immovable as Paterson. "If no state will part with any of its sovereignty"—the issue of representation seemed an insurmountable obstacle.

When the Convention met again on June 11 after a restful weekend pause, Roger Sherman proposed a compromise: representation in the first branch of the legislature would be according to population; and in the second branch every state would have one vote. Sherman's compromise would save the Convention,

but its time had not yet arrived. It was defeated.

It was exasperating to debate and then debate again points on which there seemed no possibility of resolution. The heavy, humid heat, hanging like a pall over Philadelphia, made matters worse. Tempers frayed; voices rose in anger. Yet through it all the delegates kept at their work, modifying, clarifying, enlarging the Virginia Plan. Finally on June 13 they finished; the fifteen resolutions originally presented by Randolph had become nineteen, and the Convention would begin the debate on them the following day. The next morning, however, Paterson of New Jersey asked for more time; he had an alternative plan to offer.

Paterson's New Jersey Plan was a modest revision of the Articles of Confederation. It let the small states retain their cherished sovereignty, for there would be a legislature of one house in which each state would have an equal vote. The new Congress would be given some additional powers not possessed by the Congress of the Confederation, such as that of levying import duties. In addition, there would be an executive of more than one man appointed by Congress and a supreme court appointed by the executive.

The weary argument was back at the beginning: big states against small states, a strong central government or a weak one, proportional voting or one state-one vote. On the second day of debate on the New Jersey Plan, Alexander Hamilton took the floor. Though he more than any other man except Madison was responsible for the Convention, Hamilton had said very little as a delegate. Now in a speech lasting four or five hours, he outlined an extraordinary plan that amounted to an elective monarchy. Among other things he proposed an executive and a Senate elected for life, or at least during good behavior. No one interrupted the long speech, although some of Hamilton's audience must have been acutely embarrassed; no one spoke when he finished; no mention was made of his plan when debate resumed the next morning. Why Hamilton offered such an extreme proposal, which he knew would never be accepted and would put him in an unfavorable light, is puzzling. One theory is that he wanted to present a plan that would make the Virginia Plan look mild by comparison. If so, he succeeded, for the day after he spoke the New Jersey Plan was defeated. Hamilton left the Convention soon thereafter, discouraged by his inability to accomplish anything in the face of opposition from his New York colleagues.

On June 20 the Convention returned to regular sessions with Washington once again presiding. For almost a month the delegates had been sitting as a committee of the whole; now, for the second time they began to go over the Virginia Plan item by item. For many days the delegates dealt with matters of secondary importance. They decided that the term of the first branch of the legislature should be two rather than three years, that of the second branch six instead of seven. They agreed that the second branch should be chosen by state legislatures. And all the time they were aware that the issue that could make or break the Convention remained unsolved.

On June 27 they faced that issue: was representation to be by states or proportional to population? The large states were easily able to carry the vote for proportional representation in the first branch. When the delegates turned to the second branch, Roger Sherman again offered his compromise—proportional representation in the first branch, equal votes by states in the second branch—but the large states refused.

On July 2 the unhappy delegates, realizing that they could argue forever, appointed a committee, one man from each state, to work out a compromise. The committee reported back the day after Independence Day. It had accepted Roger Sherman's compromise, with some elaboration. There would be proportional representation in the first branch of the legislature, with each state allowed one member for every 40,000 inhabitants (counting three-fifths of the slaves). In the second branch each state would have an equal vote.

There was not much support for the compromise, and the possibility of an agreement seemed to grow more remote as the days passed. "We were on the verge of dissolution, scarce held together by the strength of a hair, though the public papers were announcing our extreme unanimity," wrote Maryland delegate Luther Martin.

The Convention might well have ended then if there had not been a break in the heat. On Friday, July 13, cool weather moved into Philadelphia. Raw nerves healed; irritation was dispelled. On Monday a number of the delegates from large states accepted the compromise with its equality of voting in the second branch. The impasse was broken.

The delegates then proceeded to consider the remaining resolves of the Virginia Plan. It took them sixty ballots to decide how the executive should be elected. Five times they voted to have him appointed by Congress; once they agreed to have him chosen by the state legislatures; then they changed their minds and thought the governors should do it; they changed their minds again and again. They were equally indecisive about the term of the executive; should it be seven years, six years, or perhaps eight? Should he be eligible for reelection? Could he be impeached?

In time the end was reached and the last resolution voted on. On July 26 the Convention turned its work over to a small committee of detail to be arranged and systematized. The committee of detail produced a document that in many ways sounded strange: the legislative branch with its first and second houses was now Congress, the House of Representatives, and the Senate. The executive had become the President. And everything was organized into articles and sections.

This forerunner of the Constitution had to be exam-

The Near War with France

"It is No! No! Not a sixpence," replied an American diplomat in Paris whom French agents had asked for a bribe in 1798. The agents became known as "X, Y, and Z" when the insult was reported to President Adams. That affair and Napoleon's hostile attitude convinced Congress to fund a powerful navy. The new frigates *United States, Constitution,* and *Constellation* were fitted for sea and others completed as an unofficial war commenced. Naval life at the time was severe; above, a sailor is lashed for a breach of discipline. U.S. frigates and armed merchant vessels acquitted themselves well in action: below, the *Planter* bests a French privateer. Adams kept his head and resisted pressure to enter a full-scale war. He regarded the 1800 Treaty of Morfontaine (presented by Napoleon to American commissioners, at right) as his greatest achievement.

THE PROVIDENTIAL DETECTION

The "Revolution" of 1800

Conservatives saw their fears of revolution confirmed in 1801 when newly installed President Thomas Jefferson wore shoes with democratic laces rather than shoes with high-class buckles.

Only a few years earlier Federalists had reacted with genuine horror to news of French King Louis XVI's execution by revolutionaries (above); Hamilton had urged that, with the king dead, the treaty of alliance no longer existed. Jefferson agreed the treaty was invalid but maintained his own friendships with French philosophers of human liberty.

Critics also accused Jefferson of radicalism because he advocated a "frugal and simple" government, not a strong, centralized state. The cartoon at left shows the federal eagle preventing Jefferson from burning the Constitution.

Yet Jefferson tried to bring his states-rights men together with nationalists and expansionists. At his inauguration he remarked, "We are all Republicans, we are all Federalists."

ined clause by clause. For instance, what should be the qualifications of a voter? That had been left rather vague. In a convention with so many men of means, there was strong sentiment for setting up property qualifications both for voting and office holding, but republican spirit prevailed; no such qualifications were written into the Constitution.

The section written by the committee of detail which aroused the most emotion was that on slavery. The committee had stated that "no tax or duty shall be laid by the Legislature . . . on the migration or importation of such persons as the several states shall see proper to admit; nor shall such migration or importation be prohibited." The word "persons," of course, meant slaves. The section set off a storm of oratory that was not always divided along North-South lines. Roger Sherman of Connecticut, though opposed to slavery, recommended a hands-off policy. On the other hand, George Mason, owner of 200 slaves in Virginia, bitterly denounced the "infernal traffic." Charles Pinckney was bluntly honest: "South Carolina can never receive the plan if it prohibits the slave trade."

In the end, there was another compromise. The new Congress was denied authority to interfere with the trade until twenty years had passed. However, it could levy a tax of not more than ten dollars on each slave imported. It was a necessary compromise; without it there would have been no Constitution. The question of slavery, however, was not settled; it would fester in the American body politic for three-quarters of a century and almost tear the nation apart.

The final subject on which there was a long and sometimes rancorous debate was the manner of ratifying and putting the Constitution into effect. It was finally decided that the Constitution should be ratified in each state by a popularly elected convention and that the new government should become operative after nine states had ratified.

On September 8 the Convention turned its work over to a committee of style to be put into final shape. Madison was one member of the committee. Hamilton, now returned, was another, but most of the drafting was done by Gouverneur Morris, whose facility with the pen matched his oratorical ability. The committee returned a document that, with minor alterations, became the Constitution of the United States. The committee had done its work well, beginning with the sonorous Preamble: "We the People of the United States, in Order to form a more perfect Union, establish Justice, insure domestic Tranquility . . ."

There was one remarkable omission, however. The document contained no reference to a bill of rights that would guard the individual against federal tyranny. Such protection was judged unnecessary since the central government had only delegated powers.

The Constitution was engrossed on parchment, and on September 17, 1787, the delegates signed. Of the fifty-five who had attended the Convention at one time or another, forty-two were present at the end. Three of these—Mason, Randolph, Gerry—refused to sign, arguing that the Constitution had been formed "without the knowledge or idea of the people."

Although the public had known something momentous was occurring behind the closed doors in Philadelphia, it was not prepared for what emerged. Many were shocked, perceiving the seeds of tyranny in a strong central government. Others believed the country too large for one central authority. A great many were simply afraid of the new and strange. Sides were quickly drawn up, the Federalists or supporters on the one hand, the Antifederalists or opposition on the other. The battle was fought in the press, on the stump, in village taverns. Alexander Hamilton, John Jay, and James Madison argued the case for the Constitution in *The Federalist* papers; Randolph, Mason, and Gerry published objections in the newspapers.

Jefferson's secretary, Meriwether Lewis (29), headed the exploratory team with William Clark (33).

The Louisiana Purchase

Though he had favored a limited government, Jefferson changed his mind about the power of the presidency once he achieved it. The Constitution said nothing about acquiring foreign territories, but Jefferson leaped at the opportunity to buy Louisiana's 830,000 square miles from France for $15 million, doubling the nation's size. Napoleon thought by the sale he had built a mighty adversary against England. Jefferson, man of the Enlightenment, immediately made plans to explore the territory's distant reaches.

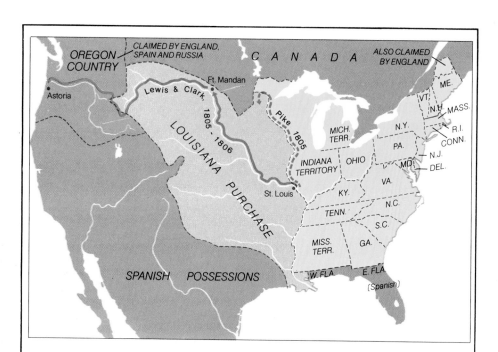

States and Territories in 1803

Taking off from St. Louis on May 14, 1804, Lewis and Clark's expedition of 23 young frontiersmen poled its way up the Missouri until winter forced a halt at Fort Mandan, near present-day Bismarck, N. Dak. There they met Sacagawėa, the 17-year-old Shoshoni girl who guided them over the Bitterroot Range through Lemhi Pass to the Clearwater and Snake rivers that led to the Pacific.
At nearly the same time, another zestful American explorer was sent northwest: Zebulon Pike to find the Mississippi's headwaters; he failed, but told great tales.

LIBRARY OF CONGRESS

From the expedition's first published account, two quaint sketches: "Captain Clark building a Hut" and "Canoe striking on a Tree."

Opposite:
Troops celebrate Louisiana Purchase at New Orleans on December 20, 1803.

174

On December 6, 1787, Delaware became the first state to ratify the new Constitution. Pennsylvania followed six days later, but only after a long and acrimonious convention in which James Wilson masterfully defended and explained the document. Georgia and then Connecticut were easy Federalist victories, but Massachusetts was a different matter. There it was largely the back-country farmers against the Federalist merchants and lawyers of the east, but the latter argued their case so adroitly, so reasonably and unemotionally, that a good many of Daniel Shays's followers decided the Constitution was not as iniquitous as they had first thought. Even Sam Adams, the old revolutionary, agreed to vote for the Constitution on the condition that a bill of rights be submitted for action by the first Congress. The final vote was close, but the Constitution carried, 187 to 168.

Maryland's ratification—with a list of amendments —followed by that of South Carolina made the count eight states. The fight was long and bitter in Virginia, where aging Patrick Henry thundered away, day after day, with his powerful oratorical guns. "Whither is the spirit of America gone?" he demanded. "We drew the spirit of liberty from our British ancestors. But now, Sir, the American spirit, assisted by the ropes and chains of consolidation, is about to convert this country into a powerful and mighty empire." Supporting Henry was a phalanx that included George Mason, Richard Henry Lee, and James Monroe, who would one day become President. Madison was prominent among the Federalists; so was a future chief justice, John Marshall. And there was an unexpected ally: Edmund Randolph, after inveighing against the Constitution and refusing to sign, now rose to announce that though he was still for amendment, he was supporting the document. And support it he did, opposing Henry step by step in debate. The Federalists won by a narrow margin, 89 to 79. Victory was due largely to the Federalists' agreement to support the addition of a bill of rights. Virginia believed that it was the ninth state to ratify, thus making the Constitution operative, but within a day came news that New Hampshire had already approved.

Since ten states had already ratified, New York in theory was not necessary to put the new government into effect, but in fact the new nation could not possibly survive if such a large, centrally located state remained aloof. The New York convention was dominated by Antifederalist Governor George Clinton, and the odds seemed impossible. Only nineteen of the sixty-five delegates were in favor of ratification at the outset. But the Federalists, and particularly Alexander Hamilton, argued so effectively, that when the vote was taken on July 26, the Constitution won by 30 to 27.

The North Carolina convention met on August 2, 1788, but did not even vote on the Constitution. It decided instead neither to accept nor reject the document until another national convention had acted on amendments it proposed. Not until November, 1789, after the new national government had been functioning several months did it ratify. And not till May of 1790 did Rhode Island accept the new government; then, its trade with the United States cut off by Congress, it voted 34 to 32 to become the thirteenth state.

But that is looking ahead of events. The Congress of the Confederation met on July 2, 1788, after receiving word that the ninth state had ratified, and appointed a committee to "report an act . . . for putting the new Constitution into operation." On September 13 it performed its last significant act when it set the date of its own demise; the new Constitution would go into effect on March 4, 1789. Actually, it would be later than that, for bad roads and other obstacles would delay the assembly of a quorum in Congress. Not until April 30 would George Washington be inaugurated and a new era in American history begun.

176

9

"Don't Give up the Ship"

On June 22, 1807, the British frigate *Leopard* intercepted the American frigate *Chesapeake* off Norfolk and insisted upon searching her for deserters. When Commodore James Barron refused, the *Leopard* opened up at close range with a series of broadsides, crippling the *Chesapeake* and killing three of her crew. The American ship, caught unsuspecting and unprepared, fired a token shot, then struck her colors. A boarding party seized four men, one of them British, and the *Chesapeake* limped back to Norfolk. To Britain, embroiled in a war with France, the incident seemed minor; but to Americans, who believed the sovereignty of their nation had been violated, the *Chesapeake* affair was a major affront.

As news of the incident spread, the country clamored for war. In a letter to James Monroe, his minister in London, President Thomas Jefferson stressed the belligerent mood of the nation. The British, he wrote, "have often enough, God knows, given us cause for war before; but it has been on points which would not have united the nation. But now they have touched a chord which vibrates in every heart. Now . . . is the time to settle the old and the new." Although his letter threatened war, Jefferson hoped to avoid it. Monroe was instructed to work out a diplomatic settlement that would include the return of the men taken from the *Chesapeake* and the abolition of Britain's practice of searching American vessels for deserters.

It soon became apparent that Jefferson's hopes for a diplomatic solution to the maritime problem were doomed. In December, 1807, Britain issued a proclamation reasserting its right to search any merchant vessel for British seamen. At about the same time,

Stephen Decatur, who broke Mediterranean pirates' hold on U.S. shipping in 1804, wrestles a Tripolitan corsair (foreground opposite). Sailing fast frigates authorized by Congress in 1794, Decatur and his fellow officers later won fame in the impending War of 1812.

Napoleon announced that any vessel submitting to a British search would be seized and its crew imprisoned. He also stepped up enforcement of the Berlin Decree of 1806, which declared the ports of France and her allies off limits to any vessel that stopped at a British port.

It was clear that Britain and France were not going to ease their maritime practices unless the U.S. resorted to stronger measures. Still opposed to war, Jefferson proposed "to starve the offending nations." He called for a permanent embargo, which would shut off American shipping to all foreign ports. The Embargo Act, passed in December, 1807, aimed to damage the trade of the two European powers, but it wrought a greater disaster at home. Shops closed, banks collapsed, farms failed, plantation owners—Jefferson included—sank deeply into debt, and ships rotted in harbors. In the port of New York, a British visitor observed, "grass had begun to grow upon the wharves."

Congressman John Randolph, Jefferson's barbed-tongued cousin, accused embargo supporters of trying "to cure the corns by cutting off the feet." The act's unkindest cut denied American ships the right to call at nearby Canadian ports, a restriction that prompted widespread flouting of the law. Smuggling became general, especially along the Canadian frontier and coast. Jefferson, determined to force observance of the embargo, declared the existence of an open insurrection in the North and stationed the army along the Canadian boundary. To prevent New England coasting vessels from stopping at Canadian ports, he issued orders calling for the detention in port of any vessel that seemed suspicious. American gunboats and frigates were soon forced to keep up a constant patrol of the northeastern coast.

The President's attempts to enforce the Embargo Act were met by open defiance. In one New England town, an armed mob prevented customs officials from detaining a vessel that was ready to sail. Elsewhere, customs collectors closed their eyes to smuggled goods; and juries, ignoring both court officials and the President, refused to indict violators.

Confronted with increasingly widespread disobedience and rising public anger, Jefferson finally had to accept the fact that the embargo could not be enforced. Three days before his retirement from the presidency, he authorized its repeal. Soon thereafter, Congress replaced the embargo with non-intercourse, a policy which, according to historian Henry Adams, "merely sanctioned smuggling."

In the election of 1808, James Madison, Jefferson's chosen successor, easily ascended to the presidency when Federalists and insurgent Republicans split the opposing vote. Madison immediately began to use the executive powers granted in the non-intercourse provisions to bait the warring nations. In essence, he planned, through proclamation, to shed American neutrality by favoring commercially the nation that would "revoke or modify her edicts."

Britain ostensibly was the first to bite; in 1809, the English minister to the U.S., David Erskine, negotiated an agreement that assured revocation of the Orders in Council in return for a resumption of American trade. Erskine, however, failed to obtain from the U.S. a promise to let the British navy enforce American regulations against France. The British government, which had insisted that this condition be included in any pact, repudiated the agreement and recalled Erskine. The United States in turn reactivated non-intercourse.

In 1810 the non-intercourse law expired and was replaced by Macon's Bill No. 2, which reopened trade with both Britain and France, but promised that if one of the belligerents lifted its restrictions on American shipping, the U.S. would reimpose a trade ban on the other. Napoleon, seeing an opportunity for some shady dealing, agreed to lift his decrees, and Madison

promptly cut off all trade with Britain. Meanwhile, Napoleon secretly ordered his navy to continue confiscating American ships. Pictured as a dupe of the French, Madison, one diplomat said, "does not know the wheel within the wheel on which they roll him. . . ."

Duped or not, Madison had nonetheless tilted toward France and consciously or not, brought American foreign policy into closer harmony with the course of events unfolding at home. That course was primarily one of restless expansion directed against the Indian lands to the west and the British territory in the north.

Americans had long coveted British Canada. After the Revolution, Ben Franklin had attempted to gain at the peace table in Paris what American soldiers had failed to win in 1775 and 1776. Though Britain had refused to yield Canada, the United States had not accepted this as the final reckoning. To expansion-minded America, Canada seemed a logical and inevitable acquisition.

Expansion—often at the expense of the Indians and

Howard Pyle's drawing of a tense moment on the high seas (below) shows a British officer inspecting an American merchantman's crew to find any deserters from the Royal Navy. Deeply resented, Britain's highhanded impressments (numbering nearly 9,000) helped bring on the War of 1812.

for the profit of land speculators—had been going on for some time. Poet and land speculator Joel Barlow had caught the prevailing mood in a burst of July Fourth oratory, declaring in 1787: "Every free citizen of the American empire ought now to consider himself the legislator of half mankind." That year the Northwest Ordinance had opened for settlement and ultimate statehood the fruitful ground wedged between the Ohio and Mississippi rivers.

South of the Ohio, land-hungry hordes had streamed through Cumberland Gap into Kentucky and Tennessee, spilling down the Natchez Trace into Mississippi Territory. In 1803 the United States had jumped the banks of the Mississippi when Napoleon unexpectedly committed, as he put it, "Louisianacide." He sold New Orleans and more than 800,000 square miles of trans-Mississippi lands to the United States for $15 million— less than three cents per acre. Jefferson, dispatching William Clark and Meriwether Lewis to survey the far-flung domain, foresaw a western migration resulting in "range after range" of states, "advancing as we multiply."

The Louisiana Purchase created a new American frontier and, in the eyes of Aaron Burr, new opportunities. A political outcast after killing Alexander Hamilton in a duel, Burr apparently dreamed of creating a huge personal estate in the West. Although the full extent of his plans has never been revealed, Burr supposedly planned to invade Mexico with a private army of westerners, detach it from Spain, and then combine it with Louisiana to form a vast empire. His scheme died aborning when one of his fellow conspirators, James Wilkinson, an army general and the governor of the Louisiana Territory, told Washington officials about the plan. Burr was arrested, accused of seeking to seize American territory for himself, and unsuccessfully tried for treason. His plan for conquest in the Spanish southwest, however, was not so much foolish as premature, as expansionists of the next generation were to prove.

Meanwhile in the southeast, settlers and speculators were moving toward the Floridas, an advance which Spain, her colonial dominion crumbling, did not have the power to stop. While still secretary of state, Madison had pressured Spain to sell her American territories, which he viewed as "a source of irritation and ill blood with the United States." But whether or not Spain sold, he declared, the Floridas' "position and the manifest course of events guarantee an early and reasonable acquisition of them."

Thus, both in the North and the South, foreign-owned territories beckoned. And to congressmen from

Thomas Burch's painting of the frigate *Constitution* giving the *Guerrière* a broadside blast (below) commemorates a key 1812 victory. War also brought naval defeats: in the sketch opposite, Capt. James Lawrence of the *Chesapeake* is seized by a British officer (sword in hand). Dying, Lawrence ordered, "Don't give up the ship!" Stitched onto banners, his words rallied the navy.

the northwestern frontier states, the prospects of winning Canada at small cost seemed especially good now that Britain's armies were bogged down in Europe.

There was much to be gained by annexing Canada: the lucrative fur trade, rich farmlands, control of fisheries. But perhaps most alluring was Canada's seemingly inexhaustible supply of timber. Americans, doubling their numbers every twenty years, depended on wood as upon no other product. It was the source of fuel for iron furnaces and home hearths; the building material for houses, factories, mills, ships, and wagons; the substance of barrels, looms, furniture, and a thousand other items. It was the stuff from whence came potash, used to make soap, glass, and gunpowder. No less importantly, wood was a profitable export. With New England forests falling at an ever accelerating rate, the vast virgin stands in Canada were increasingly tempting. Moreover, as far as frontier expansionists could see, the only obstacles to success were a handful of British forts and a few Indians, neither of which had been sufficient to check expansion south of the Great Lakes.

Indian opposition in the northwest, however, was to prove more formidable than expected. Flinging himself in America's path was a young Shawnee warrior named Tecumseh (Shooting Star). Stumping Indian villages in the Northwest Territory and ranging far afield to New York and Florida, he implored tribes to bury their differences and unite. "Where today are the Pequot?" he demanded. "Where the Narragansett, the Mohican, the Pokanoket and many other once powerful tribes of our people? They have vanished before the avarice and oppression of the white man, as snow before a summer sun." He warned that a similar fate awaited them if they did not heed his pleas for confederation.

In Vincennes, he confronted William Henry Harrison, son of a Signer of the Declaration of Independence and the governor of the Indiana Territory. Harrison, for a few thousand dollars and a few kegs of liquor, had acquired 75,000 square miles of Indian lands. "No tribe has a right to sell, even to each other, much less to strangers," contended Tecumseh. "Sell a country? Why not sell the air, the clouds and the great sea, as well as the earth?" In another meeting, as the two sat on a bench, Tecumseh gradually crowded the governor toward the end of the bench. As he was about

182

to be shoved over the edge, Harrison demanded an explanation. Tecumseh laughed and said he was illustrating a point: how white settlers pushed Indians off their land.

Harrison scoffed at Tecumseh's Indian Confederation, arguing that it was futile for the Indians to count on British aid: "Do you think that the redcoats can protect you? They are not able to protect themselves. They do not think of going to war with us. If they did, in a few months you would see our flags on all the forts of Canada."

Despite his boast, Harrison decided to strike before Tecumseh could assemble his union and hitch it to the Union Jack. As soon as Tecumseh departed on another recruiting mission, Harrison, ignoring a presidential directive discouraging a march into Indian territory, marshalled a thousand men and set out for Prophet's Town, at the junction of the Wabash and Tippecanoe rivers.

Cradle of the Indian Confederation, Prophet's Town was named after Tecumseh's one-eyed brother Tenskwatawa, also known as The Prophet. A reformed drunk, he became a religious zealot renowned for performing miracles. In 1806 he had enhanced his reputation at Harrison's expense. Challenged by the governor to produce a miracle, The Prophet, learning of an imminent solar eclipse, had commanded the sun to darken.

In the predawn hours of November 7, 1811, he attempted a miracle of warfare. Heedless of Tecumseh's warning to avoid battle until the confederacy was strong, The Prophet attacked Harrison's armed camp, pitched several miles from the village. After killing 61 soldiers and wounding 127 others, the Indians were forced to withdraw, leaving 38 dead on the field. Harrison followed and burned The Prophet's mission house and the surrounding wigwams. He then marched home, boasting that the Indians had "never sustained so severe a defeat since their acquaintance with the white people." Harrison also reported that the Indians had been equipped with British guns and powder, a fact which convinced many Americans that the English were inciting the Indians to attack the United States.

Tecumseh, returning to Prophet's Town, "stood upon the ashes" of his home and "summoned the spirits of the braves who had fallen in their vain attempt to protect their homes from the grasping invader. . . . As I snuffed up the smell of their blood from the ground, I swore once more eternal hatred—the hatred of an avenger." Americans were equally outraged by the Battle of Tippecanoe. When fiery Andrew Jackson learned of the encounter, he wrote Harrison: "The blood of our murdered countrymen must be revenged."

Vengeance, in a war long coming, was about to be taken in full measure—and with it, many Americans hoped to take the trophies of conquest as well. Congressman Henry Clay, the "Hotspur of Kentucky," had advocated a move against the north in 1810. "The conquest of Canada is in your power," he had declared on the floor of the House. "I trust I shall not be deemed presumptuous when I state that I verily believe that the militia of Kentucky are alone competent to place Montreal and Upper Canada at your feet."

After the Battle of Tippecanoe, other members of Congress took up the cry. "We shall drive the British from our Continent," vowed Felix Grundy of Tennessee. "They will no longer have an opportunity of intriguing with our Indian neighbors, and setting on the ruthless savage to tomahawk our women and children." To John A. Harper of New Hampshire, it appeared that "the Author of Nature has marked our limits in the south, by the Gulf of Mexico, and in the north, by the regions of eternal frost." Young John Calhoun from South Carolina predicted, "In four weeks from the time that a declaration of war is heard on our frontier the whole of Upper and a part of Lower Canada will be in our possession."

Gaunt John Randolph, never lacking an epithet, labeled the bellicose congressmen War Hawks. Strategically deployed by Clay, who was elected Speaker of the House in 1811, they chaired key committees, including those on Foreign Relations and Military Affairs.

Late in November, the War Hawks on the Foreign Relations Committee engineered the writing of a report reviewing Britain's aggressive maritime policies and other misdeeds. The report concluded by calling for a military buildup on both land and sea—the army should be increased to 35,000 men, the handful of existing naval vessels should be outfitted, and merchant vessels should be armed. These recommendations brought a stinging denunciation from Randolph who felt that the War Hawks were more interested in obtaining Canada than in protecting America's rights at sea. "Sir, if you go to war it will not be for the protection of, or defense of your maritime rights," he shrilled. "Agrarian cupidity, not maritime right, urges the war. Ever since the Committee on Foreign Relations came into the House, we have heard but one word—like the whippoor-will, but one eternal monotonous tone—Canada! Canada! Canada!"

While the debate raged, newspapers clamored for war. The Philadelphia *Aurora*, fanning the embers of Tippecanoe, declaimed that "war has been begun with British arms and by the Indians instigated by British emissaries. The blood of American citizens has already been shed in actual war, begun undeclared."

As the war fever mounted, President Madison deliberated. Although British minister Augustus Foster had informed him in the summer of 1811 that Britain had nothing new to offer in the way of maritime concessions, Madison still hoped for a change in British policy. Bombarded by constant calls for war from Clay and other belligerent congressmen, the President finally agreed in April, 1812, to sign into law a ninety-day embargo. If no change in European policy was forthcoming in that period, the embargo would be replaced by a declaration of war. On May 22 a ship arrived from London with instructions for Foster. These, however, merely repeated what Americans had been told before: there would be no change in British policy until France repealed its maritime decrees.

On June 1, Madison submitted his war message to Congress. The bulk of the document reviewed Britain's hostile acts against U.S. shipping. But toward the end of the statement, Madison invoked the issue—although not by name—of Tippecanoe. He cited the instance of "warfare just renewed by the savages on one of our extensive frontiers," and without directly accusing Britain, he made it clear that Americans believed British officials in Canada were behind the uprisings.

Short of a ringing call to arms, Madison's message invited rather than urged Congress to levy war. But that was enough to satisfy the War Hawks. The vote, on June 18, favored a declaration 79 to 49 in the House, 19 to 13 in the Senate.

As the war would end on an ironic turn—the last battle being fought after the peace was signed—so it began. Five days after Congress declared war, the British government, petitioned by hard-pressed manufacturing interests, finally repealed the Orders in Council, thus substantially removing the major *casus*

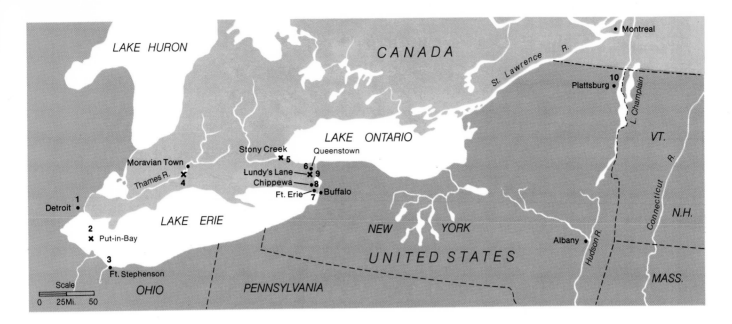

War Flames on the Border

Bitter and futile battles blazed along the U.S.-Canadian border in the War of 1812. The four major points:

Detroit. In the summer of 1812, Gen. William Hull invaded Canada from Detroit (**1**) with more than 2,000 troops. Harassed by Tecumseh's braves, he fell back on the city and soon surrendered to a lesser British force.

The Great Lakes. Oliver Hazard Perry crushed the British fleet at Put-in-Bay (**2**) in September, 1813, allowing William Henry Harrison to launch another U.S. invasion from Fort Stephenson (**3**). He won a notable victory at the Thames (**4**), where Tecumseh was killed and hopes for an Indian confederation died. Then a second American force was defeated by the hard-pressed British at Stony Creek (**5**) near Lake Ontario's western end.

Niagara. Early in the war an American attack on Queenstown (**6**) collapsed when New York militiamen (at left in painting below) declined to cross the river and bolster troops scaling the heights. Two years later Gen. Jacob Brown, driving north from Fort Erie (**7**), managed to win at the Chippewa River (**8**) and to draw against heavy odds at Lundy's Lane (**9**). But again the campaign failed as the Americans withdrew across the Niagara.

Lake Champlain. Climax of the war, a southward drive by the British in the fall of 1814 was led by Gen. George Prevost commanding 10,000 veterans of the European campaigns. At Plattsburg, Prevost's armada was smashed by 30-year-old Capt. Thomas Macdonough.

The war in the North's indecisive results helped convince both sides that peace was preferable.

Mr. Madison's War

Statesman rather than politician, President James Madison (left) had not been able to hold out against the War Hawks' fever; succumbing, he had urged Congress to declare war on June 18, 1812—just a few days after the British repealed the offensive Orders in Council.

Thereafter the war was his: "Mr. Madison's War." The opposition Federalists, traditionally inclined for England and against anything that interfered with international trade, would not support the American campaign. They and isolationist Republicans in Congress voted against increasing naval strength; Chief Justice John Marshall condemned the war as submission to Napoleon.

And in New England antipathy turned to near-desertion. Though merchants and manufacturers profited during the war, many traded illicitly with the enemy, pleading ruination. (Yet Samuel Eliot Morison points out that New England provided more regiments for the war than any other region.) Rabid Federalists such as Massachusetts's Timothy Pickering, once Adams's secretary of state, began to speak of separation. In the etching below, he prays that the southern three New England states take the fatal leap and make their own peace with England.

That secessionist tendency was brought to a head in the Hartford Convention of 1814. With moderates in charge and extremists sputtering, the convention broke up after little more than three weeks.

The unpopular war would continue until diplomats and further disasters brought it to an end.

belli. Fifty ships left for America laden with goods and bearing the good news from the British ministers. But, as the *Raleigh Star* commented, "Their wit has come too late." American forces were by then committed to a campaign against Canada. Even had the news arrived in time, the attack might still have proceeded. So great was the War Hawks' ardor for an invasion, said a correspondent of the *Aurora*, that "if England were to restore all impressed seamen and make compensation for all her depredations we should listen to no terms that did not include Upper Canada."

War Hawk predictions that Canada would quickly fall deceived the country into preparing for a short war. Writing off the navy as a lost cause—despite the sloganeering for "Free Trade and Sailors' Rights"—the administration modestly authorized a regular army of 35,000 men, settling for a fifth of that number and what militia could be induced to leave their hearthsides. Competent generals to lead the men proved even scarcer. Madison called into service two distinguished veterans of the Revolution—William Hull and Henry Dearborn—but unfortunately, as one historian noted, their abilities seemed "to have evaporated with age and long disuse." Instead of planning a concentrated attack along the St. Lawrence River, Canada's lifeline, the aged generals worked out a complicated three-stage campaign.

Hull, a "short, corpulent, good natured old gentleman, who bore the marks of good eating and drinking," was given the honor of triggering the campaign. On June 15, three days before war was officially declared, he broke camp in Dayton, Ohio, and marched toward Detroit. From that point, if all went according to plan, he would mount an attack on Canada's Fort Malden at the western end of Lake Erie. His 2,500 troops, seasoned with Tippecanoe campaigners, were expected to easily overrun the weakly defended fort and gain a commanding foothold in Upper Canada.

That it didn't turn out that way has been attributed to Hull's cowardice. Indeed, he was court-martialed and sentenced to be hanged until Madison intervened. While Hull did nothing right in the campaign, surrendering Detroit—and all of Michigan Territory—without a fight, it is doubtful that anyone else in the army, save perhaps General Andrew Jackson, could have done much better. For Hull faced, in Sir Isaac Brock and the dauntless Tecumseh, an alliance of the most brilliant military minds of the war. Though outnumbered, they outsmarted Hull at every turn, bluffing him back to Detroit after he had crossed into Canada, then demanding that city's surrender lest the Indians "be beyond controul the moment the contest commences." Salvos from Brock's short batteries and a show of force by the Indians lent authority to the threat. Hull, his nerves shot, ordered a white flag raised over Detroit on August 16.

That same day a band of Potawatomi burned Fort Dearborn (Chicago). Its ninety-one occupants, obeying Hull's order to evacuate, had done so at their peril the previous morning. All but twenty-seven were killed, including Hull's messenger, Captain William Wells. The Indians beheaded him, then cut out his heart and ate it.

A month earlier, a small American garrison at Fort Mackinac—which first learned of the war from its captors—had surrendered without "one drop of either man's or animal's blood" being spilled. The sixty-one men, outnumbered ten to one by the British on the heights and the Indians in the woods, had deemed it wiser to hold their fire. They had surrendered, among other things, more than 600 gallons of wine and whiskey.

Three days after Detroit fell, Captain Isaac Hull, the general's nephew, regained a measure of family and national pride at sea. On the afternoon of August 19, about 800 miles east of Boston, Hull, who was in command of the frigate *Constitution*, also known as "Old Ironsides," sighted a ship that turned out to be the British frigate *Guerrière*. Like many British naval officers, its commander, Captain James R. Dacres, was supremely confident that the seamanship of His Majesty's Navy was the best in the world. A few weeks earlier, he had hailed the American ship *John Adams* and issued a challenge to Commodore John Rodgers, commander of the United States Navy. "Captain Dacres," his message read, "presents his compliments to Commodore Rodgers . . . and will be very happy to meet . . . any American frigate . . . for the purpose of having a few minutes tête à tête." Captain Hull was more than willing to give Dacres his desired "tête à tête."

For a while the two ships maneuvered at a distance, then the *Constitution* closed in. Hull held his fire until he was within fifty yards of the *Guerrière*, at which time he ordered his men to "pour it into them." In very little time, the *Constitution* had battered the *Guerrière* into splinters. Dacres, realizing that further resistance was hopeless, surrendered. The crew of the *Constitution* worked all night removing survivors from the sinking ship and then sailed back to Boston, where Hull was hailed as a hero.

Dacres was full of praise for Hull's generous treatment of him and his crew, but in London the news was received with dismay and anger. "Never before in the history of the world did an English frigate strike to an American," lamented *The London Times*.

During the next four months, the small but superbly manned American navy scored three more triumphs. The sloop-of-war *Wasp* outdueled the brig *Frolic*, both carrying eighteen guns; Stephen Decatur's *United States* pounded the *Macedonian* into submission, then sent aboard a prize crew to bring her in; and the *Constitution*, now commanded by William Bainbridge, defeated the frigate *Java* off the coast of Brazil. After

"Old Ironsides'" victory over the Java, Britain clamped a blockade on the American coast to avoid further embarrassment.

Those early successes at sea helped sustain sagging American morale. Although General Hull's pathetic performance along the border of Upper Canada was a hard one to beat, sixty-two-year-old Major General Henry Dearborn, who was in charge of Fort Niagara and everything to the east, equalled or surpassed it. While 6,000 American troops assembled on the Niagara frontier, the old Bunker Hill soldier remained in Boston, worrying about the geographical extent of his command. In a letter to the secretary of war, he inquired: "Who is to have command of the operation in Upper Canada? I take it for granted that my command does not extend to that distant quarter."

By contrast, Brock, in command of the defenses on the Canadian side of the Niagara River, was eager for battle. Despite being outnumbered two to one by the Americans, he believed that "I could at this moment sweep everything before me from Fort Niagara to Buf-

British troops under Gen. Ross and Sir George Cockburn set Washington ablaze (left) to repay American burning of York (Toronto). They missed destroying such White House treasures as Gilbert Stuart's portrait of Washington because courageous, ebullient Dolley Madison (right) had whisked them to safety. Much of White House pillage was accomplished by Washington rabble.

falo." But he was held in check by his commander in chief, Sir George Prevost, who proposed an armistice based on the repeal of the Orders in Council. Dearborn, jumping at any excuse for delay, accepted the offer, only to be overruled by Washington.

While Dearborn searched for ways to avoid his command, the politically appointed commander in chief of the New York militia, Stephen Van Rensselaer, and regular army general Alexander "Apocalypse" Smyth tugged for control of the troops gathering along the Niagara frontier.

Van Rensselaer seized the initiative in mid-October. He ferried the river with some 200 troops and attacked Queenstown Heights. The brilliant British commander, Isaac Brock, was killed during this assault, but his troops remained undaunted. British light infantry, Canadian militia, and war-whooping Indians counterattacked, winning the day when New York militia reinforcements refused to budge from the American side of the river.

Van Rensselaer resigned in disgust, and Smyth,

platitudes rolling off his tongue, took command in November. "Neither rain, snow, or frost will prevent the embarkation," he promised while postponing one crossing after another. "Hearts of War!" he postured. "Tomorrow will be memorable in the annals of the United States!" Not tomorrow, not ever did Smyth cross the Niagara.

On the day appointed for embarkation, Smyth called a council of war. His officers, when asked whether the crossing should proceed, unanimously voted against it. The invasion was abandoned, and Smyth's 4,000 soldiers, upon being informed of the decision, discharged their muskets "without order or restraint," and disbanded.

Two strikes against Canada having failed, it was up to "Granny" Dearborn to make the third one—at Montreal—count. Under his command at Plattsburg were 6,000 to 8,000 troops, the largest American force yet mustered. Dearborn, though burdened with laggard militiamen, made a half-hearted stab at the border, then decided, as *The London Times* jeered, "to

189

advance backward." Weary of war, he asked Madison "to be permitted to retire in the shade of private life, and remain a mere but interested spectator of passing events."

At the close of 1812, Canada not only remained intact; it had sunk its claws into the Northwest Territory. Harrison, with 10,000 troops at his disposal, was given the task of removing the irritation. In January an advance party of about 1,000 men commanded by General James Winchester, another old revolutionary war soldier, advanced too far—to Frenchtown. Situated on the River Raisin, it was within eighteen miles of Fort Malden, now strongly fortified. Some 1,200 to 1,400 British soldiers and Indians under the command of Colonel Henry Proctor, Brock's successor, swooped down on Winchester's garrison on the morning of the twenty-first. Half the Americans were captured; the rest were either killed or wounded. Proctor marched his prisoners to Malden, leaving the injured to the mercy of the Indians. They showed no mercy. Maddened with whiskey, they massacred perhaps a hundred soldiers.

"Remember the River Raisin!" became the rallying cry as Harrison renewed his march northward. Tecumseh, returning from the Wabash, was infuriated at Proctor's assent to the barbarism. "Go and put on petticoats," he snarled. "I conquer to save, and you to murder."

On June 1 was heard another rallying cry from another massacre. As British tars from the *Shannon* swarmed aboard the crippled *Chesapeake* locked in a death struggle off Cape Cod, Captain James Lawrence begged as he lay dying, "Don't give up the ship."

In September, Oliver Hazard Perry flew those words from the mast of his flagship *Lawrence* and thus signaled the start of battle on Lake Erie. A struggle between vessels fashioned from green timber and manned by green crews, it ended when Perry,

battle flag in hand, changed ships in mid-stream to carry on the fight. After accepting surrender but not the officers' swords, he wrote Harrison: "We have met the enemy and they are ours: Two Ships, two Brigs one Schooner & one Sloop." With control of Lake Erie, the way was clear for Harrison to recover Detroit and invade Canada.

Proctor, not one for a fight unless the odds favored him, abandoned Fort Malden and retreated up the Thames River. Tecumseh called him "a miserable old squaw" and threatened to shoot him if he didn't make a stand. Reluctantly Proctor relented. When the battle started on October 5, he fled, leaving the Shawnee to break Harrison's cavalry charge. In savage hand-to-hand combat, Tecumseh was killed. The Thames River battle was a major victory for the United States. For without Tecumseh, the Indian confederacy was doomed; and without the menace of the

After the smoke cleared in Plattsburg's harbor, and Gen. Prevost saw that anchored American ships had defeated his armada, he stopped trying to cross the Saranac River (below) and retreated to Canada—a "lamentable event" according to *The London Times.*

Indians, Detroit and the area to the west of it were safe.

In Upper Canada, the war sputtered throughout 1813 in border clashes that drained resources and accomplished little. Wresting for control of Lake Ontario, an American raiding party looted, burned, and abandoned York (Toronto) in April. A month later, a British force made a futile attack on Sackett's Harbor. Action seesawed on the Niagara frontier from May to December, the Americans capturing Fort George, only to eventually lose it and Fort Niagara as well.

Niagara's fall and the destruction of several American villages, including Buffalo, resulted in part from defenders' having been pulled away for a two-pronged attack on Montreal. That campaign, directed by General James Wilkinson, Aaron Burr's former confidant, foundered as badly as Dearborn's attempt the year before. While General Wade Hampton marched 4,000 men northward from Plattsburg, New York, Wilkinson loaded 8,000 troops in boats at Sackett's Harbor for a thrust down the St. Lawrence. Hamp-

ton, striking out westward near the Canadian border, ran into a small force of French-Canadians at the Chateauguay River. After a brief skirmish on October 26, he turned around and marched back to Plattsburg. On the St. Lawrence, two weeks later, Wilkinson halted his flotilla to do battle in a muddy field about ninety miles from Montreal. The opposition, a British "corps of observation" with less than a thousand men, routed the American force, a detachment twice its strength. The defeat coupled with news of Hampton's retreat killed Wilkinson's appetite for Montreal. He retired to winter quarters.

Except for the victories of Jackson's Indian fighters against the Creek "Red Sticks" in the South, there was little for Americans to cheer about in the spring of 1814. The fall of Napoleon in April promised an even bleaker summer, for 15,000 of the Duke of Wellington's battle-hardened veterans had embarked for America: some of them were bound for Jamaica, from which point they would sail northward to attack New Orleans and attempt to cut off the West from the rest of

America's Last-Minute Victories

When reports of the unsuccessful British attempt to bomb Baltimore into submission (opposite) reached Europe in October, 1814, British negotiators at the Ghent peace table reviewed the bidding. Baltimore's news, taken with word of the Plattsburg repulse, indicated that demands on U.S. boundaries could not be enforced.

But the greatest aid to peace was the forthright opinion of Napoleon's conqueror, the Duke of Wellington, who, pondering the North American chessboard, denounced further attempts on American territory as futile. Wellington's brother-in-law Gen. Pakenham died in the slaughter of British troops at New Orleans (below) a month after the peace treaty was signed.

Francis Scott Key, having won the release of a
friend from a British prison ship, beholds the
"star-spangled banner" still flying the morning
after the bombardment of Baltimore. His poem,
written on the back of an old letter, appeared as a
broadside in the delivered city's streets even before
the British fleet had cleared the Chesapeake.
Set to a ballad's tune, it soon became popularly
regarded as the national anthem and was belatedly
recognized as such by Congress in 1931.

193

WE OWE ALLEGIANCE TO NO CROWN.

the U.S. Most, however, were headed for Canada.

Before the Canada-bound troops arrived, disciplined American soldiers under young Generals Jacob Brown and Winfield Scott won a measure of glory across the Niagara. On July 3 they overwhelmed Fort Erie, then advanced up the river to Chippewa. There, on July 5, a bayonet charge by Scott's infantry broke the British line. "Those are Regulars, by God," cried the startled British general, Phineas Riall. Three weeks later he was captured in the battle of Lundy's Lane, near Niagara Falls. A standoff, it produced the fiercest fighting on the frontier. Each side suffered about 900 casualties—more than 40 percent of their forces—and both Scott and Brown were severely wounded. Yielding the field but not their honor, the Americans withdrew to Fort Erie, where the British besieged them for two months at a cost of several hundred lives.

By mid-August, 10,000 of Wellington's redcoated infantry had landed in Montreal, and Sir George Prevost was preparing to lead them in an invasion of the United States. At the same time General Robert Ross, at sea with another army, was "to effect a diversion" on the U.S. coast. Vice Admiral Alexander Cochrane, meanwhile, had ordered his royal fleet "to destroy and lay waste such towns and districts upon the coast as you may find assailable."

His second in command, Rear Admiral George Cockburn, prowling and pillaging along the Chesapeake, advised Cochrane that "the City of Washington might be possessed without difficulty or opposition of any kind." Dramatic proof of that statement was soon forthcoming. At dawn, August 19, British transports entered the Patuxent River, and Ross's army disembarked without opposition. A leisurely trek through pleasant countryside brought it to the backdoor of Washington—the crossroads village of Bladensburg, Maryland.

There on the twenty-fourth, battle lines were drawn. Spectators—including President Madison—hurried to the scene. As a reporter described, "It was something like the community turning out to see a fire." After the first clash of arms, the battle was over. Deprived of leadership, 7,000 militia broke and ran rather than face the British assault. Later that day, Ross entered the capital "city in the woods" and found that most of its 10,000 citizens had fled.

Dolley Madison provided a running account of the day's events in a letter to her sister Lucy Washington Todd:

> Since sunrise I have been turning my spy-glass in every direction, and watching with unwearied anxiety, hoping to discover the approach of my dear husband and his friends; but, alas! I can descry only groups of military, wandering in all directions, as if there was a lack of arms, or of spirit to fight for their own fireside.
>
> Three o'clock. Will you believe it, my sister? we have had a battle, or skirmish, near Bladensburg, and here I am still, within sound of the cannon! Mr. Madison comes not. May God protect us! Two messengers covered with dust come to bid me fly.

Delaying long enough to remove the full-length painting of George Washington hanging in the dining room, she departed shortly before Madison returned to the White House. He soon followed, taking refuge across the Potomac in Virginia.

That evening Ross put the torch to the city, burning the White House and the Capitol. A British officer recorded that he had never witnessed "a scene more striking or sublime."

The next day a tornado roared through Washington, inflicting more damage. Ross, his pockets "full of old Madison's love letters," decided against spending another day in the smoldering city. He slipped out after dark, retracing his steps through Bladensburg.

On the twenty-eighth, Alexandria, Virginia—which, like Georgetown, had been trying to surrender before being asked—finally got its death wish. A British squadron sailed up the Potomac and held it for ransom. Now, wrote Cochrane, "Baltimore may be destroyed, or laid under a severe contribution." A nest for privateers and America's third largest city with a population of 45,000, it was too inviting a target to pass up.

Anticipating the worst, Senator Samuel Smith, general of the militia, marshalled the city's defenses, erecting a series of earthworks from which to deploy 13,000 men. Guarding the harbor was Fort McHenry, commanded by Major George Armistead.

On September 12, Ross landed his army at North Point and, vowing to eat supper that night in Baltimore—"or in hell"—began the twelve-mile hike to the city. Firing and falling back, Smith's militia slowed the British advance and, aiming at an officer on a white horse, mortally wounded General Ross.

Next morning British bomb ships opened up on Fort McHenry, continuing the bombardment all day and through the night. By the dawn's early light, Maryland lawyer Francis Scott Key, detained on a British sloop while negotiating the release of a prisoner, saw the fort's star-spangled banner still flying. Fort McHenry had not fallen. "My heart spoke," Key said, and he scribbled a few words on the back of an envelope. Set to the tune of an old English ballad, they survived to be sung as the national anthem.

Coincident with the punitive expeditions against Washington and Baltimore, Prevost was making his bid in the North. His army, 10,000 strong, cautiously filed down the west bank of Lake Champlain to Plattsburg. Before striking at the inferior American force dug in near the Saranac River, Prevost ordered his freshwater fleet into action against the ships and gunboats of Captain Thomas Macdonough.

On the morning of September 11, the two flotillas clashed at short range in Plattsburg Bay. The outcome of the battle hinged on the duel between Macdonough's *Saratoga*, twenty-six guns, and the frigate *Confidence*, thirty-six. By turning his ship around while at anchor, Macdonough was able to bring all his guns to bear. The pivoting maneuver proved decisive. The frigate struck. With the loss of the *Confidence*, Prevost refused to commit his army, and hightailed it back to Canada.

For several months, U.S. and British commissioners had been meeting in the Flemish town of Ghent. Their respective demands changed with each development of the war: the British pressing for the guarantee of Indian lands and the right to conquered territory; the Americans raising and—as the war soured—dropping maritime issues. In the end, both sides agreed to the *status quo ante bellum*. In essence the Treaty of Ghent, signed on Christmas Eve, said the War of 1812 was a draw, that neither side had lost.

The Battle of New Orleans, fought two weeks after the peace was signed, didn't change a thing; but it might have if Jackson had lost. For General Sir Edward Pakenham, the Duke of Wellington's brother-in-law, carried a commission giving him—as would-be territorial governor—authority "over all the territory fraudulently conveyed by Bonaparte to the United States."

But governor of Louisiana he was not to be. Shot in the neck, he died among the sugarcane stubble as his army, packed in tight formation, marched into a withering fire from Jackson's breastworks along Rodriguez Canal. After the slaughter—the Americans suffered 20 casualties to more than 2,000 for the British—Pakenham's body was shipped back to England in a cask of rum.

"Old Hickory" Jackson emerged from the battle as presidential timber. He had won the nation's gratitude for the war's greatest victory.

Carriers to the Far Frontier

"The true history of the United States," wrote an English observer, "is the history of transportation." Pioneer ingenuity built wagon homes to cross a continent, flatboats to float rivers, sharp ships to knife waves, and developed steam engines to run boats and railroads. Using leather thoroughbraces instead of steel springs, and an oval body for lightness and strength, the Concord coach, after 1827, set the American pattern. By 1860 coaches ran from California to Oregon, passing Mt. Shasta (below) en route.

Trenton to Philadelphia by diligence was a rough ride. From there to Baltimore took five more days.

Roads Across the Mountains

At first, many roads were stumpy paths. The best were stone covered with gravel. Sectional rivalry and doubtful legality slowed federal building; finally the National Road reached the Ohio. In the 1790s there was a rash of road building, mostly by states or private companies which expected to profit from tolls.

New roads led west; this one by way of Pennsylvania's Alleghenies. Most remarkable was
the rugged National opened from Cumberland, Maryland, to Wheeling in 1818. A New Yorker
marveled at its stone bridges, "monuments of taste and power that will speak well for
the country when the brick towns they bind together shall have crumbled in the dust."

199

Flatboating the Westward Rivers

People and produce moved west or east by river, often on primitive but effective flatboats which could be broken up and sold at the end of the trip. Better-designed keelboats were towed or poled back upriver.

DAVY CROCKETT ALMANAC

PRINTS DIVISION, NEW YORK PUBLIC LIBRARY

THE ST. LOUIS ART MUSEUM

Flatboat crew at left celebrates journey's end. Keelboatmen exaggerated their exploits, as implied by sketch of dolphin driver. One tall-tale teller, Mike Fink, claimed, "I'm a land-screamer . . . I can lick five times my own weight in wildcats."

Migrants' boats (above and at right) on western rivers ranged from the "stately barge" to dugouts. Favored for large groups were "broadhorns . . . 15 feet wide, from 40 to 100 feet in length" with "comfortable and separate apartments, fitted up with chairs . . . old and young, servants, cattle . . . bringing to recollection the cargo of the ancient ark."

A Craze for Canals

From 1816 to 1840 Americans built
3,226 miles of canals. The canal
of canals was the Erie. Finished
in 1825, the Erie paid for itself
many times over before tolls were
eliminated in 1882. Settlers going
west could make the 360-mile trip
from Albany to Buffalo for $8.00.

NEW-YORK HISTORICAL SOCIETY

Packets, like the one opposite rounding a bend near Little Falls, could travel the Erie in seven days. Line boats took longer, about twelve days. Local craft, cargo boats, tradesmen added to the bustle. Waiting for water levels to equalize and lock gates to open was a good time for a wayside stroll (above). Where grades were very steep, lock piled upon lock (left). Many other canals were built, but no other route west was so direct, none so profitable as DeWitt Clinton's "big ditch." Relocated, modernized, the Erie carries on.

Ships Powered by Steam

Even as flatboats drifted down the Delaware, delegates to the 1787 Constitutional Convention watched with interest as an embryonic steamboat chugged along the waterfront. In 1807 Fulton's *Clermont* began a profitable New York to Albany service. Henry Shreve added power, second deck, adapting the boat to turbulent western rivers.

TULANE UNIVERSITY

The shallow-draft Mississippi sidewheeler had, *Harper's* magazine said, "grown out of the needs of our commerce, is not only original to us in its form of construction, but . . . splendid in appearance." By 1849 there were 1,000 on western rivers, many crowding New Orleans levees. John James Audubon did not share the general enthusiasm; steamboats were "the very filthiest of all filthy old rat-traps I ever travelled in."

Mississippi pilots memorized ''the longest river in the world—four thousand three hundred miles . . . also the crookedest river in the world.'' You steered, Mark Twain said, ''by the shape that's in your head, and never mind the one that's before your eyes.''

Wagons Winding to the West

Two trails, the northern Oregon and southern Santa Fe, were followed by most who made the arduous cross-country trek. Many families chose a high-sided wagon drawn by oxen or mules. Combination rolling home and moving van, the Conestoga could be adapted to float across rivers.

COLLECTION OF C. R SMITH

Few families dared attempt the long westward march alone. Banding into wagon trains, they chose officers and guards (left), shared dangers and hardships of the trail. The first big train, 1,000 persons, some 120 wagons, and hundreds of cattle, left Independence, Missouri, on May 22, 1843.

Spreading out across the countryside, a wagon train begins the day's travel, some twenty miles. Small groups have ridden ahead to scout, others to hunt. Crossing the Platte River (right) was horrendous: shifting islands blocked the way; wading through water "a mile wide and six inches deep," travelers were snared in quicksand.

A rider made two round trips a week, each "run" being about 100 miles. He averaged nine miles an hour, taking two minutes to change horses (above). Weight was kept to a minimum to ensure speed. Preference for orphans —with no family complications, in case of fatal meeting with Indians—adds wry note to advertisement, left.

PONY EXPRESS

   CHANGE OF **TIME!**   REDUCED **RATES!**

EFFECTIVE JULY 1st, 1861

10 Days to San Francisco!

LETTERS

WILL BE RECEIVED AT THE

OFFICE, 84 BROADWAY,

NEW YORK,

Up to **4 P. M.** every **TUESDAY,**

AND

Up to **2½ P. M.** every **SATURDAY,**

Which will be forwarded to connect with the PONY EXPRESS leaving ST. JOSEPH, Missouri, the following SATURDAY and WEDNESDAY, respectively, at 11:00 P.M.

TELEGRAMS

Sent to Fort Kearney on the mornings of MONDAY and FRIDAY, will connect with PONY leaving St. Joseph, WEDNESDAYS and SATURDAYS.

EXPRESS CHARGES.

LETTERS weighing half ounce or under (reduced from $5.00) $1.00
For every additional half ounce or fraction of an ounce $1.00
In all cases Express CHARGES are to be Pre-paid.

RIDERS WANTED

Young, skinny, wiry fellows. Anxious for adventure and chance to see our great WEST. Must be expert riders, willing to risk death daily. Orphans preferred. $60 PER MONTH and keep. Apply at above address.

Lean Riders of the Pony Express

Conceived to speed messages between east and west, the Pony Express began its spectacular eighteen-month life in April, 1860. Changing mounts at 190 way stations, riders took mail from Missouri to California, 2,000 miles in ten—later eight—days. It was fast, but not enough to compete with the telegraph, completed in October, 1861.

Indians, wary of white invaders, resented Pony Express. Real trouble came after two stationmasters kidnapped an Indian girl. Attacks on riders (below) and relay stations were frequent, especially in Nevada among the Paiutes.

Clippers for Frisco

Fleet and lovely, American clippers had already cut the China run to 100 days when gold made California a mecca. Piling on canvas, the daring builders and more daring captains pushed the slim ships to record speeds in the race for San Francisco.

PEABODY MUSEUM

Sleepy San Francisco (above) became a metropolis overnight after gold was found in 1848 at Sutter's mill on the American River. When the news reached the East, men left everything to look for the shiny metal. Clippers raced around the Horn, carrying gold seekers and supplies to California. The ultimate clipper, Donald McKay's *Flying Cloud* (right), set a record never broken, eighty-nine days to the Golden Gate. Even in storms, such as the one *Young America* is riding out (opposite), some captains thought nothing of sending a man aloft to add sails. Steam ultimately won the battle, but in the 1840s and '50s these knife-edged beauties wrote a brilliant final chapter for American sailing ships.

211

Salute to the Future

In a symbolic tableau, the sturdy covered
wagon rides into the past. America began a new
era when Union Pacific met Central Pacific
at Promontory Point, May 10, 1869.

PART THREE

Manifest Destiny 1816-1860

Chronology:

Jacksonian Era

Struggles on the Borders

Antebellum Period

Jackson: The People's Friend 10

"It was like the inundation of northern barbarians into Rome. . . . Strange faces filled every public place and every face seemed to bear defiance on its brow." Thus did one observer describe the crowds of people that streamed into Washington to attend the inauguration ceremonies of 1829.

From North, from South, and especially from the West they came—soldiers, backwoodsmen, farmers, laborers, sightseers, in short, the common people—to witness the inauguration of General Andrew Jackson, the Nation's Hero and the People's Friend.

The crowds overflowed the city. They slept on benches and billiard tables or camped five to a bed. They flowed in and out of taprooms faster than bartenders could pour. And above all, they lay siege to Gadsby's Indian Queen Tavern, Jackson's headquarters, seeking to congratulate their hero. Despite the efforts of Jackson's aides to preserve order, so many admirers and office-seekers gained entrance to the hotel, cramming the stairways and jostling one another, that the owners feared the building might collapse.

On March 4, Jackson emerged from the Indian Queen and strode down Pennsylvania Avenue toward the Capitol. "The Avenue was crowded with carriages of every description," noted one eyewitness, including "wagons and carts, filled with women and children, some in finery, some in rags. . . ." In contrast to the brightly dressed, cheering crowd, the tall gaunt Jackson, his face etched with lines of sorrow, was attired in a suit of deepest mourning for the recent death of his wife. As the sixty-one-year-old general made his slow way down the avenue, even those who had come to laugh at the spectacle of the common people and their rough military hero were touched. Exclaimed one

Andrew Jackson—nicknamed during the War of 1812 when his men thought him "tough as hickory"—doffs his hat in this heroic lithograph. As a result of his New Orleans victory (background), Old Hickory became the 1820s' most popular national figure.

fashionable Washington lady, "It is *true* greatness which needs not the aid of ornament and pomp."

Such was the crush that the general had to outflank the eager crowds by clambering over a wall and entering the Capitol through the basement. When he reappeared, a mighty cheer went up, and he stood for a moment bowing with "grace and composed dignity."

After being sworn in by Chief Justice John Marshall, Jackson mounted a horse for the triumphal ride to the White House. The cheering, shouting crowd fell in behind. At the gates of the Executive Mansion, the mob pushed past the guards and followed the new President inside. They overwhelmed the official guests, elbowing them aside, breaking the furniture, and roaming through the rooms. Women fainted; men fought. Priceless wine goblets and china were hurled to the floor. When waiters attempted to bring out refreshments, the people surged forward, knocking the food to the floor. A cordon of gentlemen locked arms around the shaken Jackson and escorted him back to his lodging at Gadsby's. Supreme Court Justice Joseph Story, a Boston conservative, observed dolefully that "The reign of King 'Mob' seemed triumphant."

But to others, notably newspaperman Amos Kendall, "It was a proud day for the people. . . .General Jackson is *their own* president."

Much of Jackson's appeal for the people lay in the fact that unlike the Presidents who had come before him, he was a self-made man. His career, unfolding amid the freedom and fierce competition of the frontier, epitomized the western belief that any individual might rise to greatness.

Born in the "Garden of the Waxhaws," the upland frontier region of the Carolinas, in 1767, he was the son of Scotch-Irish immigrants. The senior Andrew Jackson died two months before his third son and namesake was born. Thus Andy grew up under the roof of his uncle, James Crawford. The boy manifested

215

unusual intelligence; he could read by the time he was five and write in a clear hand by the age of eight. Young Andrew, however, was less interested in learning than in riding, fighting, and shooting. He was impetuous and courageous. "I could throw him three times out of four," related one of Jackson's burlier classmates. "But he would never *stay throwed*. He was dead game and never would give up."

During the Revolution, he served in the patriot militia, first as a mounted courier, then as a trooper. The Waxhaws were the scene of much irregular fighting, and during one British foray, thirteen-year-old Andrew was captured and imprisoned. Elizabeth Jackson subsequently obtained her son's release, then rode off to help two nephews being held prisoner in Charleston. She died there of typhus in 1781. Andrew Jackson would long remember her last advice. Make friends by being honest and keep them by being steadfast, she had told her son. "Never tell a lie, nor take what is not your own. . . ." Throughout his life, Jackson's honesty would impress both friend and foe. He was "utterly honest, naturally honest; would beggar himself to pay a debt and did so," wrote one man who had business dealings with Jackson.

After his mother's death, Andrew went to stay with Major Robert Crawford, a family friend and one of the wealthiest landowners in the Waxhaws. Horses, cock-fighting, and gambling were his main preoccupations for the next few years. In 1783 he inherited £300 from his grandfather in Ireland, which he promptly lost in the gambling halls and on the racetracks of Charleston. After losing his inheritance, Jackson taught school for a few months and then moved to Salisbury, North Carolina, where at the age of eighteen, he began to read law. His lust for gambling and good times unabated, he was long remembered as "the most roaring, rollicking, game-cocking, horse-racing, card-playing, mischievous fellow, that ever lived in Salisbury."

Yet Jackson still found time to study; at the age of twenty, he passed his law examination and was appointed public prosecutor of North Carolina's Western District, a sparsely settled strip of land extending from the Great Smoky Mountains to the Mississippi River. Jackson headed west in 1788, arriving at Nashville, a small, lawless settlement on the Cumberland River, in October. The young prosecutor rapidly brought the frontier town to order, forcing rebellious pioneers to pay their debts and in general respect the law.

While the court was sitting at Nashville, Jackson boarded at the Widow Donelson's blockhouse, about ten miles away. There he met and fell in love with his landlady's dark-eyed, dimpled daughter Rachel Donelson Robards. Rachel had married Captain Lewis Robards of Kentucky at the age of seventeen, but their life together had been less than happy. The intensely jealous Robards grew enraged at the sight of his wife talking with another man. Finally, after numerous separations and reconciliations, Robards obtained permission from the Virginia Assembly (Kentucky was

Jackson's fighting spirit against British and Indians alike dated back to a frontier youth and a revolutionary incident. His brow forever bore a scar from the sword slash received for sassing a cavalry officer. Embattled with Creeks in 1814, he ultimately received the sword of Red Eagle, also known as William Weatherford, who enters tent opposite below.

OVERLEAF: George Caleb Bingham's *Verdict of the People* depicts American politics as Monroe's Era of Good Feelings gave way to Jackson's Era of the Common Man.

not yet a state) to sue for a divorce. Jackson, mistaking this step for the divorce itself, married Rachel in August, 1791. Two years later Robards finally completed the divorce action. Jackson, learning with deep shock that he and his Rachel were not really married, went through a second ceremony, but their unwitting mistake would haunt the couple for the rest of their lives.

Jackson's business affairs prospered. His law practice grew steadily, as did his wealth in land, slaves, and horses. He seems to have had little interest in politics at this time, but in 1796 he received the first of many calls to serve in a political capacity.

Back in 1789, when North Carolina had ratified the federal Constitution, its Western District had been incorporated into the United States as a territory. By 1795 the region had enough inhabitants to apply for statehood. To pave the way for admission to the Union, the territorial legislature called for a constitutional convention. Andrew Jackson was elected to attend, and according to tradition, he proposed the new state's name—Tennessee. At the first election, voters chose John Sevier, an Indian fighter of legendary prowess, to be their governor and Andrew Jackson to be their representative in Congress.

Jackson declined a second term in the House; but after Tennessee Senator William Blount was expelled from Congress for "a high misdemeanor," he agreed to take that gentleman's place in the Senate. Jackson, however, resigned the seat before his term was up and returned to Tennessee, where he became judge of the state superior court. Little is known about his decisions, but he is reputed to have frequently exhorted juries to "do what is *right* between these parties. That is what the law always *means.*"

Jackson and "his Lady" celebrate the New Orleans victory in the folk painting at right. Yet Rachel (who died in 1828) took little joy from public affairs: "You have served your Country Long Enough . . . Oh Lord of heaven, how can I beare it."

In 1801 he was voted head of the state militia, with the rank of major general, over Governor John Sevier. Not long after the election, the two men clashed when Sevier insulted Jackson's wife. The two met on neutral ground, but the proposed duel became a brawl, from which both emerged unharmed.

The Sevier affair would not be the last. Jackson's political success created enemies and—inevitably—besmirching references to his wife's unwitting adultery. Whispers circulated around Nashville for years and resulted in numerous challenges.

The War of 1812 signalled the beginning of a new phase in Andrew Jackson's career—his rise to fame as a military commander. Possessed of an undying hatred

BOSTON MUSEUM OF FINE ARTS

for England, engendered by his experiences during the Revolution, Jackson welcomed the news that Congress had declared war on England and offered his services. He was given command of Tennessee's militia, which was to be sent on an expedition to Spanish Florida, but was told that he would not be in charge of the campaign. Instead he would serve under General James Wilkinson. This was a bitter blow to Jackson, but he consented to join the expedition anyway. Upon reaching Natchez, Jackson and his men were told to wait and then were dismissed. By this maneuver, Wilkinson hoped to get Jackson's troops without their fiery commander. Jackson, however, refused to leave his troops stranded 800 miles from Tennessee. Lack of food, much sickness, and heavy winter rains made the march back to Tennessee an ordeal. Commanding one of the sick men to ride his horse, General Jackson moved up and down the line on foot, encouraging

stragglers and clearing obstacles from the trail. Appreciating his selfless endurance and understanding the reasons for his stern discipline, the militiamen affectionately nicknamed their commander "Old Hickory."

In August, 1813, the Creek Indians, grasping the opportunity to strike while the United States was at war with Britain, surprised and massacred 260 Americans at Fort Mims, a small stockade near what is now Mobile, Alabama. Jackson was recovering from gunshot wounds received in a tavern brawl, but he promptly led a force of 2,500 men against the Creeks. In a series of lightning strikes and rapid marches across what is now Alabama, Old Hickory demolished the Creek army and compelled the tribe to cede 23 million acres of its territory to the United States.

After defeating the Creek Indians, Jackson, by now a major general in the regular army, turned his attention back to Florida. Having heard rumors that British marines were arming Florida Indians and that English ships were lurking off the West Florida Coast, he wrote to Washington, advocating an attack on Florida.

John Armstrong, the secretary of war, sent Jackson a reply that seemed to encourage him to enter Florida but permitted the federal government to disavow him if necessary. The letter, however, was—perhaps intentionally—delayed, and Jackson plunged on down to Mobile, where he learned that the British had already established themselves at Pensacola. On November 7, 1814, Jackson invaded the city and accepted its surrender from the Spanish. Meanwhile the British quickly retreated to their anchored ships, and sailed off towards New Orleans. With a force of six ships-of-the-line, fourteen frigates, and transports capable of carrying 7,000 soldiers, they hoped to capture and isolate

President-elect Jackson accepts the crowd's adulation as he progresses toward his inauguration. He went by steamboat to Pittsburgh, by coach to Washington. President J.Q. Adams, recognizing Jackson's popularity, had declined to campaign.

Louisiana and much of the territory to the north.

Jackson, although unaware of the full extent of British plans, was certain that New Orleans would be the object of a major attack. He marched his forces west and deployed them along the northern (and eastern) bank of the Mississippi, some six miles down river from

"To the victor belong the spoils," remarked a senator of Jackson's presidency. Yet Jackson gave this 1,400-pound cheese to the crowd at one of his public receptions; little stuck to his fingers.

New Orleans. Three days before Christmas, 1814, 2,000 British troops landed in darkness on the shores of a bayou at the western end of Lake Borgne. After some indecisive night fighting, Jackson withdrew his men to a fortified line some 1,300 yards inland from the river. In order to reach New Orleans, the British would have to break through Jackson's defenses.

On Christmas Day, Major General Sir Edward Pakenham, the hero of Salamanca and the brother-in-law of the Duke of Wellington, took command of the British land forces. After twice attempting to force the American stockade with infantry and artillery, Pakenham mounted, on the morning of January 8, what he hoped would be the decisive assault.

At the first glow of dawn, the American guns opened fire on the advancing British lines, dimly visible through the fog. Three hundred yards from the parapet the British infantry moved from a walk to a fast trot, then into a full-blooded charge. On Jackson's command a sheet of flame cut across the top of the American works. The British staggered, then came on again. Jackson fired two more volleys in rapid succession. By now the sun had risen and the cane stubble was crimson with British coats. Under a constant fusillade of fire the line slowed and began to disintegrate. When they rode up to urge it onward, three British

221

Machines made the economy hum faster in Jackson's America. But work in North and South was dramatically different.

After the introduction and widespread utilization of Eli Whitney's 1793 cotton gin (left), farmers required vast lands with numerous slaves to produce massive cotton crops. Risk-minded southerners gambled all to get plantations in deltaland. If their gamble paid off—by means of blacks who grew and picked and cleaned the cotton (100 slaves for every 1,000 acres)— they built porticoed mansions and enjoyed an elegant life.

The Currier and Ives print above shows delta field hands harvesting a crop. Other slaves crank the gin (right) whose toothed cylinders remove the seeds. Next pressed into bales, the cotton was carted to the levee and taken by paddlewheeled riverboat to New Orleans.

Industry in the North

Given the concept of machines to make interchangeable parts—like the drill press for Whitney's musket factory (right)—northerners began to invest in machine shops (below) and mechanized mills. Industrialized cities grew. President Jackson visited the pioneer mill town of Lowell, Massachusetts, and was amazed at the sight of 2,500 factory girls parading with regulation parasols.

The Industrial Revolution, arrived from Europe, drove the two American cultures farther and farther apart.

AMERICAN ANTIQUARIAN SOCIETY

NEW-YORK HISTORICAL SOCIETY

Eli Whitney began making muskets with interchangeable parts at his Hartford factory (below) after he had returned from the South. Dismayed that his cotton gin's success had called for more slaves, he hoped that factory workers would never be so oppressed as blacks.

generals, including Pakenham, fell mortally wounded.

General Lambert, one of the few ranking British officers left alive on the field, ordered a general retreat. By 8:30 A.M. the American riflemen had ceased firing. On the field before them lay 1,971 dead and wounded British soldiers, including 3 generals, 8 colonels and 54 lieutenants. The Americans, safe behind their barricade, suffered only 13 dead and 58 wounded.

Jackson's campaign against the Creeks had already made him a popular hero. His triumph at New Orleans rendered him a figure of world renown. His rough border upbringing, his plain-spoken—even peremptory—manner, and his taproom vendettas clearly appalled the tidewater gentry, but these characteristics merely enhanced Jackson in the eyes of the multitude, who welcomed him as one of their own. Indeed, he had not been back at his plantation, the Hermitage, more than a few weeks when his name was raised in connection with the presidency.

Jackson, however, disclaimed any interest in the office and threw his support to James Monroe in 1816. Soon thereafter he was given command of the southern division of the U.S. army, with the rank of major general, and in 1817 he returned to active service to put down a Seminole Indian uprising on the border of Georgia and Spanish Florida. Marching into western Florida in search of the elusive Seminoles, Jackson captured a number of Spanish forts, executed two men alleged to be British agents, and finally seized the territory's capital, Pensacola. Leaving one of his officers there as military governor, Jackson returned home.

Spain, outraged, demanded that Jackson be punished and that the forts be restored. In a cabinet meeting held by President Monroe, Secretary of State John Quincy Adams staunchly upheld Jackson's action (he was the only member to do so) and finally prevailed upon Monroe to dispatch a stern note to Spain. Afraid that impetuous Americans might next invade Mexico,

Spain ceded Florida to the U.S. for $5 million in February, 1819. Jackson was appointed first American governor of the new territory. But an economic depression, the Panic of 1819, and lean times on his cotton plantations forced him to return to the Hermitage.

After his return from Florida, Jackson disavowed any further interest in public life, but he reckoned without the machinations of certain of his Tennessee friends who were determined to push him into the presidential race of 1824. This group of political schemers, some of whom would later belong to Jackson's famed Kitchen Cabinet, included Senator John H. Eaton, John Overton, William Berkeley Lewis, Congressman Felix Grundy, and newspaper editor George Wilson, among others. In July, 1822, the Nashville Junto, as the group came to be called, placed before the Tennessee legislature a resolution calling for the nomination of Andrew Jackson as a candidate for President of the United States. It passed unanimously. Jackson, however, refused to acknowledge the nomination publicly, and privately he wrote: "I have no desire, nor do I expect ever to be called to fill the Presidential chair, but should this be the case . . . it shall be

without exertion on my part." The Nashville Junto, undaunted by their candidate's unenthusiastic response, continued to work on his behalf. In 1823, they engineered Jackson's election as senator, and Old Hickory, adhering to his personal belief that when called a man must serve, returned to Washington.

In 1824 the country was restless and discontented. The Panic of 1819 had bred widespread dissatisfaction with the economic order of things, and sectional cleavages over major policies were becoming apparent. Nationally only one major political party remained. The Federalists had dealt themselves a deathblow by

opposing the War of 1812 and as a result had not even attempted to contest Monroe's reelection in 1820. The Republican party still existed, but was in the process of splitting into two factions. One wing eventually would be led by men like Henry Clay, who believed in a strong national government; the other would be headed by those who wanted a return to the Jeffersonian ideal of limited national government. Martin Van Buren, the powerful New York State politician and future supporter of Andrew Jackson would become a leader of this faction. But at the time of the election of 1824, these new parties had not yet coalesced.

In addition to Andrew Jackson, four men were active contenders for the presidency in 1824: Monroe's secretary of state, John Quincy Adams; Secretary of the Treasury William H. Crawford of Georgia; the brilliant South Carolina politician John C. Calhoun; and Speaker of the House Henry Clay. Three of these men—Adams, Clay, and Calhoun—favored Clay's "American System." Clay pictured an America in which an industrial East would provide a market for southern cotton and western food crops and meat. In turn, an agrarian West and South would provide a market for eastern manufactured goods. He proposed a protective tariff for the East and a system of "internal improvements" such as canals and railroads, which would lower transportation costs, for the West and South. To facilitate transactions between the sections, he proposed a stable credit system based on a strong national bank. William Crawford, who received the endorsement of Jefferson and Madison, was a states-rights man, opposed to both the tariff and internal improvements.

Jackson's position was less clear. He made no pronouncements on any of the major issues except to say vaguely that he was in favor of a "judicious" tariff. It was well known that as a lawyer he had espoused the cause of the creditor, the large landowner, and the

wealthy man in general. Yet because Jackson tended to judge a man on his ability instead of his background, his supporters were able to present him as the champion of the common man. Moreover, his popularity as a military hero prompted many to consider him above politics; the general, people felt, had no need to discuss the issues.

As the campaign progressed, the list of serious candidates narrowed. Calhoun's hopes were dashed when a nominating convention in Pennsylvania declared for Jackson, choosing the South Carolinian as the vice-presidential candidate. Crawford's popularity suffered when he was nominated by a caucus of Republican congressmen. This method, which allowed a small group of congressmen to choose the political candidate of their party, had been used in all previous elections, but by 1824, the people had come to regard it as a symbol of aristocratic power. Gradually throughout most of the West and North, the franchise had been extended to all free white males, regardless of whether they owned property, and with the extension of the right to vote had come a belief that the voters should have a larger share in actually naming the candidates. When it was learned that only sixty-six congressmen had shown up at the caucus which nominated Crawford, there was a nationwide outcry against his candidacy. Adams, Massachusetts's favorite son, gained the support of all New England. Clay, regarded as the candidate of the West, was strong in Missouri, Ohio, and Kentucky. But by far the most popular candidate was Andrew Jackson.

When the election results were added up, Old Hickory had a plurality of the popular votes but only 99 electoral votes—32 short of a majority. Adams had 84 votes, Crawford 41, and Clay 37. The election was thrown into the House of Representatives. Clay, with the lowest number of electoral votes, was eliminated but was in a position to decide the winner. After a

long talk with Adams, who supported many of the Kentuckian's ideas, Clay threw his support to the New Englander. Adams was elected on the first ballot, with Calhoun, who had the support of both the Jackson and Adams forces, as Vice President.

Soon after his inauguration, Adams appointed Clay secretary of state. Immediately Jackson's followers charged that a "corrupt bargain" had been made at the Adams-Clay talk. This accusation would haunt Adams throughout his administration and would become the Jacksonians' slogan for the campaign of 1828.

By the time of the congressional elections of 1826, Adams's supporters had come to be called National Republicans, while his opponents, consisting primarily of supporters of Jackson, Calhoun, and Crawford, now formed the Democratic Republican party. Under the leadership of Martin Van Buren, the Democratic Republicans captured control of the House of Representatives and proceeded to bring about the President's downfall.

In 1828, the Democratic Republicans led by Van Buren concocted a tariff which they hoped would help them pose as friends of both the North and the South. Its schedule of duties was so high that the Jacksonians believed not even New Englanders would vote for it. To their surprise, this Tariff of Abominations passed both the House and Senate and was signed into law

"Black Dan" Webster rises before the Senate in G.P.A. Healy's painting of the 1830 Webster-Hayne debate. Deploring nullification, Webster cried, "Liberty *and* Union, now and forever, one and inseparable!"

by Adams, who thereby also signed his political death warrant in the South. The tariff would become one of the major issues of the campaign of 1828, and southern states-right support would go to Jackson even though his supporters had originally proposed the tariff.

Above all else, the presidential campaign of 1828 marked a new high in vindictive personal abuse. Jackson's supporters charged Adams with corruption and labeled him a spendthrift and a monarchist. Some of Adams's followers, however, went far beyond the limits of accepted political abuse when they accused Jackson and his wife of having knowingly lived in adultery.

Such vehemence fired the popular imagination. In 1824 only 360,000 votes had been cast for presidential electors; four years later no less than 1,155,000 men cast their ballots, of which Adams received 508,000 to Jackson's 647,000. But Jackson's political machine had created a far wider base of support, and its candidate received 178 electoral votes to Adam's 83. John Calhoun was returned to the vice presidency.

The Jackson forces were exultant. But two months before the inauguration their leader was crushed by the death of his wife. For the rest of his life Jackson held the campaign, and its calumnies, largely responsible for Rachel's death.

Unlike his predecessor, Jackson entered office without any definite program to lay before Congress. In-stead, he brought with him a deep belief in his kinship with the people. Martin Van Buren later summarized Jackson's attitude in these terms: the President felt that the people were his "blood relations—the only blood relations he had . . . [he believed that] to labor for the good of the masses was a special mission assigned to him by his Creator. . . ."

This belief led Jackson to develop a principle of executive supremacy. In his opinion, the President alone was elected by all the people, and therefore, he alone was the chief instrument of their will. Jackson, moreover, was the first President to make full use of the chief executive's constitutional power to participate in the making—or better yet the unmaking—of laws. During his two terms, Jackson, who came to regard Congress as the home of "aristocratical establishments" such as the National Bank and himself as the people's only protection against such "interests," would veto more legislation than all the former Presidents combined.

Jackson's policy in relation to the civil service was consistent with his view of the presidency as an instrument of the people's will. He recommended a system of rotation in office to nullify the idea that "office is a . . . species of property and government . . . an engine for the support of the few at the expense of the many." He advocated the passage of a law to limit most appointments to four years. It was not passed, but Jackson's men did so well in finding rewards for loyal party workers that "the spoils system," as rotation in office came to be called, soon became one of the leading issues in American politics.

Also consistent with his view of the presidency was Jackson's use of close personal friends as political advisers. Members of his inner circle, known as the Kitchen Cabinet, included Martin Van Buren, who was the only man to remain both a member of this group and the regular cabinet; John H. Eaton, who also served as

227

secretary of war for a short while; and William Berkeley Lewis. To this group were added two brilliant polemicists, Amos Kendall and Frank Blair, both newspapermen by trade. These two provided the main intellectual thrust to Jackson's administration. Another close ally of the new President was Andrew Jackson Donelson, one of Old Hickory's nephews. With Rachel's death, Jackson called upon Donelson's young wife Emily to perform the social functions of First Lady; her inability to keep Washington society in line was to present the Jackson administration with its first crisis, the Eaton Affair (see box at right).

Eventually this social problem turned political. The urbane secretary of state, Martin Van Buren, had no qualms about accepting the Eatons' invitations and soon earned Jackson's gratitude for sponsoring the couple socially. Vice President Calhoun, who had never been an enthusiastic supporter of Jackson, became head of the anti-Eaton faction. Jackson soon began to measure the loyalty of his advisers by the Eaton Affair, seeing Van Buren as his champion and Calhoun as his enemy. Finally Van Buren, realizing that the affair was making the government appear ludicrous, resigned as secretary of state and convinced Eaton to do the same. Soon thereafter Jackson asked three of the remaining four cabinet members to resign, but for somewhat different reasons. They were supporters of John C. Calhoun, and Jackson and the Vice President were rapidly diverging on the most basic of issues—the powers of the federal government.

The struggle between Jackson and Calhoun over the extent of the federal government's power arose in connection with the Tariff of Abominations.

Many southerners, including Calhoun, had once been in favor of protective tariffs, but as congressmen from the northeast progressively pushed the duties on imports higher and higher, the southern attitude changed. In 1828, Vice President Calhoun anonymous-

Scandal in the Cabinet

A cabinet fall because of a woman? Difficult to believe—until we recall the prudery that co-existed with the lustiness of the 19th century.

"If you love Margaret Timberlake, go and marry her . . . forthwith," Jackson had urged his friend John Henry Eaton of Tennessee. And when Eaton became secretary of war, Peggy Eaton became Jackson's social problem.

Her promiscuous past was no secret (her late husband had cut his throat because of her affair with Eaton). And the beauty of the 29-year-old bride was too much for the other cabinet wives. (The Brady portrait of her above was made many years later.) Mrs. Calhoun, who led the attack, ordered Jackson out of her house when he came to beg her to visit Peggy socially.

Lady or otherwise, Peggy Eaton provided lively copy: the cartoonist below imagines that Jackson has asked her to appear before the cabinet—the cabinet whose resignations she finally forced when neither President nor wives would budge.

ly published an antitariff essay, *The Exposition and Protest*, in which he claimed that the South had been reduced to serfdom by northeastern industrialists. Through the use of the tariff, he argued, the North could make the South pay exorbitant prices for its manufactured goods. At the same time, America's protective tariffs goaded Europe into levying duties against southern cotton and rice.

Calhoun realized that northerners outnumbered southerners two to one and that the North could therefore argue that a majority of people favored the tariff. But, he claimed, this tyranny of the majority could be counteracted by the constitutional right of each state to "nullify" unconstitutional acts of Congress.

In January, 1830, Senator Robert Y. Hayne of South Carolina introduced the doctrine of nullification into a debate over western land policy, asserting that each state had the right to set aside any federal law it considered insupportable. The Constitution, maintained Hayne, was a compact between sovereign states, which had delegated certain powers to the federal government and therefore could rightfully determine when that government had exceeded those powers.

Senator Daniel Webster of Massachusetts vehemently opposed Hayne, arguing that the Union was the "creature of the people." They had erected it and they alone were sovereign in it. The "God-like Daniel" argued that if a single state had the right to decide whether laws should be set aside, then the Union was dissolved and liberty itself menaced. Webster closed his speech with a passage of such eloquence that schoolchildren across the nation were henceforth sentenced to learn it by heart. "When my eyes shall be turned to behold for the last time the sun in heaven," declaimed Webster, "may I not see him shining on the broken and dishonored fragments of a once glorious Union; on States dissevered, discordant, belligerent; on a land rent with civil feuds, or drenched, it may be,

Jackson steps on Van Buren's tail (below) to keep him from running away with other cabinet members after the Peggy Eaton affair. The cartoonist also showed Jackson's "Altar of Reform" falling, his wall cluttered with resignations.

in fraternal blood!" Not "Liberty first, and Union afterwards," he thundered to a spellbound Senate, "but Liberty and Union, now and forever, one and inseparable!"

The public followed the Webster-Hayne debate with close attention. Eyes turned to the White House. Where did Old Hickory stand? In an attempt to draw out the old general, Vice President Calhoun invited Jackson to a Jefferson Day dinner in April, 1830. Twenty-four prepared toasts in favor of nullification

Powerful Nicholas Biddle (left), president of the National Bank located in Philadelphia (opposite), represented the eastern oligarchy that Jackson disdained. Biddle boasted, "I can remove all the constitutional scruples in the District of Columbia." But even his bribes did not avail; Old Hickory finally and legally outmatched him.

were on the program, and the President patiently sat through all of them. As guest of honor he would make the first volunteer toast. When the time came, Jackson stood, raised his glass, and fixing a baleful glare upon Calhoun, uttered the words: "Our Union: it must be preserved." (The toast was later amended to read "Our Federal Union," which is what Jackson intended to say.) The Vice President and his flustered supporters retained enough composure to raise their glasses, but they were staggered by what they chose to view as Jackson's betrayal. Finally, Calhoun responded with the words: "The Union: next to our Liberty, most dear."

The battle lines had been drawn. When the President departed a few minutes later, two-thirds of the company followed him out into the night, leaving just thirty nullifiers at the table.

The battle over nullification did not end with the Jefferson Day banquet. In December, 1831, in a conciliatory gesture toward the South, Jackson urged that the tariff be reduced, and in July, 1832, Congress lowered the duties. Southerners, however, were not appeased; they still felt the rates were too high.

That autumn, South Carolina called a special convention, which nullified the tariffs of 1828 and 1832 and prohibited the collection of import duties in that state after February 1, 1833. The convention further resolved that if the federal government tried to use force, South Carolina would secede.

At the first hint of trouble, Jackson had alerted the forts in Charleston harbor, sent warships to the city, and dispatched General Winfield Scott to take command in the South. Now he prepared to make a public response. On December 10, 1832 he issued the Nullification Proclamation, considered to be his greatest state paper. In it, President Jackson took a firm stand against disunion: "I consider . . . the power to annul a law of the United States, assumed by one State,

incompatible with the existence of the Union. . . ."

The Constitution, he continued, "forms a *government* not a league. . . . To say that any State may at pleasure secede from the Union is to say that the United States is not a nation." The proclamation concluded with this warning: "Disunion by armed force is treason. Are you really ready to incur its guilt?"

The more timid South Carolinians began to have doubts. To stiffen them Robert Hayne, now governor of the state, penned a counterproclamation, later declaring that he would protect the sovereignty of South Carolina or die "beneath its ruins." Old Hickory, however, had played his cards shrewdly. Not a single state came to South Carolina's support; even those in the South repudiated nullification.

But the crisis was far from over. In February 1833, Jackson asked the Senate to pass a "Force Bill," empowering him to use the armed forces if South Carolina resisted federal customs officials. At the same time, Henry Clay introduced a compromise tariff bill calling for a gradual reduction of the 1832 duties. Even Calhoun, now a senator, supported Clay's bill, which easily passed the Senate. But Jackson's Force Bill passed as well.

Clay's tariff combined with Jackson's admirable restraint averted the crisis. After the passage of the tariff, South Carolina withdrew its nullification ordinance, but to save face it then nullified the Force Act. Since the act was no longer needed, Jackson wisely ignored this final gesture of defiance.

Though relieved that no blood had been shed, Jackson had few illusions about the permanence of the peace. "The nullifiers in the south," he wrote to his friend John Coffee in April, 1833, "intend to blow up a storm on the slave question . . . be assured these men would do any act to destroy this union and form a southern confederacy." Some historians have surmised that had Jackson been led to crush the nullifiers with

100,000 men in 1833, the South might have learned the bloody cost of such policies and spared the next generation the prolonged havoc of Civil War.

Jackson's policies were often contradictory, based more on personal loyalties than on abstract reasoning. He had denied South Carolina's right to nullify a federal tariff; he would uphold another state's right to void a federal treaty. In the years after the battles of 1813-14, four Indian tribes (the Creeks, Choctaws, Cherokees and Chickasaws) lived peacefully on lands guaranteed them by federal treaty. But as the years went by, the white settlers of Georgia, Alabama, and Mississippi began to view the rich cotton lands of these tribes with mounting envy and pressured President Monroe into rewriting the treaties. During his administration, Adams investigated the Indian problem and tried to negotiate a fairer treaty with the Creeks. But he could not restrain the Georgians, who initiated a campaign of such flagrant abuse that he threw up his hands and urged the Indians (for their own safety) to move west of the Mississippi.

As President, Andrew Jackson, the old Indian fighter, implicitly supported the white Georgians, whose avarice was fanned to fever pitch by the discovery of gold in Cherokee territory. In 1830 the Georgia legislature decreed that state laws rather than federal laws would govern the Cherokee lands in their state. Thereafter many Georgians simply appropriated thousands of fertile acres, often executing the Indian owners and their families without fear of legal reprisals. When two New England missionaries named Samuel Worcester and Elizur Butler objected to such depredations, they were jailed and sentenced to four years hard labor. Their appeal was brought before the U.S. Supreme Court, where Chief Justice John Marshall reversed the conviction and ordered the prisoners released. The state refused to comply. Andrew Jackson, however, seemed unperturbed by Georgia's flagrant challenge to federal authority. "John Marshall has made his decision," the President is reputed to have declared, "now let him enforce it."

The Cherokees remained in Georgia for five more years, despite the mounting brutality of the whites. Many women and children, their men dead, their land stolen, were left to starve in the woods. In 1835 the federal government signed a new treaty that required the tribe to leave their land once and for all. Three years later troops, bayonets fixed, drove the surviving Cherokees across the Mississippi. Along the "trail of tears" as the appalling winter march came to be known, a quarter of the remaining tribesmen died of sickness and starvation.

As the pathetic remnants of once-great tribes were being bundled off to oblivion, westerners and poorer citizens in general were beset by a new, and perhaps more destructive menace: the annihilating boom-bust cycles of the adolescent American economy.

In 1816 Congress had tried to stabilize the financial affairs of the nation by chartering, for a period of twenty years, the second bank of the United States. (The charter of the first bank had expired in 1811.) The new bank had a total capitalization of $35 million (one-fifth subscribed by the government) and twenty-five directors of whom twenty were appointed by private

stockholders. The bank, in return for services to the government, would hold federal funds in its vaults interest free.

Due to inexperienced and incompetent management, the new bank was in trouble from the first. Since 1811 the federal government had transacted its business through ninety-four state-chartered banks, which held some $23 million in federal deposits. Unlike modern banks, these state institutions had the right to print their own money, so long as it was backed by an adequate amount of bullion or coin reserves. Many banks had been using their federal deposits for this purpose, and no small number had their gold illegally locked up in long-term real estate speculation. Thus when the new bank demanded the return of these deposits, many state banks were unable to comply. In an effort to pry the bullion loose, the U.S. Bank proceeded to accumulate large quantities of state bank paper and then present them to the parent banks for redemption in gold.

Such demands drove banks, particularly those in the West, to contract loans, foreclose mortgages, and in many cases file for bankruptcy. To the ordinary people, who had to surrender the farms they had carved out of the wilderness, it seemed as if the bank was determined to acquire all the property in the land.

In 1823 Nicholas Biddle, a facile and well-connected young Philadelphian, became the bank's president. Though shrewd enough to avoid the mistakes that had exacerbated the recession of 1819, he kept the pressure on the surviving state banks, often causing their paper money to fluctuate wildly in value. Indeed, so volatile had the nation's currencies become by 1828 that Jackson, in his inaugural address, warned Biddle's bank that it might be disbanded if it failed to establish "a uniform and sound currency."

Two years later, in his annual message of 1831, Jackson reaffirmed his view of the bank "as at present or-

ganized." Believing that some of the problems of state and local banks could be solved if the U.S. bank were made more responsive to the needs of the different regions of the country, Jackson sought to find a way of restructuring the institution. But despite the help of James Hamilton, the able son of the first secretary of the treasury, it seemed impossible to devise a directorate that would neither be open to flagrant political influence on the one hand, nor engage in a blind pursuit of private profit on the other.

Biddle sought to divert the Jacksonians from restructuring the bank by offering to take over the national debt—then about $50 million—in return for a recharter of the bank four years ahead of time. Jackson, however, had begun to have doubts about the neutrality of the bank in politics. It was well known that many congressmen, government officials, and influential newspapers had received low-interest loans and other special services from the bank. On the basis of such evidence, Jackson denounced the existing bank as a "hydra of corruption, dangerous to our liberties everywhere." But his advisers still could not fashion a replacement; consequently, they persuaded Biddle to postpone his push for a recharter bill until after the election of 1832, after which, they seemed to imply, renewal of the bank would be certain.

Unhappily for Biddle, however, the bank issue would not die. In 1831 supporters of the bank won a local election in Kentucky. This convinced Henry Clay that he could use the bank as a major issue against Jackson in the presidential election. The Kentuckian thereupon convinced Nicholas Biddle to ask Congress for a new bank charter before the election. Biddle at last yielded to Clay's advice, and on July 3, 1832, the recharter bill passed both houses of Congress.

While Biddle and Clay attended celebration banquets, the Jackson men, led by new Attorney General Roger Taney, prepared a formidable veto message,

232

Proud epitome of the "Five Civilized Tribes" on the southern U.S. border, the Cherokee artist and inventor Sequoya (right) created his people's alphabet. Neighboring Seminoles waged a bitter defensive war (1835-42) against Jackson's remorseless forces; in the drawing opposite the Seminoles attack an American fort.

charging that the bank made "the rich richer and the potent more powerful." This veto was to form the foundation of Jackson's campaign for reelection.

Biddle promptly dubbed the veto statement a "manifesto of anarchy" and—totally misreading the public mood—rashly reprinted 30,000 copies of the message for campaign distribution.

But Jackson had outfoxed his man. He arranged to have himself nominated, with Van Buren replacing Calhoun as the Vice President, by a device known as a national convention, which had first been used by a

"The Trail of Tears," subject of Robert Lindneux's dramatic painting below, led Indians from the southeastern states to reservations across the Mississippi. The Choctaw removal treaty stated "no part of the land granted them shall ever be embraced by any state"; yet their new land became a part of Oklahoma.

little known political party, the Anti-Masons, in 1831. Afterwards, Jackson made a leisurely trip across the country to the Hermitage, lambasting the "hydra of corruption" at every opportunity and paying all wayside bills in gold coin. When the electoral votes were counted, Jackson had 217 votes to Clay's 49.

Although its recharter had been vetoed, the bank still had four years to run. Jackson ordered all future federal deposits, which up to then had been held by the bank interest free, to be channeled into state banks. Biddle responded by tightening credit, thereby throwing the country into a contrived recession. Loans to state banks were called in, and acceptance of their paper money was further limited so that westerners and southerners could neither purchase manufactures nor move their crops to market. In seven months the

dying bank squashed $18 million of credit out of state banks. "Nothing but the evidence of suffering abroad," Biddle crowed to an assistant, would bring about recharter.

Jackson, however, remained adamant. To one group of New York merchants who petitioned him for help, he replied, "Go to the monster, go to Nicholas Biddle. . . . I never will recharter the United States Bank. . . ."

By the spring of 1834, Pennsylvania and New York had become so irked by the lack of credit that the latter recommended a state-based issue of currency. Biddle opposed this vehemently, and the public began to realize that he was the true author of the recession. In a second miscalculation Biddle reversed his policy and unleashed a wave of credit upon the nation, which further emphasized his responsibility for the recession.

Though his final victory was sweet, Jackson knew he had not resolved the underlying problem. The answer to the currency question, he now believed, was a new concept of paper money issued by the United States Treasury and based upon the bullion in its vaults.

During the eight years of his presidency, Jackson's policies frequently appeared to contradict one another: federal law was blandly violated in three states but vigorously upheld in a fourth; a great engine of financial stability, the bank, was torn apart in the name of financial stability. Indeed there seems to have been no guiding principle save one: the single-minded enhancement of the concept of a nation whose only true embodiment was the people and whose only true agent —in the view of Andrew Jackson—was the President of the United States.

Jackson wielded his power as no President before him had done. If Congress passed legislation that conflicted with his view of what the people wanted, he vetoed it. If the Supreme Court made a decision he disliked, he ignored it.

He manipulated the power of appointment so as to bring into the government men who agreed with his views. This is especially true with the Supreme Court, on which Jackson left a lasting imprint. During his two terms of office, Jackson was able to appoint six out of eight justices, and when Chief Justice Marshall died in 1835, Jackson appointed one of his closest advisers, Roger B. Taney, as his successor.

Under Marshall, whose famous decision in the case of *Marbury vs. Madison* had determined the Supreme Court's power to declare acts of Congress unconstitutional, the Court had been a powerful force for nationalism, establishing the supremacy of the federal government and Supreme Court over state governments and courts as far as constitutional issues were concerned. Marshall's Court was also a fortress of Federalist conservatism. In his decisions, he had consistently upheld the sanctity of property rights and contracts, thereby enlarging the rights of corporations. Under Taney, the Court would move toward a greater consideration of the rights of the people by widening the scope of social legislation and limiting the privileges of business corporations. In one of his most famous cases, that of Boston's Charles River Bridge, Taney established the Jacksonian principle that when rights of private property conflicted with the rights of the community, the public's right would prevail.

By the time Jackson vacated the presidency in 1837 for his protégé, Martin Van Buren, he had forged the office into a nearly invincible instrument of the popular will. At the same time he had helped build an extra-Constitutional political institution—the new Democratic party—that was to become a nearly invincible machine for electing Jacksonians to the presidency— even if they were sometimes neither the best nor the most popular men for the job. Old Hickory's decisive imprint lay upon the government, upon the party, and upon the American electorate, until all were ripped asunder by the Civil War.

Call of the West

11

The brash confidence of the whole West rang out in boasts attributed to Tennessee's folk hero, Davy Crockett. "I'm a screamer," he reputedly told his fellow congressmen one day in Washington. "I can run faster, dive deeper, stay under longer, and come out drier than any *chap* this side of the big *Swamp*. I can outlook a panther and outstare a flash of lightning, tote a steamboat on my back and play at rough and tumble with a lion. . . ."

It was the voice of a people proud of their past and eager for their future. They had breached the Alleghenies, defeated the formidable Indians of the deep forests, and opened the dark woods to sunlight with their axes. Their stand under Andrew Jackson at New Orleans in 1815 had proved for the second time, in their own minds, that England was no match for their young democracy.

Spain, too, had felt their muscle. In 1818 a force under the command of Andrew Jackson had seized the Floridas. The invaders had later withdrawn, but Spanish minister, Luis de Onís, afraid that the aggressive Americans might next take Mexico, agreed to cede the Floridas in return for $5 million. The Adams-Onís Treaty also delineated California's northern boundary as the forty-second parallel and thus shifted to the United States shadowy Spanish claims to the Pacific Coast as far north as 54°40′, the southern tip of today's Alaska. So far, so good. But then, by accepting the Sabine River as the southeastern boundary of Louisiana, Adams had relinquished whatever rights the Louisiana Purchase had given this country to the lush Texas plains that stretch toward the Rio Grande.

Movement along that frontier, however, could not be restrained for long by mere paper agreements. By putting one of their own kind, Andrew Jackson, into the presidency, the rambunctious voters of the West had at last broken (so they thought) the domination of the cautious East.

Westering was ingrained so deep in their bones that it was almost an instinct. Consider Crockett. He had been born in 1786 in a pioneer cabin in eastern Tennessee and had received less than six months of schooling. After fighting Indians under Jackson in 1813-14, he had drifted on to Shoal Creek in western Tennessee. When the district became a county, he was appointed justice of the peace, relying, he said later, not on law books but on "natural-born sense" in reaching his decisions. He did so well that his neighbors sent him to the legislature in 1821 and then to Congress for the terms of 1827-1831 and 1833-1835.

As a Whig he came into contention with his one-time military commander, Andrew Jackson, a Democrat. One quarrel arose over a proposal to dispossess certain squatters who had settled in western Tennessee in advance of surveys. Many of these squatters were employed by speculators and land companies to grab large tracts of land before the government opened the area for settlement. Speculators could then sell the land to later settlers for a huge profit. Often, moreover, they seized lands before Indian titles to them had been cleared. Other squatters, however, were merely small independent farmers who did not want to be hemmed in by civilization. No law was on their side—just custom and the spirit of Davy Crockett.

A squatter himself, Crockett knew the life that was being threatened. Personal freedom in backwoods Tennessee in those days was almost complete. The Indians were peaceful. Nature was bountiful. A man spent a minimum of effort on his farm and as much as he chose on hunting, fishing, loafing, and, now and then, cooperating with his neighbors on such chores as barn raising and butchering.

Terrified horses leap in their traces as Indians attack a wagon on the Oregon Trail. On the alternate Santa Fe Trail steady oxen were more commonly used. Bleached bones (lower right) show that despite scouts and rifles many pioneers did not survive the gauntlet.

In Congress, Crockett spoke out for those who, in his words, had "mingled the sweat of their brows with the soil they occupied." That concern, plus his droll country flavor, caught the fancy of the Whigs. Seeking a homespun hero popular enough to offset Jackson, they sent him on a tour of the East to see what the response would be.

It was by no means enough. During the upsurge of Jacksonian popularity that occurred in 1834, Crockett's constituents turned him out of office. Despondent, he and a few followers sought the standard release of their time. They turned west. In their case, in the late months of 1835, that meant Texas, or, more specifically, an abandoned Spanish mission of crumbling adobe brick known as the Alamo.

For decades Spain had feared that enemy powers might reach Mexico's rich silver mines by striking from the north. In order to forestall the threats, the Dons had sought to establish, over the course of many decades, an arc of settlements stretching from the Gulf of Mexico across the southern spurs of the Rocky Mountains to the coast of California. Earliest and most flourishing of those northern provinces was New Mexico, founded by Juan de Oñate in 1598 as a means of blocking the supposed Northwest Passage between the Atlantic and Pacific. No passage materialized, however, and another century passed before missionaries and rancheros reached southern Arizona. Then, early in the 1700s, a new threat appeared—Frenchmen descending the Mississippi. To check them the Spanish spaced six stations, including San Antonio, home of the Alamo, across southern Texas. Still later, in 1769, rumors of British and Russian activity in the Pacific led to the occupation of California.

Three elements were twined together in Spain's strategy—the presidio, the mission, and the pueblo. The presidios consisted of barracks that housed a few dextrous but poorly equipped cavalrymen, whose duty was to look after local defense. The missions, often located at some distance from the presidios, were dedicated to training nearby Indians to be Catholic workers and farmers. The pueblos, which could be formed only with government permission, were civilian settlements. The principal duty of their inhabitants was to grow supplies for the soldiers in the presidios. It was also expected that in time the townsmen would mingle with and absorb the Christian Indians turned out by the missions. In this way, it was hoped, self-supporting communities capable of deterring foreign thrusts would be formed along the northern rim of Mexico.

With the modest exception of Santa Fe and its neighboring towns in New Mexico, the scheme did not work well. Reaching Texas from the heart of Mexico involved crossing hundreds of miles of forbidding desert. Contrary winds howling out of the North Pacific buffeted the clumsy sailing vessels that tried to supply California. There were no population pressures within Mexico to push settlers northward and no mystique about land to lure them, as land lured Americans. Although the padres nominally converted, over the years, scores of thousands of Indians, only a relative few became self-sufficient in the Spanish definition of the term; the rest remained dependent throughout their lives on the missions.

The need for stronger barriers became evident first in Texas. Revolutions that erupted in Mexico in September, 1810, prevented Spain from exerting authority in the distant north. Indians raided to the very gates of the Alamo, the Mexican population of Texas shrank to fewer than 4,000 souls, and American adventurers maneuvered restlessly along the border. How, the government wondered, could stability be restored?

In 1820, Moses Austin, born in Connecticut but a resident of Missouri since 1798, rode to San Antonio with a plan. If he brought into Texas 300 reputable

South and West to Texas

Across the Sabine River, western boundary of the Louisiana Purchase, beckoned the rich plains of Texas. Land-hungry Moses Austin and other adventurous Americans saddled up.

The territory, named after the Tejas Indians, had been weakly held by Spain since the arrival of conquistadors in the 16th century. When Mexico won its independence from Spain in the 1820s, Texas seemed all the more available.

Increasing numbers of American *empresarios* followed Austin's lead and moved in; schemes abounded for making Texas a separate state. Mexico resisted, jailed the troublemakers. Former Tennessee governor Sam Houston (right) then considered an uprising with his Cherokee Indian allies. Austin's son Stephen mounted an attack on San Antonio, captured the city in December, 1835.

Now about 30,000 Americans in Texas faced the national army of Mexico under dictator general Lopez de Santa Anna. Washington offered no hint of aid (though some Southern states sent assistance). An abandoned mission named the Alamo (below), which sheltered the San Antonio task force, became focus of the rebellion that would finally give Texas freedom.

THE SAN JACINTO MUSEUM OF HISTORY ASSOCIATION

OVERLEAF:
Ammunition gone, Davy Crockett tries to beat off attackers with his riflestock. He and 180 fellow Alamo defenders—including fever-stricken Jim Bowie, who fought from a cot—perished before the assault of 2,500 Mexicans. Texas lost the battle but gained a battle cry: Remember the Alamo!

239

The Lone Star Republic

Texan independence seemed to go up in smoke along with farms put to the torch by Santa Anna's 1,400-man force in the spring of 1836.

But at the San Jacinto River, General Sam Houston saw that he could trap the Mexicans. Dispatching men to destroy an escape bridge, he sprang a surprise attack (left). Though wounded in the ankle and his white stallion shot out from under him, he led the final charge to victory.

In the painting below, Santa Anna (captured after fleeing through a swamp) surrenders to wounded Houston and companion "Deaf" Smith. Soon Mexican armies withdrew; Houston became first president of the republic beneath the lone star banner (opposite). The U.S. delayed recognition for nearly a decade, fearing international repercussions.

American families who promised to embrace Catholicism and swear allegiance to Spain, would the government give them land—plus extra amounts to him for his work?

Depending on outsiders for strength was obviously dangerous. Yet what other way was there of populating the border with at least nominal citizens? Hopeful that Austin could control his own imports, the government agreed.

Hitches soon developed. Moses died in 1821, and his son Stephen took over his work. Simultaneously Mexico won her independence from Spain. What now? Worried, Stephen rode all the way to Mexico City to press his case.

The new Mexican nation proved friendly, in part because the United States was the first major power to recognize the rebel government. After the hurly-burly of change was completed, the new administration confirmed Austin's grant and then, in 1824, extended similar privileges to other Americans who agreed to act as *empresarios*, or colonizers, for Texas.

This friendship extended all along the northern border. Three small parties of traders, fur trappers, and hunters of wild horses, who worked around the edges of New Mexico, were rousingly welcomed into once-forbidden Santa Fe and given permission to extend their activities throughout the province. Out of that welcome grew the custom of independent merchants banding together for protection against the Indians of the plains and each spring rolling their caravans of canvas-covered wagons to Santa Fe. There they swapped cotton goods and hardware for pesos, gold dust, fur, wool, and mules, which they took back to the trade-starved frontier towns of Missouri. Meanwhile, California opened her ports to ships from New England, which were eager to exchange clothing, kettles, gunpowder, and tools for mission-produced cowhides needed in eastern shoe factories. For the nation as a whole, the result of the activity was a growing body of information about the attractions of those once isolated parts of the North American continent.

Of all the attractions, land was the most powerful. In the United States a prospective settler had to buy his piece of the public domain at $1.25 an acre for a minimum of eighty acres. In Texas a Mexican citizen could buy a *labor* (177 acres) for farming or a *sitio* (4,426 acres) for grazing for only $30. Moreover, most land in southeastern Texas was suitable for growing cotton. Values, in short, were certain to soar.

The magnet attracted thousands of Americans, mostly from the South. Cultural conflicts soon sparked. For although the Anglo-Saxon immigrants accepted the Roman Catholic Church and Mexican citizenship in return for their land, they did not forget either their protestantism or their Americanism. They looked down on the Mexicans, many of whom showed traces of Indian blood, as being somehow inferior. They disliked the leisurely, juryless Mexican system of justice and resented the fact that Texas was a mere administrative appendage of the province of Coahuila to the south. The legislature met in distant Saltillo, and the northerners were not allowed enough seats to make their wishes heard.

On their part the Mexicans considered the new immigrants to be crude, untrustworthy, quarrelsome materialists. They scorned the clumsy efforts of President Jackson's emissary, Anthony Butler, to bribe Mexican officials into selling Texas to the United States for $5 million. Above all, they did not like either slavery or the loud protests that came from southern-born Texans when the Mexican government abolished the institution in 1829. How strange these *Norteamericanos* were! Only a few of them actually owned slaves, but the mere expectation that some day they might want to was enough to stir them into defying the

243

government and bringing about changes in the decree.

When the friction continued in spite of the concessions, the government sought to slow immigration from the United States while speeding it from Europe and the Mexican provinces to the south. Grim officials strengthened the military garrisons in Texas and slowed commerce by cracking down on the smugglers who brought their little ships into the river mouths along the southeastern coast. Acts of petty tyranny accompanied the restrictions. Then in the summer of 1832, an extraordinary adventurer, General Antonio Lopez de Santa Anna, seized control of the central government. To the Americans the time seemed ripe to press for a redress of grievances. In August, 1832, a call went out to all American communities, asking them to send delegates to a convention at San Felipe de Austin on October 1. The men who attended professed their loyalty to Mexico and then proceeded to draw up a list of demands, the most important of which was a request that Texas be detached from Coahuila and made into a separate state.

The Americans' request for reforms was ignored by the Mexican government; so in April, 1833, they held another meeting. This time in addition to drawing up a petition of grievances they drafted a constitution for the Texan state they hoped to form. Both documents were given to Stephen Austin, who hastened south to deliver them to Santa Anna. He reached Mexico City in July but was forced to wait months for an audience with Santa Anna. Finally, in November, the Mexican leader agreed to grant all of Texas's demands except statehood. Austin started north, but was stopped and arrested in Saltillo on charges of treason. A letter which he had angrily written some months earlier, urging Texas to form a state government even if his mission failed, had been intercepted by Mexican officials. He was sent back to Mexico City and jailed for eighteen months.

Outraged, Texans gathered to protest the arrest. The Mexican government ordered them dispersed and sent soldiers north. Then in April, 1834, Santa Anna repudiated his reform program, abolished all state governments, and declared himself dictator of Mexico. Word of these changes, accompanied by rumors that Santa Anna intended to drive all American settlers back into the United States reached Texas late in 1834. Soon Mexican soldiers arrived to strengthen the garrison at Anahuac and patrol the border. Angered, a handful of Texas radicals led by William B. Travis marched on Anahuac and forced the garrison there to surrender. Santa Anna immediately marched an army north to bring the province to heel.

The excitement reached into the United States. Armed volunteers, Davy Crockett among them, rode across the border to help. Other sympathizers in the United States sent money. Meanwhile the Texans formed a provisional government which, on March 2, 1836, declared its independence. Sam Houston was named commander in chief of the tiny army.

Before Houston could gather his forces, however, Santa Anna's army of more than 5,000 men occupied San Antonio. Defenders of the town numbered less than 200, but as their leader, Colonel William B. Travis put it, they were "resolved to make victory worse to the enemy than defeat." Taking refuge behind the stout walls of an ancient mission, the Alamo, they prepared to defend the city or die. On February 24, Travis wrote a message to "the people of Texas and all the Americans of the world," in which he stated his determination "to sustain myself as long as possible and die like a soldier who never forgets what is due to his own honor and that of his country. VICTORY or DEATH." On March 6 the entire Mexican army stormed the Alamo. Twice the Mexicans were driven back, but on the third attack they breached the walls and exterminated the handful of defenders who were

Dreams of Expansion

In 1845 an expansionist magazine coined the memorable phrase "Manifest Destiny"; by that bold ethic, Americans would "overspread the continent." Symbolically, in the November elections a year earlier a dark horse Democrat had won with the slogan "Polk and Dallas—Texas and Oregon."

Grasping Texas and Oregon may not have been quite such a national preoccupation as implied by the contemporary British cartoon below. But Polk's narrow victory confirmed the mood of the populace: no longer would sectionalist concerns restrain national ambitions.

Yet after his close victory, people still asked, "Who *is* James K. Polk?" He became known as the President who pushed the U.S. to its western and southwestern bounds.

JAMES K. POLK.
THE PEOPLES CHOICE

COURTESY OF THE JAMES K. POLK HOME, COLUMBIA, TENNESSEE

THE LAND OF LIBERTY.

RECOMMENDED TO THE CONSIDERATION OF "BROTHER JONATHAN."

PUNCH, 1847, NEW YORK PUBLIC LIBRARY

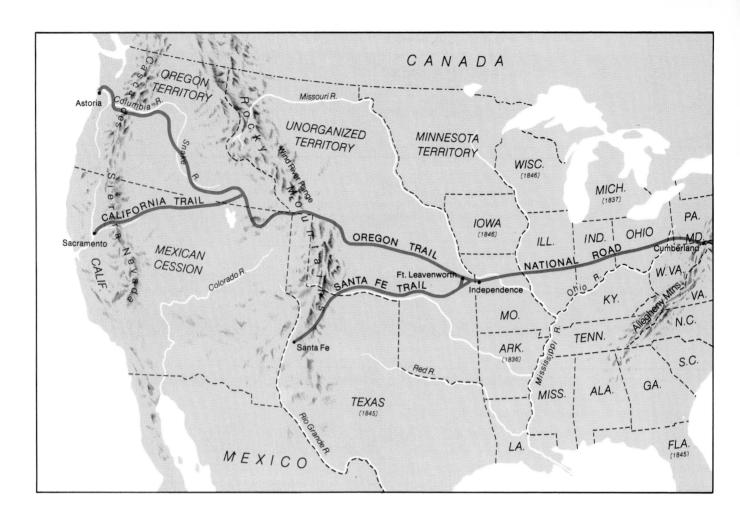

Wagon Trails of the Pioneers

"Oregon or bust!" cried pioneer families of the 1830s and 40s. First one or two, then scores and hundreds more, with wagon wheels following the ruts of others, they set out upon the 2,000-mile route from Independence, Missouri, to the mouth of the Columbia River—where survivors arrived six months later.

Yet before the Great Migration of 1843 could get under way, negotiable trails had to be found for the wagons. Early motivation for exploration of the river valleys into the mountains had been provided by the beaver: trade in fur made fortunes. Lured by Indian tales of beaver-rich glades, such trappers as Jim Beckwourth and Jim Bridger became mountain men of the Rockies.

Yet it was Jedediah Smith (below at left) who first crossed the Great Divide from east to west. In 1824 Smith—who once survived a head-in-mouth encounter with a grizzly—found a way over the Wind River range and used it as a gateway for trapping expeditions in the interior.

Other explorers opened routes through old Spanish territories to California and Mexico (map above). Reproduced below is a view of the Santa Fe Trail, taken from the notebooks of surveyor Joseph C. Brown. He carefully sketched water sources and such features as "Rabbit Ears" hills for the aid of travelers. Neither map nor waterhole helped Jed Smith's 1831 trip on the Santa Fe; the Comanches got him.

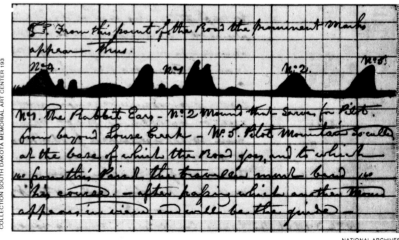

still alive. Travis and Davy Crockett were among the last to die. The rallying cry "Remember the Alamo" swept across Texas and brought hundreds of Texans out to revenge the slaughter.

Not long after, another American setback occurred at Goliad, where more than 300 Texans were killed. Refugees streamed in panic toward the Louisiana border. Houston's army of 700 men retreated behind them as far as the San Jacinto River. There, on April 21, the Texians (as they spelled the word) turned and caught the overconfident Mexicans by surprise. During a fifteen-minute battle they killed 630 of the enemy and captured 760, including Santa Anna. He was released on his promise to press independence on the Mexican Congress. Later, claiming duress, he repudiated the bargain. Mexico, however, was too beset by foreign difficulties and internal discord to make any immediate attempt to recover the lost province.

Exuberantly the voters of the new republic declared in favor of annexation to the United States. To their astonishment they were rejected. Many northern Whigs were convinced that Jackson, a crony of Houston's, had fomented the rebellion so as to add another state to those controlled by the Democrats. Abolitionists suspected a plot to extend slavery. New England businessmen, sorely hurt by a growing economic depression, feared that annexation would bring war with Mexico. Because of these obstacles, the most that the Republic of Texas could gain from the United States was official recognition.

Texas was on her own now, tormented by Indian wars, threatened by a hostile neighbor to the south, and beset by a chronically empty treasury. Her only resource was land. Her officials threw it open to claiming, and during the next few years some 100,000 persons flocked in from the United States and Europe to take advantage of that ever-beckoning New World hope.

Turmoil succeeded turmoil. In 1842 Mexican raiders captured San Antonio and precipitated another panic. When Texians struck back both at Mexico proper and at New Mexico, the results were disastrous. Harried by persistent bad luck and a continuing financial crisis, Sam Houston, president of the republic, began maneuvering with increased urgency for annexation. In 1844 sentiment in America finally veered in his favor.

There were several reasons for the shift. America was growing rapidly, both through natural increase and immigration. The overflow of people filled the states and territories immediately west of the Mississippi, and railroads began inching over the Alleghenies. Pressure for space seemed to come more quickly than ever before, but this time when the pioneers looked westward they felt trapped.

Immediately ahead of them was an unfamiliar type of land, dry and treeless, the Great American Desert of the early explorers. Last home of the Indians, the vast stretches appeared unsuited to the farming techniques of the time. But according to rumor, the land near the Pacific was better and the climate superb. That land, however, was not unreservedly American. In the Northwest, citizens of the United States shared equal rights of settlement with the British. Southward, the Mexicans held loose sway over California, a hegemony that might not last, for it was widely believed that Britain was interested in that area, too.

As for Texas, the British definitely wanted the republic to stay independent, for then its fields would furnish England's textile mills with an alternative supply of cotton and its buyers would provide British manufacturers with a market free of American tariff levies. British humanitarians hoped, moreover, that they could prevail on independent Texans to emancipate their slaves, something that would not happen, abolitionists feared, if the republic became part of the slaveholding United States. Thus the shadow of Great Britain lay everywhere. With her influence paramount in the Canadas, in Oregon, perhaps in California, and in Texas—where could the ever-mobile, ever-seeking westerners turn?

Houston played skillfully on western fears. He let it be known that he was seeking commercial treaties not only with Great Britain but with France. Reaction in the United States split along sectional lines. The South, eager for new slave states that might restore her slipping political power, and many western agrarians, long committed to expansionism, favored annexation as a way of forestalling Houston's dalliance with Britain. Most northerners, on the other hand, were opposed to the entrance of another slave state. The cleavage over Texas shook both major parties, but in general the Whigs opposed annexation on the grounds that it might cause war with Mexico, while the Democrats lined up, by and large, on the side of western and southern expansionists.

The President of the United States, spare, stubborn John Tyler, was a Whig. He had gained his office through being Vice President at the time of William H. Harrison's death on April 4, 1841. Whig leaders, disliking their own man thoroughly, called him "His Accidency" and ignored him as much as possible. Only a popular issue could save Tyler's political fortunes, and the uproar over Texas looked like opportunity.

During the early months of 1844 his State Department negotiated a treaty of annexation with its counterpart in Texas. To become effective as a treaty the document would have to be approved by a two-thirds majority of the Senate. But when Tyler's secretary of state, John C. Calhoun, equated annexation with the protection of slavery against the plotting of British abolitionists, he alienated the antislavery North and much of the West. The treaty was resoundingly defeated.

Tyler had been right, nevertheless. Expansionism was in the air. The movement, which would dominate the mood of the country for the next ten years, had developed for many reasons. Pride in America and its way of life and government was one factor. Hunger for new lands, combined with contempt for the "lesser breeds without law," was another. Still a third reason for the growth of expansionism was fear of the foreign influence of Britain in the West and Spain in the South. Sensing the new mood, the Democratic party snatched the issue away from the unfortunate President, and began to lay the groundwork of an expansionist ideology. American-type democracy, their theme went, was particularly suited to the New World. It was therefore the mission of the United States to extend the blessings of freedom to all peoples on the continent who wished to enter the Union—voluntarily, of course, for a nation devoted to self-determination in government would not force its views on others by conquest. But if the people of Texas truly wished annexation . . .

The Whigs sought to submerge the issue. They did not mention Texas in their platform for the election of 1844. Repudiating Tyler, they chose as their candidate that master of compromise, Henry Clay.

The Democrats, meanwhile, decided to espouse an expansionist platform. At first the obvious choice for candidate seemed to be Martin Van Buren, Andrew Jackson's old protégé. Jackson, however, had said that no one who opposed the annexation of Texas could be elected President, and Van Buren, it turned out, had written a long open letter stating that it would be inexpedient to admit Texas into the Union because war with Mexico might result.

After vainly appealing to Van Buren to change his stand, Jackson switched his support to a dark horse, Tennessee Congressman James K. Polk, whom he described as "the most available man."

West to Oregon

"The cowards never started and the weak died on the way," said those who remembered the early Oregon Trail voyages. The painting above shows a fur trading caravan of 1837 halted for a parley with Indians on the sun-seared prairies; ahead lay the mountains.

Gradually forts were built and the route secured. After the climactic year of 1843 (which boosted Americans in Oregon to 1,500), the settlers determined to form a U.S.-style government. Not for them was the paternalistic embrace of the Hudson Bay Company, which sought to assert British claims on the territory and its people. Backing up the American settlers, voters in the 1844 election took up the cry "54-40 or fight!"—which meant that the U.S. should win exclusive right to the region up to that parallel.

When asked how he intended to resolve the boundary dispute, President Polk answered, "The only way to treat John Bull is to look him straight in the eye." But, in 1846 when the British backed off from earlier claims and suggested a settlement at the 49th parallel, Polk took counsel with the Senate and reluctantly agreed. The next year some 4,500 Americans arrived in Oregon.

To Convert the Heathen

One of the first two women to traverse the Oregon Trail, lovely blonde Narcissa Whitman arrived at Fort Vancouver in 1836. She and her husband, Dr. Marcus Whitman—missionary, skillful healer, and dedicated promoter of Oregon settlement— represented the westernmost thrust of the evangelical revival that was then agitating American protestantism. From their mission in the rich Walla Walla Valley they taught and served red and white alike.

But as the newly settled farmers prospered, interest in Christianizing the Indians dwindled. The Indians became hostile; when measles wiped out half the Cayuse tribe, they believed the disease a white conspiracy. On November 29, 1847, a band of Cayuse braves broke into the mission and slew the Whitmans.

MASSACRE OF REV. DR. WHITMAN OF THE PRESBYTERIAN MISSION.

249

Rendezvous Along the Trail

Mountain man Kit Carson met his Arapaho wife at one of the unrestrained fall rendezvous that trappers held with Indian colleagues. When his wife died, Carson took his beloved daughter to a convent school in St. Louis. Returning from that trip on a Missouri River steamboat in 1842, he encountered young, ambitious John Charles Frémont, the army officer later hailed as the Pathfinder. Both men appear at right (Frémont is seated); the photograph was taken in 1849 after Carson had guided Frémont on historic treks west.

By then the wild times of the mountain men were yielding to settlement and military maneuvers. Fort Laramie, once a fur trading post and rendezvous site (above) was taken over by the army: it guarded approaches to vital South Pass which took the Oregon Trail over the Rockies.

250

Nevertheless, at first it appeared that Van Buren would still be able to muster enough votes to win the nomination: a simple majority was all that he needed. Then the expansionist forces succeeded in getting the convention to adopt a two-thirds rule for nomination. There was no way Van Buren could drum up that many votes. Finally, after seven inconclusive ballots, the Democratic leaders settled on Polk as a compromise candidate. After the eighth ballot, Van Buren withdrew his name and on the ninth, the dark horse, Polk, was unanimously nominated. The Democrats then extended the scope of their expansionism to include the Oregon country as well as Texas. The result was victory, by 38,000 votes, for the Democratic candidate, James K. Polk of Tennessee.

Thin though the winning margin was, Tyler, the outgoing President, read it as a mandate for expansionism. Having advocated that program in the first place, he meant to have the fruits. Accordingly he asked Congress to annex Texas by joint resolution, which required only a simple majority for passage. The House concurred by a vote of 120 to 98; the Senate more narrowly, 27 to 25. Branding the step as naked aggression, the Mexican minister left for home. Undeterred by the implied threat of war, Tyler signed the resolution three days before his retirement. If the Texas congress agreed, and no one seriously doubted the outcome, the Lone Star Republic's stormy life would end with absorption into the Union. That done, the nation could turn to the potentially more dangerous part of the new President's program, the "re-occupation" of Oregon as far north as 54° 40'.

In insisting that American rights to Oregon extended from California and the Rocky Mountains as far as Alaska, President Polk was relying on Spanish claims that had been transferred to the United States in 1818—claims that the Russians had recognized a few years later. In speaking of "re-occupying" that vast tract, Polk was saying, in effect, that Americans had been there first. His claims were based first on the travels of Robert Gray and his sailors, who had entered the mouth of the Columbia River in 1792; next on the Lewis and Clark expedition, which had descended the same stream in 1805; and finally on the explorations of John Jacob Astor's fur traders, who had built the settlement known as Astoria on the Columbia in 1811.

The British retorted with strong claims of their own. Navigators from their country had entered the Columbia a few weeks behind Gray and had gone a hundred miles farther up stream than the American had. Canada's famed Alexander Mackenzie had reached the Pacific by way of today's British Columbia in 1793, well ahead of Lewis and Clark. British fur men had scoured the upper reaches of the Columbia and Fraser rivers in advance of Astor's men. Finally, during the War of 1812, when supplies had failed to reach Astoria from New York and capture by British warships had seemed imminent, Astor's American fur traders had sold their holdings to blustering rivals from the North West Fur Company of Montreal. In the minds of the British diplomats hammering out the Treaty of Ghent that closed the war (1815), their sovereignty had been clinched by that sale.

American negotiators refused to concede the point. They wanted to retain a good harbor for the future, in case the United States ever did extend to the Northwest. Few ports were available on the Pacific Coast. San Diego and San Francisco bays were then in Spanish (later in Mexican) hands. The usefulness of the Columbia was diminished by a tumultuous bar across the river's mouth. Only the magnificent waters of Puget Sound in present-day Washington state would serve. Accordingly the Americans refused to let the Sound go. So did the British.

Weary of the impasse, the negotiators in 1818 compromised on a Convention of Joint Occupancy: citizens of either country could settle in the area without prejudice to the other nation's claims. In 1827 the arrangement was extended indefinitely, with the proviso that either nation could terminate it by giving one year's notice to that effect.

Throughout those years the British were busy. The world's greatest fur trading monopoly, the Hudson's Bay Company, absorbed the North West Company and spread its posts throughout the disputed area. Their hunting brigades were so efficient and their hold on the loyalties of the Indians was so strong that little incentive existed for American trappers in the Rockies to try to break into the closed circle. American traders working the coast by ship fared no better in competition with the company's sailing fleet. All agreed in essence with that most energetic of the American mountain men, Jedediah Smith, when he wrote in disgruntlement to the secretary of war in 1830 that Oregon was not "jointly" occupied. It was as British as if the title deed had already been delivered to London.

What commercial interest could not do, however, missionaries to the Indians did. Aided by John McLoughlin of the Hudson's Bay Company, a handful of American Methodists under Jason Lee in 1834 established themselves in the Willamette Valley south of the Columbia. Two years later, Marcus Whitman, Henry Spalding, and most significantly, their wives—the first white women to cross the continent by land—built stations farther to the east. Of necessity all had to farm to support themselves. Partly to attract attention to what they were doing, they sent home glowing reports of the productive land. A few missionary reinforcements traveled from the East to join them. As the beaver trade died, a few mountain men settled nearby with their Indian wives. Gradually it occurred to the leaders, notably Jason Lee, that the future might lie not so much in administering to the Indians as in preparing the way for an American type of civilization.

The tides were running their way. In 1841 and annually thereafter Senator Lewis Linn of Missouri introduced bills into the Senate to fortify the Oregon Trail, extend American laws to United States citizens living in Oregon, and grant each settler a square mile of free land—all, obviously, in defiance of British claims. Because of the convention, Linn's bills failed to pass. In 1842, however, the government did order a contingent of soldiers led by Lieutenant John Charles Frémont of the Army Corps of Topographical Engineers to examine the Oregon Trail as far as the crest of the Continental Divide at South Pass (now in Wyoming, but in those days on the Oregon border). The next year Frémont extended his trail marking to the Columbia. In his reports he described routes, topography, camp sites, water holes, and such other details as would assist wagon trains along the way. Prospective settlers naturally deduced that if they went to Oregon to confront the British, their government would stand behind them.

A score or more settlers traveled west in 1841, upwards of a hundred in 1842. The next year was marked by the so-called "Great Migration" of nearly a thousand men, women, and children guided by missionary Marcus Whitman. In 1845, five times that many people were on the trail, traveling in several columns.

There was excitement at first—breaking the animals to yoke, fighting stampedes, learning camp routines under the eyes of hired guides and captains whom they elected to impose order and then defied at will. The start from the Missouri border came as soon as the spring grass was high enough to feed livestock. Wildflowers sparkled; cumulus clouds rode the wind and sometimes discharged savage thunderstorms. Then, as the wagons creaked along the shallow Platte River of Nebraska, boredom and aridity grew. Trees disappeared; meals had to be cooked over buffalo

Newcomers to California

By the mid-1840s, certain go-for-broke settlers were turning south off the Oregon Trail beyond Fort Hall. Their goal: California, reached along the Humboldt River and over the towering Sierra Nevada. Some parties, like the well-remembered Donners of 1846, lost half their number on the snowy heights. But still the attraction of California's green valleys tempted the westward wagons.

Tranquil California succumbed slowly to boisterous American

ways. Mission friars (on white horses in the contemporary scene above) and military noblemen still supervised an economy based on Indian labor. The Mexican-imposed administration—which had favored the establishment of John Sutter's hospitable ranch on the Sacramento River—began to suspect the intentions of such American scouts as Frémont and the loyalty of many immigrants.

Their fears were justified: on June 14, 1846 (a month after the U.S. declaration of war against Mexico over the annexation of Texas), a band of settlers at Sonoma declared themselves independent; their brash republic's banner appears at right.

Zach Taylor's Call to Arms

"Not withstanding all our efforts to avoid it . . ." war was recommended to Congress by President Polk on May 11, 1846. He had already dispatched General "Rough and Ready" Zachary Taylor—a hero of the Seminole War of 1835 (at left with horse Old Whitey)—to occupy the contested piece of Texas soil between the Nueces and the Rio Grande rivers (map, page 257).

The Mexicans for their part had broken off diplomatic relations early in 1845 when a joint resolution annexing Texas passed the U.S. Congress. They wanted no war with the industrialized U.S., but honor was dearer. They saw Taylor's men as an invading force and attacked, seizing or killing 63.

American blood having been shed, Polk could call for war, focusing attention on Zach Taylor's needs. Congress authorized an army of 50,000 volunteers. Though some in New England opposed the southern campaign, many patriots harkened to the call of recruitment posters (left below). The enlistees in the contemporary sketch below are learning the true horrors of war.

FROM THE JOURNAL OF WILLIAM H. RICHARDSON, 1846

254

dung smoldering in shallow trenches. Wyoming's alkali dust caked everyone's clothing, reddened eyes, dried skins. And then, as they looked across the endless sagebrush west of South Pass, a new fear quickened. Would they reach land's end before snow fell?

The pace slowed as the animals grew thinner and the way rougher—the dangerous fords of the Snake River, the weary haul over the Blue Mountains of western Oregon, the desperate raft rides through the Columbia gorge. The people of the Hudson's Bay Company helped the destitute with loans of seed and tools and then steered them south into valleys that even England was conceding to be American territory.

But where should the exact dividing line between the nations be drawn? Britain wanted to extend the forty-ninth parallel, which was the border east of the Rockies, on to the Columbia and then follow the river to the sea. The American negotiators, determined to have Puget Sound, countered with a compromise: the forty-ninth parallel all the way to salt water, with enough dip south to let the British control Vancouver Island and the potential harbors opening out of the Strait of Georgia.

Before Britain could consider the proposal seriously, expansionism in the United States flared hot again. The Hudson's Bay Company, the argument ran, would keep the Northwest a wilderness for the sake of fur trapping, whereas American plowmen would turn the land into a garden for everyone's benefit. The settlers south of the Columbia had already (1843) formed a provisional government and were asking for American jurisdiction. Therefore expansion was not aggression but—and here, in the summer of 1845, a dynamic new phrase entered the American lexicon—the fulfillment of Manifest Destiny. If England interfered, it would be at her own risk.

Fifty-Four Forty or Fight!—bellowed the expansionists as they clamored for the United States to take all of Oregon. Slogans, however, do not always reflect practicality. Privately Polk believed that there was nothing in the shaggy lands north of Puget Sound worth a war, especially since conflict with Mexico over Texas already loomed as a sobering possibility. Quietly he let it be known that since his predecessors had proposed a boundary that followed the forty-ninth parallel to the Pacific, he would accept the same shrunken area.

Knowing by then that further stubbornness on its part would bring on costly clashes with the Oregon pioneers, the Hudson's Bay Company decided to remove its western headquarters from the Columbia to Vancouver Island. At that the British government, beset by troubles at home, gave way. By June, 1846, the Oregon crisis was over, and the United States, having fit its desires to possibility, stretched unbroken from sea to sea.

Although there had been little mention of California in the presidential campaign of 1844, the motives for acquiring the province were the same as those involving Texas and Oregon: the logic of continental geography, millions of acres of fertile land, a healthful climate, and an advanced column of American emigrants eager for United States jurisdiction to follow them.

The first Americans to penetrate the area had been hide traders arriving by sea. Shortly thereafter occasional trapping brigades had found their way across the deserts and mountains; and when they returned home, they invariably left a few deserters behind. During the late 1830s and early 1840s, when the government was secularizing the province's twenty-one missions, several of these newcomers adopted Mexican citizenship and thus acquired, along with native Californios, enormous grants of land.

Paramount among the adventurers were John Marsh and John Augustus Sutter. A graduate of Harvard College, dour John Marsh had had a checkered

The War With Mexico

Ulysses Grant called it "one of the most unjust [wars] ever waged by a stronger against a weaker nation." But it would give fighting men on both sides of the Civil War an opportunity to learn their skills, and it added 500,000 square miles to the U.S. at a cost of 17,000 casualties. Though the Mexican army was longer on dash than military strength, its soldiers fought on native soil—and treacherous mountain terrain it was. Zach Taylor's and other attempts to take the rugged country from the north failed to bring the Mexicans to bay. It was left to Winfield Scott to push from the coast "to the Halls of Montezuma."

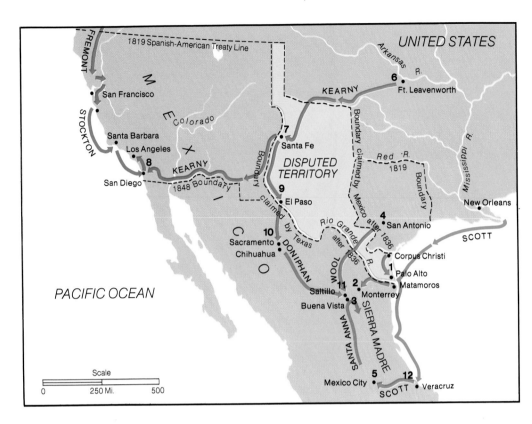

The Mexican War was planned in four phases. Despite complications, the strategy was carried out in 18 months (May, 1846-September, 1847):

Zachary Taylor's first victories at Palo Alto (**1**) and Monterrey (**2**) almost ended in defeat by Santa Anna at Buena Vista (**3**).

John Wool's drive from San Antonio (**4**) brought him to Buena Vista in time to help Taylor; thence he proceeded 800 miles to Mexico City (**5**).

Stephen Kearny's "Army of the West" campaigned almost bloodlessly from Leavenworth (**6**) to Santa Fe (**7**); he then went on with partial forces to San Diego (**8**) and helped Frémont and Stockton take California; other forces under Doniphan went south to El Paso (**9**), Sacramento (**10**), and Saltillo (**11**).

Winfield Scott smashed from Veracruz (**12**) to Mexico City to bring the war to a successful conclusion.

The Battle of Buena Vista was fought beneath the fierce heights of Mexico's Sierra Madre (below).

Scott's 10,000 land at Veracruz (opposite), largest U.S. amphibious maneuver yet.

Conquest of Mexico

The sand and rock road from Veracruz to Mexico City was some 250 miles long and passed over 10,000-foot heights. At times Scott's engineers had to hoist cannon up by rope. After bouts with malaria, enemy skirmishes, critical battles, Scott faced the final test at the Castle of Chapultepec, the summit where Montezuma's palace once stood. Fiercely defended by Mexican cadets, it fell when Thomas Jackson (later nicknamed "Stonewall") kept a single cannon firing and broke through the walls. Then the punctilious general entered the capital in triumph (left). He is seen below on a brown horse in Mexico City's main square.

career as an Indian agent, trapper, and storekeeper on the Missouri frontier. Threatened with arrest for illegally selling guns to the Indians during his time as an agent, he fled through the deserts of the Southwest to the tiny adobe village of Los Angeles. Setting himself up as a doctor, he earned enough money—it did not take much during the 1830s—to buy a newly granted, completely unimproved 50,000-acre ranch on the lower San Joaquin River. (The San Joaquin flows north through the southern part of California's long central valley, joins the south-flowing Sacramento River, and then bends abruptly west into the northeastern arm of San Francisco Bay.)

Knowing that his lands would rise in value if population grew, Marsh sent letters to the Missouri newspapers, extolling California's charms. In 1841 the Bidwell-Bartleson party responded—thirty-one men and the first white woman to reach California directly by land, Benjamin Kelsey's teenage wife Nancy, who rode and walked across the Sierra Nevada with her baby in her arms after the party's wagons had collapsed west of Great Salt Lake. Marsh let the Missouri papers know of the feat. A woman with a baby! Each year thereafter a few more people made the crossing, veering away from the easier Oregon Trail in what is now southern Idaho.

And then there was Sutter. After emigrating from Switzerland in 1834 to escape being jailed for debt, he tried his hand unsuccessfully in the Santa Fe trade and then traveled to the Northwest in 1837 with a party of missionaries. A Hudson's Bay Company ship took him to Hawaii. There he recruited three white followers and hired several devoted Kanaka laborers. With them he sailed to California via Alaska and in 1838 won a land grant in the lower Sacramento Valley by promising to introduce Swiss colonists after the fashion of the *empresarios* of Texas.

Aided by Indians, over whom he exerted magnetic influence, he built a huge fort, nucleus of his wilderness empire. No Swiss appeared. But American pioneers did. Sutter's Fort was the handiest settlement on the west side of the difficult Sierra passes, and most immigrants paused there to get their bearings. By 1845 the establishment was the psychological center of restless immigrants scattered throughout the lower San Joaquin and Sacramento valleys and on around the northern rim of San Francisco Bay.

California politics grew increasingly chaotic. Factions struggled for power. Governors appointed by Mexico City were blown hither and yon by excited marchings and battles that consisted mostly of sonorous proclamations. Any outside power that wished the province could take it at will, or so the alarmists said.

Americans in California feared Britain. Rumor said that London meant to accept the province as payment for debts owed by the Mexican government to British citizens. The opening of a Hudson's Bay Company post in San Francisco looked to some like an entering wedge. Another grave portent, it seemed, was the awarding of a land grant in the San Joaquin Valley to an Irish priest who proposed to introduce 10,000 Irish Catholics as a barrier to "an irreligious and anti-Catholic nation"—obviously the United States. In the meantime, speculation about the drift of British and French commercial activities in the Pacific filled the reports of the U.S. consul in Monterey, Thomas O. Larkin.

All this, coupled with the interest that New England whalers and leather importers had in San Diego and San Francisco bays, led President Polk to send an emissary, John Slidell, to Mexico City, with an offer to pay up to $40 million for certain disputed areas in southern Texas, New Mexico, and California. Since the Mexicans might refuse, he prepared alternative plans. Through his secretary of state, James Buchanan, he instructed Consul Larkin to assure influential Californians that the United States would welcome them into

Gold in California

It weighed a quarter of an ounce; no bigger than a dime. But the golden nugget discovered by carpenter James Marshall at Sutter's Mill on the American River had enormous consequences: it triggered the greatest surge of western migration. The discovery occurred almost simultaneously with the drafting of the treaty that gave California to the U.S. early in 1848.

As a result of the gold rush, Sutter (bottom) lost his holdings, Marshall lost his sanity. But from California's placer beds others took fortunes: miners at a location called Carson Hill produced $2,800,000 in ten months. Gradually techniques of gravel washing improved; in the

MARRIED MUM ? **NO SIR!**

painting above, the big wheels on the North Yuba River feed water into "long tom" troughs.

Such a flood of emigrants to California left the East that a town like Plymouth, Massachusetts, lost a fifth of its male voters by mid-January, 1849. The forty-niners settled in boom towns lacking safe whiskey, real justice, and good women. In the cartoon at top, miners hear the hoped-for response: No, sir, the lady is not yet married.

260

the Union if they chose to come. And finally, there was the mysterious case of John C. Frémont.

In the spring of 1845, Frémont headed west again, ostensibly to explore immigrant trails into California. With him he took sixty heavily armed soldiers, trappers, and Delaware Indians—a stronger force, the authorities in California felt, than was needed for so routine a mission. Because of his blustering they ordered him out of the province. He had barely crossed the border into Oregon, however, when he was overhauled on May 6, 1846, by a special courier from Washington, naval lieutenant Archibald Gillespie.

To this day no one knows what dispatches Gillespie carried. In any event, Frémont turned back into the Sacramento Valley. There he found the American settlers highly agitated over rumors that persons without valid passports, and that meant most of them, were to be expelled. In reaction certain hotheads, acting without Consul Larkin's knowledge, were calling for revolution. Encouraged by Frémont (who, however, did not join them), thirty of the rebels captured the village of Sonoma, its recently abandoned presidio, and the presidio's former commander. Hastily manufacturing a flag emblazoned with a shapeless animal they claimed was a bear, the rebels then proclaimed the Republic of California.

Larkin, his own peaceful maneuverings undercut, was dismayed. All turned out to be irrelevant, however. On July 28, 1846, U.S. naval vessels put into Monterey harbor with word that the United States and Mexico were at war and that California was being occupied by right of conquest, regardless of whose revolution had been most in accord with Washington's original script.

A skillful opportunist always, Frémont enrolled his own men and many of the Sacramento Valley settlers into what he called the California Battalion. This small army, acting in conjunction with the American naval squadron, then occupied the other principal towns in the province. By the end of August, 1846, California was safely in American hands—or so it seemed.

When it annexed Texas in 1845, the United States also annexed the new state's quarrel with Mexico about the southern boundary. The Mexicans insisted that even if Texas were independent, which they refused to admit, the boundary would be the Nueces River. The Texans pointed instead to the Rio Grande. As we have seen, Polk sought to bolster the American contention by offering, through John Slidell, $40 million for the disputed strip, plus New Mexico and California. Simultaneously, General Zachary Taylor was ordered to drop a broad hint by taking a small force first to the south bank of the Nueces and later, in February, 1846, to the Rio Grande.

The Mexican government refused to receive Slidell. To the impatient Polk this rudeness, coupled with Mexico's failure to pay debts owed certain American citizens, constituted grounds for war. As he was preparing a message to Congress outlining his stand, a courier arrived from Taylor with better justification. On April 25, Mexican cavalry had crossed the Rio Grande and had killed or captured every man of an American patrol. Belligerently Polk redrafted his message: war existed by act of Mexico.

Taylor meantime soundly defeated a Mexican army that crossed the Rio Grande to attack him. Then, fording the river himself, he seized the town of Matamoras. There he settled down in the sledgehammer heat of summer to wait for orders from Washington.

The first plan was to seize northern Mexico and use the territory as a lever for, as the pet phrase of the time became, "conquering a peace." Naval squadrons already in the Pacific were ordered to California, where they were to be joined by dragoons dispatched overland through New Mexico under General Stephen Watts Kearny. Two columns were to drive simultaneously south from Texas: General J. E. Wool toward Monclova and Taylor toward Monterrey.

Problems were formidable. Although enlistment quotas were oversubscribed in southern and western states, they lagged in the Northeast, where "Polk's War" was regarded at worst as a plot to extend slavery and at best as a Democratic scheme to reduce the power of the Whigs. Tropical diseases killed hundreds of recruits in unsanitary camps along the Rio Grande. Information about and transportation facilities into the deserts of northern Mexico were almost non-existent. Uprisings in supposedly conquered California drove the startled Americans out of the southern part of the province.

Triumphs nonetheless followed swiftly. A prodigious summer march carried Kearny's dragoons and volunteers to Santa Fe, which they occupied bloodlessly on August 18, 1846. From there Kearny marched on with part of his force to California. Although Mexican lancers hit him hard at San Pasqual, he linked up with the American contingent at San Diego and soon reconquered California. At the same time General Wool was plodding south through Monclova to Parras. From there he swung east to join Taylor, who had taken Monterrey in September and then, sorely hurt, had limped on to Saltillo, capital of Coahuila province.

In spite of the losses, the Mexicans showed no disposition to make peace. Worse, the Whigs were booming Taylor for the presidency. Polk's Democrats accordingly shifted strategy. After ordering Taylor onto the defensive, they gave his best men to General Winfield Scott, who was preparing to seize the Gulf port of Veracruz as the first step in a drive to Mexico City. In a bold counterstroke General Santa Anna fell on Taylor's outnumbered forces on February 22, 1847, at a place called Buena Vista, south of Saltillo. Taylor beat him back with severe losses. Scott then captured Veracruz and during the summer of 1847 pushed against dogged resistance into Mexico City.

The formal end came February 2, 1848, with the signing of the Treaty of Guadalupe Hildago. In return for $15 million and the assumption of private American claims against the Mexican government, Mexico confirmed the Rio Grande as the boundary with Texas and ceded to the United States much of today's Colorado and all of Utah, Nevada, New Mexico, Arizona and California.

Manifest Destiny! By the time the treaty was executed, a vanguard of Mormon pioneers, seeking a haven in what they supposed would be Mexican territory, had founded Salt Lake City and had started tilling the fertile lands of central Utah, a blessed oasis for migrants bound to California. Soon the number of travelers would pass all expectations, for less than two weeks before the execution of the treaty of peace a carpenter named James Marshall, busy building a sawmill for Sutter in the foothills of the Sierra, discovered gold. The word spread with unbelievable speed, and soon one of the greatest folk migrations of history was gathering momentum.

At once, sleepy California leaped into the Union as a full-fledged state. The territories of Oregon and Washington prospered by providing supplies. Prospectors trained in the Sierra Nevada fanned out through the mountainous West, made new discoveries, and quickened the settlement of the last empty spaces. That was one part of destiny. There was another. It had been inherent in the westward surge ever since the Davy Crocketts of the nation, eager for the promises held out by the virgin land, had first listened to the call of the unknown. How big could a country racked by the animosities born of slavery grow before it split completely apart?

John Brown's Body

12

On March 4, 1850, the Sentinel of the South, John C. Calhoun, old and mortally ill, entered the Senate chamber to deliver his final speech. An angry indictment of the North's attitude toward slavery and the South, it threatened the nation with Southern secession unless the government admitted slavery to the western territories, unless the North granted the South equal rights, unless the North gave up even criticizing the institution of slavery. Their parting, said the fiercely defiant Calhoun, should preferably be peaceful, but if it could not be done in peace, "Then we shall know what to do."

Gradually, inexorably, the issue of slavery had split the nation in two. Although a few statesmen had repeatedly tried to reconcile the differences of the North and the South, by the time of Calhoun's speech hardly any middle ground remained. Yet there had been a time when the bondage of black people seemed destined to disappear. During the hot summer of 1787, when the men at Philadelphia had worked to create the Constitution, there had been bitter opposition to slavery. It had already been abolished or was on the way out in most Northern states, and the slave trade had been forbidden in every state but two from New England south to Virginia. Only South Carolina and Georgia, whose rice fields demanded—and killed—large numbers of blacks, insisted on continuing the slave trade and refused to enter a union that forbade it. And so the Founding Fathers compromised, as they did so many times, and permitted the importation of slaves—but only until 1808.

In spite of the compromise many Americans, including such slave-owning Southerners as George Washington, Thomas Jefferson, and George Mason, believed

that slavery was doomed. The reasons for the change in Southern attitudes over the ensuing years were complex, involving such intangibles as regional pride and a defensive attitude toward outside criticism. But one major reason for the change was economic. In 1793 Eli Whitney invented the cotton gin, making it profitable to grow short fiber upland cotton, a crop which quickly exhausted the soil and sent growers westward in search of new lands. From a beginning in South Carolina and Georgia, cotton culture spread throughout the lower South, in time reaching into Alabama, Mississippi, Tennessee, Arkansas, and eventually Texas. The cultivation of cotton also required a large work force, and in the opinion of most planters, the only way that problem could be solved profitably was through the continued use of slaves.

Fear was another compelling reason for the South's change in attitude. In 1822 Denmark Vesey, a free Negro, planned to raise an army of slaves and take over Charleston. Before he could do so, he was betrayed by one of his men. In 1831 a group of slaves led by Nat Turner, a fanatic who claimed to be guided by voices from heaven, slaughtered fifty-seven whites in Southampton County, Virginia, and sent an even deeper chill through the slave-owning states. Blacks were dangerous, not to be trusted; blacks could not possibly be freed and permitted to become neighbors to whites, Southerners told each other. Increasingly stringent laws were enacted to control both slaves and free Negroes: it became illegal to teach a slave to read and write; curfews were established for Negroes; night patrols were organized to insure that no slave without a pass was abroad during the dark hours. In North Carolina, a law was passed to prevent free Negroes from leaving the state and returning at will.

Where first the South had been apologetic and argued that it would like to abolish slavery but could not, it gradually came to defend the institution as an

Arms swept wide to embrace the nation in his antislavery cause, fiery-eyed fanatic John Brown raises the wild wind of the Civil War. John Steuart Curry's mural at the Kansas state capitol shows Brown with his rifle in one hand, his Bible in the other.

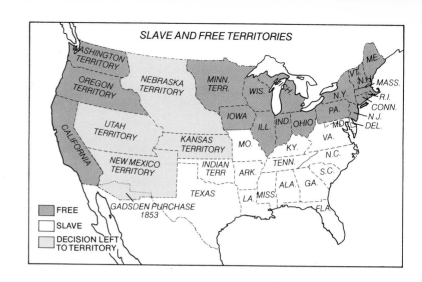

SLAVE AND FREE TERRITORIES

FREE
SLAVE
DECISION LEFT TO TERRITORY

arrangement ordained by Providence, a system that contributed to the well-being of the black man as well as the white. Calhoun wrote, "We of the South will not, cannot surrender our institutions. To maintain the existing relations between the two races, inhabiting that section of the Union, is indispensible to the peace and happiness of both."

The South did its best to draw a picture of a gracious plantation chivalry, where Massa and Mistress ruled benignly over a feudal world where crinolined belles and their beaus danced through the night while carefree Sambo and Dinah, still fresh after a day in the cotton fields, were joining in the revels down in the slave quarters. It was not quite that way, but Southerners liked to pretend it was and spent much time and effort contriving elaborate defenses of their system. George Fitzhugh, a leading apologist for slavery, included this paragraph in his *Sociology of the South:*

> Until the last fifteen years, our great error was to imitate Northern habits, customs and institutions. Our circumstances are so opposite to theirs, that whatever suits them is almost sure not to suit us. Until that time, in truth, we distrusted our social system. We thought slavery morally wrong, we thought it would not last, we thought it unprofitable. The abolitionists assailed us; we looked more closely into our circumstances; became convinced that slavery was morally right, that it would continue ever to exist, that it was as profitable as it was humane.

Although Fitzhugh's position was hardly defensible, he had touched on a raw nerve in his mention of abolitionist attacks and the Southern reaction to them. The South was sensitive, and the voices of the abolitionists were strident and uncompromising. As early as 1817, an abolitionist newspaper had been published in Ohio, but the most famous was the *Liberator,* launched by William Lloyd Garrison in 1831.

In the first issue of his journal, Garrison demanded the immediate liberation of all slaves. Although he realized that freeing more than two million slaves without some preparation might pose dangers to both blacks and whites, he denounced the concept of gradual abolition as a "sentiment . . . full of timidity, injustice, and absurdity."

"I will be as harsh as truth and as uncompromising as justice," he wrote. "I am in earnest—I will not equivocate—I will not excuse—I will not retreat a single inch —and I WILL BE HEARD." And indeed he was. Although at the end of its first three years the *Liberator* had only four hundred subscribers, it had gained a national reputation for impassioned invective and vitriolic indictments of Southern slaveholders.

Garrison's rapid climb up the ladder of notoriety was due largely to his skillful manipulation of the press. By mailing copies of his journal to Southern newspapers, he triggered a chain reaction of public comment that spread across the nation. Southern editors angrily reprinted his editorials to show that the North was trying to rob the South of its heritage; then Northern newspapers reprinted the Southern comments and added editorials of their own. Garrison soon became the most celebrated—and hated—of all abolitionists. One Southern newspaper accused him of "poisoning the waters of life" of the American community. Another, the South Carolina *Free Press,* claimed that Garrison was sending "secret agents" to the South to foment slave rebellions and suggested that if any such traitors were found they should be roasted alive. The Georgia legislature offered $5,000 for his arrest.

Although the abolitionist movement gradually gained thousands of adherents, at first it was nearly as unpopular in the North as it was in the South. Early speakers for the movement were bombarded by "harsh words . . . stale eggs . . . brick-bats and tar." After one meeting, William Lloyd Garrison was seized by a Bos-

Vainly seeking to hold slave and free states together, Henry Clay (foreground below) urges his 1850 compromise on the Senate. By his plan, the newly won western lands would be split: California admitted as a free state, New Mexico and Utah to make their own decisions (map opposite). President Zachary Taylor, who had opposed the compromise, then died; the bill was passed under successor Millard Fillmore's approval.

ton mob and paraded around the city with a rope around his neck; he was eventually released shaken but not seriously harmed. Not so fortunate was Elijah Lovejoy, in whom the abolition movement found its first martyr. Lovejoy was a bigot as well as an abolitionist and used his *Observer* in St. Louis to attack Catholics as zealously as he did slaveholders. After a mob wrecked his office, he moved across the river to Alton, Illinois, where his presses were destroyed three times. When in 1837 Lovejoy and a group of his followers attempted to defend a newly arrived fourth press, he was shot and killed. Revulsion against the mob action and the killing gained new supporters for abolitionism, but it would still be a number of years before the movement would be generally accepted.

Moreover, despite the spread of abolitionist sentiment, there was no great warmth for the Negro in the North. Although the free states disliked slavery, most of them restricted the voting of their own free Negroes and in other ways treated them as second-class citizens. When a woman named Prudence Crandall opened a school for Negro girls in a small Connecticut community, townspeople wrecked the building and ended the project. A man who attempted to open a school for blacks in Canaan, New Hampshire, fared no better; villagers hitched oxen to his school building and hauled it into a swamp. At the same time, there were many people in the North who risked their lives to help free the slave; the operations of the Underground Railroad brought a great many slaves out of the South at considerable hazard and no personal gain to helpful whites along the way.

Thus at the outset, many Northerners were perfectly content to let slavery exist in Southern states provided

267

it was not imposed on the free states. But the slave states wanted more; they demanded a stifling of all criticism everywhere. Among the most flagrant of their acts was the passage of so-called "gag resolutions," beginning in 1836, in the House of Representatives. The gag rules, which declared that any petitions "relating in any way to slavery" should be tabled, unread, were passed after abolitionist societies began sending Congress petitions to end the slave traffic in the District of Columbia. Former President John Quincy Adams, who had returned to Washington as a Massachusetts congressman, considered the gag rules a threat to freedom of speech and fought them session after session. Finally in 1845 public opinion in the North came to his support, and the rules were repealed. It was by such arrogance as much, perhaps, as by slavery itself, that the South drove the North toward a stronger antislavery position.

The extension of slavery into western territories had long been a matter of contention between the two sections. A balance of power had been maintained in the Senate by alternately admitting free and slave states, and neither section wanted that balance upset in the other's favor. The vast region added to the United States by the Louisiana Purchase had precipitated a long power struggle that was finally resolved in 1820 by the Missouri Compromise. This act allowed Missouri to enter the Union as a slave state, but prohibited slavery in the rest of the territory north of the latitude 36° 30′, the line that forms the southern boundary of Missouri. To maintain sectional balance, the act had also authorized the admittance of Maine as a free state.

The Missouri Compromise was scrupulously respected for years, but other problems arose. Texas became independent of Mexico in 1836 but had to wait nine years for annexation by the United States because

Frederick Douglass escaped from Maryland slavery in 1838, became one of abolitionism's most effective leaders. Sojourner Truth, freed along with other New York slaves in 1827, took that name to symbolize her travels "to declare truth unto people."

free-state senators objected to the entrance of another slave state. The dust of Texas had scarcely settled when war with Mexico was declared; at its end in 1848 the huge southwestern corner of the United States had been added, from the Continental Divide to the Pacific. Meanwhile, during the war President Polk had negotiated with Great Britain a settlement of the status of the Oregon country, adding to the nation the great Pacific Northwest, an area that contained five future states or parts of states.

It was not easy to work out agreements for the regulation of slavery in the new lands. Oregon Territory was finally organized without slavery in 1848 because two Southern senators voted with their Northern colleagues, but debate over the region taken from Mexico dragged on for more than two years after the war. Actually, the first indication of the ensuing controversy had come during the war when President Polk had asked Congress for $2,000,000 with which to conclude peace by offering to buy California. David Wilmot, a Pennsylvania congressman, attached an amendment to the appropriations bill prohibiting slavery in any territory acquired from Mexico. The Wilmot Proviso, as it was called, was not passed; but during the long debates that followed, the South developed completely new theories about the relationship between Congress, slavery, and the territories.

It was Senator John C. Calhoun, idol of the South, the shining advocate of states' rights, the great nullifier whom Andrew Jackson had once faced down, who bent doctrine to fit the occasion. For many years, the clause in the Constitution which states that Congress has the power to "make all needful rules and regulations respecting the territory or other property belonging to the United States" had been interpreted as giving Congress the right to admit slavery into a territory or to exclude it. The Missouri Compromise of 1820 had been based on this interpretation. But according

CULVER

to Calhoun, Congress had exceeded its rights when it barred slavery from the northern half of the Louisiana Territory. The term "United States" as used in the Constitution, he claimed, was only a phrase, for that document had been drawn up by delegates representing the separate states; so when the Constitution says "United States" it really means the States United. The territories, then, belonged to one state as much as to any other, and every state had a right to the protection of its citizens' property, including slaves, in any territory. Hence, Calhoun's reasoning continued, the Missouri Compromise was unconstitutional because it prohibited slavery in part of a territory, and, of course, any attempt to keep even part of the new regions west of the Rockies free of slavery would likewise be unconstitutional.

Calhoun's extreme and uncompromising stand was matched by that of free-soil senators, such as William H. Seward of New York, who insisted that every bit of the new territory must remain free. As a result of the

269

deadlock, nothing was done about organizing the former Mexican territories until California, tired of having its petitions ignored, bypassed the territorial stage completely. A state constitution outlawing slavery was drawn up and overwhelmingly ratified by the voters, a governor and legislature were elected, and the state government began operating in 1850 without waiting for formal admission to the Union.

Southerners were dismayed and Northerners elated at this turn of events. Meanwhile, other factors continued to exacerbate ill will on both sides: demands for an end to the slave trade in the District of Columbia grew more strident; chained slaves being driven in the shadow of the nation's Capitol was hardly an edifying sight for foreign visitors. Quarrels continued over free-states' flouting of the fugitive slave law; Northerners took umbrage at Southern arrogance; Southerners reacted bitterly to Northern criticism. Southern hotheads talked openly of secession, and a few in the North, mostly Garrisonian abolitionists, were beginning to agree that it just might be a good idea.

From his Senate seat the aging Henry Clay marked the disarray into which his country had fallen and was deeply troubled. From his reflections on the problem came a great compromise, an "omnibus bill" aimed at giving both sections at least part of what they wanted. The bill provided for California's admission as a free state, while the rest of the region taken from Mexico would be organized into the territories of New Mexico and Utah, with no mention of slavery one way or the other. The slave trade would be prohibited in the District of Columbia, but the owning of slaves would still be permitted. And there would be a new and tough fugitive slave law.

Clay, a Kentuckian, loved the Union. Although he was seventy-three years old and weary, he somehow summoned up strength and eloquence as he pleaded with both North and South to compromise their differences for the sake of unity. "The Constitution," he reminded the senators and the crowded galleries that had come once again to hear Harry of the West, ". . . was made, not merely for the generation that then existed, but for posterity, undefined, unlimited, permanent, and perpetual . . . and for every subsequent state which might come into the Union, binding themselves by that indissoluble bond."

Clay's arguments were effective, but they did not move old John Calhoun. The South Carolinian was a sick man when he came into the Senate chamber on March 4 to reply to Clay, and so weak that he had to have his speech read for him by Senator Mason of Virginia; but there was no hint of frailty in the words he had written: "I have, Senators, believed from the first that the agitation of the subject of slavery would, if not prevented by some timely and effective measure, end in disunion." He went on to enumerate the South's grievances: it was being kept from the Mexican territories it had helped win; states' rights were being trampled on; power had been concentrated in the federal government; and the North had seized control of that power to the detriment of the South. Clay's compromise could not right these wrongs. Slavery must be admitted to all territories—not only to New Mexico and Utah but also to California. There must be a strong fugitive slave law, the speech continued. The North must refrain even from criticizing slavery. And there must be a constitutional amendment to redress the balance of power between North and South. The speech closed with its warning of secession, peaceful or otherwise, if these things were not accomplished.

Three days later Daniel Webster rose to speak for the compromise. Like Clay and Calhoun, Webster was aging and weary. His voice had lost some of its old thunder, but his love for the Union was as strong as ever. "Mr. President," he began, "I wish to speak today, not as a Massachusetts man, not as a Northern man,

Vivid scenes from the verbose *Uncle Tom's Cabin* by Harriet Beecher Stowe brought to personal life the abstract horrors of slavery. Spun out first as a serial for an antislavery magazine, her text appeared fully in 1852—the most immediately popular book ever published. An 1853 children's edition appears below. Stage renditions (poster below right) contained a scene not in the book—Eliza fleeing across the Ohio River's ice (opposite).

but as an American. . . . I speak today for the preservation of the Union. Hear me for my cause." Both the North and South had reasonable cause for complaint, he said, mentioning Northern obstacles to the return of fugitive slaves, Southern resentment of abolitionist activities, Northern complaints that the South was attempting to extend slavery in spite of early understandings not to do so. But, said Webster, secession was another matter. "What am I to be? An American no longer? I would rather hear of natural blasts and mildews, pestilence and famine, than to hear gentlemen talk of secession. . . . No, Sir! No, Sir! There can be no secession!"

It was Webster's last Senate speech of a long career, for soon thereafter he became secretary of state. A splendid effort, it strengthened the sentiment that was now running against disunion and in favor of compromise. But though the Omnibus Bill gathered momentum in the debate that followed and seemed assured of passage, its enemies suddenly killed it by using a parliamentary stratagem. Younger hands then took over the fight, chief among them Senator Stephen A. Douglas of Illinois; they were able to guide the various provisions of the Omnibus Bill through Congress, one after another, as individual measures. Before the end of August the entire Compromise of 1850 had become law.

Calhoun did not live to see his defeat; mortally ill the day his speech was read, he died four weeks later. Clay and Webster survived him by only two years, dying within months of each other. The abolitionists never forgave Webster for calling for the passage of a

Flight to Freedom

To escape human bondage, thousands of blacks fled north each year. Many were aided by the Underground Railroad or "Liberty Line," a loosely organized group of abolitionists, many of whom lived along the Ohio River, the border between free and slave states. At considerable risk, these selfless individuals

CAUTION!!
COLORED PEOPLE
OF BOSTON, ONE & ALL,

You are hereby respectfully CAUTIONED and advised, to avoid conversing with the

Watchmen and Police Officers of Boston,

For since the recent ORDER OF THE MAYOR & ALDERMEN, they are empowered to act as

KIDNAPPERS
AND
Slave Catchers,

And they have already been actually employed in KIDNAPPING, CATCHING, AND KEEPING SLAVES. Therefore, if you value your LIBERTY, and the *Welfare of the Fugitives* among you, Shun them in every possible manner, as so many *HOUNDS* on the track of the most unfortunate of your race.

Keep a Sharp Look Out for KIDNAPPERS, and have TOP EYE open.

APRIL 24, 1851.

Riding a stolen horse, a black family heads north (below). Along the way, weary fugitives could expect shelter at Levi Coffin's Indiana farmhouse, a station on the Underground Railroad (opposite). But once in the North, blacks were not yet safe. The poster above warns them to stay clear of lawmen—who would return them to the South as stolen property.

*sheltered runaways in their homes during the day,
then guided them at night along an intricate and constantly
changing network of back roads to another stop on
the route to freedom. To angry Southerners, aid to
fugitives was deliberate theft; to Northerners it was
obedience to a higher morality.*

fugitive slave law as part of the Omnibus Bill and refused to join in ceremonies of mourning at his death.

It was the Fugitive Slave Law as passed, more than anything else, that caused Northern revulsion at the Southern system. It was one thing to have slavery in the distance; it was quite another to have it brought home, for under the new law professional slave hunters ranged through the free states, seizing escaped slaves —and occasionally infuriating Northerners by illegally claiming free Negroes as fugitives and whisking them into the South before they could prove their identity. Any person harboring or aiding an escaped slave was subject to a heavy fine; citizens could obtain possession of an escaped slave—or alleged escaped slave— simply by claiming ownership, for the Negro was denied the right to trial by jury. The power of enforcing the law was given to federal commissioners who received ten dollars for every conviction, but only five dollars if the Negro was freed. Outraged, the abolitionist Wendell Phillips claimed that this provision put the price of a Southern slave at a thousand dollars but that of a Yankee's soul at five.

The South's insistence on rubbing free-state noses in the Fugitive Slave Law had an inevitable reaction. The abolition movement rapidly gained recruits. The Underground Railroad became more active and more ingenious at finding ways of spiriting slaves over the Mason-Dixon Line and sending them to safety in Canada. Yet by and large, the free states abided by the Fugitive Slave Law, distasteful though it was. Not till later would there be widespread contempt for the law.

One who became aroused by the situation of the slaves was the wife of a college professor in Maine; the result was the most effective attack yet made on slaveholding. According to Harriet Beecher Stowe, the death scene of Uncle Tom came to her "like the unrolling of a scroll" while she was at a communion service. That same day she wrote out the episode and then

SALES BY AUCTION OF MEN, WOMEN, AND CHILDREN,

WITH HOUSES, LANDS, AND CATTLE, &c.

Husbands, Wives, and Families sold indiscriminately to different purchasers, are violently separated—probably never to meet again.

"Slavery must be overthrown!" preached William Lloyd Garrison from his *Liberator* (top), founded in 1831. Resented at first, his militant message gradually gained acceptance—and readership (his American Anti-Slavery Society had 250,000 members by 1840). Propagandists also used emotional techniques (above) which characterized both slavery and the South as immoral.

developed a novel around it, which appeared serially in the abolitionist magazine *The National Era* in 1851 and as a book the next year. That book, *Uncle Tom's Cabin, or Life Among the Lowly,* was an immediate success.

Mrs. Stowe's firsthand knowledge of her subject was slight. She had lived for eight years in Cincinnati across the Ohio River from the slave state of Kentucky, but only once, it appears, had she visited that state and then only for a few days. Moreover, conditions in Kentucky were not at all like the Deep South locale of her story. At one time during the writing she had to ask a former slave what a cotton plantation looked like.

Uncle Tom's Cabin is wordy, given to long exposition, and loaded with improbable coincidences, but it is a powerful indictment of slavery, and it had an electric effect on the nation. It circulated even in the South, despite strenuous efforts to keep it out. Shipments of the book were burned in Alabama, and a free Negro preacher was jailed in Maryland for having a copy. Yet a bookseller in South Carolina complained that he could not get enough copies, and one observer saw it being sold on a Mississippi steamboat. For all its faults, the book did one thing all the abolitionist tracts with their horror tales of slavery had failed to do; it personalized the institution. Slaves and their masters were no longer faceless generalizations but people with names: Uncle Tom, Little Eva, Eliza, Simon Legree, Topsy. During the Civil War, when President Lincoln met Mrs. Stowe, he asked, "Is this the little woman who made this big war?"

AMERICAN ANTI-SLAVERY ALMANAC, 1839

Slavery advocates wreck Elijah P. Lovejoy's abolitionist press at Alton, Ill. in 1837. Later Lovejoy was killed, the cause's first martyr. His death, according to John Quincy Adams (then in Congress), sent "a shock as of an earthquake throughout this continent."

Stephen Douglas had been instrumental in pushing the Compromise of 1850 through Congress. Four years later he became responsible for a piece of legislation that had an opposite effect, one that brought the nation to the edge of the precipice. In 1854, as chairman of the Senate Committee on Territories, he reported out a bill for organizing the vast Great Plains region as Nebraska Territory. Douglas had been urging a territorial government for this area ever since 1844, but Southerners in Congress had objected because slavery was prohibited in the region by the Missouri Compromise. In January, 1854, Douglas modified his bill; the question of slavery would be decided by the people of the territory. This principle became known as popular sovereignty—"squatter sovereignty" its critics called it—and if applied to Nebraska it would mean that the Missouri Compromise was dead.

Douglas's motives have been debated ever since. One theory is that he wanted to gain Southern support for a bid for the presidency. It is also known that he was anxious to have a proposed transcontinental railroad follow a northerly route, one that would enhance his holdings in Chicago real estate and western land. A northern route, however, could not be planned until a government was established in the country through which it would pass. Thus to get Southern support for organizing Nebraska Territory, Douglas proposed to abandon the Missouri Compromise, which Northerners considered almost as untouchable as the Constitution. But though the Nebraska Bill would have implicitly killed the Missouri Compromise, Southerners demanded even more; they wanted it stated in so many unequivocal words. Douglas, though unhappy, gave in and rewrote his bill again. This time he added another change; the territory was to be divided into Kansas and Nebraska.

When the Kansas-Nebraska Bill was unveiled, fury gripped the North. Protest meetings were held in which conservative merchants and professional men spoke on the same platform as the once disreputable abolitionists. Democratic as well as Whig newspapers in the North condemned Douglas, and the clergy united in sending Congress petitions protesting the new bill.

While debate continued in Congress, an incident occurred in Massachusetts which demonstrated the full extent of the North's change in mood. On the evening of May 24, 1854, Anthony Burns, a fugitive slave, was seized in Boston. When his hearing was convened, crowds of people from surrounding towns flocked to the city to attend. At one point they attempted to rush the courthouse and free Burns; the rescue failed, but a special deputy was shot and killed. After the hearing, it took a thousand troops to escort the Negro through protesting crowds to a ship that would return him to the South. The cost of returning this one man to slavery was somewhere between $40,000 and $100,000, and he was the last ever to be returned from Boston.

Douglas fought for his bill during three months of angry debate, and thanks to a large Democratic majority that even many Northern defections could not wipe out, it was passed. The popular sovereignty fea-

Holding a copy of his Kansas speech, Charles Sumner falls beneath the blows of South Carolina Congressman Preston Brooks.

SOUTHERN CHIVALRY — ARGUMENT versus CLUB'S.

ture in the bill, Douglas said during the debate, "would avoid the slavery agitation for all time to come." But he had stirred a stew that was already bubbling and had, among other things, hastened the split of the Democratic party. The Whig party was already breaking up under sectional stresses. An anti-Nebraska party began coalescing in 1854, drawing together a mixture of free-soilers, antislavery Democrats, Northern Whigs, and other elements. The new party, adopting the name Republican, entered the 1854 midterm elections for the first time. The resulting House of Representatives consisted of 108 Republicans, 83 Democrats, and 43 members of the nationalistic American, or Know-Nothing, party.

The competition between free-soilers and slavery men for Kansas had begun even before the debate ended in Congress. In April, 1854, the Massachusetts (later New England) Emigrant Aid Society was incorporated to raise money and recruit settlers for Kansas. Though the society itself sent only a modest number of settlers into Kansas, it did encourage a general movement of free-soilers into the new territory. It also had another effect. Rumors reached the border areas of Missouri, distorted as rumors always are, that the New England Aid Society was an abolitionist scheme to capture Kansas by force and to kidnap slaves. The border Missourians, in general a rough and bellicose crew, organized for mutual protection; a gathering at Independence formed a vigilance committee and exhorted all Missourians in counties bordering Kansas to take "action, that we may meet and repel the wave of

"Bleeding Kansas" was swept by violence in the mid-1850s as proslavery forces sought to prevent the state from voting for freedom. Their "Sack of Lawrence" was followed by John Brown's bloody revenge at Pottawatomie Creek. That produced such repercussions as the Marais des Cygnes massacre (opposite) in which five free-soilers were killed. As Kansas bled, the compromise seemed less possible.

fanaticism which threatens to break upon our border."

President Pierce established a territorial government for Kansas in the fall of 1854, appointing as governor Andrew H. Reeder, a lawyer who had never before held office. Reeder's first act was to hold an election for the territory's delegate to Congress. "Border Ruffians" swarmed across from Missouri to vote and carry the election. It was later estimated that only 1,114 of the 2,871 votes cast that day were legal; in one district only 20 of 604 were legitimate.

Except for the Border Ruffians, who were not even residents, few in Kansas were much excited about slavery. There were not many abolitionists; only a small proportion of the settlers came from Northern states where antislavery feeling was high, and fewer still came from the Deep South. Most settlers were opposed to slavery but had no missionary spirit about it. They did not much care if there were slaves in the South but wanted none among themselves. Left alone, Kansas would have gone free-soil without fuss or turmoil. But it was not left alone.

An election to select a legislature was held on March 30, 1855. Disregarding Governor Reeder's stipulation that every voter must be a resident of Kansas, the Border Ruffians once again came out in force. One group of about a thousand arrived with flags, a band, and two cannon. Senator David R. Atchison of Missouri personally led a group of about eighty, all armed. "There are eleven hundred coming over from Platte County to vote," he told his followers, "and if that ain't enough we can send five thousand—enough to kill every God-damned abolitionist in the Territory." It was more than enough; the proslavery vote was 5,427, free-soil 791—but a check showed that 4,908 votes were illegal.

Free-soilers protested to Governor Reeder, but that unhappy man had no idea of the extent of the frauds. When the men claiming election called on him to demand their certificates, he only had enough proof to withhold certificates of election from about one-third of the men; later, when he learned the full extent of the knavery, Reeder went to Washington to set the case before President Pierce. The President tut-tutted but in the end did nothing except admonish Reeder for not also attacking frauds by the free-soilers—frauds that had not occurred.

The Bogus Legislature then set about passing flagrant proslavery laws: any person who claimed that slavery was not legal in Kansas could be sentenced to hard labor for not less than two years; only proslavery men were declared eligible for office; aiding a runaway slave or circulating any book or literature that incited slaves to rebellion was made punishable by death. Governor Reeder vetoed the bills, but they were passed over his head. In the summer of 1855, Reeder's enemies were able to talk the pliant President Pierce into replacing him with Wilson Shannon, a former governor of Indiana.

The free-soilers, in their turn, held a Free State convention at Topeka in the fall of 1855. The delegates drew up a constitution prohibiting slavery in Kansas after July 4, 1857, and named Topeka the temporary capital. Submitted to the people of Kansas that winter, the constitution was approved by an overwhelming majority of 1,731 to 46. The Topeka government then forwarded the document to Congress and asked to be admitted to the union.

When Congress met in January, 1856, it was confronted with two rival Kansas delegations, each claiming to represent the territory. President Pierce, after avoiding a decision for as long as possible, took counsel with his Southern attorney general and finally sent a special message to Congress in which he upheld the proslavery legislature and proposed that it organize the territory for statehood. He then denounced the free-soil movement as being "of revolutionary character" and warned the free-staters that any resistance

on their part would be considered "treasonable insurrection."

Stephen Douglas backed the proslavery legislature, arguing that the government recognized by the President must be upheld as the embodiment of law and order. William H. Seward of New York, a staunch antislavery man, championed the free-soil cause. Debate continued in both the House and Senate into the spring of 1856. Outside Congress supporters of each side aided the Kansas cause in their own fashion. Southern men, volunteering to farm and fight in Kansas, were financed and given free transportation. In the North clergyman Henry Ward Beecher gave a sermon urging that free-soil settlers be sent forth well armed because "one Sharps rifle will have more moral influence upon slaveholders than a hundred Bibles." From then on the rifles were known as Beecher's Bibles.

There had been occasional crimes of violence in Kansas—a free-soil settler waylaid and murdered, another attacked and shot in his home—but most activity had been limited to boasts and threats. Then, in May, 1856, a proslavery grand jury indicted several members of the Topeka government for treason, among them Charles Robinson, the free-state "governor," who was seized and jailed. The jury also brought charges of sedition against two newspapers in Lawrence, a free-soil stronghold, and against the fortress-like Free-State Hotel in Lawrence.

Following the indictments, the federal marshal, J.B. Donaldson, issued a proclamation in which he asserted that a group of disorderly men had violently resisted a deputy marshal's efforts to serve a summons in Lawrence. Further resistance was certain, he warned, and called upon all good citizens to come to his aid. With tremendous enthusiasm, seven to eight hundred proslavery men, armed with four brass cannon, hastened to oblige. On May 21 they surrounded Lawrence, emplacing cannon at strategic points and stationing part

Dred Scott's Fate

Could a Negro be a citizen? No. Could slavery be excluded from a U.S. territory? No. So proclaimed the Supreme Court's Chief Justice Taney (below) in the 1857 decision against Dred Scott (above). Negroes "had no rights which the white man was bound to respect."

This shocking decision, founded on the letter rather than the spirit of the Constitution, shattered the moral authority of the Court for decades. Fortunately, Scott's owner freed him soon after the decision. But his enjoyment of freedom was tragically short; after working as a hotel porter in St. Louis for a year, he died in 1858.

of their force on a hill overlooking the town. The deputy marshal, with a small posse, entered the town and arrested two men for whom he had warrants.

There was no resistance. A committee of safety, elected some days earlier by the citizens of Lawrence, had forbidden any violence whatsoever, even warning men not to gather in groups on the street. After the arrests were made, Donaldson and several other leaders accepted an invitation to dine at the Free-State Hotel as guests of the owner and turned the "army" over to S.J. Jones, a county sheriff who had a private score to settle with Lawrence; some months earlier he had been wounded there by an unknown assailant.

Under his leadership the mob began sacking the city. Declaring that the grand jury had ordered the two newspapers to be "abated as nuisances," Jones led his men to the offices of the *Herald of Freedom*. The mob hoisted a red flag, studded with a white star and emblazoned with "Southern Rights" on one side and "South Carolina" on the other over the building. Then they smashed the presses of both papers, tossed them into the river, and destroyed all the papers and books they could find. Their thirst for violence unabated, the excited mob then dragged three cannon up to the hotel and fired over thirty shots in an effort to batter its walls down. This failing, they tried to blow it up with a keg of gunpowder and finally just set it on fire. Next they ransacked the home of free-state "Governor" Charles Robinson, destroying his furniture and library. One of the wreckers was accidently killed when a wall fell on him, but there were no other casualties.

This, the so-called "Sack of Lawrence," was a moral victory for the free-staters since it revealed their enemies as lawless and irresponsible. It also gave the Republican party the issue of "Bleeding Kansas" and marked the beginning of civil war in that unhappy territory. Popular sovereignty was not working out as Douglas had promised.

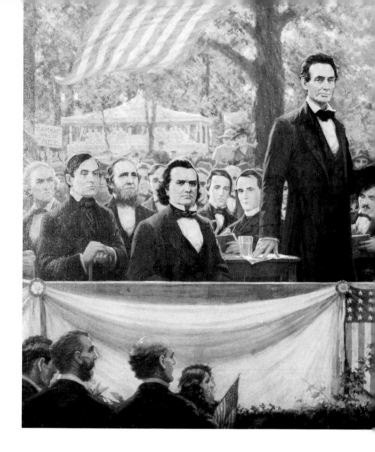

Accounts of the Sack of Lawrence reached the North at the same time as news of another event, which also concerned Kansas. On May 19, Senator Charles Sumner of Massachusetts had begun a two-day speech, which he called *The Crime Against Kansas*. Sumner was an uncompromising antislavery man, who was admired in New England as much for his commanding appearance as for his views. He was, however, arrogant, self-righteous, egotistical, humorless, and completely without taste. He had made himself so disliked by his fellow senators that many of them would not speak to him. And now, true to form, he delivered himself of a carefully prepared oration that had few redeeming passages. As he railed against the treatment of free-soil Kansas, his principal targets were Stephen Douglas and Senator Andrew Butler of South Carolina, a courteous, white-haired gentleman who was not even present at the time. Using a deliberate *double-entendre* of miscegenation, he described Butler as having "chosen a mistress to whom he has made his vows and who, though ugly to others, is always lovely to him; though polluted in the sight of the world, is chaste in his sight—I mean the harlot, Slavery." In an exchange with Douglas, he addressed the senator from Illinois in these choice words: "I will say it—no person with the upright form of man can be allowed, without violation of all decency, to switch out from his tongue the perpetual stench of offensive personality. Sir, this is not a proper weapon of debate, at least, on this floor. The noisome, squat, and nameless animal, to which I now refer, is not a proper model for an American Senator. Will the Senator from Illinois take notice?"

All who heard the speech were angered and offended and, had the affair gone no further, only Sumner's reputation would have suffered. But Butler's nephew, Congressman Preston Brooks of South Carolina, brooded over the insults to his uncle. Two days after the speech he entered a nearly empty Senate chamber and began beating Sumner over the head with a cane as the senator sat working at his desk. Brooks's assault injured Sumner so badly that it was more than three years before he could return to the Senate; during his absence he was reelected almost unanimously.

Sumner became a Northern martyr. Meetings of protest were held in Boston, in New York, in Albany, in dozens of other cities, and the news of the Sack of Lawrence, following almost within hours on reports of the attack on Sumner, brought gloomy forebodings

MISSOURI HISTORICAL SOCIETY

NATIONAL PORTRAIT GALLERY

"This government cannot endure permanently half slave and half free," said Abraham Lincoln upon accepting the Republican nomination for senator from Illinois. Then followed the famous debates with Stephen A. Douglas (above) who supported the Dred Scott decision. Folk artists were soon depicting the two politicians' contrasting shapes (opposite below).

that order and restraint were breaking down completely. As for Brooks, he was an instant hero in the South. Censured by the House of Representatives, he resigned but was immediately reelected by his district and returned to Washington in triumph.

The Sack of Lawrence had occurred without bloodshed, but blood soon flowed in Kansas. A settler named John Brown, an ardent abolitionist but a perennial ne'er-do-well, decided that vengeance must be had for the attack on Lawrence. Two days after the Lawrence episode Brown, with four of his sons—he had twenty children by two wives—and two other men, went to a small settlement on Pottawatomie Creek. There they shot and hacked to death five men and boys with Southern sympathies.

From then on, throughout the summer and fall, there was open civil war in Bleeding Kansas. Armed men from both sides roamed the territory. Free-soilers worked their fields in groups for protection, ready to grab their rifles. In the so-called battle of Osawatomie, proslavery forces attacked John Brown's headquarters; a dozen men were slain and several wounded before

the defenders fled. Men were killed in pitched battles and ambushes; houses and barns were burned; settlers were driven away. A proslavery mob took control of Leavenworth and, blacklisting some fifty free-state leaders, gave them three days to leave Kansas. Governor Shannon, unnerved by events, resigned and was replaced in September by John W. Geary, a strong and capable figure, who was able to bring order to the territory before winter set in. It was an uneasy peace, however, and Kansas would become a devastated land of guerilla warfare during the Civil War.

By the time Buchanan became President in 1857, free-soil settlers in Kansas greatly outnumbered proslavery men, but the latter still controlled the Bogus Legislature and later that year held a convention which drew up a proslavery constitution. By manipulating the vote, proslavery forces managed to get their constitution approved. Their machinations were so unabashed that the nation was shocked; nevertheless, Buchanan, in his December, 1857, message to Congress announced that the proslavery constitution was the legitimate one and urged Congress to approve it. Stephen Douglas opposed the President and, insisting on the principle of popular sovereignty, demanded a fair election in Kansas.

Two elections were held. The first, which most free-staters boycotted, was won by the proslavery forces 6,226 to 569. In a second referendum, arranged to discourage chicanery, 10,266 voters rejected the proslavery constitution, 162 accepted it, most with reservations. Once again the battle went into Congress. Buchanan's forces won in the Senate, but Douglas continued to fight, using all his powers of persuasion to convert the House of Representatives to his point of view. Finally, instead of voting on the proslavery constitution, the House passed a measure calling for another Kansas vote on the question. When a third and fair election was held in Kansas, the voters rejected the

Above: a contemporary view of Harpers Ferry; arsenal buildings are off to right, engine house (where Brown barricaded his forces) is brick structure at far left. After Col. R. E. Lee stormed the building (left), Brown—holding dying son's hand, below—surrendered with seven others. Opposite: on his way to the gallows, John Brown stopped and kissed a black child, according to Horace Greeley (who was not there). Brown died unrepentant, confident that his avenging spirit would march on.

**Assault on
Harpers Ferry**

*Long ago the quaint old village stopped keeping up with time.
Here in 1747 Robert Harper located a mill and ferry, bases for a little
industrialized community. Here in 1797 George Washington urged that
a gun factory be established (by the War of 1812 it was turning out
10,000 muskets a year). Here grew the armory that attracted the eye of
John Brown, on the lookout for weapons for a slave rebellion. Through
the covered railroad bridge from Maryland he came with his 18 followers
on the drizzly night of October 16, 1859. The war that his assault helped
precipitate soon destroyed Harpers Ferry. Walls that withstood
Confederate and Union shells fell before flood waters. Today those
battered ruins continue to evoke the past at a National Parks site.*

proslavery constitution by a vote of 11,812 to 1,926.

Kansas was still inflaming national passions when the Supreme Court delivered the historic Dred Scott decision. Dred Scott, a slave, had been taken by his army surgeon owner from Missouri, first to an army post in the state of Illinois, then to Fort Snelling, Minnesota, at the time part of Wisconsin Territory. He was brought back to Missouri and some time later sued—undoubtedly with outside connivance—for freedom on the grounds that both residence in a free state and in a territory where slavery was prohibited by the Missouri Compromise made him free. The case made its slow way through lower courts and eventually reached the Supreme Court, where Chief Justice Roger Taney, a Southerner—though one who hated slavery—saw in it an opportunity to settle for good the question of slavery in the territories. Four other Southerners sat on the court; they were joined by two Northern justices in what amounted to a majority opinion, although they disagreed on some points. Nonetheless, the majority opinion, delivered March 6, 1857, was a bombshell that blew apart existing laws and notions regarding the power of Congress to regulate slavery.

Dred Scott, said Taney, reading his opinion, was a Negro, and as such was not a citizen of the United States. He therefore had no right to sue in a federal court. Secondly, when Scott returned to Missouri he had once again come under the laws of that state, and his prior residence in the free state of Illinois had ceased to be germane. Finally his residence in territory north of 36° 30' could not make him a free man because Congress had no right to deprive a person of property without due process of law and a slave was property. By this reasoning the Missouri Compromise was unconstitutional. Even popular sovereignty was dead. There was no way to keep slavery out of a territory.

The North was infuriated. Attacks on the Supreme Court were the most bitter in history, and it was condemned for making a political decision—as indeed it had. Not for years would it recover its prestige. Legal scholars have pointed out that only on the second point, that relating to Dred Scott's residence in Illinois, was the Court's reasoning sound or an opinion even necessary. Instead of helping to settle the troubled question of slavery, as Taney had hoped, the decision had raised it to a new pitch.

Almost like a man in a trance the nation had gone from crisis to crisis, approaching ever nearer to the precipice of secession and war. Each time that passions appeared to be cooling and common sense taking over, something else occurred to nudge the country further toward the brink. In mid-October of 1859 it was John Brown, who appeared traveling down a dusty road toward Harpers Ferry, Virginia (now West Virginia), that set things awry. He

☞ THE QUESTION

IF LINCOLN

will be elected or not, is one which interests all parties, North and South. Whether he

IS ELECTED

or not, the people of

SOUTH CAROLINA

(whose rights have been for a number of years trampled upon) have the advantage of supplying themselves with CLOTHING, at the well-known CAROLINA CLOTHING DEPOT, 261 King-street, at such prices as

WILL LEAD

them to be satisfied that the reputation of this Establishment has been

BOLDLY

and fearlessly maintained

FOR A

number of years, supplying its

SOUTHERN

Customers with all the Latest Styles, and at as low prices as any Clothing House in *the present*

CONFEDERACY

of all the States.
Thankful for the liberal patronage extended, the Proprietors desire merely to inform their customers and the public generally, that their present STOCK OF CLOTHING IS COMPLETE in all its departments, and are now prepared to offer Goods on the most reasonable and satisfactory terms. A call is therefore solicited by
OTTOLENGUIS, WILLIS & BARRETT,
November 5   261 King-street.

led an army of thirteen whites and five Negroes, and his baggage included a wagonload of pikes to arm the slaves he expected to free.

Brown had fled Kansas when it became too hot for him and had gained a hearing and money from New England abolitionists to whom he apparently never quite divulged his plans. He had, it seems, a hazily conceived scheme to foment a slave uprising and create a Negro republic in the Appalachian Mountains; from there war would be waged against the slave states. His first objective was Harpers Ferry, and the arms and ammunition in the government arsenal there.

Brown and his legions struck on the evening of October 16, seizing the arsenal without resistance from its unsuspecting watchman. An hour after midnight they stopped the Baltimore-bound express train, but later, for unknown reasons, Brown let it proceed. Ironically, the first person to die was a free Negro, mortally wounded when he tried to escape from one of Brown's patrols. Brown sent out men to bring in hostages and to free slaves; they returned with two angry planters and ten bewildered slaves who showed no interest when told that they were now part of an army of freedom.

During the night the little town had awakened to the danger in its midst. Citizens took up arms and surrounded the arsenal; a company of militia arrived from nearby Charlestown in response to a Paul-Revere summons. Brown soon realized that there would be no slave uprising; he prepared for a siege by taking his men into the enginehouse, the most substantial structure in the arsenal.

Twice, as the next day dragged on, Brown sent men out with a white flag to negotiate, but the besiegers, bitter because their mayor had been slain, shot the first emissary to death and mortally wounded the second, Brown's son. Meanwhile, the telegraphs flashed fragmentary and wildly distorted stories across the nation: a Negro insurrection was reported to be underway at Harpers Ferry.

A detachment of marines under Colonel Robert E. Lee and Lieutenant J.E.B. Stuart arrived at Harpers Ferry late the second night, but nothing was done during darkness for fear of harming the hostages Brown held. After daybreak Stuart went up to the enginehouse door and parleyed with Brown through a crack. If Brown would surrender, said Stuart, he and his men would be protected from mob action and handed over to proper authorities. Brown refused, demanding that he and his men be allowed to leave and given a decent head start on their pursuers. Stuart thereupon signaled to his men, who rushed at the door with a battering ram and broke through, two of them dying before they subdued the defenders. Brown calmly knelt and fired his rifle until an officer beat him unconscious with the hilt of his dress sword. Ten of his army were dead or fatally injured, including two of his sons; seven were taken captive. The rest escaped.

John Brown went on trial a week later, though still so weak from his wounds that he had to lie on a cot. He showed an admirable dignity throughout this ordeal and refused to permit his lawyers to plead insanity, his one hope of escaping a death sentence. Convicted of criminal conspiracy, murder, and treason against Virginia, he was sentenced to death (as were, in a separate trial, the six men captured with him). He died on December 2, 1859, showing no trace of fear or remorse. Among those who saw him hanged was a twenty-one-year-old Virginia militiaman named John Wilkes Booth and a group of cadets from Virginia Military Institute with their professor, Thomas J. Jackson, very soon to be known as Stonewall. John Brown's raid and his death acted on the nation like an alarm bell. Most people in the South viewed the raid as part of an abolitionist plot, a Northern plan to destroy the slave states. There were some farseeing Southerners, however, who advised the governor of Virginia to commute Brown's death sentence instead of making a martyr of him and deepening even further the gulf between North and South.

And a martyr is just what Brown became in the North. Flags were lowered to half-mast at the hour of his death, buildings were draped in black, and church bells tolled. Though responsible men condemned his lunatic act, there was widespread admiration for his bravery and for his dignified demeanor during his trial and at his death. The abolitionists hailed Brown as a prophet, quoting these words from his last speech: "I . . . am now quite certain that the crimes of this guilty land will never be purged away but with blood." Ralph Waldo Emerson described Brown as a "new saint" who had made "the gallows glorious like a cross." The murders on Pottawatomie Creek in Kansas were completely forgotten as John Brown's soul went marching on.

The final parting of the ways had become foreseeable and almost inevitable. In 1856 the Republican party had nominated John C. Frémont for President, its first entry in the presidential race; and Frémont had made a very respectable showing, getting some 1,340,000 votes to 1,833,000 for James Buchanan, Democrat and the winner (Millard Fillmore, the American, or Know-Nothing, party candidate had received 872,000 votes). The Republican party's stand against the spread of slavery had not endeared it to the slave states, and only 1,200 of Frémont's votes had come from the South. In the next four years the party gained no favor in the slave states, for there Black Republicanism was lumped with abolitionism.

In 1860 the Republican party nominated a prairie politician from Illinois, a man who had served only one term in Congress as an obscure Whig representative from Illinois, but who had established in his own frontier community a reputation for incisive thinking and clear speaking that eventually reached far beyond Illinois. Two years earlier Abraham Lincoln had said that "a house divided against itself cannot stand." Although he would accept slavery in the states where it existed, Lincoln was opposed to its extension. That alone made him unacceptable to the South, which, citing the Dred Scott decision, considered all territories open to slavery.

The Democratic convention of 1860 nominated Stephen Douglas, but the Southern wing of the party refused to accept him, blaming Douglas for the loss of Kansas to the free-soilers, and nominated instead John C. Breckinridge of Kentucky. To add to the confusion, a Constitutional Union party, attempting to take whatever middle ground might remain, nominated John Bell of Tennessee. Lincoln, however, easily won a majority in the electoral college, getting more votes than the combined opposition.

For years the bellicose states of the South had threatened secession whenever any law had been passed or action taken that they considered inimical to their interests. Much of this was bluff; much of it the threats of loud-mouthed extremists. But when those same states warned that the election of a Republican President would be cause for secession, they were not bluffing. South Carolina, always the hotbed of secessionist sentiment, waited only until Lincoln's election was certain, then called a state convention that met in Charleston on December 20, 1860. The delegates enthusiastically repealed South Carolina's ratification of the American Constitution of 1787, proclaiming that the union between South Carolina and the United States was thereby dissolved. When the cheering died down and the enthusiasm ebbed a bit, the secessionists in Charleston looked out at Fort Sumter, and perhaps some of the wisest of them wondered if disunion was going to be as easy and festive as they had thought.

In Their Own Words

America's past flashes to life when told by eyewitnesses. The early Americans who speak in the following pages tell us about themselves, their individual lives, and their private concerns for the future. From their reports we catch a glimpse of what it was like to be that "new creature" —an American—during the years between the French and Indian War and the Civil War.

Through letters, diaries, documents, and songs these eyewitnesses invite us to enter their various worlds. Patrick Henry sparks the bonfire of change in prerevolutionary America when he cries, "If we wish to be free . . . we must fight!" Literature and legalism culminate in Thomas Jefferson's Declaration of Independence. The ideals of the Revolution are carried forward by America's early reformers, stimulating Ralph Waldo Emerson to exult, "What is man born for but to be a Reformer, a remaker of what man has made."

Life in revolutionary America can be read from either side—from that of patriot soldiers or from that of British loyalists. Abner Stocking, a private in Benedict Arnold's army, wearily describes his march into the unknown vastness of Canada: "When we arose this morning many of the company were so weak that they could hardly stand on their legs.

Reading's merit is trumpeted on the frontispiece of a 1798 book on "Female Education."

When we attempted to march they reeled about like drunken men, having now been without provisions five days." Captain John André, who would later be hanged as a conspirator in Benedict Arnold's act of treason, writes about an extravaganza staged by the British during the winter they occupied Philadelphia: "The ball was opened by the knights and their ladies. . . . [We were served supper by] twenty-four black slaves in Oriental dresses and with silver collars and bracelets."

American life between the Revolution and the Civil War speaks to us from authentic sources in language vivid and variegated. A visiting Englishman, Basil Hall, describes the 1828 election in Albany, New York: "The Americans . . . are infinitely more occupied about bringing in a given candidate than they are about the advancement of those measures of which he is conceived to be a supporter."

We wince at the crude vigor of early America at play as Thomas Hughes remembers the game of cudgeling in early Virginia. We feel the individual and mass tragedy of slavery as Frederick Douglass asks, "Why am I a slave?"

The search for a more prosperous future is a continuing and typically American theme. Our hearts are stirred as Meriwether Lewis sees the Rocky Mountains for the first time and comprehends the potential of this continent. A half century later Forty-Niners haul themselves over those peaks to the tune of "Sweet Betsey From Pike."

In intimate papers we also learn of the passions and prejudices of famous Americans. George Washington rose above his contemporaries and had few detractors. But literature takes a vindictive slant as we hear John Adams in his *Autobiography* say of Alexander Hamilton, "Although I have long since forgiven this Arch Enemy, yet Vice, Folly and Villany are *not* to be forgotten, because the guilty Wretch repented in his dying Moments."

What we see emerging in these pages is a distinctively American way of looking at life. Founded in experiences of our past, it is an energetic, hopeful look, a look into the future to a world that can be changed by tough politics and hard work.

Spokesmen for Liberty

*As the 1760s gave way to the 1770s,
American resentment of the British crown's control of
the colonies turned into a call for rebellion.*

BEFORE THE STORM

John Adams, later to become the infant nation's first Vice President, argued that the 1760s and early 1770s were the years when the real revolution occurred:

What do we mean by the Revolution? The war? That was no part of the Revolution; it was only an effect and consequence of it. The Revolution was in the minds of the people, and this was effected, from 1760 to 1775, in the course of fifteen years before a drop of blood was shed at Lexington. The records of thirteen legislatures, the pamphlets, newspapers in all the colonies, ought to be consulted during that period to ascertain the steps by which the public opinion was enlightened and informed concerning the authority of Parliament over the colonies.

∽

TOWNSHEND ACTS

The Townshend Acts were the culmination of the king's ministers' attempts to tax the colonies. John Dickinson, a conservative lawyer, argued in 1767 that these acts were unconstitutional:

Here we may observe an authority expressly claimed and exerted to impose duties on these colonies; not for the regulation of trade; not for the preservation or promotion of a mutually beneficial intercourse between the several constituent parts of the empire, heretofore the sole objects of Parliamentary institutions; but for the single purpose of levying money upon us.

That we may be legally bound to pay any general duties on these commodities relative to the regulation of trade is granted; but we being obliged by the laws to take from Great Britain, any special duties imposed on their exportation to us only with intention to raise a revenue from us only are as much taxes upon us as those imposed by the Stamp Act.

Here, then, my dear countrymen, ROUSE yourselves and behold the ruin hanging over your heads. If you ONCE admit that Great Britain may lay duties upon her exportations to us, for the purpose of levying money on us only, she then will have nothing to do but to lay those duties on the articles which she prohibits us to manufacture—and the tragedy of American liberty is finished.

∽

BOSTON MASSACRE

The Boston Massacre was the costliest confrontation between patriots and British soldiers until then. The widely read *Boston Gazette* reported the 1770 incident in these inflammatory words:

Thirty or forty persons, mostly lads, being by this means gathered in King Street, Capt. Preston, with a party of men with charged bayonets, came from the main guard to the Commissioners house, the soldiers pushing their bayonets, crying, Make way! They took place by the custom-house, and continuing to push to drive the people off, pricked some in several places; on which they were clamorous, and, it is said, threw snow-balls. On this, the Captain commanded them to fire, and more snow-balls coming, he again said, Damn you, Fire, be the consquence what it will! One soldier then fired, and a townsman with a cudgel struck him over the hands with such force that he dropt his firelock; and rushing forward aimed a blow at the Captain's head, which graz'd his hat and fell pretty heavy upon his arm: However, the soldiers continued the fire, successively, til 7 or 8, or as some say 11 guns were discharged.

By this fatal manoeuvre, three men were laid dead on the spot, and two more struggling for life; but what shewed a degree of cruelty unknown to British troops, at least since the house of Hanover has directed their operations, was an attempt to fire upon or push with their bayonets the persons who undertook to remove the slain and wounded!

The people were immediately alarmed with the Report of this horrid Massacre, . . . and great Numbers soon assembled at the Place where this . . . Scene had been acted.

∽

BEWARE OF TYRANNY

In 1771, in one of Sam Adams's weekly articles in the *Boston Gazette*, he chastized those who did not rise to the challenge of the king's tyrannical powers:

Our enemies would fain have us lie down on the bed of sloth and security, and persuade ourselves that there is no danger. . . . With what resentment and indignation did we first receive the intelligence of a design to make us tributary, not to natural enemies, but infinetely more humiliating, to fellow subjects! And yet, with unparalleled insolence, we are told to be quiet when we see that very money which is torn from us by lawless force made use of still further to oppose us, to feed and pamper a set of infamous wretches who swarm like the locusts of Egypt, and some of them expect to revel in wealth and riot on the spoils of our country. Is it a time for us to sleep when our free government is essentially changed, and a new one is forming upon a quite different system? A government without the least dependence on the people—a government under the absolute control of a minister of state, upon whose sovereign dictates is to depend not only the time when, and the place where, the legislative assembly shall sit, but whether it shall sit at all; and if it is allowed to meet, it shall be liable immediately to be thrown out of existence, if in any one point it fails in obedience to his arbitrary mandates.

∽

"RALLYING SONG OF THE TEA PARTY"

The Sons of Liberty demonstrated their hatred for British taxes and regulations by dumping a cargo of tea into Boston harbor in 1773. Their valor was then saluted in song:

Rally, Mohawks! bring out your axes,
And tell King George we'll pay no taxes
　　On his foreign tea;
His threats are vain, and vain to think
To force our girls and wives to drink
　　His vile Bohea!
Then rally, boys, and hasten on
To meet our chiefs at the Green Dragon.

Our Warren's there and bold Revere,
With hands to do, and words to cheer,
　　For liberty and laws;
Our country's "braves" and firm defenders
Shall ne'er be left by true North-Enders
　　Fighting Freedom's cause!
Then rally, boys, and hasten on
To meet our chiefs at the Green Dragon.

∽

BOSTON PORT ACT

In 1774 Parliament passed the Boston Port Act, which cut Boston's economic lifelines. This typical handbill, posted in Farmington, Conn., called patriots to a protest meeting:

To pass through the fire at six o'clock this evening, in honour to the immortal goddess of Liberty, the late infamous Act of the British Parliament for farther distressing the American Colonies; the place of execution will be the public parade, where all Sons of Liberty are desired to attend.

"WE MUST FIGHT!"

As reported by William Wirt, Patrick Henry's long fight against the king's usurpation of colonial freedom climaxed in his speech before the 1775 Virginia Convention:

I have but one lamp by which my feet are guided; and that is the lamp of experience. I know of no way of judging of the future but by the past. And judging by the past, I wish to know what there has been in the conduct of the British ministry for the last ten years, to justify those hopes with which gentlemen have been pleased to solace themselves and the house? . . . I ask gentlemen, sir,

In this cartoon Benjamin Franklin set forth his cohesive sentiments on American colonial unity.

what means this martial array, if its purpose be not to force us to submission? Can gentlemen assign any other possible motive for it? Has Great Britain any enemy in this quarter of the world, to call for all this accumulation of navies and armies? No, sir, she has none. They are meant for us: they can be meant for no other. They are sent over to bind and rivet upon us those chains which the British ministry have been so long forging. And what have we to oppose to them? Shall we try argument? Sir, we have been trying that for the last ten years. . . .

. . . If we wish to be free—if we mean to preserve inviolate those inestimable privileges for which we have been so long contending—if we mean not basely to abandon the noble struggle in which we have been so long engaged, and which we have pledged ourselves never to abandon until the glorious object of our contest shall be obtained—we must fight!—I repeat it, sir, we must fight! An appeal to arms and to the God of Hosts is all that is left us!

. . . The war is inevitable—and let it come! I repeat it, sir, let it come!

COMMON SENSE

Thomas Paine was one of early America's most powerful pamphleteers. His *Common Sense*, published in 1776, did much to urge popular support for the patriot cause:

I have heard it asserted by some, that as America has flourished under her former connection with Great Britain, the same connection is necessary towards her future happiness. . . . I answer roundly that America would have flourished as much, and probably much more, had no European power taken any notice of her. The commerce by which she hath enriched herself are the necessaries of life and will always have a market while eating is the custom of Europe.

But Britain is the parent country, say some . . . Europe, and not England, is the parent country of America. This new world hath been the asylum for the persecuted lovers of civil and religious liberty from *every part* of Europe. Hither have they fled, not from the tender embraces of the mother, but from the cruelty of the monster; and it is so far true of England, that the same tyranny which drove the first emigrants from home pursues their descendants still. . . .

I challenge the warmest advocate for reconciliation to show a single advantage that this continent can reap by being connected with Great Britain. . . .

O ye that love mankind! Ye that dare oppose not only the tyranny but the tyrant, stand forth! Every spot of the old world is overrun with oppression. Freedom hath been hunted round the globe. Asia and Africa have long expelled her. Europe regards her like a stranger, and England hath given her warning to depart. O receive the fugitive, and prepare in time an asylum for mankind!

BIBLIOGRAPHIC CREDITS: Lester J. Cappon, *The Adams-Jefferson Letters*, University of North Carolina Press, 1957, published for the Institute of Early American History and Culture; John Dickinson, *Political Writings* (1801); Edwin Emery, *The Story of America as Reported in its Newspapers from 1690-1965*, Simon Schuster, 1965; H.V. Wells, *The Life and Public Service of Sam Adams* (1866); Elbridge Henry Goss, *Life of Colonial Paul Revere* (1891); Peter Force, *American Archives: Fourth Series, Containing a Documentary History of the English Colonies in North America from the King's Message to Parliament of March 7, 1774, to the Declaration of Independence by the United States* (1837–1846); William Wirt, *Sketches of the Life and Character of Patrick Henry* (1818); Thomas Paine, *Additions to Common Sense: Addressed to the Inhabitants of America* (1776).

Loyalists in Revolutionary America

Initially, the loyalists, of high or low estate, looked upon the war as an annoyance to be dispensed with quickly: "the rabble" could not win. From their accounts we are allowed to view the Revolution through disapproving, incredulous eyes.

LOYALISM DEFENDED

Many Americans declined to break their ties with Great Britain. Jonathan Boucher, an Anglican minister, argued that disloyalty to government meant disobedience to God:

Obedience to government is every man's duty, because it is every man's interest; but it is particularly incumbent on Christians, because (in addition to its moral fitness) it is enjoined by the positive commands of God; and, therefore, when Christians are disobedient to human ordinances, they are also disobedient to God. If the form of government under which the good providence of God has been pleased to place us be mild and free, it is our duty to enjoy it with gratitude and with thankfulness and, in particular, to be careful not to abuse it by licentiousness. If it be less indulgent and less liberal than in reason it ought to be, still it is our duty not to disturb and destroy the peace of the community by becoming refractory and rebellious subjects and *resisting the ordinances of God.* However humiliating such acquiescence may seem to men of warm and eager minds, the wisdom of God in having made it our duty is manifest.

∽

TREATMENT FOR A LOYALIST

In the heat of prerevolutionary flames, patriots had little sympathy for loyalists. Alexander Graydon, one of the Revolution's outstanding historians, remembered this incident in Philadelphia:

An extremely zealous Loyalist, and impetuous in his temper, . . . [Doctor Kearsley] had given much umbrage to the whigs; and if I am not mistaken, he had been detected in some hostile machinations. Hence he was deemed a proper subject for the fashionable punishment of tarring, feathering and carting. He was seized at his own door by a party of the militia, and, in the attempt to resist them, received a wound in his hand from a bayonet. Being overpowered, he was placed in a cart provided for the purpose, and amidst a multitude of boys and idlers, paraded through the streets to the tune of the rogue's march. I happened to be at the coffeehouse when the concourse arrived there. They made a halt, while the Doctor, foaming with rage and indignation, without his hat, his wig dishevelled and bloody from his wounded hand, stood up in the cart and called for a bowl of punch. It was quickly handed to him; when so vehement was his thirst that he drained it of its contents before he took it from his lips.

I must confess, [that I was most] revolted at the spectacle. I was shocked at seeing a lately respected citizen so cruelly villified. . . .

Not long after these occurences, Major Skene of the British Army ventured to show himself in Philadelphia. Whatever might have been his inducement to the measure, it was deemed expedient by the newly constituted authorities to have him arrested and secured. . . .

I well recollect the day that the guard was paraded to escort him out of the city on his way to some other station. An immense crowd of spectators stood before the door of his quarters, and lined the street through which he was to pass. The weather being warm, the window sashes of his apartment were raised, and Skene, with his bottle of wine upon the table, having just finished his dinner, roared out in the voice of a Stentor, *"God save great George our king!"*

PATRIOTS THROUGH LOYALISTS' EYES

Loyalists looked down upon the patriot army as a band of wretches. Ann Hulton, a resident of Boston during the battle of Bunker Hill, compared the two opposing armies:

In this army are many of noble family, many very respectable, virtuous and amiable characters, and it grieves one that gentlemen, brave British soldiers should fall by the hands of such despicable wretches as compose the banditti of the country; amongst whom there is not one that has the least pretension to be called a gentleman. They are a most rude, depraved, degenerate race, and it is mortification to us that they speak English and can trace themselves from that stock.

∽

LIFE IN EXILE

As described by Samuel Curwen, who lived out the war years in England, loyalist refugees experienced embarrassing financial problems:

Those who bring property here may do well enough, but for those who expect reimbursement for losses, or supply for present support, will find to their cost the hand of charity very cold; the latter may be kept from starving, and beyond that their hopes are vain. "Blessed is he (saith Pope) that expecteth nothing, for he shall never be disappointed"; nor a more interesting truth was ever uttered.

I find my finances so visibly lessening that I wish I could remove from this expensive country (being heartily tired of it) and, old as I am, would gladly enter into a business connection anywhere consistently with decency and integrity, which I would fain preserve. The use of the property I left behind me I fear I shall never be the better for; little did I expect from affluence to be reduced to such rigid economy as prudence now exacts. To beg is a meanness I wish never to be reduced to, and to starve is stupid; one comfort, as I am fast declining into the vale of life: my miseries cannot probably be of long continuance.

∽

CIVILIANS IN SAVANNAH

Not all loyalists could—or would— flee their native shores; many stayed to endure the sieges and privations of the war as best they could:

The guns seemed to approach on each side, and about three o'clock on Wednesday morning a shell whistled close by Captain Knowles' house. Soon afterwards another came nearer and seemed to strike my quarters, and I thought I heard the cry of people in distress. We all jumped up, and before I could dress myself, my quarters were so much in flames that I could not venture further than the door, for fear of an explosion from the rum. George and Jemmy were over with me in Captain Knowles' cellar; the others were at my quarters. George ran over before me, and fortunately for me drew out of the flames the two black trunks with some of my apparel, etc., that I brought out with me, and then removed them over to Captain Knowles' passage which was all the property I saved, except a little black trunk that was put into one of the larger ones by accident; for I momently expected that the explosion of the rum would blow up the house and kill every one near it.

∽

THE MESCHIANZA

During the winter of 1777, when the British occupied Philadelphia, they staged a huge extravaganza. Captain John André, who later would conspire in the treason of Benedict Arnold, described the evening's activities:

The ball was opened by the knights and their ladies, and the dances continued till ten o'clock, when the windows were thrown open, and a magnificent bouquet of rockets began the fireworks . . . [which] consisted of twenty different exhibitions. . . .

At twelve supper was announced, and large folding doors, hitherto artfully concealed, being suddenly thrown open, discovered a magnificent saloon of two hundred and ten feet by forty, and twenty- two in height. . . . Fifty-six large pier-glasses, ornamented with green silk, artificial flowers, and ribbons; a hundred branches with three lights in each, trimmed in the same manner as the mirrors; eighteen lusters, each with twenty-four lights, suspended from the ceiling and ornamented as the branches; three hundred wax tapers disposed along the supper tables; four hundred and thirty covers; twelve hundred dishes; twenty-four black slaves in Oriental dresses with silver collars and bracelets, ranged in two

Philadelphia loyalists entertained with lavish social events while British troops were nearby.

lines and bending to the ground as the general and admiral approached the saloon—all these, forming together the most brilliant assemblage of gay objects . . . exhibited a coup d'oeil beyond description magnificent.

Toward the end of the supper, the Herald of the Blended Rose, . . . attended by his trumpeteers, entered the saloon and proclaimed the King's health, the Queen and royal family, the army and navy, with their respective commanders, the knights and their ladies, and the ladies in general. Each of these toasts were followed by a flourish of music. After supper, we returned to the ballroom and continued to dance until four o'clock.

THE WORLD TURNED UPSIDE DOWN

At Yorktown, according to tradition, the following words were sung as the British band sadly played farewell:

If buttercups buzzed after the bee,
If boats were on land, churches on sea,
If ponies rode men and grass ate the
    cows,
And cats should be chased to holes by
    the mouse,
If the mamas sold their babies to the
    gypsies for half a crown,
Summer were spring and t'other way
    round,
Then all the world would be upside
    down.

∽

RETURN FROM EXILE

Many loyalists anxiously awaited the day they could return to America. Samuel Curwen described the reentry process, and his feelings as he landed in Boston:

July 10, 1784. To the Treasury; found the American door besieged by a score of mendicants like myself, waiting their turns. Though I thought my early attendance would have entitled me to No. 1, I was glad to stand No. 21. So great was the crowd that I was more than once about to depart and leave them.

Sept. 25. Arrived at Boston, and at half past three o'clock landed at the end of Long Wharf, after an absence of nine years and five months, occasioned by a lamented civil war, excited by ambitious, selfish men here and in England, to the disgrace, dishonor, distress and disparagement of these extensive territories. By plunder and rapine some few have accumulated wealth, but many more are greatly injured in their circumstances; some have to lament over the wreck of their departed wealth and estates, of which pitiable number I am; my affairs having sunk into irretrievable ruin.

BIBLIOGRAPHIC CREDITS: Jonathan Boucher, *A View of the Causes and Consequences of the American Revolution* (1797); Alexander Graydon, *Memoirs of His Own Time, with Reminiscences of Men and Events of the Revolution* (1840); Ann Hulton, *Letters of a Loyalist Lady; Being the Letters of Ann Hulton, Sister of Henry Hulton, Commissioner of Customs of Boston, 1767-1776,* Harvard University Press, 1927; Samuel Curwen, *The Journal and Letters of Samuel Curwen, an American in England, from 1775-1783* (1864); Frank Moore, *Diary of the American Revolution, From Newspapers and Original Documents* (1860); Benson J. Lossing, *Two Spies: Nathan Hale and John André,* (1866); *Gentlemen's Magazine,* XXXVI, (March, 1776); Curwen, *Journal and Letters.*

Soldiers in the Patriot Army

The Thirteen Colonies' revolutionary contingents were gradually moulded into an effective army. Far down the line from high level problems of organization and supply toiled the common infantryman. His GI observations sound timeless.

THE PROBLEM OF REENLISTMENTS

Enlistees often abandoned the army at its most pressing moments. Simeon Lyman related some methods employed by Washington's generals to encourage men to reenlist:

Thursday, [November] 30th [1775]. About 12 o'clock they fired about 10 cannon to salute. In the afternoon we was ordered out to see who would stay 3 weeks longer, and there was but three that would stay and they had listed to stay another year, and they dismissed them.

December, Friday, 1st. We was ordered to parade before the general's door, the whole regiment, and General Lee and General Solivan came out, and those that would not stay 4 days longer after their enlistments was out they was ordered to turn out, and there was about 3 quarters turned out, and we was ordered to form a hollow square, and General Lee came in and the first words was "Men, I do not know what to call you; [you] are the worst of all creatures," and flung and curst and swore at us, and said if we would not stay he would order us to go on Bunker Hill and if we would not go he would order the riflemen to fire at us, and they talked they would take our guns and take our names down, and our lieutenants begged of us to stay and we went and joined the rest, and they got about 10 of their guns, and the men was marched off, and the general said that they should go to the work house and be confined, and they agreed to stay the four days, and they gave them a dram, and the colonel told us that he would give us another the next morning, and we was dismissed. There was one that was a mind to have one of his mates turn out with him, and the general see him

and he catched his gun out of his hands and struck him on the head and ordered him to be put under guard.

Saturday, 2d. . . . then they read some new orders to us and they said that we must not go out of our brigade without a written pass from our captain, and before night there was a paper set up on the general's door not to let the soldiers have any victual if they would not stay 3 weeks longer.

∽

THE BITE OF STARVATION

From the outset of the war the common soldier suffered. Abner Stocking, a private in Benedict Arnold's army, remembered the starvation during the march to Canada:

When we arose this morning many of the company were so weak that they could hardly stand on their legs. When we attempted to march, they reeled about like drunken men, having now been without provisions five days. As I proceeded, I passed many sitting wholly drowned in sorrow, wishfully placing their eyes on everyone who passed by them, hoping for some relief. Such pity-asking countenances I never before beheld. My heart was ready to burst and my eyes to overflow with tears when I witnessed distress which I could not relieve.

∽

"YANKEE DOODLE"

This delightful tune was one of the most popular revolutionary songs:

Father and I went down to camp
    Along with Captain Gooding,
And there we see the men and boys
    As thick as hasty pudding.

And there we see a thousand men,
    As rich as 'Squire David,
And what they wasted every day,
    I wish it could be saved.

And there we see a swamping gun,
    Big as a log of maple,
Upon a deuced little cart,
    A load for Father's cattle.

And every time they shoot it off
    It takes a horn of powder,
And makes a noise like Father's gun,
    Only a nation louder.

And there was Captain Washington,
    And gentlefolks about him.
They say he's grown so tarnal proud
    He will not go without 'em.

I see another snarl of men
    A-digging graves, they told me,
So tarnal long, so tarnal deep,
    They 'tended they should hold me—

It scared me so I hooked it off,
    Nor stopt as I remember,
Nor turned about till I got home
    Locked up in Mother's chamber.

∽

THE JOY OF VICTORY

Victory is an army's most powerful medicine for her beleaguered soldiers. Thomas Rodney, who served under General Cadwalader, described the capture of Trenton:

The enemy have fled before us in the greatest panic that ever was known; we heard this moment that they have fled from Princeton, and that they were hard pressed by Washington. Never were men in higher spirits than our whole army is; none are sick, and all are determined to extirpate them from the Jersey, but I believe the enemy's fears will do it before we get up with them.

THE LACK OF SUPPLIES

Provisions and clothing were scarce during the excruciating winter at Valley Forge. James Martin remembered eating a "special" thanksgiving dinner:

While we lay here there was a Continental thanksgiving ordered by Congress; and as the army had all the cause in the world to be particularly thankful, if not for being well off, at least that it was no worse, we were ordered to participate in it. We had nothing to eat for two or three days previous, except what the trees of the fields and forests afforded us. But we must now have what Congress said—a sumptuous thanksgiving to close the year of high living we had now nearly seen brought to a close. Well—to add something extraordinary to our present stock of provisions—our country, ever mindful of its suffering army, opened her sympathizing heart so wide, upon this occasion, as to give us something to make the world stare. And what do you think it was, reader?—You cannot guess, be you

Typical patriot soldiers, camp in background, were crudely depicted by a contemporary artist.

as much of a Yankee as you will. I will tell you: it gave each and every man *half a gill* of rice, and a *table spoon full* of vinegar!

After we had made sure of this extraordinary superabundant donation, we were ordered out to attend a meeting and hear a sermon delevered upon the occasion. . . .

The army was now not only starved but naked; the greatest part were not only shirtless and barefoot, but destitute of all other clothing, especially blankets. I procured a small piece of raw cowhide and made myself a pair of moccasons,

which kept my feet (while they lasted) from the frozen ground, although, as I well remember, the hard edges so galled my ancles, while on a march, that it was with much difficulty and pain that I could wear them afterwards; but the only alternative I had was to endure this inconvenience or to go barefoot, as hundreds of my companions had to, till they might be tracked by their blood upon the rough frozen ground. But hunger, nakedness and sore shins were not the only difficulties we had at that time to encounter; we had hard duty to perform and little or no strength to perform it with.

෴

THE AGONY OF BOREDOM

For George Rogers Clark's army in the west, the wilderness was the enemy. A frontiersman himself, Clark permitted his men many liberties, and thus held his band together:

My object now was to keep the men in spirits. I suffered them to shoot game on all occasions and feast on them, like Indians' war dances, each company by turns inviting the other to their feasts, which was the case every night. . . . Myself and principal officers hailing on the woodsmen, shouting now and then, and running as much through the mud and water as any of them.

Thus insensibly without a murmur was those men led on to the banks of the Little Wabash, which we reached the thirteenth, through incredible difficulties far surpassing anything any of us had ever experienced.

෴

"AT EUTAW SPRINGS THE VALIANT DIED"

The common soldier may eventually be glorified—sometimes beyond recognition. Revolutionary poet Philip Freneau romanticized the brave men of Eutaw Springs:

At Eutaw Springs the valiant died;
Their limbs with dust are covered o'er—
Weep on, ye springs, your tearful tide;
How many heroes are no more!

They saw their injured country's woe:
The flaming town, the wasted field;
Then rushed to meet the insulting foe;
They took the spear—but left the shield.

Led by thy conquering genius, Greene,
The Britons they compelled to fly;
None distant viewed the fatal plain,
None grieved, in such a cause to die—

Now rest in peace, our patriot band;
Though far from nature's limits thrown,
We trust they find a happier land,
A brighter sunshine of their own.

෴

A VIEW OF YORKTOWN

Here we are allowed to view Yorktown through the eyes of James Martin, a private in Washington's army:

We waited two or three hours before the British made their appearance. They were not always so dilatory, but they were compelled at last, by necessity, to appear, all armed, with bayonets fixed, drums beating, and faces lengthening. They were led by General [Charles] O'Hara, with the American General Lincoln on his right, the Americans and French beating a march as they passed out between them. It was a noble sight to us, and the more so, as it seemed to promise a speedy conclusion to the contest. The British did not make so good an appearance as the German forces, but there was certainly some allowance to be made in their favor. The English felt their honor wounded, the Germans did not greatly care whose hands they were in. The British paid the Americans, seemingly, but little attention as they passed them, but they eyed the French with considerable malice depicted in their countenances. They marched to the place appointed and stacked their arms; they then returned to the town in the same manner they had marched out, except being divested of their arms.

BIBLIOGRAPHIC CREDITS: Simeon Lyman, "Journal of Simeon Lyman of Sharon, Aug. 10–28, 1775," Connecticut Historical Society *Collections, VII* (1891); Abner Stocking, "Journal," reprinted from Kenneth Roberts, *March to Quebec,* Doubleday, 1940; Edmund C. Stedman and E.M. Hutchinson, *Library of American Literature* (1891); Hezekiah Niles, *Centennial Offering, Republication of the Principles and Acts of the Revolution in America* (1876); Joseph Plumb Martin, *Private Yankee Doodle,* edited by George Scheer, Little Brown and Company, 1962; *George Rodgers Clark Papers,* Illinois State Historical Society Collections; Philip Freneau, *Poems Written and Published During the American Revolutionary War* (1809); Martin, *Private Yankee Doodle.*

The Founding Documents

The ideals within our founding documents had roots that stretched back to the Magna Carta and to the English Bill of Rights of 1688. The ideals also expressed the distinctive philosophy of the 18th century.

TOWARD THE DECLARATION OF INDEPENDENCE

The arguments set forth in the Declaration of Independence were based on English legal tradition as influenced by the Enlightenment. This tradition had been enhanced in the political treatises of John Locke, in legislation passed by both colonial legislatures and Parliament, and in American and British lawyers' interpretations:

English philosopher John Locke's *Second Treatise on Civil Government* (1689):

When any one, or more, shall take upon them to make laws whom the people have not appointed so to do, they make laws without authority, which the people are not therefore bound to obey; by which means they come again to be out of subjection, and may constitute to themselves a new legislative, as they think best, being in full liberty to resist the force of those who, without authority, would impose anything upon them.

Boston lawyer James Otis's *The Rights of the British Colonies Asserted and Proved* (1764):

The Sum of my argument is, . . . That no parts of his Majesty's dominions can be taxed without their consent: That every part has a right to be represented in the supreme or some subordinate legislature: That the refusal of this, would seem to be a contradiction in practice to the theory of the constitution.

Suffolk Resolves (1774):

If we successfully resist that unparalleled usurpation of unconstitutional power, whereby our capital is robbed of the means of life; whereby the streets of Boston are thronged with military execution- ers; whereby our coasts are lined and harbours crouded with ships of war; whereby the charter of the colony, . . . the unalienable and inestimable inherit- ance, which we derived from nature, the constitution of Britain, and the privileges warranted to us in the charter of the province, is totally wrecked, annulled, and vacated, posterity will acknowledge that virtue which preserved them free and happy.

Declaration of Resolves of the First Continental Congress (1774):

1. That they are entitled to life, liberty, and property, & they have never ceded to any sovereign power whatever, a right to dispose of either without their consent.

4. That the foundation of English lib- erty, and of all free government, is a right in the people to participate in their legis- lative council: and as the English colo- nists are not represented, . . . they are entitled to a free and exclusive power of legislation in their several provincial leg- islatures, where their right of representa- tion can alone be preserved, in all cases of taxation and internal polity, subject only to the negative of their sovereign.

Excerpts from the Declaration:

We hold these truths to be self-evident, that all men are created equal, that they are endowed by their Creator with cer- tain unalienable Rights, that among these are Life, Liberty, and the pursuit of Happiness. That to secure these rights, Governments are instituted among Men, deriving their just powers from the con- sent of the governed, That whenever any Form of Government becomes destruc- tive of these ends, it is the Right of the People to alter or to abolish it, and to in- stitute new Government, laying its foun- dation on such principles and organizing its powers in such form, as to them shall seem most likely to effect their Safety and Happiness.

∽

TOWARD THE CONSTITUTION OF THE UNITED STATES

The Articles of Confederation, America's first governing document, did not provide an adequate base for the young republic. Among its inadequacies was the assumption that the central government derived power from the states. The new government, by contrast, found that power originated in the people:

Ordinance for Virginia (1621):

II. . . . there shall be Two Supreme Coun- cils in Virginia, for the better Govern- ment of the said Colony aforesaid.

III. The one of which Councils, to be called The Council of State . . . shall be chosen, nominated, placed and dis- placed, from time to time, by Us, the said Treasurer, Council, and Company, and our Successors.

IV. The other Council, more generally to be called by the Governor, . . . shall consist, . . . of the said Council of State, and of two Burgesses out of every Town, . . . to be respectively chosen by the In- habitants.

French philosopher Montesquieu's *The Spirit of Laws* (1748):

Here then is the fundamental constitu- tion of the government we are treating of. The legislative body being composed of two parts, they check one another by the mutual privilege of rejecting. They are both restrained by the executive pow- er, as the executive is by the legislative.

Albany Plan of Union (1754):

1. That the said general government be administered by a President-General, to be appointed and supported by the crown; and a Grand Council, to be chosen by the representatives of the people of the several colonies.

9. That the assent of the President-General be requisite to all acts of the Grand Council, and that it be his office and duty to cause them to be carried into execution.

14. That they make laws for regulating and governing such new settlements, till the crown shall think fit to form them into particular governments.

16. That for these purposes they have power to make laws, and lay and levy such general duties, imposts, or taxes, as to them shall appear most equal and just.

23. That all military commission officers, whether for land or sea service, to act under this general constitution, shall be nominated by the President-General; but the approbation of the Grand Council is to be obtained. . . . And all civil officers are to be nominated by the Grand Council, and to receive the President-General's approbation before they officiate.

Excerpts from the Constitution:

We the people of the United States, in Order to form a more perfect Union, establish Justice, insure domestic Tranquility, provide for the common defence, promote the general Welfare, and secure the Blessings of Liberty to ourselves and our Posterity, do ordain and establish this Constitution for the United States of America.

Art. I

Sec. 1. All legislative Powers herein granted shall be vested in a Congress of the United States, which shall consist of a Senate and a House of Representatives.

Art. II

Sec. 1. The executive Power shall be vested in a President of the United States of America.

Art. III

Sec. 1. The judicial Power of the United States, shall be vested in one supreme Court, and in such inferior Courts as the Congress may from time to time ordain and establish.

TOWARD THE BILL OF RIGHTS

The new constitution possessed one major deficiency. It contained no bill of rights, no guarantee of personal liberty, desired by many of the Founding Fathers. This was rectified by the first ten amendments to our Constitution, which were based on documents previously accepted by several states:

Maryland Act of Toleration (1649):

Be it Therefore . . . enacted . . . that noe person or persons whatsoever with this Province, . . . belonging professing to believe in Jesus Christ, shall from henceforth bee any waies troubled, Molested or discountenanced for or in respect of his or her religion ore in the free exercise thereof within this Province.

Virginia Bill of Rights (1776):

8. That in all capital or criminal prosecutions a man hath a right to demand the cause and nature of his accusation, to be

The Liberty Bell pealed with joy when both the Declaration and the Constitution were signed.

confronted with the accusers and witnesses, to call for evidence in his favour, and to a speedy trial by an impartial jury of his vicinage, without whose unanimous consent he cannot be found guilty; nor can he be compelled to give evidence against himself; that no man be deprived of his liberty, except by the law of the land or the judgment of his peers.

9. That excessive bail ought not to be required, nor excessive fines imposed, nor cruel and unusual punishment inflicted.

10. That general warrants, . . . whose offence is not particularly described and supported by evidence, are grievous and oppressive, and ought not to be granted.

12. That the freedom of the press is one of the great bulwarks of liberty.

Massachusetts Bill of Rights (1780):

XIV. Every subject has a right to be secure from all unreasonable searches, and seizures, of his person, his houses, his papers, and all his possessions.

XVII. The people have a right to keep and bear arms for the common defence. . . . and the military power shall always be held in an exact subordination to the civil authority, and be governed by it.

XIX. The people have a right, in an orderly and peaceable manner to assemble to consult upon the common good; give instructions to their representatives; and to request of the legislative body, by the way of addresses, petitions, or remonstrances, redress of the wrongs done them, and of the grievances they suffer.

XXVII. In time of peace, no soldier ought to be quartered in any house without the consent of the owner; and in time of war, such quarters ought not to be made but by the civil magistrate, in a manner ordained by the legislature.

Excerpts from the Bill of Rights:

Art. I

Congress shall make no law respecting an establishment of religion, or prohibiting the free exercise thereof; or abridging the freedom of speech, or of the press; or the right of the people peaceably to assemble, and to petition the government for a redress of grievances.

Art. VI

In all criminal prosecutions, the accused shall enjoy the right to a speedy and public trial, by an impartial jury of the State and district wherein the crime shall have been committed, which district shall have been previously ascertained by law, and to be informed of the nature and cause of the accusation; to be confronted with the witnesses against him; to have compulsory process for obtaining witnesses in his favor, and to have the Assistance of Counsel for his defense.

Reformers of the New Nation

America has always been a nation of change—old ideas giving way to new. In these excerpts we see the American reformer fighting to realize the promises set forth in our founding documents.

MAN THE REFORMER

Ralph Waldo Emerson, nineteenth century lecturer and essayist, argued that the rejection of false ideas should be our greatest joy:

What is a man born for but to be a Reformer, a Remaker of what man has made; . . . a restorer of truth and good, imitating that great Nature which embosoms us all, and which sleeps no moment on an old past, but every hour repairs herself, yielding us every morning a new day, and with every pulsation a new life? Let him renounce everything which is not true to him, and put all his practices back on their first thoughts, and do nothing for which he has not the whole world for his reason. . . .

The power which is at once spring and regulator in all efforts of reform is the conviction that there is an infinite worthiness in man, which will appear at the call of worth, and that all particular reforms are the removing of some impediment. Is it not the highest duty that man should be honored in us?

ABOLITION OF SLAVERY

The emancipation of slaves was fought for from the nation's inception. In 1831 William Lloyd Garrison, a Boston publisher, made abolition an aggressive crusade:

During my recent tour for the purpose of exciting the minds of the people by a series of discourses on the subject of slavery, every place that I visited gave fresh evidence of the fact, that a greater revolution in public sentiment was to be effected in the free states—and *particularly in New England*—than at the south. I found contempt more bitter, opposition more active, detraction more relentless, prejudice more stubborn, and apathy more frozen, than among slave owners themselves. . . . I determined, at every hazard, to lift up the standard of emancipation in the eyes of the nation, *within sight of Bunker Hill and in the birth place of liberty.* That standard is now unfurled; and long may it float, unhurt by the spoliations of time or the missiles of a desperate foe—yea, till every chain be broken, and every bondman set free! Let Southern oppressors tremble—let their secret abbettors tremble—let their Northern apologists tremble—let all the enemies of the persecuted blacks tremble.

. . . I will be as harsh as truth, and as uncompromising as justice. On this subject, I do not wish to think, or speak, or write, with moderation. No! No! Tell a man whose house is on fire, to give a moderate alarm; tell him to moderately rescue his wife from the hands of the ravisher; tell the mother to gradually extricate her babe from the fire into which it has fallen;—but urge me not to use moderation in a cause like the present. I am in earnest—I will not equivocate—I will not excuse—I will not retreat a single inch—AND I WILL BE HEARD.

"COME HOME, FATHER"

The American Temperance Union was formed in 1836 to fight the growing use of alcohol. At ATU meetings, songs like this one were sung with strenuous piety:

Father, dear father, come home with me
 now!
The clock in the steeple strikes one.—
You said you were coming right home
 from the shop,
As soon as your day's work was done.—
Our fire has gone out, our house is all
 dark,
And mother's been watching since tea,—
With poor brother Benny so sick in her
 arms,
And no one to help her but me.—
Come home, come home, come home!—
Please,—father, dear father,
 come home!—

Father, dear father, come home with me
 now!
The clock in the steeple strikes three;
The house is so lonely!—the hours are
 so long
For poor weeping mother and me.
Yes, we are alone—poor Benny is dead,
And gone with the angels of light;
And these were the very last words that
 he said—
"I want to kiss Papa good night."
Come home! come home! come home!
Please, father, dear father, come home.

PLIGHT OF THE INSANE

Dorothea Dix devoted her life to improving the conditions of the insane. Her 1843 plea to the Massachusetts legislature stirred consciences across the land:

I proceed, gentlemen, briefly to call your attention to the present state of insane persons confined within this Commonwealth, in *cages, closets, cellars, stalls, pens! Chained, naked, beaten with rods, and lashed* into obedience.

I offer the following extracts from my notebook and journal.

Springfield: In the jail, one lunatic woman, furiously mad, a state pauper, improperly situated, both in regard to the prisoners, the keepers, and herself. It is a case of extreme self-forgetfulness and oblivion to all the decencies of life, to describe which would be to repeat only the grossest scenes. In the almshouse of the same town is a woman apparently only needing judicious care and some well-chosen employment to make it unnecessary to confine her in solitude in a dreary unfurnished room. Her appeals for employment and companionship are most touching, but the mistress replied "she had no time to attend to her."

Injustice is also done to the *convicts:* it is certainly very wrong that they should be doomed day after day and night after night to listen to the ravings of madmen and madwomen. This is a kind of punishment that is not recognized by our statutes, and is what the criminal ought not to be called upon to undergo. The confinement of the criminal and of the insane in the same building is subversive of that good order and discipline which should be observed in every well-regulated prison.

ⵏⵓ

BROOK FARM

The energetic American search for utopias gave rise to a variety of experiments in communal living. The goals of Brook Farm, established in 1841, were set forth in its preamble:

In order more effectually to promote the great purposes of human culture; to establish the external relations of life on a basis of wisdom and purity; to apply the principles of justice and love to our social organization in accordance with the laws of Divine Providence; to substitute a system of brotherly cooperation for one of selfish competition; to secure to our children and those who may be entrusted to our care, the benefits of the highest physical, intellectual and moral education, which in the progress of knowledge the resources at our command will permit; to institute an attractive, efficient, and productive system of industry; to prevent the exercise of worldly anxiety, by the competent supply of our necessary wants; to diminish the desire of excessive accumulation, by making the acquisition of individual property subservient to upright and disinterested uses; to guarantee to each other forever the means of physical support, and of spiritual progress; and thus to impart a greater freedom, simplicity, truthfulness, refinement, and moral dignity, to our mode of life;—we the undersigned do unite in a voluntary Association.

WOMEN'S RIGHTS

Reformers also challenged women's subservient status to men. The women who met in Seneca Falls, New York, in 1848 declared:

The history of mankind is a history of repeated injuries and usurpations on the part of man toward woman, having in direct object the establishment of an absolute tyranny over her. . . .

He has never permitted her to exercise her inalienable right to the elective franchise.

He has compelled her to submit to laws, in the formation of which she had no voice.

He has made her, if married, in the eye of the law, civilly dead.

. . . In the covenant of marriage, she is compelled to promise obedience to her husband, he becoming, to all intents and purposes, her master—the law giving him power to deprive her of her liberty, and to administer chastisement.

After depriving her of all rights as a married woman, if single, and the owner of property, he has taxed her to support a government which recognizes her only

Classrooms such as this, with a teacher towering over hapless pupils, were a target of reformers.

when her property can be made profitable to it.

He has endeavored, in every way that he could, to destroy her confidence in her own powers, to lessen her self-respect and to make her willing to lead a dependent and abject life.

Now, in view of this entire disfranchisement of one-half the people of this country, their social and religious degradation—in view of the unjust laws above

mentioned, and because women do feel themselves aggrieved, oppressed, and fraudulently deprived of their most sacred rights, we insist that they have immediate admission to all the rights and privileges which belong to them as citizens of the United States.

ⵏⵓ

THE GREAT EQUALIZER

When Horace Mann became secretary of the Massachusetts Board of Education in 1837 the state's educational system badly needed reforming. In his 1848 annual report he showed the need for education:

Now surely nothing but universal education can counterwork this tendency to the domination of capital and the servility of labor. If one class possesses all the wealth and the education, while the residue of society is ignorant and poor, it matters not by what name the relation between them may be called: the latter, in fact and in truth, will be the servile dependents and subjects of the former. But, if education be equally diffused, it will draw property after it by the strongest of all attractions. . . . The people of Massachusetts have, in some degree, appreciated the truth that the unexampled prosperity of the State—its comfort, its competence, its general intelligence and virtue—is attributable to the education, more or less perfect which all its people have received. . . .

Education then, beyond all other devices of human origin, is a great equalizer of the conditions of men,—the balance wheel of the social machinery. I do not here mean that it so elevates the moral nature as to make men disdain and abhor the oppression of their fellow men. This idea pertains to another of its attributes. But I mean that it gives each man the independence and the means by which he can resist the selfishness of other men.

BIBLIOGRAPHIC CREDITS: Ralph Waldo Emerson, *Nature: Addresses and Lectures* (1903); William Lloyd Garrison, *The Liberator*, Vol. I, No. 1, January 1, 1831; John Krout, *The Origins of Prohibition*, Alfred A. Knopf, Inc., (1925); Dorothea Dix, Memorial to the Legislature of Massachusetts, January, 1843, *Old South Leaflets*, No. 148 (no date); Octavius D. Frothingham, *Transcendentalism in New England* (1876); Elizabeth C. Stanton et al, *The History of Woman Suffrage* (1881); *Annual Reports of the Board of Education of Massachusetts for the Years 1845-1848* (1891).

Lewis and Clark's Journey of Discovery

*When Thomas Jefferson purchased the Louisiana Territory
from France, Americans had little knowledge of what their $15 million
had bought. In the diaries of the Lewis and Clark expedition,
we find an invitation to explore with them the wonders and the
realities of a new continent.*

LEGEND OF THE "DEAVELS"

The travelers met Indians on the upper Missouri who retold a frightful legend which was faithfully recorded by William Clark:

24th August Friday 1804
In a northerley derection from the Mouth of this Creek in an emence Plain a high Hill is Situated, and appears of a Conic form, and by the different nations of Indians in this quarter is Suppose to be the residence of Deavels. that they are in human form with remarkable large heads, and about 18 Inches high, that they are very watchfull and are arm'd with Sharp arrows with which they Can Kill at a great distance; they are Said to kill all persons who are So hardy as to attempt to approach the hill; they State that tradition informs them that many Indians have Suffered by these little people, and among others three *Mahar* Men fell a sacrefise to their murceless fury not many Years Sence. So Much do the Maha, Soues, Ottoes and other neighbouring nations believe this fable, that no Consideration is Suffecient to induce them to approach the hill.

∽

CHRISTMAS AT FT. MANDAN

The expedition wintered at Ft. Mandan in present-day North Dakota. Sgt. John Ordway, next in command to Lewis and Clark, described the company's attempt to celebrate a joyous Christmas:

Tuesday 25th Decr 1804, cloudy
we fired the Swivels at day break & each man fired one round. our officers Gave the party a drink of Taffee. we had the Best to eat that could be had, & continued firing dancing & frolicking dureing the whole day. the Savages did not Trouble us as we had requested them not to come as it was a Great medicien day with us. We enjoyed a merry cristmas dureing the day & evening untill nine oClock—all in peace & quietness.

∽

'A FORMIDABLE GRIZZLY BEAR

The wild mammals of North America challenged the explorers' progress. Meriwether Lewis caught every detail of their first western grizzly bear:

Monday April 29th 1805.
I walked on shore with one man. about 8 A.M. we fell in with two brown or yellow bear; both of which we wounded; one of them made his escape, the other after my firing on him pursued me seventy or eighty yards, but fortunately had been so badly wounded that he was unable to pursue me so closely as to prevent my chargin my gun; we again repeated our fir and killed him. it was a male not fully grown, we estimated his weight at 300 lbs. . . . The legs of this bear are somewhat longer than those of the black, as are it's tallons and tusks incomparably larger and longer. . . . it's colour is yellowish brown, the eyes small, black, and piercing; the front of the fore legs near the feet is usually black; the fur is finer thicker and deeper than that of the black bear. . . . it is a . . . furious and formidable anamal, and will frequently pursue the hunter when wounded. it is asstonishing to see the wounds they will bear before they can be put to death. the Indians may well fear this anamal equiped as they generally are with their bows and arrows or indifferent fuzees, but in the hands of a skillfull riflemen they are by no means as formidable or dangerous as they have been represented.

LAND OF "VISIONARY INCHANTMENT"

With poetic pen and atrocious spelling, the explorers extolled the beauties of the land. Of the White Cliffs of the Missouri, Lewis wrote:

Friday May 31st 1805.
The hills and river Clifts which we passed today exhibit a most romantic appearance. The bluffs of the river rise to the hight of from 2 to 300 feet and in most places nearly perpendicular; they are formed of remarkable white sandstone which is sufficiently soft to give way readily to the impression of water; . . . The water in the course of time in decending from those hills and plains on either side of the river has trickled down the soft sand clifts and woarn it into a thousand grotesque figures, which with the help of a little immagination and an oblique view, at a distance are made to represent eligant ranges of lofty freestone buildings, having their parapets well stocked with statuary; collumns of various sculpture both grooved and plain, are also seen supporting long galleries in front of those buildings; . . . we see the remains or ruins of eligant buildings; some collumns standing and almost entire with their pedestals and capitals; others retaining their pedestals but deprived by time or accident of their capitals, some lying prostrate an broken othe[r]s in the form of vast pyramids of connic structure bearing a serees of other pyramids on their tops becoming less as they ascend and finally terminating in a sharp point. . . . As we passed on it seemed as if those seens of visionary inchantment would never have and [an] end; for here it is too that nature presents to the view of the traveler vast ranges of walls of tolerable workmanship.

FIRST SIGHT OF THE ROCKIES

A long-sought achievement loomed before Lewis's eyes when he finally glimpsed the Continental Divide:

Sunday May 26th 1805.
In the after part of the day I also walked out and ascended the river hills which I found sufficiently fortiegueing on arriving to the summit [of] one of the highest points in the neighborhood I thought myself well repaid for my labour; as from this point I beheld the Rocky Mountains for the first time, ... while I viewed these mountains I felt a secret pleasure in finding myself so near the head of the heretofore conceived boundless Missouri; but when I reflected on the difficulties which this snowey barrier would most probably throw in my way to the Pacific, and the sufferings and hardships of myself and party in thim, it in some measure conterballanced the joy I had felt in the first moments in which I gazed on them; but as I have always held it a crime to anticipate evils I will believe it a good comfortable road untill I am compelled to believe differently.

Lewis and Clark held numerous parleys with Indians they met during their westward struggle.

∽

INDIAN COURAGE

The explorers keenly—and sympathetically—observed the Indians' way of life. Lewis recounted Indian courage in a buffalo hunt:

Wednesday May 29th 1805
Today we passed on the Stard. side the remains of a vast many mangled carcases of Buffalow which had been driven over a precipice of 120 feet by the Indians and perished; ... in this manner the Indians of the Missouri distroy vast herds of buffaloe at a stroke; for this purpose one of the most active and fleet young men is scelected and disguised in a robe of buffaloe skin, ... thus caparisoned he places himself at a convenient distance between a herd of buffaloe and a precipice proper for the purpose, ... the other indians now surround the herd on the back and flanks and at a signal agreed on all shew themselves at the same time moving forward towards the buffaloe, the disguised indian or decoy has taken care to place himself sufficiently nigh the buffaloe to be noticed by them when they take to flight and runing before them they follow him in full speede to the precipice, the cattle behind driving those in front over ... forming one common mass of dead an[d] mangled carcases: the decoy in the mean time has taken care to secure himself in some cranney or crivice of the clift which he had previously prepared for that purpose. the part of the decoy I am informed is extreamly dangerous, if they are not very fleet runers the buffaloe tread them under foot and crush them to death.

∽

ENCHANTING NEZ PERCÉ INDIANS

Most prosperous of the Indians the explorers encountered, the Nez Percé were also the most cordial. Clark took particular pains to describe their unique civilization:

October 10th Wednesday (Thursday)
The *Cho-pun-nish* or Pierced nose Indians are Stout likely men, handsom women, and verry dressey in their way, the dress of the men are a White Buffalow robe or Elk Skin dressed with Beeds which are generally white, Sea Shells & the Mother of Pirl hung to the[i]r hair & on a piece of otter skin about their necks hair Ceewed in two parsels hanging forward over their Sholder, feathers, and differnet Coloured Paints which they find in their Countrey Generally white, Green & light Blue. Some fiew were a Shirt of Dressed Skins and long legins & Mockersons Painted, which appear to be their winters dress, with a plat of twisted grass about their Necks.

The women dress in a Shirt of Ibex or Goat (bighorn) Skins which reach quite down to their anckles with a girdle, their heads are not ornemented, their Shirts are ornemented with quilled Brass, Small peces of Brass Cut into different forms, Beeds, Shells & curious bones &c. ...

Their amusements appear but feiw as their Situation requires the utmost exertion to pr[o]cure food they are generally employed in that pursute, all the Summer & fall fishing for the Salmon, the winter hunting the deer on Snow Shoes in the plains and takeing care of ther emence numbers of horses, & in the Spring cross the mountains to the Missouri to get Buffalow robes and meet &c. at which time they frequent[ly] meet with their enemies & lose their horses & maney of their people.

∽

REACHING THE PACIFIC

After an arduous voyage down the roaring Columbia River, Clark finally sighted the mouth of the river, which he mistook for the Pacific Ocean:

November 7th Thursday 1805
Great joy in camp we are in *view* of the *Ocian*, this great Pacific Octean which we been so long anxious to see. and the roreing or noise made by the waves brakeing on the rockey Shores (as I suppose) may be heard disti[n]ctly.

∽

RETURN TO CIVILIZATION

The expedition emerged from the wilderness two and a half years after leaving civilization. We can feel the jubilation of their first signs of home in Clark's narrative:

Sunday 21th Septr. 1806
Saw Several persons also stock of different kind on the bank which reviv'd the party very much. at 3 P M we met two large boats assending. at 4 P M we arrived in Sight of St. Charles, the party rejoiced at the Sight of this hospita[b]l[e] village plyed thear ores with great dexterity and we Soon arived opposit the Town this day being Sunday we observed a number of Gentlemen and ladies walking on the bank, we saluted the Village by three rounds from our blunderbuts and the Small arms of the party, and landed near the lower part of the town. we were met by great numbers of the inhabitants.

BIBLIOGRAPHIC CREDITS: Meriwether Lewis and William Clark, *The Journals of Lewis and Clark,* edited by Bernard deVoto. Houghton, Mifflin Company, 1953.

Pioneers to the West

Each pioneer who trekked across the little-known continent remembered a thousand tales of his challenging adventure. Their accounts allow us to capture the spirit of a bygone era.

DETERMINING TO GO WEST

Pioneers challenged the unknown West for mixed reasons. Peter Burnett's personal goals for undertaking this adventure were perhaps typical:

There was a bill pending in Congress. . . which proposed to donate to each immigrant six hundred and forty acres of land for himself, and one hundred and sixty acres for each child. I had a wife and six children, and would, therefore, be entitled to sixteen hundred acres.

I saw that a great American community would grow up, in the space of a few years, upon the shores of the distant Pacific; and I felt an ardent desire to aid in this most important enterprise. At that time the country was claimed by both Great Britain and the United States; so that the most ready and peaceable way to settle the conflicting and doubtful claims of the two governments was to fill the country with American citizens. If we could only show by practical test, that American emigrants could safely make their way across the continent to Oregon with their wagons, teams, cattle, and families, then the solution of the question of title to the country was discovered. Of course, Great Britain would not covet a colony settled by American citizens.

ESSENTIAL PROVISIONS

Since supplies could only be purchased at few stops during the trip west, an ample stock had to be laid in at the journey's outset. Forty-Niner diaries yield this individual shopping list:

For every man we carried a hundred twenty-five pounds of flour, fifty pounds of cured ham, fifty pounds of smoked side bacon; thirty pounds of sugar, six pounds of ground coffee, one pound of tea, a pound and a half of cream of tartar, two pounds of soda or good saleratus, three pounds of salt, a bushel of dried fruit, one sixth of a bushel of beans, twenty-five pounds of rice, sixteen and a half pounds of hard or "pilot" bread, and pepper, ginger, citric acid, and tartaric acid "to suit."

ELECTING OFFICERS

Organization was a wagon train's first order of business. An eastern newspaper reporter, Matthew C. Field, colorfully portrayed an election of officers for the journey:

The Oregonians were assembled here to the number of six or eight hundred, and when we passed their encampment they were engaged in the business of electing officers to regulate and conduct their proceedings. It was a curious and unaccountable spectacle to us, as we approached. We saw a large body of men wheeling and marching about the prairie, describing evolutions neither recognizable as savage, civic, or military. We soon knew they were not Indians and were not long in setting them down for the emigrants, but what in the name of mystery they were about, our best guessing could not reduce to anything in the shape of a mathematical probability. They were only going on with their elections, in a manner perhaps old enough, but very new and quizzical to us. The candidates stood up in a row before the constituents, and at a given signal they wheeled about and marched off, while the general mass *broke* after them, "lickaty-split," each man forming in behind his favorite, so that every candidate flourished a sort of tail of his own, and the man with the longest tail was elected! These proceedings were continued until a Captain and a Council of Ten were elected.

FIRST BUFFALO HUNT

With eager anxiety, westbound travelers awaited their first sight of buffalo. As told by Josiah Gregg, a trader on the Santa Fe Trail, the first buffalo hunt soon followed:

Early on the second day after leaving Cottonwood (a few miles beyond the principal Turkey creek), our eyes were greeted with the sight of a herd amounting to nearly a hundred head of buffalo, quietly grazing in the distance before us. Half of our company had probably never seen a buffalo before (at least in its wild state); and the excitment that the first sight of these prairie beeves' occasions among a party of novices, beggars all description. Every horsemen was off in a scamper: and some of the wagoners, leaving their teams to take care of themselves, seized their guns and joined the race afoot. Here went one with his rifle or yager—there another with his double-barrelled shot-gun—a third with his holster-pistols—a Mexican perhaps with his lance—another with his bow and arrows—and numbers joined without any arms whatever, merely for the 'pleasures of chase'—all helter-skelter—a regular John Gilpin race, truly 'neck or naught.' The fleetest of the pursuers were soon in the midst of the game, which scattered in all directions, like a flock of birds upon descent of a hawk.

AN INDIAN ATTACK

The fear of Indian attacks was a constant worry to overland pioneers. James Ohio Pattie, an early Santa Fe trader told of his narrow escape during an Indian raid:

We pushed on as rapidly as possible, fearful that these red children of the desert, who appear to inherit an equal hatred of all whites, would follow us, and attack us in the night. . . . To prevent, as far as might be, such accidents, we raised a fortification round our camp every night, until we considered ourselves out of their reach. . . . This evening we erected no breast-work, placed no other guard than one person to watch our horses, and threw ourselves in careless security around our fires. We had taken very little rest for four nights, and being exceedingly drowsy, we had scarcely laid ourselves down, before we were sound asleep. The Indians had still followed us, too far off to be seen by day, but had probably surveyed our camp each night. At about 11 o'clock this night, they poured upon us a shower of arrows, by which they killed two men, and wounded two more; and what was most provoking, fled so rapidly that we could not even give them a round. One of the slain was in bed with me. My own hunting shirt had two arrows in it, and my blanket was pinned fast to the ground by arrows. There were sixteen arrows discharged into my bed. We extinguished our fires, and it may easily be imagined, slept no more that night.

∽

HARDSHIP ON THE TRAIL

Overland pioneers overcame immense hardships. John Townsend, a Philadelphia naturalist, vividly portrayed thirst on the desert of present-day Idaho and Washington:

We were moving this morning with the dawn, and travelled steadily the whole day, over one of the most arid plains we have seen, covered thickly with jagged masses of lava, and twisted wormwood bushes. Both horses and men were jaded to the last degree; the former from the rough, and at times almost impassable nature of the track, and the latter from excessive heat and parching thirst. We saw not a drop of water during the day, and our only food was . . . dried meat . . .

After a hard day's journey, overland pioneers enjoyed relaxing around the evening's campfire.

which we carried, and chewed like biscuits as we travelled. . . . The air feels like the breath of a sirocco, the tongue becomes parched and horny, and the mouth, nose, and eyes are incessantly assailed by the fine pulverized lava, which rises from the ground with the least breath of air. Bullets, pebbles of chalcedony, and pieces of smooth obsidian, were in great requisition today; almost every man was mumbling some of these substances, in an endeavor to assuage his burning thirst. The camp trailed along in a lagging and desponding line over the plain for a mile or more, the poor horses heads hanging low, their tongues protruding to their utmost extent, and their riders scarcely less drooping and spiritless. We were a sad and most forlorn looking company, certainly; not a man of us had any thing to say, and none cared to be interrupted in his blissful dream of cool rivers and streams.

∽

"SWEET BETSEY FROM PIKE"

The overland journey of these hardy pioneers is summed up in this humorous song, popular at the time:

Oh, don't you remember sweet Betsey from Pike,
Who cross'd the big mountains with her lover Ike,
With two yoke of cattle, a large yellow dog,

A tall Shanghai rooster and one spotted hog.

They soon reached the desert, where Betsey gave out,
And down in the sand she lay rolling about;
While Ike, half-distracted, looked on with surprise,
Saying, "Betsey, get up, you'll get sand in your eyes."

Their wagon broke down with a terrible crash,
And out on the prairie rolled all kinds of trash;
A few little baby clothes done up with care—
'Twas rather suspicious, though all on the *square*.

The shanghai ran off, and their cattle all died;
That morning the last piece of bacon was fried;
Poor Ike was discouraged, and Betsey got mad;
The dog drooped his tail and looked wondrously sad.

Sweet Betsey got up in a great deal of pain.
Declared she'd go back to Pike Country again;
But Ike gave a sigh and they fondly embraced,
And they traveled along with his arm round her waist.

They suddenly stopped on a very high hill,
With wonder looked down upon old Placerville;
Ike sighed when he said, and he cast his eyes down:
"Sweet Betsey, my darling, we've got to Hangtown."

BIBLIOGRAPHIC CREDITS: Peter H. Burnett, "Recollections and Opinions of an Old Pioneer" *Oregon Historical Society Quarterly*, Vol. V, No. 1, March, 1904; Archer Butler Hulbert, *Forty-Niners*, Atlantic—Little, Brown and Co., 1931; Matthew C. Field, *The Daily Picayune* (New Orleans) November 21, 1843; Josiah Gregg, *Commerce of the Prairies* (1844); James O. Pattie, *Personal Narrative of James O. Pattie of Kentucky* (1833); John K. Townsend, *Narrative of a Journey across the Rocky Mountains to the Columbia River* (1839); John A. Stone, *Put's Golden Songster* (1858).

Foreign Travelers' Tall Tales

The most objective accounts of early American civilization were written by travelers from abroad. Their candid observations tell us much about the nature of life in the young nation.

WHAT IS AN AMERICAN?

From colonial days America has been a melting pot of nations and races. In 1782 Hector St. Jean de Crèvecoeur, a naturalized British subject, sketched the western pilgrim:

What then is the American, this new man? He is either a European or the descendant of a European; hence that strange mixture of blood which you will find in no other country. I could point out to you a family whose grandfather was an Englishman, whose wife was Dutch, whose son married a French woman, and whose present four sons have now four wives of different nations. He is an American who, leaving behind him all his ancient prejudices and manners, receives new ones from the new mode of life he has embraced, the new government he obeys, and the new rank he holds. . . . Here individuals of all nations are melted into a new race of men whose labors and posterity will one day cause great changes in the world. Americans are the western pilgrims, who are carrying along with them the great mass of arts, sciences, vigor, and industry which began long since in the East. They will finish the great circle. The Americans were once scattered all over Europe. Here they are incorporated into one of the finest systems of population which has ever appeared and which will hereafter become distinct by the power of the different climates they inhabit. The American ought therefore to love this country much better than that in which either he or his forefathers were born. Here the rewards of his industry follow with equal steps the progress of his labor. . . . The American is a new man who acts on new principles; he must therefore entertain new ideas and form new opinions. From involuntary idleness, servile dependence, penury, and useless labor, he has passed to toils of a very different nature, rewarded by ample subsistence. This is an American.

∽

LAND OF MILK AND HONEY

Some travelers were so taken with America that they stretched the truth to cover the subject. Samuel Crabtree, who visited in 1818, was one of these Bunyanesque promoters:

This is the country for a man to enjoy himself: Ohio, Indiana, and the Missouri Territory; where you may see prairie sixty miles long and ten broad, not a stick nor a stone in them, at two dollars an acre, that will produce from seventy to one hundred bushels of Indian corn per acre: too rich for wheat or any other kind of grain. I measured Indian corn in Ohio State last September more than fifteen feet high, and some of the ears had from four to seven hundred grains. I believe I saw more peaches and apples rotting on the ground than would sink the British fleet. I was at many plantations in Ohio where they no more knew the number of their hogs than myself. And they have such flocks of turkeys, geese, ducks, and hens as would surprise you; they live principally upon fowls and eggs, and in summer upon apple and peach pies. The poorest family has a cow or two and some sheep and in the fall can gather as many apples and peaches as serve the year round. Good rye whiskey; apple and peach brandy, at forty cents per gallon, which I think equal to rum. Excellent cider at three dollars per barrel of thirty-three gallons, barrel included. The poorest families adorn the table three times a day like a wedding dinner—tea, coffee, beef, fowls, pies, eggs, pickles, good bread; and their favorite beverage is whisky or peach brandy. Say, is it so in England?

If you know the difference between this country and England you would need no persuading to leave it and come hither.

∽

ELECTIONEERING IN ALBANY

While traveling through America during the era of Jacksonian Democracy, Basil Hall tried to comprehend the goals of an American election:

The most striking peculiarity of this spirit [of politics], in contradistinction to what we see in England, is that its efforts are directed more exclusively to the means, than to any useful end. The Americans, as it appears to me, are infinitely more occupied about bringing in a given candidate, than they are about the advancement of those measures of which he is conceived to be the supporter. They do occasionally advert to these prospective measures, in their canvassing arguments in defense of their own friends, or in attacks upon the other party; but always, as far as I could see, more as rhetorical flourishes, or as motives to excite the furious acrimony of party spirit, than as distinct or sound anticipations of the line of policy which their candidate, or his antagonist, was likely to follow. The intrigues, the canvassing for votes, all the machinery of newspaper abuse and praise, the speeches and maneouvres in the Legislature, at the bar, by the fireside, and in every hole and corner of the country from end to end, without intermission, form integral parts of the business—apparently far more important than the candidate's wishes—his promises—or even than his character and fitness for the office.

All these things, generally speaking, it would seem, are subordinate considerations; so completely are men's minds swallowed up in the technical details of the election.

∽

NO CLERGY IN POLITICS

Alex de Tocqueville, a young Frenchman in America to study penitentiaries, journeyed through America in 1831 and rejoiced in Americans' freedom from clerical interference:

Upon my arrival in the United States, the religious aspect of the country was the first thing that struck my attention; and the longer I stayed there the more did I perceive the great political consequences resulting from this state of things, to which I was unaccustomed. . . .

This led me to examine more attentively than I had hitherto done, the station which the American clergy occupy in political society. I learned . . . that they filled no public appointments; not one of them is to be met with in the administration, and they are not ever represented in the legislative assemblies. In several States the law excludes them from political life, public opinion in all. And when I came to inquire into the prevailing spirit of the clergy I found that most of its members seemed to retire of their own accord from the exercise of power, and that they made it the pride of their profession to abstain from politics.

The Church cannot share the temporal power of the State without being the object of a portion of that animosity which the latter excites.

∽

THE ALMIGHTY DOLLAR

Frances Trollope, who had almost nothing good to say about the young nation she saw in the late 1820s, wrote this biting description of Americans in pursuit of the dollar:

Nothing can exceed their activity and perseverance in all kinds of speculation, handicraft, and enterprise, which promises a profitable pecuniary result. . . . The result is exactly what might be anticipated. This sordid object, for ever before

their eyes, must inevitably produce a sordid tone of mind, and, worse, still, it produces a seared and blunted conscience on all questions of probity. I know not a more striking evidence of the low tone of morality which is generated by this universal pursuit of money, than the manner in which the New-England states are described by Americans. All agree in saying that they present a spectacle of industry and prosperity delightful to behold, and this is the district and the population most constantly quoted as the finest specimen of their admirable country; yet I never met a single individual in any part of the Union who did not paint these New-Englanders as sly, grinding, selfish, and tricking. The Yankees (as the New-Englanders are called) will avow these qualities themselves with a complacent smile, and boast that no people on the earth can match them at overreaching in a bargain. I have heard them unblush-

An early cartoonist portrayed visiting English authoress Frances Trollope as a crotchety biddy.

ingly relate stories of their cronies and friends, which, if believed among us, would banish the heros from the fellowship of honest men for ever; and all this is uttered with a simplicity which sometimes led me to doubt if the speakers know what honour and honesty meant. Yet the Americans declare that 'they are the most moral people upon earth.' Again and again I have heard this asserted, not only in conversation, and by their writings, but even from the pulpit. Such broad assumption of superior virtue demands examination, and after four years of attentive and earnest observation and inquiry, my honest conviction is, that the standard or moral character in the United States is very greatly lower than in Europe.

SOUTHERN HOSPITALITY

William Thomson, a Scottish weaver, traveling in America in the 1840s, was quite taken by Southern life-style and by the attitude of a prospective employer:

I will now describe a planter's house in the State of Georgia, about eight miles from Augusta, who owned a manufacturing establishment, to whom I went in search of employment. It was a handsome, but not large frame house, with everything in good taste about it. I went up to the front door, and asked if Judge Sley was at home: a lady answered "No, that he was on his circuit (he was a district judge), and that it would be some days before he returned." She shewed me into an elegantly-furnished room; I then told the lady, who was the judge's wife, my name, and that I was a wool-carder and spinner, wanting employment. A lady in her circumstances in this country (Scotland), would very quickly have changed her manners on such a piece of information; but such was not the case here. I was treated with the greatest consideration and unobtrusive politeness, and desired to make myself at home, and remain with them till the judge returned, which he did in a few days. . . . In speaking, he treated me with perfect equality, called me "Mr. Thomson," said "Yes, Sir," or "No, Sir," just as I would do, in speaking to a gentleman I held in high estimation. I sat at the same table. . . . And all this, not to please, and make comfortable, a gentleman who could repay them in kind, but to a stranger seeking employment. . . .

The character of the southern states, for hospitality, stands high and it is not overrated. They are quite a distinct race from the "Yankees". They have a high sense of honour; treating every white man as a gentleman.

BIBLIOGRAPHICAL CREDITS: Hector St. Jean de Crevecoeur, *Letters from an American Farmer, Written for the Information of a Friend in England* (1782); Samuel Crabtree, *Important Extracts from Original and Recent Letters Written by Englishmen, in the United States of America & Their Friends in England* (1818); Basil Hall, *Travels in North America in the Years 1827-1828* (1829); Alex de Tocqueville, *Democracy in America* (1900); Frances Trollope, *Domestic Manners of the Americans* (1832); William Thomson, *A Tradesman's Travels in the United States in the Years 1840, 41 & 42* (1842).

Americans at Play

*Early Americans found time to frolic even amidst
colonial and postrevolutionary turmoil*

LOTTERIES

**Lotteries were popular in a number
of the colonies. In 1752 the *Virginia
Gazette* published this "meditation"
for the consolation of readers who
didn't win:**

Why frets my Soul because of a Blank!
or why doth it lament at having missed
of a Prize? Suppose I had got one of the
Ten Thousands, what then?—Why then,
slap dash down at a Blow, with the whole
Catalogue of my Wants. But soft—Would
not the Destruction of those Wants
be the Generation of others; and the
Destruction of these the Generation of
more? and so on?—As sure as a Gun.—
At this Rate, what would be gained by a
Ten Thousand Pound Prize?—Nothing—
Or, what have I lost by a Blank?—Nothing at all.—Why then, a Blank is as good
as a Ten Thousand Pound Prize.—Who
then in their Wits can doubt it? and consequently better than an Inferior Prize.—
As plain as a Pike Staff. Then what are
they who rejoice at the Prize?—Prize
Fools. And what are they who grieve at
a Blank?—Blank Fools.—*Sing tan-tara-ra-
ra, Fools all, Fools all, &c.*

☙

A TASTE FOR DANCING

**Baron von Closen, stationed at
Williamsburg in 1781 with
Rochambeau, compared the dance
styles of the colonial ladies:**

M. de Rochambeau gave a large dinner for the leading residents of Williamsburg, and a ball to which all the Ladies
were invited. . . .

The fair sex in this city like minuets
very much. It is true that some of them
dance them rather well, and infinitely
better than those up North; to make

amends for this, the latter dance the
Scottish (reels) better. All of them like
our French quadrilles, and in general,
they find French manners to their taste.

☙

BOAT RACING

**Philip Fithian, a tutor at a Virginia
plantation, vividly described a
1774 boat race along with its
accompanying betting:**

The boats were to start, to use the language of jockeys, immediately after dinner; a boat was anchored down the river
at a mile distance—Captain Dobby and
Captain Benson steered the boats in the
race—Captain Benson had five oarsmen;
Captain Dobby had six—It was ebbtide—
The betts were small—chiefly given to
the negroes who rowed—Captain Benson
won the first race—Captain Purchace
offered to bett ten dollars that with the
same boat and same hands, only having
liberty to put a small weight in the stern,
he would beat Captain Benson—He was
taken, and came out best only half the
boat's length—about sunset we left the
ship and went all to Hobb's Holl, where
a ball was agreed on.

☙

COCKFIGHTING

**A visiting New England merchant,
Elkanah Watson, viewed a Virginia
cockfight in 1787 and left us this
ghastly description:**

The roads as we approached the scene
were alive with carriages, horses, and
pedestrians, black and white, hastening
to the point of attraction. Several houses
formed a spacious square, in the center
of which was arranged a large cock-pit;
surrounded by many genteel people pro-

miscuously mingled with the vulgar and
debased. Exceedingly beautiful cocks
were produced, armed with long, steel-
pointed gaffles, which were firmly at-
tached to their natural spurs. The moment the birds were dropped, bets ran
high. The little heroes appeared trained
to the business; and were not the least
disconcerted by the crowd or shouting.
. . . Advancing nearer and nearer, they
flew upon each other at the same instant
with a rude shock, the cruel gaffles being
driven into their bodies, and, at times,
directly through their heads. Frequently
one, or both would be struck dead at the
first blow. I soon sickened at this barbarous sport, and retired under the shade
of a wide-spread willow.

☙

CUDGELING

**The rough sport of cudgeling has
long since lost favor. Thomas Hughes
remembered this contest taking place
at Virginia fairs in the early 1800s:**

The weapon is a good stout ash-stick
with a large basket handle, heavier and
somewhat shorter than a common single-
stick. The players are called "old gamesters"—why, I can't tell you, —and their
object is simply to break one another's
heads: for, the moment that blood runs
an inch anywhere above the eyebrow,
the old gamester to whom it belongs is
beaten and has to stop. A very slight
blow with the sticks will fetch blood, so
that it is by no means a punishing pas-
time, if the men don't play on purpose,
and savagely, at the body and arms of
their adversaries. The old gamester going
into action only takes off his hat and coat,
and arms himself with a stick, . . . and
he faces his man armed in like manner,

and they stand some three feet apart, often nearer, and feint, and strike, and return at one another's heads until one cries "hold," or blood flows; in the first case they are allowed a minute's time, and go one again; in the latter, another pair of gamesters are called on. If good men are playing, the quickness of the returns is marvellous; you hear the rattle like that a boy makes drawing his stick along palings, only heavier, and the closeness of the men in action to one another gives it a strange interest, and makes a spell at back-swording a very noble sight.

∽

"SHUCKIN' OF THE CORN"
Corn-shucking parties, important social events, were celebrated in this popular song:

I have a ship on the ocean,
All lined with silver and gold.
Before I'd see my true love suffer,
That ship should be anchored and sold.

Chorus:
I'm a-goin' to the shuckin' of the corn,
I'm a-goin' to the shuckin' of the corn,
A shuckin' of the corn and a-blowin'
    of the horn,
I'm a-goin' to the shuckin' of the corn.

The wind blows cold in Cairo,
The sun refuses to shine.
Before I'd see my true love suffer,
I'd work all the summer time.

∽

LACROSSE
Many games played by early Americans were adapted from the Indians. Lacrosse, described by visiting Englishman Basil Hall in 1828, was one of these:

One of the chiefs, having advanced to the centre of the arc cast the ball high in the air. As it fell, between twenty and thirty players rushed forward and leaping several feet off the ground, tried to strike it. The multiplicity of blows, acting in different directions, had the effect of bringing the ball to the ground where a fine scramble took place. . . . At length an Indian, more expert than the others, contrived to nip the ball between the end of his two sticks and ran off with it like a deer, with his arms raised over his head pursued by a whole party engaged in the

first struggle. The fortunate youth was, of course, intercepted in his progress twenty different times by his antagonists, who shot like hawks across his flight, from all parts of the field, to knock the prize out of his grasp, or to trip him up—in short by any means to prevent his throwing it through the opening between the boughs at the end of the playground. Whenever this grand purpose of the game was accomplished the successful party announced their right to count one by a fierce yell of triumph which pierced the very depths of the wilderness.

Rounders, very popular in colonial America, later became our national sport—baseball.

TOUR OF THE SPRINGS
Any Tidewater resident who could afford it took a tour of the mineral springs in the Appalachian Mountains each summer. Perceval Reniers described a typical 1830s tour:

By the 1830's, after more than half a century of trial and error, the Southerner had evolved his method of taking the waters: he took them in quantity and he took them seriatim. That is, he made the Springs Tour, visiting as many resorts in a season as time and money would allow. The phrase at home in the lowlands was, he was going "up to the Springs," always in the plural. He might own a cottage at the White Sulphur and expect to put in most of his time there, but he went to "the Springs" just the same; it was taken for granted that before he returned to the lowlands again he would sample the water and the company at anywhere from three to half a dozen other places, a few days here and a week there. . . .

The popular thing was, to alight at the Warm and then be off again with all possible speed. . . .

Their overnight stay [at the Warm Springs] was just long enough to see colored bartender, in the basement story, where the wine was cooled in a spring and stag horns bristled from the walls. It was just time to sink like a sigh into the soft warm liquid of the pool, just time to inquire what was the news from the White and to get it.

After the White there was no hard and fast rule; which Springs came next depended on many things and not the least of these was what the White Sulphur water had done to the working parts. The patient might now need the Sweet for the "tonic" which rehabilitated the overpurged, or he might need the Salt for its Glauber salt or its iodine. Dr. Horner, continuing his prescription, routed them first to the Salt, then on to the Red Sulphur, seventeen miles, then doubled them back through the Salt to the Sweet, recommending a week at each. By that time the animal economy . . . would be ready for the bathing at the Hot and Warm, thermal springs which Nature had so conveniently placed near the main exit from the region.

. . . There was an immutable law that required everybody in the fashion to converge on the Sweet for the last week in August and the first week in September, from whatever direction, whether from the White or the Salt or the Hot. There, after the unspeakable hilarity of crowding together for another fortnight, they separated, some striking straight South to Tennessee and the Carolinas, some going back east the Fincastle way, but most of them returning to the Warm for a last lingering farewell.

BIBLIOGRAPHIC CREDITS: *Virginia Gazette* (Williamsburg) April 24, 1752, reprinted from Jane Carson, *Colonial Virginians at Play*, University Press of Virginia, 1965, reprinted for Colonial Williamsburg; Jean Christophe, Baron von Closen, "The Journal of Baron Von Closen," *William and Mary Quarterly*, 3rd Series, X (1953), reprinted from Carson, *Colonial Virginians*; Philip Fithian, *Journal and Letters 1767-1774* (1900), reprinted in Krout, "Annals of American Sport", Vol. XV, *Yale Pageant of America*, by permission of United States Publishers Assn., Inc.; Elkanah Watson, *Men and Times of the Revolution* (1856), reprinted from Krout, "Annals of American Sport"; Thomas Hughes, *Tom Brown's School Days* (1856), reprinted from Carson, *Colonial Virginians*; Margaret Boni, *The Fireside Book of Favorite American Songs*, Simon & Schuster, 1952; Basil Hall, *Travels in the United States in 1827-1828* (1829), reprinted from Krout, "Annals of American Sport"; Perceval Reniers, *The Springs of Virginia: Life, Love, and Death at the Waters (1775-1900)*, University of North Carolina Press, 1941.

The Slaves' America

The horror of American slavery stretched from earliest colonial times through the Civil War. In accounts from the eighteenth and nineteenth centuries we trace the blacks' epic journey from the African coast to the southern plantation and eventually on freedom's road to the North.

LIFE ON A SLAVER

Slavery began with capture in Africa and then shipment to America. Gustavus Vasa, who survived this journey, would not forget its wretchedness:

The first object which saluted my eyes when I arrived on the coast was the sea, and a slaveship, which was then riding at anchor, and waiting for its cargo. These filled me with astonishment, which was soon converted into terror, which I am yet at a loss to describe, not the then feelings of my mind. When I was carried on board I was immediately handled, and tossed up, to see if I were sound, by some of the crew; and I was now persuaded that I had got into a world of bad spirits, and that they were going to kill me. . . .

I was not long suffered to indulge my grief; I was soon put down under the decks, and there I received such a salutation in my nostrils as I had never experienced in my life; so that, with the loathsomeness of the stench, and crying together, I become so sick and low that I was not able to eat, nor had I the least desire to taste anything . . . but soon, to my grief, two of the white men offered me eatables; and, on my refusing to eat, one of them held me fast by the hands, and laid me across, I think, the windlass, and tied my feet, while the other flogged me severely. . . .

One day, when we had a smooth sea, and moderate wind, two of my wearied countrymen, who were chained together (I was near them at a time), preferring death to such a life of misery, somehow made through the nettings, and jumped into the sea; immediately another quite dejected fellow, who, on account of his illness, was suffered to be out of irons

also followed their example; and I believe many more would very soon have done the same, if they had not been prevented by the ship's crew.

∽

A FIELD HAND'S DAY

The economy of the antebellum South was built on the backs of slaves. Solomon Northup, a Northern black sold into slavery, describes cotton picking on a typical plantation:

The hands are required to be in the cotton field as soon as it is light in the morning, and, with the exception of ten or fifteen minutes, which is given them at noon to swallow their allowance of cold bacon, they are not permitted to be a moment idle until it is too dark to see, and when the moon is full, they often times labor till the middle of the night. They do not dare to stop even at dinner time, . . . however late it be, until the order to halt is given by the driver.

The day's work over in the field, the baskets are "toted," or in other words, carried to the gin-house, where the cotton is weighed.

. . . This done, the labor of the day is not yet ended, by any means. Each one must then attend to his respective chores. One feeds the mules, another the swine—another cuts the wood, and so forth; besides, the packing is all done by candlelight. Finally, at a late hour, they reach the quarters, sleepy and overcome with the long day's toil. Then a fire must be kindled in the cabin, the corn ground in the small hand-mill, and supper, and dinner for the next day in the field, prepared. All that is allowed them is corn and bacon, which is given out at the corncrib and smoke-house every Sunday morning. Each one receives, as his week-

ly allowance, three and a half pounds of bacon, and corn enough to make a peck of meal. That is all—no tea, coffee, sugar, and, with the exception of a very scanty sprinkling now and then, no salt.

∽

HUMAN AUCTION

Slaves were bought and sold like animals. The breakup of his slave family, and his mother's grief, were described with revulsion by Josiah Henson:

My brothers and sisters were bid off first, and one by one, while my mother, paralyzed by grief, held me by the hand. Her (my mother's) turn came, and she was bought by Isaac Riley of Montgomery county. Then I was offered to the assembled purchasers. My mother, half distracted with the thought of parting forever from all her children pushed through the crowd, while the bidding for me was going on, to the spot where Riley was standing. She fell at his feet, and clung to his knees, entreating him in tones that a mother could only command, to buy her baby as well as herself, and spare to her one, at least, of her little ones. Will it, can it be believed that this man, thus appealed to, was capable not merely of turning a deaf ear to her supplications, but of disengaging himself from her with such violent blows and kicks, as to reduce her to the necessity of creeping out of his reach, and mingling the groan of bodily suffering with the sob of a breaking heart? As she crawled away from the brutal man I heard her sob out, "Oh, Lord Jesus, how long, how long shall I suffer this way!"

"GO DOWN, MOSES"

Laboring mainly on cotton and rice plantations, slaves frequently sang this spiritual as they toiled away their lives:

Go down, Moses,
   'Way down in Egypt land,
Tell ole Pharaoh,
   To let my people go.
Go down, Moses,
   'Way down in Egypt land,
Tell ole Pharaoh,
   To let my people go.

When Israel was in Egypts land:
   Let my people go,
Oppressed so hard they could not stand,
   Let my people go.

"Thus spoke the Lord," bold Moses said;
   Let my people go,
If not I'll smite your first born dead,
   Let my people go.

Go down, Moses,
   'Way down in Egypt land,
Tell ole Pharaoh,
   To let my people go.
O let my people go.

§

"WHY AM I A SLAVE?"

From his youngest days in the South Frederick Douglass asked this question. Though he never got a satisfactory answer, he penetrated to the heart of the problem:

By some means I learned . . . that "God, up in the sky," made everybody; and that he made white people to be masters and mistresses, and black people to be slaves.

I found that there were puzzling exceptions to this theory of slavery on both sides, and in the middle. I knew of blacks who were not slaves; I knew of whites who were not slaveholders; and I knew of persons who were nearly white, who were slaves. Color, therefore, was a very unsatisfactory basis for slavery.

Once, however, engaged in the inquiry, I was not very long in finding out the true solution of the matter. It was not color, but crime, not God, but man, that afforded the true explanation of the existence of slavery; nor was I long in finding out another important truth, viz: what man can make, man can unmake.

Abolitionist sentiment was spread throughout the antebellum nation by drawings such as this.

§

NAT TURNER'S REVOLT

An outcry against the cruelty of slavery was written by David Walker. As if in response, Nat Turner led his revolt the following year, and later described his quest for freedom:

It was quickly agreed we should commence at home (Mr. J. Travis') on that night; and until we had armed and equipped ourselves, and gathered sufficient force, neither age nor sex was to be spared—which was invariably adhered to. . . .

I took my station in the rear, and, as it was my object to carry terror and devastation wherever we went, I placed fifteen or twenty of the best armed and most to be relied on in front, who generally approached the houses as fast as their horses could run. . . . .

The white men pursued and fired on us several times. Hark had his horse shot under him, and I caught another for him as it was running by me; five or six of my men were wounded, but none left on the field. Finding myself defeated here, I instantly determined to go through a private way, and cross the Nottoway River at Cypress Bridge, three miles below Jerusalem, and attack that place in the rear, as I expected they would look for me on the other road, and I had a great desire to get there to procure arms and ammunition. After going a short distance in this private way, accompanied by about twenty men, I overtook two or three, who told me the others were dispersed in every direction.

UNDERGROUND RAILROAD

To man a way station on the Underground Railroad, the road to freedom, required steady nerves and a full purse. Levi Coffin dared to tell his part in the perilous adventure:

In the winter of 1826-27, fugitives began to come to our house, and as it become more widely known on different routes that the slaves fleeing from bondage would find a welcome and shelter at our house, and be forwarded safely on their journey, the number increased. Friends in the neighborhood, who had formerly stood aloof . . . were encouraged to engage in it when they saw the fearless manner in which I acted. . . .

. . . the Underground Railroad business increased as time advanced, and it was attended with heavy expenses, which I could not have borne had not my affairs been prosperous. I found it necessary to keep a team and a wagon always at command, to convey the fugitive slaves on their journey. Sometimes, when we had large companies, one or two other teams and wagons were required. These journeys had to be made at night, often through deep mud and bad roads, and along byways that were seldom traveled. Every precaution to evade pursuit had to be used, as the hunters were often on the track, and sometimes ahead of the slaves. . . .

I soon became extensively known to the friends of the slaves, at different points on the Ohio River, where fugitives generally crossed, and to those northward of us on the various routes leading to Canada. . . . Three principle lines from the South converged at my house: one from Cincinnati, one from Madison, and one from Jeffersonville, Indiana. The roads were always in running order, the connections were good, the conductors active and zealous, and there was no lack of passengers. Seldom a week passed without our receiving passengers by this mysterious road.

BIBLIOGRAPHIC CREDITS: Gustavus Vasa, *The Interesting Narrative of the Life of Olandah Equiano or Gustavus Vasa, Written by Himself* (1793); Solomon Northup, *Twelve Years a Slave* (no date); Willard Thorp, *The Southern Reader*, Alfred Knopf, 1955; Josiah Henson, *Truth Stranger Than Fiction, Father Henson's Story of His Own Life* (1858); Frederick Douglass, *Narrative of the Life of Frederick Douglass* (1845); Nat Turner, *The Confessions of Nat Turner, Leader of the late insurrection in Southampton, Virginia*, edited by Thomas R. Gray, (1831); Levi Coffin, *Reminiscences of Levi Coffin* (1876).

Great Americans' Views of Each Other

Americans tend to eulogize past political leaders, placing them on lofty pedestals. Yet as we view these famous men through their associates' eyes, we catch a glimpse of their many dimensions.

Thomas Jefferson on George Washington (1814)

Perhaps the strongest feature in his character was prudence, never acting until every circumstance, every consideration, was maturely weighed; refraining if he saw a doubt, but, when once decided, going through with his purpose, whatever obstacles opposed. His integrity was most pure, his justice the most inflexible I have ever known, no motives of interest or consanguinity, of friendship or hatred, being able to bias his decision. He was, indeed, in every sense of the words, a wise, a good, and a great man . . . and it may truly be said, that never did nature and fortune combine more perfectly to make a man great.

John Marshall on George Washington (c. 1810)

Though prizing popular favor as highly as it ought to be prized, he never yielded principle to obtain it, or sacrificed judgment on its altar. This firmness of character added to his acknowledged virtue enabled him to stem a torrent which would have overwhelmed almost any other man, and did, I believe, save his country.

Thomas Jefferson on John Adams (1787)

He is vain, irritable, and a bad calculator of the force and probable effect of the motives which govern men. . . . He is as disinterested as the being who made him: he is profound in his views; and accurate in his judgment, except where knowledge of the world is necessary to form a judgment.

Alexander Hamilton on John Adams (1800)

Not denying to Mr. Adams patriotism and integrity, and even talents of a certain kind, I should be deficient in candor, were I to conceal the conviction that he does not possess the talents adapted to the *administration* of government, and that there are great and intrinsic defects in his character, which unfit him for the office of chief magistrate.

Benjamin Rush on Thomas Jefferson (1800)

He possessed a genius of the first order. It was universal in its objects. He was not less distinguished for his political than his mathematical and philosophical knowledge. . . . He was not only the friend of his country, but of all nations and religions.

John Marshall on Thomas Jefferson (1801)

His foreign prejudices seem to me totally to unfit him for the chief magistracy of a nation which cannot indulge those prejudices. . . . Mr. Jefferson appears to me to be a man who will embody himself with the House of Representatives. By weakening the office of President he will increase his personal power. He will diminish his responsibility, sap the fundamental principles of the government, and become the leader of that party which is about to constitute the majority of the legislature.

Alexander Hamilton on Thomas Jefferson (1801)

I admit that his politics are tinctured with fanaticism; that he is too much in earnest in his democracy; that he has been a mischievous enemy to the principal measures of our past administration; . . . that he is not scrupulous about the means of success, nor very mindful of truth, and that he is a contemptible hypocrite.

Thomas Jefferson on Alexander Hamilton (1791)

Hamilton was, indeed, a singular character. Of acute understanding, disinterested, honest, and honorable in all private transactions, amiable in society, and duly valuing virtue in private life, yet so bewitched and perverted by the British example, as to be under thorough conviction that corruption was essential to the government of a nation.

John Adams on Alexander Hamilton (1816)

Although I have long since forgiven this Arch Enemy, yet Vice, Folly and Villany are not to be forgotten, because the guilty Wretch repented, in his dying Moments. . . . Nor am I obliged by any Principles of Morality or Religion to suffer my Character to lie under infamous Calumnies, because the Author of them, with a Pistol Bullet through his Spinal Marrow, died a Penitent.

Ambrose Spencer on Alexander Hamilton (c. 1840)

Alexander Hamilton was the greatest man this country ever produced. . . . In power of reasoning Hamilton was the equal of Webster; and more than this can be said of no man. . . . It was he, more than any other man, who thought out the . . . details of the government of the Union; and, out of the chaos that existed after the Revolution, raised a fabric every part of which is instinct with his thought.

Thomas Jefferson on John Marshall (1807)

His twistifications of the law in the case of Marbury [and] in that of Burr . . . shew how dextrously he can reconcile law to his personal biasses.

Daniel Webster on John Marshall (1814)

There is no man in the court who strikes me like Marshall. . . . I never have seen a man of whose intellect I had a higher opinion.

John Quincy Adams on John Marshall (1835)

By the ascendancy of his genius, by the amenity of his deportment, and by the imperturbable command of his temper, [he] has given a permanent and systematic character to the decisions of the Court, and settled many great constitutional questions favorably to the continuance of the Union.

Thomas Jefferson on James Madison (c. 1800)

He acquired a habit of self-possession which placed at ready command the rich resources of his luminous and discriminating mind, . . . Never wandering from his subject into vain declamation, but pursuing it closely in language pure, classical, and copious, soothing always the feelings of his adversaries by civilities and softness of expression, he rose to the eminent station which he held in the great National convention of 1787.

Henry Clay on James Madison (1812)

Mr. Madison is wholly unfit for the storms of War. Nature has cast him in too benevolent a mould. Admirably adapted to the tranquil scenes of peace —blending all the mild & amiable virtues, he is not fit for the rough and rude blasts which the conflicts of Nations generate.

Daniel Webster on James Madison (1824)

Mr. Madison was the wisest of our Presidents, except Washington.

Henry Clay on Andrew Jackson (1825)

I can not believe that killing two thousand five hundred Englishmen at New Orleans, qualifies for the various, difficult, and complicated duties of the chief magistracy.

Sam Houston on Andrew Jackson (1827)

Your virtues, your qualifications, and your distinguished services to the country have rendered you the rallying point of the friends of principle [those opposed to John Quincy Adams] throughout the Union; . . . the Republicans ask nothing in return but that pleasure and joy of seeing the destinies of this country wrested from the hands of a corrupt Dynasty, and guided by an enlightened Patriot, who will regard the principles of our Government, and administer its laws agreeably to the constitution!

This patriotic memorial symbolizes Americans' long-held, idealized opinion of our first President.

Daniel Webster on Andrew Jackson (1829)

General Jackson will be here about the
   15th of February.
Nobody knows what he will do.
Many letters are sent to him; he answers
   none of them
My opinion is
That when he comes he will bring a
   breeze with him.
Which way it will blow I cannot tell.

Henry Clay on Daniel Webster (1824)

I rejoice to find such men as yourself [Edward Everett] and Mr. Webster cherishing correct opinions, as I think, on the great subject of Internal Improvements. It would certainly be a very narrow and selfish principle to oppose them, upon the ground that New England would not participate in their benefit, to the same extent as can other sections. And yet it is only the liberal & enlightened that can, in the first instance, withstand the influence of that principle.

Rev. Theodore Parker on Daniel Webster (1850)

No living man has done so much to debauch the conscience of the nation. . . . I know of no deed in American history done by a son of New England to which I can compare this [7th of March speech supporting the Compromise of 1850], but the act of Benedict Arnold.

Andrew Jackson on Henry Clay (1829)

He is certainly the bases[t], meanest scoundrel that ever disgraced the image of his god—nothing too mean or low for him to condescend to to secretly carry his cowardly & base *slander* into effect; even the aged and Virtuous female is not free from his secrete combinations of base slander—*but enough—you know me.* . . . retributive *justice* will visit him and his pander[er]s heads.

Daniel Webster on Henry Clay (1852?)

Mr. Clay is a great man; beyond all question, a true patriot. He has done much for his country. He ought long ago to have been elected President.

John Quincy Adams on John Calhoun (1837)

Calhoun looks like a man racked with furious passions and stung with disappointed ambition, as undoubtedly he is.

Daniel Webster on John Calhoun (1844)

John C. Calhoun [was] longheaded, a man of extraordinary power,—much the ablest man in the Senate.

Thomas Hart Benton on John Calhoun (c. 1849)

Anybody else—anybody; you may tell me to go and ask the pardon of a negro in the jail, and I will go and do it. But I won't be reconciled to Calhoun,—I won't, sir! Calhoun is a humbug.

Sam Houston on John Calhoun (1849)

Upon what authority does Mr. Calhoun assume the character of guardian of the whole South? Whence does he derive the privilege of holding the Senators of the other States accountable before his constituents of South Carolina, as betrayers of them and the whole South?

THE NATION'S FATHER

George Washington, the man who led the infant nation through revolution and its initial experiment in self-government, had appeared until recently as a one-dimensional hero. The complexity of his brilliance has been fully revealed by his modern biographer, James Thomas Flexner:

To an extent which under examination becomes shocking, the passage of years has buried in historical memory the living Washington. The charm and the splendor of his character, the greatness of his contribution to the United States and to human freedom everywhere, have been distorted into various caricatures, which are now regarded as the true man.

Even as it would be ridiculous to attribute a volcanic eruption to a molehill, so it is ridiculous to define Washington as a man incapable of achieving what Washington achieved. The cold hero who never smiled or loved or told a lie; the comic figure characterized by wooden false teeth; the hypocritical crook who refused any salary as Commander in Chief and then forged his expense account; the autocrat chuckling as he undermined the republican aspirations of American people; the self-congratulatory stuffed shirt—none of these could possibly have done what the record reveals Washington did. Not one of these would as a stripling have been entrusted with a dangerous and vital diplomatic mission through a frozen wilderness; not one could have kept, year after year, an unfed and naked army in the field to win a seemingly hopeless war against the might of Great Britain; not one would have repelled the possibility opened to him of being dictator or king; not one could have led a far-flung nation into a stronger constitutional union and then steered to solidity the first major republican government in the modern world; not one could have directed a mercantile nation torn by ideological disputes on the path of peace through the wars of the French Revolution; not one would have, in a position of perhaps unassailable power, always put first what he considered the welfare of the people.

Washington had to have the fierceness necessary to a successful soldier, the self-will necessary for a leader of men, the self-interest essential to the amassing of a large estate. He exploded sometimes into actions of which his best judgment disapproved. He could be very overbearing to his subordinates, even to fellow statesmen of such stature as Jefferson and Hamilton. In his private life as in his public, he was not always understanding, not always kind. Yet Washington wished to be wise and good.

Which of the triumphant generals, which of the great rulers in all time have so willingly relinquished power, have inspired so little fear among their contemporaries, so much love? Only after Washington's death could Jefferson have been correctly styled "The Man of the People." While Washington lived, even in his last unhappy years, the majority of the people followed, often in opposition to the expressed convictions of the Jeffersonians, wherever Washington led.

Washington's character comprised that pull of opposites which give color and depth. His heart was warm; his emotions fierce; his gentleness both deep and the result of control; his prudence due as much to self-education as to temperament; his intentions (although he sometimes slipped) altruistic; his force tremendous; his feelings oversensitive; his charm usually overwhelming. His motions were graceful although he had the physical strength of a giant. Conscious of an inadequate education, he was always slow of speech, seeking the right word. If he became sometimes self-righteous, he was always self-demanding. Although he was an aristocrat by temperament and achievement, his kindness knew no class or economic bounds.

Had Washington refused a second term or been unable to serve, the United States would quite probably have slipped into the wars touched off by the French Revolution, which wrecked much of Europe. Such involvement abroad might well have incited at home civil dissension that could have broken the union into two or more mutually hostile nations. The area now covered by the United States might well have become, in its political divisions, another Europe. Not even historians now most strongly interventionist believe that the newly formed republic would have been better off had it been caught up, while still weak and coalescing, in foreign politics.

It has been assumed (even by Jefferson, who did not then object) that Washington would, like the kings who ruled around him, stay in power until death required a new President. Washington himself believed that the American experiment needed, to complete its demonstration that humanity could rule itself, the orderly relinquishment of power by one elected representative to his elected successor. This would be a prodigy in a world of kings. Although he might well have sought vindication from attacks in the overwhelming suffrage he would undoubtedly have received had he run again, Washington made his last major gift to the nation and the world by returning of his own free will to the private life for which part of his nature had always hankered. The republican system was thus sent rolling down its own road.

According to modern ideas, Washington was not at sixty-seven a truly old man. Yet his thread had been spun and he knew it. As soon as his final illness came upon him, he was sure—and not altogether regretfully—that this was the end.

BIBLIOGRAPHIC CREDITS: Jefferson Papers, Library of Congress, Series 1, Vol. XIII, No. 244; Marshall Papers, Library of Congress; Jefferson Papers, Library of Congress, Series 1, Vol. II, No. 215; Alexander Hamilton, *Letter from Alexander Hamilton, concerning the public conduct and character of John Adams, Esq.* (1800); George W. Corner, *Autobiography of Benjamin Rush; His "Travels Through Life" Together with His Commonplace Book for 1789-1813*, Princeton University Press, copyright 1948 by the American Philosophical Society; Marshall Papers, Library of Congress; Hamilton Papers, Library of Congress; Thomas Jefferson, *Anas* (1854); Hamilton Papers, Columbia University Library; John Adams, *Autobiography* (1816); Jefferson Papers, Library of Congress, Series 5, Vol. XV, No. 99; Peter Harvey, *Reminiscences and Anecdotes of Daniel Webster* (1882); Quotations from the Adams Papers are from the microfilm edition, by permission of the Massachusetts Historical Society; Jefferson, *Anas;* James F. Hopkins, *The Papers of Henry Clay,* Vol. I, University of Kentucky Press, 1959; Walker Lewis, *Speak for Yourself Daniel,* Houghton, Mifflin Co., 1969; Hopkins, *Henry Clay,* Vol. IV, 1967; Jackson Manuscripts, Library of Congress; Reprinted from *An Epoch and a Man: Martin Van Buren and His Times* by Denis Tilden Lynch, by permission of Kennikat Press Inc., copyright 1961 by Kennikat Press Inc.; Hopkins, *Henry Clay,* Vol. III, 1963; Francis P. Cobbe (ed.), *Theodore Parker's Works* (1863); Jackson Manuscripts, Library of Congress; Charles Lanman, *Haphazard Personalities* (1886); The Adams Papers; Harvey, *Reminiscences;* Harvey, *Reminiscences; The Northern Standard,* May 12, 1849; From the Introduction to *George Washington: Anguish and Farewell (1793-1799)* by James Thomas Flexner, copyright © 1972 James Thomas Flexner, reprinted by permission of Little, Brown and Company.

PICTURE CREDITS: p. 291—Library of Congress; p. 293—by H.A. Ogden; p. 295—Chicago Historical Society; p. 297—Huntington Library, San Marino; p. 299—Free Library of Philadelphia; p. 301—Library of Congress; p. 303—Culver; p. 305—*Comic Almanac,* 1834; p. 307—The Bettmann Archive, Inc.; p. 309—Library of Congress; p. 311—The Metropolitan Museum of Art

A Presidential Gallery

WASHINGTON THROUGH BUCHANAN

"I do solemnly swear that I will faithfully execute the Office of President of the United States, and will to the best of my ability, preserve, protect and defend the Constitution of the United States."

All the chief executives of our nation have sworn this oath. They have then gone on—both the great and the middling—to lead the country in a term or series of terms that would test their personal capacities to the utmost.

That heroic and occasionally tragic story is best told in the faces of the men who lived it. Fortunately, most Presidents were painted while in office, and their portraits have been preserved either at the National Portrait Gallery or in other collections.

In the next several pages, as if in the chambers of a gallery, one encounters the first fifteen Presidents. Their common purpose and grandest accomplishment was the shaping of their unique office.

All but the foremost lived in the White House (Abigail Adams becoming its first First Lady). In the 1839 view above, the executive mansion rather fittingly bespeaks both the log cabin of the frontier and the palace of kings.

George Washington (1789-1797)

After the victory at Yorktown, one of his colonels proposed that General Washington be crowned king. The thought of heading the nation, as king or otherwise, appalled Washington; he wished only to retire to his fields. But the qualities he had demonstrated in war rendered him invaluable to his country in peace as well. For Washington's greatness as a general lay not so much in tactical brilliance as in his ability to hold a ragtag army together in defeat and adversity. As the liberated states drifted toward anarchy, Washington seemed—even, reluctantly, to himself—the logical choice to weld the Union.

His influence on the executive office began even before there was a presidency. Its powers, wrote a delegate to the Convention of 1787, would not "have been so great had not many of the members cast their eyes toward General Washington as President."

He was acutely aware that the "first of everything, *in our situation* will serve to establish a precedent." One of his first precedents was to name a cabinet; the Constitution made no mention of such a body. One of his last was to decline a third term, a tradition broken only by Franklin Roosevelt.

Although careful not to usurp the powers of Congress, Washington was a strong chief executive. Congress alone could declare war, but Washington could and did declare neutrality during the Franco-British war. His two terms left foreign policy firmly in the hands of the President.

In 1794 he ordered militia to suppress the Whisky Rebellion, thus affirming Congress's right to tax the people and the executive's power to enforce the law.

Tall and charismatic, Washington was well on his way to patron sainthood in his own lifetime. Portraits of him proliferated; this exceptional likeness is by Gil-

Life	Born Feb. 22, 1732, Westmoreland County, Va. Married widow, Martha Custis; two stepchildren. Died December 14, 1799.
Campaigns	Only President to receive unanimous vote of the electoral college (twice: 1789, 1793). Delegates voted for two men; runner-up became Vice President.
Milestones	Put a new and mistrusted office on sound footing. Presided over creation of national bank, adoption of first ten Amendments (the Bill of Rights).
Image	Honest, fair, high-principled. Slowed by caution, sometimes seemed indecisive. Aristocratic, aloof, formal to a fault.

bert Stuart. "All his features," said Stuart, "were indicative of the strongest and most ungovernable passions" —but always, he added, under complete control.

Typically the conciliator, the deliberator, the methodical seeker of advice, Washington drew into his cabinet two opposed titans: Alexander Hamilton, leader of the Federalists, served as secretary of the treasury; Thomas Jefferson, soon to win the presidency as a Democratic-Republican, was his secretary of state. Yet Washington kept his office above the two parties while deriving the best qualities of both. On occasion he aggravated their worst qualities. "Curse on his virtues," Jefferson once blurted, "they have undone his country."

But when Washington died, the country mourned for months. His friend Fisher Ames wrote of "The unambitious life of Washington, declining fame, yet courted by it. . . . His presidency will form an epoch [known] as the age of Washington."

MOUNT VERNON

A silver eagle, symbol of the nation he helped unite, adorned the general's hat.

John Adams (1797-1801)

While serving as Washington's Vice President, John Adams complained (as have most Vice Presidents) that the country "has in its wisdom contrived for me the most insignificant office that ever the invention of man contrived. . . ." But if eclipse under the Father of His Country irked the brilliant, ambitious John Adams, succeeding him proved even worse.

Just getting elected mired Adams in the politicking that Washington had soared above. There was a "natural division," Adams believed, between "the gentlemen and the simple men;" the masses he mistrusted in turn found little to idolize in the scholarly Massachusetts aristocrat. But the "simple men" had no vote in 1796. The landed gentlemen of the Federalist party did, and they found much to admire in John Adams's philosophy. He squeaked past Jefferson, leader of the Democratic-Republicans, by three electoral votes—then by the system of the day won Jefferson as Vice President.

The two began well, but ideological differences drove them apart. By term's end they were no longer on speaking terms. A more disastrous rift split the Federalist party itself as Alexander Hamilton sought time and again to manipulate the President; John Adams proved equally as often that an opinionated, determined, and—by his own candid analysis—"puffy, vain, conceited" chief executive would not be anyone's tool.

Nor had he ever been. He had advocated liberty at the Continental Congress, helped produce the Declaration of Independence, urged the creation of an army with Washington in command, and won a sorely needed Dutch loan for the new republic. From farmer's son to historymaker, he had weighed each

Life	Born Oct. 19, 1735, Quincy, Mass. Graduated Harvard. Married Abigail Smith; five children. Died July 4, 1826.
Campaigns	First election under two-party system (candidates named by Congress in caucus). Elected 1796 with less than half the electoral votes. Defeated in 1800.
Milestones	Opposed alliance with Britain; forced to wage undeclared naval war with France. His peace overtures finally succeeded as victories brought French to terms.
Image	Haughty, fond of titles, yet respected for intellectual depth. Shyness masked strength of conviction, determination, and drive.

question objectively, then taken his stand against all comers. For love of country he had called the Boston Tea Party "magnificent"—yet for love of justice he had volunteered to defend British soldiers on trial for the mob-incited Boston Massacre. John Trumbull's portrait of Adams reflects these sterling qualities.

As President, Adams sought to strengthen his country. He created the Navy Department and, with good intentions, secured the repressive Alien and Sedition Acts; but excesses under the acts led to their repeal, leaving his image tarnished. France continued to demand his attention; when he sent peace envoys to Paris after years of rebuff and piracy, the Hamiltonians disowned him. Rather than yield to them he led a sundered party into the 1800 election and lost. But it turned out, in defeat, that he had been right all along; he had produced peace almost singlehandedly. France accepted the peace treaty the year Adams stepped down from the presidency.

Adams gave Abigail this locket; she gave him a calm hand and understanding heart.

Thomas Jefferson (1801-1809)

The third President once took time out from the burdens of office to catalog a collection of fossils. He devised a prize-winning plow, read Plato in Greek, smuggled rice out of Italy to try growing it at home, and even proposed a Panama canal. He designed the neoclassical Monticello and there charmed guests with his musical skill and horsemanship. His *Summary View of the Rights of British America*—"Open your breast, Sire, to liberal and expanded thought," it exhorted George III—brought him fame at thirty-one; two years later he authored the Declaration of Independence. Only once in the history of the presidency has there been a Thomas Jefferson, the total Renaissance man, exemplar of the Age of Enlightenment.

The highest office had little use for Jefferson's knowledge of fossils, but great need of his acute mind, which brought order and sense to any field it explored. In Jefferson's view, the Federalists' desire for a powerful central government controlled by a ruling class betrayed the ideals of the Revolution. The United States, he argued, "must show by example . . . that the will of the majority . . . is the only sure guardian of the rights of man." No longer able to stay aloof from party politics, preferring, as he put it, "the boisterous sea of liberty" to the "calm of despotism," Jefferson openly became leader of the Republican party in 1800, the year Rembrandt Peale painted this portrait. Soon thereafter he won the presidency from John Adams and promised to run a "wise and frugal government."

Ironically, in the most crucial decision of his first term, Jefferson outfederaled the Federalists in his use of sheer presidential clout. Nothing in the Constitution empowered him to buy territory; yet when Napoleon offered him the Louisiana Territory for

Always inventing, never patenting, "Long Tom" cut a hole in Monticello's floor for weights of his clock.

Life	Born April 13, 1743, Albemarle County, Va. Married Martha Skelton; six children. Died July 4, 1826.
Campaigns	His party won in 1800, but Jefferson and running mate Aaron Burr tied. Burr refused to withdraw. A Federalist-controlled House took thirty-six ballots to decide. (Twelfth Amendment later separated the contests.) Reelected 1804.
Milestones	Steered U.S. toward more local democracy. Doubled the country's size. Sent Lewis and Clark beyond the nation's frontiers.
Image	Radical to some, visionary to others, but to all a gifted writer and scholar.

$15 million, Jefferson swallowed his qualms, seized the bargain—which doubled the nation's area—and informed Congress later. Irony marked his second term as well; when Britain and France, at war again, began harassing American shipping, he sought to avoid entanglement by ordering American vessels off the sea. Merchants, sailors, farmers, fishermen howled in chorus; a judge Jefferson had appointed damned the President's Embargo Act as "an encroachment upon individual liberty." To tread on personal freedom was the next-to-last thing Jefferson wanted to do—but to lead his nation into war was the last.

A persuasive statesman, Jefferson saw many of his visionary ideas on education, religious freedom, and civil rights become law. In retirement, the two old scholars, Jefferson and Adams struck up a warm correspondence, full of memories of the great events they had helped to shape. They were the only two Signers of the Declaration of Independence to become President.

James Madison (1809-1817)

The "withered little apple-John" that Washington Irving described at the inauguration of 1809 stood barely five-foot-six, weighed a frail hundred pounds, and was the smallest of all the Presidents. Bookish, reticent, nearly inaudible in speech, Madison was viewed by many as a man of straw, likely to be swayed by the slightest breeze of opposition. Eight years as Jefferson's secretary of state had merely enhanced that impression, since Jefferson habitually handled foreign policy himself, leaving James Madison all but invisible.

But the somewhat hypochondriacal Madison already stood tall among the Founding Fathers. Though he insisted that the Constitution was "the work of many heads and many hands," his hand had written by far the largest part. A respected scion of one of Virginia's first families, he had spoken with faint voice but forceful logic at the Convention of 1787; his notes are history's clearest window into those secret proceedings. He had then urged ratification of the Constitution in *The Federalist* papers, a series of tightly reasoned, persuasive essays. As a congressman, Madison became a leader of the emerging Jeffersonian bloc and was the prime mover in shaping it into the Democratic-Republican party.

Jefferson's chosen successor, Madison came to the presidency as seeds of war were sprouting. England and France were again pestering American ships. The English habit of impressing American sailors into the Royal Navy especially galled the proud Americans. Yet even a storm of protest from War Hawks such as Henry Clay of Kentucky failed to blow the President off his course toward a peaceful settlement. France agreed to honor America's shipping rights, meanwhile continuing to seize U.S. ships, but there was no offer of a

Nostrums from an elegant medicine chest soothed the sickly Madison's many ills.

Life	Born March 16, 1751, King George County, Va. Married widow Dolley Payne Todd; no children. Died June 28, 1836.
Campaigns	In 1808 defeated Federalist Charles C. Pinckney and his own running mate, George Clinton, who had accepted vice-presidential nomination, then campaigned for the presidency. Reelected 1812.
Milestones	Let national bank expire in 1811 but sought its rebirth in 1816; annexed West Florida.
Image	Shy and bookish, yet witty in conversation. Superb political thinker; poor administrator.

change in policy from Britain. Finally on June 1, 1812, Madison asked Congress to declare war, unaware that Britain had acquiesced to his demands the day before.

"Mr. Madison's War" began badly. Defeat followed defeat, and when the British burned the White House, his tattered popularity seemed to burn with it. Once his graceful Dolley had been the toast of Washington, gay and charming at every social event; now she fled the mansion she had made a home.

Suddenly a spate of victories ended the war in a draw. Americans felt they had won, however, and high on the crest of the nation's resurgent pride rode James Madison. The Federalist party, which had opposed the war and even threatened secession, withered in disgrace.

In his second term, Madison reversed himself on many earlier stands. Once against the U.S. Bank, he sponsored its reestablishment in 1816; then later signed a tariff bill he had earlier opposed. Just before retiring, Madison sat for this portrait by Joseph Wood.

James Monroe (1817-1825)

In the election of 1816, Massachusetts—still clinging to Federalism—voted against Democratic-Republican James Monroe. But by July 12, 1817, a conciliatory Boston newspaper could boast that "many persons have met at festive boards, in pleasant converse, whom party politics had long severed." The occasion was the new President's unprecedented good will tour of the North, and the newspaper's headline stuck ever after to his presidency: "ERA OF GOOD FEELINGS."

The nation had many reasons to feel good: naval victories over the world's most formidable navy; freedom at last from Europe's squabbles. And most important, the Democratic experiment seemed to be working. Thus, a generation reared under the Stars and Stripes looked westward and rolled up its sleeves.

It looked backward, too, to the heroes of its birth. James Monroe had crossed the Delaware with Washington, nursed the wounded Lafayette, and studied law under Jefferson. The presidency would not see another revolutionary, and Monroe knew it well. John Vanderlyn in 1822 portrayed him fittingly as the last President to wear knee breeches, cockade, and sword. This portrait hangs in City Hall of New York City.

A splendid administrator, Monroe named a strong cabinet from both North and South and would have added West had not Henry Clay turned him down. He then settled down to wrestle for eight years with the nation's growing pains. For not all the era's feelings were good. Landless men wanted the vote; depression struck in 1819; and the slavery question raised hackles everywhere.

The Missouri Compromise of 1820 kept the uneasy balance of slave and free states. But like other thoughtful men since the Revolution, Monroe

Monroe penned the speech that included his Doctrine at this desk.

foresaw the inevitable showdown. He owned slaves himself, yet deplored slavery; his ambivalence reflected the nation's. He seemed ambivalent too when he urged an amendment empowering Congress to build roads and authorize other internal improvements, then vetoed the Cumberland Road bill when his proposal for an amendment was defeated.

History remembers him chiefly for the Monroe Doctrine, a single sentence in his 1823 message to Congress: "The American continents . . . are henceforth not to be considered as subjects for future colonization. . . ." The words were written by his secretary of state, John Quincy Adams, and Europe did not take them seriously until the United States became a major power toward the end of the century. But James Monroe made them a national policy; events proved them to be of immense importance; and Presidents invoked them from the Spanish-American War to the Cuban missile crisis.

Life Born April 28, 1758, Westmoreland County, Va. Married Elizabeth Kortright; three children. Died July 4, 1831.

Campaigns Opposing disgraced Federalists, he won handily as a Democratic-Republican in 1816, and by all but one electoral vote in 1820.

Milestones Missouri Compromise postponed conflict over slavery. Treaties fixed Canadian border; acquired Florida from Spain. "Principles of President Monroe" later become Monroe Doctrine.

Image Unpretentious, generous, stolid but steadfast friend. Not a brilliant statesman; more a compromiser than an innovator.

John Quincy Adams (1825-1829)

President John Quincy Adams, following the unimaginative James Monroe, must have seemed like a whirlwind. He rose at five or six in the morning, retired about midnight, and in between deluged Congress with visionary proposals. Aid to education and the arts, a naval academy, mapping expeditions, an interior department, astronomical observatories, interstate highways and canals—these and more that came to pass in time were proposed by Adams.

Conscience-stricken by the plight of the American Indians, Adams also worked out a program of aid for them, asking Congress for land in the West where they could live peacefully and undisturbed.

It is America's good fortune to produce such public men, but sometimes its misfortune—and theirs—to frustrate them. For four years a hostile Congress rejected his programs, one by one. And then the nation rejected him, choosing for President his most ardent Senate foe, Andrew Jackson.

Adams's term was blighted, ironically, by his election. He had been a brilliant diplomat and superb secretary of state; in the latter post he negotiated the treaties that acquired Florida and settled the Canadian-U.S. border dispute. His firmness kept Russia off the West Coast; his hand shaped the Monroe Doctrine. Shrill, pudgy, and doggedly independent, he was difficult to like, but in 1824, with such a shining record behind him, he was a logical choice for a presidential nomination.

Jackson polled highest, Adams second, William Crawford third, Henry Clay fourth. Since none had a majority, the House had to decide between the top three. Clay swung his support to Adams, and the House named him President on the first ballot.

When Adams named Clay secretary of state, howls of a "corrupt bargain"

ADAMS NATIONAL HISTORIC SITE

In this rocker, the unbending Adams allowed himself to bend.

rose to a crescendo that would echo through the next four years. History can neither prove nor fully refute the charge. But Adams's diaries assert that he chose Clay as the best man. Adams's integrity and disdain for party politics back up the assertion—and so does his image as painted by Gilbert Stuart. Completed by Thomas Sully, it reflects a proud, tight-lipped man who would rather lose than make a deal.

But the common man felt cheated, and in the 1820s the masses were finding their voice. Adams became the first President to lose his congressional majority in mid-term; the second to fail in his bid for reelection.

To his delight, he was voted back to Washington in 1830 as representative from Massachusetts. For eighteen years, he harangued, persuaded, and wrote in support of his views, notably against the "gag rule" that prevented debate on slavery. In the midst of a speech, a stroke cut him down—but not before friends and foes alike had dubbed him "Old Man Eloquent."

Andrew Jackson (1829-1837)

"The country is ruined past redemption," snapped Virginia Congressman John Randolph after the tumultuous inauguration of Andrew Jackson. To Randolph and other aristocratic Americans, the election of Jackson seemed to mark the end of reasonable, ordered government and the beginning of mob rule. The next eight years did little to dispel their fears. For Jackson was one of the strongest Presidents in history, one of the least educated, and in the heart of the ordinary citizen whose causes he advanced, one of the most beloved.

Jackson's image makers portrayed him as a rough-hewn, short-tempered, tobacco-chomping frontiersman and war hero—all of which he was, though wealth gained by land speculating had also made him a genteel plantation owner. He was presented as the champion of the common man, and he was that too, sharing the masses' mistrust of special privileges and breeding.

But when they hailed him as a Jeffersonian Democrat, they missed the mark. Jefferson had wanted a nation in which educated patricians governed for the good of the masses; the President's job, he felt, was to carry out the people's will as expressed through Congress. He would have stood aghast as Jackson reshaped the presidency and the whole fabric of government.

One out of five federal workers lost his job as Jackson dispensed the spoils of victory to office-seeking cronies, many of whom were qualified only by their lack of qualifications—a virtue in this heyday of commonness. His predecessors had invoked the presidential veto only nine times in all, and each time on grounds of constitutionality; Jackson vetoed a dozen bills, some simply because he did not

<table>
<tr><td>Life</td><td>Born March 15, 1767, Waxhaws in Carolinas. Married divorcee, Rachel Donelson Robards; no children. Died June 8, 1845.</td></tr>
<tr><td>Campaigns</td><td>Let supporters run mud-slinging campaign in 1828. First President nominated by national party convention (1832); first truly elected by popular vote.</td></tr>
<tr><td>Milestones</td><td>Shifted locus of power from Congress to presidency. Only President to see the national debt paid in full.</td></tr>
<tr><td>Image</td><td>Proud, stubborn, autocratic, yet true to friends and tender memory of his pipe-smoking Rachel.</td></tr>
</table>

like them. Soon cartoonists began to sketch him as "King Andrew I," crown on head, veto in hand. His answer, a gem of Jacksonian logic, was that he was the only government official elected by all the people and thus the only instrument of their will.

Jackson was no theorist. He dealt with each situation as he saw fit, whipping South Carolina into line when it tried to nullify the federal tariff, then looking the other way when Georgia nullified a federal treaty in order to seize Indian lands. He knew nothing of banking, yet slew the national bank because he felt it favored the wealthy. Hunch and intuition guided his hand, and to the ordinary citizen these were enough. Jackson not only led his America, he embodied it.

Full of drama, replete with regalia, this painting by John Wesley Jarvis portrays Old Hickory at his brusque and tousled best.

THE HERMITAGE

© WHITE HOUSE HISTORICAL ASSOCIATION

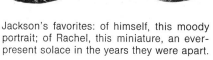

Jackson's favorites: of himself, this moody portrait; of Rachel, this miniature, an ever-present solace in the years they were apart.

Martin Van Buren (1837-1841)

Admirers dubbed five-foot-six Van Buren the "Little Magician." Detractors called him the "Red Fox of Kinderhook" after his New York State birthplace. Both were right; the tavern keeper's son was a consummate politician, a wily wizard who could yank the rug from under an opponent one week and charm him over a gourmet dinner the next.

Van Buren freely confessed to a mediocre mind. But he understood the value of patronage, compromise, and persuasion in melding factions into a smoothly running political machine, and he recognized the immense new power of public opinion in the conduct of statecraft. He was, as one observer puts it, the nation's first systematic national politician.

It was Martin Van Buren who converted Jackson's popularity into political clout and pulled together the Democratic party which nominated him. It was the Red Fox who quit the Senate and ran for governor of New York to deliver his state's votes to Jackson. And when Jackson's feuding cabinet split over the snubbing of one member's wife, it was the Little Magician who resigned as secretary of state so others would do likewise; Jackson named a new cabinet and chose Van Buren as his next Vice President. In the campaign of 1836 Van Buren emerged an easy victor, the first President born under the Stars and Stripes.

He had hardly taken office when the Panic of 1837 erupted, in part a legacy from Jackson's bank veto. As scores of banks failed, many of them still holding federal funds, Van Buren proposed —and got—the independent treasury system that still holds the nation's purse strings. But the worst depression the country had yet known dragged on for half a decade abetted by a crop failure and Van Buren's *laissez faire*

The White House now holds only a bust and this inscribed silver pitcher from Van Buren's stay.

© WHITE HOUSE HISTORICAL ASSOCIATION

Life	Born Dec. 5, 1782, Kinderhook, N.Y. Married Hannah Hoes; four children. Died July 24, 1862.
Campaigns	Van Buren defeated William Henry Harrison in 1836, then lost to him in 1840. Defeated as Free Soil candidate in 1848.
Milestones	Averted war with British by settling Canadian border wrangles, and with Mexico by refusing to seize Texas. Created U.S. Treasury after battle with Congress.
Image	Expert in acquiring power, but inept at using it. Reputation as fence-sitter persisted into more forceful later years.

view of government: "The less government interferes with private pursuits, the better for . . . prosperity."

Meanwhile the storm clouds of slavery gathered. When Van Buren tried to compromise, he alienated both sides. He was regarded as proslavery in the North, antislavery in the South. When he finally took a stand and refused to add another slave state by annexing Texas, his party disowned him, although the act would have risked war with Mexico.

Henry Inman's idealized portrait, painted near the end of Van Buren's term, reflects none of the strife—though perhaps some of the gloom—of that hour. For the magic had gone out of the Little Magician. Hung on the horns of hard times and slavery, spurned by people and party, the Red Fox went home to Kinderhook to try twice more for the presidency and fail in both attempts. It may be a measure of the turmoil of the times that no later President until Grant would win a second term in a nationwide election.

William Henry Harrison (1841)

Down Main Street they came, a squad of men pushing a long axle on which a giant paper ball festooned with slogans trundled ponderously along. They added a cliché to the language as they kept the ball rolling for William Henry Harrison and the Whig ticket on Main Streets all across the growing nation. "May times improve as on we move," it proclaimed to the voters in 1840. "Farewell dear Van, you're not the man."

But was Harrison "the man" for these troubled times? No one really knew. In his first presidential campaign four years earlier, he had been advised to "say not one word about his principles or his creed . . . about what he thinks now and will do hereafter." He lost that election, not surprisingly, to Jackson's heir apparent, Martin Van Buren—then won the next by the selfsame tactic of silence on the issues of the day.

The aim of the Whigs in both campaigns was not so much to put Harrison in the White House as to pry the Jacksonian Democrats out. They ransacked the old soldier's record as an Indian fighter; among other battles he had fought bravely against Tecumseh's confederacy at the Tippecanoe River. It was a meaningless victory, but enough for the phrasemakers; "Tippecanoe and Tyler Too" kept the general and his running mate on the tip of every tongue.

A Baltimore newspaper unwittingly provided the campaign's central theme when it tried to portray Harrison as a man of shallow mind, content to sit "in his Log Cabin" with a pension and "a barrel of Hard Cider." Old Tip's men seized the folksy image, a perfect foil to Van Buren's patrician lifestyle. Ironically, Van Buren was the self-made man; Harrison was yet another scion of the Virginia planter aristocracy. No matter. The Whigs erected

Under such homey bunting, throngs rallied around the tired old hero they scarcely knew.

Life	Born Feb. 9, 1773, Charles County, Va. Married Anna Symmes; ten children. Died April 4, 1841, Washington, D.C.
Campaigns	First presidential candidate of the new Whig party, a coalition of anti-Jacksonians. Defeated in 1836; elected in 1840 by 4-to-1 in the electoral college.
Milestones	Oldest man ever elected President; first to die in office.
Image	Successfully presented as plow-pushing frontiersman despite wealth and pedigree. Genial and considerate, though often overgenerous with promises to friends. Mediocre as congressman and senator.

log cabins everywhere; and from these campaign headquarters, they deluged the electorate with a wondrous array of trinkets, drummed up rallies and torchlight parades, and raised well-cidered voices in slogan and song. Though little was said about the issues, it was anything but a silent campaign.

Albert Gallatin Hoit went to North Bend, Ohio, to paint this portrait, now in the National Portrait Gallery. Sure enough, there was the original log cabin built by Lieutenant Harrison for his bride in 1795. But in 1840 Old Tip was sixty-seven, and the cabin was only a corner of a much-enlarged, sumptuous mansion.

Proud of his rugged frontier image, Harrison stood hatless in bitter cold to deliver his inaugural address of an hour and forty minutes. A month later he died of pneumonia and the exhaustion of trying to satisfy hordes of office seekers. Seeking to please friends, he had promised some cabinet posts twice, some thrice. His failing plea: "Don't trouble me."

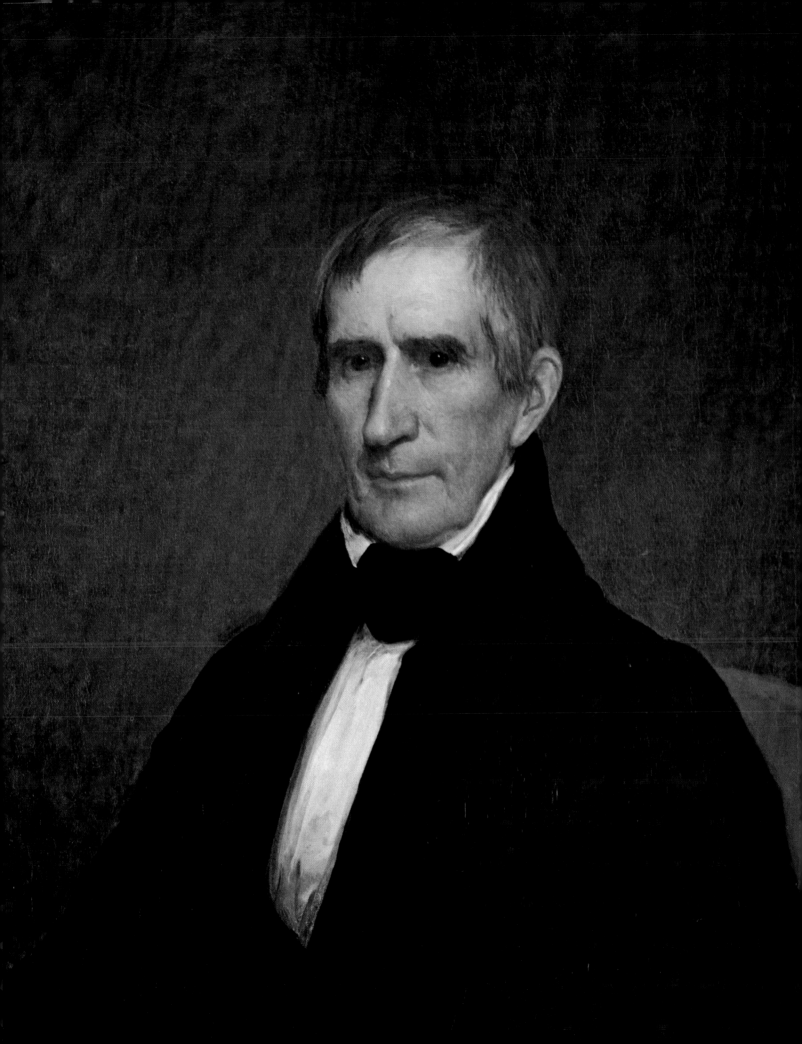

John Tyler (1841-1845)

The unthinkable had happened. Pliable old Tippecanoe had died after only one month in office, leaving an almost intact four year term to "Tyler Too." Yet John Tyler, the Whigs knew, was nobody's me-too.

Whig chieftain Henry Clay sought to limit Tyler's role to that of "acting President" lest he build up a following and rob Clay of the 1844 nomination. Then Secretary of State Daniel Webster reminded Tyler that Harrison's cabinet was to have made decisions by majority vote, the President having one vote like the rest.

Tyler, like most antebellum Southerners, was a strict constructionist, believing that "implied powers" should not be read into the Constitution. But the Constitution was vague about whether a Vice President succeeded to "the Powers and Duties of the said Office of President," or to the office itself. The decision was Tyler's, and he wasted no time making it. He kept Old Tip's cabinet but scrapped the one-vote idea; he alone would lead, and the members could act as advisers or resign. After a swearing-in ritual and an inaugural address, Tyler became President, and at fifty-one he was the youngest yet.

His troubles began almost immediately. The Whigs controlled Congress, and Tyler was, at the moment, a Whig. But at heart he had always been a Democrat, and as President he would become one again. John Tyler was one of many who had backed into the Whig amalgam because of what the Jacksonians had made of the Democratic party—a force for nationalism that threatened the states' rights so dear to Southern hearts. The Whigs, also nationalistic, had nominated Tyler to balance the ticket; now they had to fight him.

Life	Born March 29, 1790, Charles County, Va. Twice married: Letitia Christian, seven children; Julia Gardiner, seven children. Died Jan. 18, 1862.
Campaigns	Nominated for Vice President 1840 to lure Southern votes to Harrison. Splinter party candidate in 1844.
Milestones	Annexed Texas; calmed disputes with England over Canadian border; arranged treaty with China. First to face impeachment try.
Image	A cultured, charming Virginia gentleman. Facade of genteel serenity masked financial worries and tragedy of his first wife's death in 1842.

And fight him they did. Within five months "His Accidency" became "Old Veto" as the presidential "Nay" blocked bill after bill. He was burned in effigy, drummed out of the Whig party, and shorn of his cabinet when all but Webster resigned. Domestically his term was a near-fiasco—but internationally it was a success. Three days before his tenure ended, he signed Texas into the Union—a triumph of personal diplomacy and political skill.

Clutching the newspaper that first carried rumors of the annexation, Tyler gazes from G. P. A. Healy's 1859 portrait with an almost wistful grandeur, perhaps looking back on a lifetime of unswerving devotion to the supremacy of the rights of states over those of the federal government— or perhaps ahead to grim days when as a Confederate congressman, he would see those rights assayed in the awful crucible of civil war.

COURTESY OF HARRISON TYLER

Geo. H. Atwood,
Plymouth, Mass.
10th Co. H'vy Art'y

Union soldiers captured Tyler's Bible but treated it with respect; years later it was given to his son.

James K. Polk (1845-1849)

"One," counted James Knox Polk with a sharp slap of the presidential thigh, "a reduction of the tariff; another—slap!—the independent treasury; a third—slap!—the settlement of the Oregon boundary question; and, lastly—slap!—the acquisition of California." His secretary of the navy heard the slaps, and the country heard the echoes as the eleventh President attained all four goals in one term and left his nation a million square miles bigger than when it elected him, its borders stretching for the first time to the Pacific. Not bad for the first dark-horse presidential candidate, chosen by a deadlocked convention and needled by Whig opponents with the query, "Who is James K. Polk?" He was, in fact, one of the most effective Presidents in American history.

And yet the question was a valid one. Polk had few friends, and even those he had felt they scarcely knew this secretive, tenacious, sometimes sly, and often suspicious man. As he chose his cabinet members, he exacted from each a disavowal of any presidential ambitions. He mistrusted not only their loyalties, but also their ambitions, delegating little to them that he could do himself. He claimed to be "the hardest working man in this country," and in all probability he was.

Meanwhile, all around him flourished the Fabulous Forties. The last wails of a lingering depression were drowned by the rising song of the Industrial Revolution. War over the Texas border laid Mexico low in 1848; and for $15 million in "conscience money," Polk added to the United States all of California and the New Mexico area.

Life Born Nov. 2, 1795, Mecklenburg County, N.C. Married Sarah Childress; no children. Died June 15, 1849.

Campaigns Nominated on Democrats' ninth ballot. Dissident Whig James Birney took enough votes from Henry Clay to assure Polk's victory.

Milestones Only President to achieve all platform goals. Strengthened Monroe Doctrine to ban voluntary subjection to a European power. Revised the treasury.

Image A driven but colorless man who met the office's demands with dogged perseverance and great administrative skill. Dour, formal, unimaginative.

Believing that "the only way to treat John Bull was to look him straight in the eye," Polk convinced Congress to terminate the agreement that allowed Britain and the United States to share the Oregon Territory. He then got Britain to withdraw to the forty-ninth parallel, where the border between Canada and the United States still stands. In 1848 he told Congress about gold in the West—then went back to work while miners, merchants, and molls lit out for El Dorado.

By then his work was almost over. Gone was the dark-haired ramrod who had sat for artist Miner Kellogg in 1840; out of the White House in March, 1849, shuffled a bent shadow with only three months to live. People mourned his death with no great feeling, for he had had no great feeling for the people. On the other hand, his marvelous grasp of the issues and their solutions helped to make the forties fabulous.

THE JAMES K. POLK HOME, COLUMBIA, TENNESSEE

Polk and predecessors adorn a fan he gave his Sarah. Pious Mrs. Polk banned wine, cards, dancing in the White House.

Zachary Taylor (1849-1850)

"If elected I would not be the mere president of a party—I would endeavor to act independent of party domination, & should feel bound to administer the Government untrammeled by party schemes. . . ." General Zachary Taylor meant what he said to the voters in 1848. But "party schemes" are an integral part of political life, and the old hero was not always able to ignore them.

The White House had seen other generals, but Taylor was the first to move in without ever having held public office. Only through his great personal popularity and the power of the presidency was he able to hold his own among the politicians.

His popularity had been well earned on the battlefields of the Mexican War, where his victories against armies of superior number had won him such adulation that local groups began nominating him for President two years before the election. John Vanderlyn's portrait, painted about 1852, flatters him; his seamed and heavy face, his unkempt hair and baggy clothes, his large head and stubby legs gave him the look of a simple rough-hewn farmer on whom the duties of President sat no better than his suits.

They were difficult duties in 1849. For years the issue of slavery had been balanced on a delicate fulcrum; states joined the Union in twos, one slave, one free. By Taylor's time, the growing abolitionist sentiment in the North and the exclusion of slavery from the northern territories had convinced the South that it must extend its peculiar institution into the southwest in order to maintain a stalemate in Congress. But the western lands were ill suited to plantation life. As a general, Taylor had helped gather California and

LIBRARY OF CONGRESS

Even this engraving flatters "Old Rough and Ready;" as general he wore old farm clothes, often sat his horse sideways.

Life	Born Nov. 24, 1784, Orange County, Va. Married Margaret Smith; six children. Died July 9, 1850.
Campaigns	Persuaded to run, he kept aloof from party ties, declared himself a Whig six weeks before the convention.
Milestones	Gold Rush of 1849 pushed California toward statehood in 1850, intensifying the slavery issue; Taylor preferred war to compromise. Arranged treaty with England to neutralize Central America for a canal.
Image	A gruff, apolitical patriot with little idea of what his office involved. Never voted, lost a battle, or made a political deal.

New Mexico under the Stars and Stripes; now they threatened to tip the balance in favor of the North.

Let them, Taylor reasoned; let the South keep slavery, but let us stop its spread. To forestall a dispute in Congress, he invited the western territories to choose their own status, slave or free, and then apply for statehood. In March, 1850, California asked to be admitted as a free state.

Congressional leaders sought to ward off trouble by postponing the admission of New Mexico and its fellow territory, Utah; many expected support from Virginia-born Taylor. But years of soldiering had broadened his loyalties. Taylor had fought more for the Union than for any of its parts. When talk of secession grew loud in the South, he vowed not only to send an army but to lead it himself.

The Civil War might have begun then, but sudden death intervened. In eleven weeks the Compromise of 1850 became law—over the dead body of Zachary Taylor.

Who would run with Zachary Taylor? Daniel Webster was approached, but he declined to swap the Senate limelight for the obscurity of the vice presidency. Since Henry Clay and his disciples in the Whig old guard resented Taylor's meteoric rise toward the office Clay had courted for so long, a candidate to smooth their feathers would be a wise choice for the Whigs to make. And it had to be admitted that Taylor was rather slovenly and plain; the cosmetic effect of a tall, handsome running mate could do no harm.

Millard Fillmore certainly filled the latter bill, as James Bogle's 1847 portrait shows. He was log-cabin born, self-made, a typical American success story. And his middle-of-the-road political stance was certain to please Henry Clay, the great compromiser.

Taylor's running mate was no neophyte; he had served in Congress and had chaired the powerful House Ways and Means Committee. Despite his experience, Vice President Fillmore spent a sleepless night after Taylor died, and the resignation of the entire cabinet the next day did little to bolster his spirits.

Taylor had been ready for war over slavery. Fillmore was not; he had warned the President that if a Senate tie gave him the deciding vote he would cast it for compromise. When the vote came, he *was* President and thus able to sign into law the five bills known as the Compromise of 1850—a courageous act of political suicide, done for the good of the Union.

The compromise satisfied no one. Southerners, although pleased with the stiff fugitive slave law, resented the admission of California as a free state, which tipped the free state-slave state balance in favor of the North. Even worse, the federal government had legislated on slavery, which the South

Life	Born Jan. 7, 1800, Locke (now Summer Hill), N.Y. Married twice: Abigail Powers, two children; widow Caroline McIntosh, no children. Died March 8, 1874.
Campaigns	Elected Vice President as a Whig; lost 1856 election as Know-Nothing candidate.
Milestones	Temporarily drew the country back from brink of war; wooed extremists toward compromise on slavery. Sent Commodore Perry to Japan. Kept France from annexing Hawaii, U.S. from annexing Cuba.
Image	A man of hard-earned wealth and robust good looks. Skilled administrator, but lacked the force the times demanded.

considered none of its business. The North detested having to treat a runaway as a slave on its free soil. Thus the Compromise of 1850 did not resolve the conflict; it merely postponed it. Soon the simmering cauldron would boil over as *Uncle Tom's Cabin* and the impassioned rhetoric of extremists fanned the flames of hatred.

Fillmore deserves to be remembered for what he really accomplished: he kept France out of Hawaii and the United States out of Cuba, opened trade with Japan, and enforced the compromise despite his own misgivings and the howls at every hand. But the Whig Party, which would soon dissolve over its failure to settle the uncompromisable issue of slavery with compromise, refused to renominate him. And when he ran in 1856, he garnered only eight electoral votes. History does not count Millard Fillmore among the great Presidents. He did his best, but he failed to bring lasting peace to his troubled nation.

Fillmore's frail Abigail stayed out of sight, but got from Congress a good White House library.

BUFFALO AND ERIE COUNTY HISTORICAL SOCIETY

Franklin Pierce (1853-1857)

Histories like to say that Franklin Pierce took office in the eye of a hurricane. It is an exquisite image of the Union in 1853. The rising storm over slavery had buffeted generations of Americans and would soon dash another on the rocks of civil war. But Pierce began his term in a deceptive calm created by the Compromise of 1850, viewed by many as the final solution to the slavery question.

Pierce stares from G.P.A. Healy's 1853 portrait, now in the National Portrait Gallery, with a force that might have made the compromise work. But the portrait, too, is deceptive; because of his reluctance to make unpopular decisions, Pierce reaped the whirlwind and earned a place among the Presidents as one of those least equal to his time.

Handsome and likeable, Franklin Pierce had risen quickly in the world of politics: speaker of the New Hampshire legislature at twenty-six, congressman at twenty-nine, senator at thirty-three.

By 1852 the great men of the Democratic party were only great enough to cancel each other out. On the forty-ninth ballot the convention tapped dark-horse Franklin Pierce. Although a Yankee, Pierce was acceptable to the South because he felt the Union was threatened not by slavery but by efforts to abolish it.

His term was clouded even before it began. Two months before the inauguration, his youngest child died in a train mishap; his wife, a neurotic, spent his tenure in seclusion. The President set about dispensing spoils in grief-ridden distraction, changing appointees from day to day until the party factions he sought to conciliate were united only in their exasperation.

Then arose the issue that would break him: a railroad route to the

Life	Born Nov. 23, 1804, Hillsboro, N.H. Married Jane Appleton; three children. Died Oct. 8, 1869.
Campaigns	Said little on issues; party leaders drummed up support, as was custom. Popular margin small, but swept electoral college, 254 to 42. Was not renominated.
Milestones	Record number of treaties for four-year administration, including Canadian Reciprocity Treaty, trade pacts with Denmark and Netherlands. Reluctantly supported Kansas-Nebraska Act.
Image	Good-looking and gregarious, but too indecisive and inexperienced for his time.

West. He arranged to buy a small piece of Mexican land, known as the Gadsden Purchase, to make room for a Southern route. But Northern speculators wanted a route through the Great Plains, as yet unorganized. To pave the way, Northern senators drew up a bill, establishing the Kansas and Nebraska territories. It won Southern support when an amendment allowing the new territories to choose slavery if they wished was added. The Kansas-Nebraska Act defied the Missouri Compromise and alienated many Northerners, but Pierce backed it.

Kansas was born in blood as settlers chose slavery amid the crackle of gunfire. But Southerners soon repudiated Pierce when they saw that without friends in the North he could do little for them. The 1856 Democratic convention denied him the renomination he wanted. The eye of the hurricane swept on, and the gathering winds bore a bitter, uncomprehending Pierce back to New Hampshire, from whence he had risen bright with promise.

LIBRARY OF CONGRESS

Posters depicted Pierce as stern and resolute, an image contradicted by four years of inaction.

James Buchanan (1857-1861)

The son of a prosperous Pennsylvania merchant, James Buchanan came to the Executive Mansion full of promise. He was sixty-five and a veteran of four decades of public service; for two of those decades he had had his eye on the presidency. Van Buren wanted him as attorney general; Polk got him as secretary of state; Pierce sent him as minister to England. He was opposed to slavery as "a great political and a great moral evil," but felt the Union could not force states to give it up. In denouncing abolitionists as trouble-makers, he won the South's crucial support. And he had the good fortune to be in England while politicians at home were tearing each other apart over "Bleeding Kansas." It was hard to hate the unscarred statesman who just might bring peace to the troubled nation of 1856.

But peace was not to come. Two days after his inauguration the Supreme Court announced the Dred Scott decision. The North was enraged, but the South —and Buchanan—were pleased. As President-elect, Buchanan had advised friends on the court to make a decision that would define Congress's power to legislate on slavery. They had done so, declaring that Congress had no right to outlaw slavery in a territory. And by implication territorial legislatures had no right to do so either; until it became a state, a territory could not exclude slaves. Thus with one blow, the Supreme Court had slain both the Missouri Compromise and the principle of popular sovereignty.

When the South pressured Buchanan into supporting the lost cause of slavery in Kansas, his Northern support in Congress vanished. Without it he could do nothing to save the South from the rising wrath against slavery, and so lost Southern

WHEATLAND

"The Emperor's Bowl," world's largest porcelain, was presented to Buchanan by first Japanese ambassadors in 1860.

Life	Born April 23, 1791, near Mercersburg, Pa. Never married. Died June 1, 1868.
Milestones	Dred Scott decision; admission of Kansas as free state. John Brown's exploits inflamed slavery issue. Panic of 1857 worsened the crisis that finally erupted at Ft. Sumter.
Campaigns	Defeated John C. Fremont (first Republican candidate) and ex-President Fillmore (Know-Nothing party). Decided no man should serve two terms; did not run again.
Image	A statesman of unassailable integrity, well equipped for diplomacy abroad in times that called for strength at home. Skilled orator and persuasive student of law.

backing as well. Denied consensus even in his own party, paralyzed by his conviction that the Union had no means to prevent secession, reluctant to use presidential powers that an Andrew Jackson would have readily seized in the gathering crisis, Buchanan could only stand in the cross fire, appeal to reason, and fail.

In 1859, Buchanan struck a typical pose for G.P.A. Healy—head bowed and cocked a little as if in deference but actually due to nearsightedness in one eye and farsightedness in the other. This painting from the National Portrait Gallery is one of a presidential series begun by Healy for Louis Philippe I of France. But in 1848, Louis abdicated and the series was never delivered.

"I acted for some time as a breakwater between the North and the South, both surging with all their force against me," said Buchanan of his last futile months in the presidency. His attempts to pacify both sides having failed, he left office just before the waters crashed over him.

Index

ENDSHEET: The commerce and the culture of Baltimore about 1850 are caught in this colored lithograph by E. Sachse.